MW01155715

To Make a World Safe for Revolution

*Written under the auspices of
the Center for International Affairs,
Harvard University*

To Make a World Safe for Revolution

CUBA'S FOREIGN POLICY

Jorge I. Domínguez

Harvard University Press

Cambridge, Massachusetts

London, England

1989

This book is printed on acid-free paper, and its binding materials
have been chosen for strength and durability.

Library of Congress Cataloging-in-Publication Data

Domínguez, Jorge I., 1945–
To make a world safe for revolution : Cuba's foreign policy
Jorge I. Domínguez.
p.   cm.
Written under the auspices of the Center for International
Affairs, Harvard University.
Includes index.
ISBN 0-674-89325-5 (alk. paper)
1. Cuba—Foreign relations—1959–   I. Harvard University.
Center for International affairs. II. Title.
F1788.D59 1989   88–16556
327.7291—dc19   CIP

To Mary, who asked me to write this book,
and to Lara and Leslie

Preface

This study of Cuban foreign policy completes the work begun in *Cuba: Order and Revolution,* published by Harvard University Press in 1978. The earlier book dealt mainly with domestic politics; this book deals mainly with foreign policy. Each can be read, however, without reference to the other.

My own approach to the study of Cuba has not changed in the intervening years. This book, too, strives for scholarly impartiality and comprehensiveness. And this book is conditioned in the same way as the first by some circumstances of my life that are appropriate to recall. I was born in Cuba and left the country with my family in 1960 as a fifteen-year-old. For many years I found it personally difficult to engage in the scholarly study of Cuba. In some ways, I still do. This study went through five thorough revisions before final copy was delivered to the publisher. A supporter of neither the Cuban government nor of its organized opposition, I continue to agree with some of its actions (such as the social policies that have brought valuable and impressive results in education and redistribution of wealth) and condemn others (including the harsh treatment of political dissidents). Finally, in both books, I have been motivated by a love for the country of my birth and a love for the country of my choice.

One difference between the two books is that the first had to rely exclusively on research done outside Cuba. This book benefited from five trips to Cuba in January 1979, August 1980, March 1985, June 1986, and April 1988, for a combined total time in Cuba of six weeks. (A discussion of the interviews I conducted and have used appears in Appendix A.)

I have acquired a great many personal and intellectual debts in the preparation of this work. At Yale College many years ago I learned about the subject from Richard Morse and Anthony Maingot. My general intellectual work has been nurtured and supported for many years by Harvard's Center for International Affairs, directed in the 1980s by Samuel P. Huntington.

Time and again the center's scholars have driven me to develop new insights and new perspectives. This book was written and is being published under the center's auspices; the research and writing have been supported by a generous grant from the Ford Foundation.

Although no chapter of this book has been published before, parts of it have been presented at various conferences and seminars of the Institute of Cuban Studies, directed by Maria Cristina Herrera. The institute's members have provided me over the years with an attentive audience, appropriate skepticism, valuable criticism, and warm friendship. In addition, I am grateful for the close and thoughtful reading of earlier drafts of Chapter 2 by McGeorge Bundy, Michael Mandelbaum, Fen Hampson, Rafael Hernández, and Wallace Nutting; of Chapters 2–5 by Marifeli Pérez-Stable; and of Chapters 3, 4, and 7 by Jorge Pérez-López. I would also like to thank Luis Suárez and Rafael Hernández, of Cuba's Centro de Estudios sobre América, for having facilitated my research in Cuba in 1985, 1986, and 1988 and for the comments I have received from them and from their colleagues on an earlier version of the entire manuscript (see Appendix A). Timothy Prinz and Lara Dominguez provided valuable research assistance on the statistical tables.

Aida Donald and Elizabeth Suttell were helpful in their advice about the work that needed to be done on the manuscript that they first saw, and they were gracious in waiting for me to do a better job. Barbara Gale turned the manuscript into a finished book with her characteristic intelligence, tolerance, and good humor, and Darlene Bordwell shortened it effectively. Errors are mine alone.

Contents

Introduction   *1*

1 The Formative Years   *8*

2 The Security Regime   *34*

3 Cuba's Challenge to the Soviet Union in the 1960s   *61*

4 The Reestablishment of Soviet Hegemony   *78*

5 Support for Revolutionary Movements   *113*

6 Support for Revolutionary States   *147*

7 Cuba's Relations with Capitalist Countries   *184*

8 Cuba's Diplomacy in the Americas and the Third World   *219*

9 How Cuban Foreign Policy Is Made   *248*

Appendix A
Interviews Conducted in Cuba and Elsewhere   *285*

Appendix B
Technical Notes on Soviet-Cuban Economic Relations   *290*

Notes   *295*

Index   *351*

To Make a World Safe for Revolution

Introduction

This is not a book of fiction, yet much of the story seems a fantasy. Cuba, in the 1980s a country of about ten million people, brought the world near nuclear war in October 1962. Although Cuba had been closely tied to the United States for most of its modern history, the revolutionary government that came to power there in January 1959 defied the U.S. government and successfully consolidated its own power. It defeated an invasion by a brigade of exiles at the Bay of Pigs (Playa Girón) in April 1961, thus humiliating the brigade's sponsor: the U.S. government.

Cuba developed deep and far-reaching military, political, and economic relations with the Soviet Union, becoming its primary ally in Africa and in Latin America. Cuba also got elected head of the Nonaligned Movement in the late 1970s. Still economically underdeveloped, typically dependent on sugar for about four-fifths of its export earnings for decades before and since the revolution, Cuba managed, especially after 1976, to obtain enormous subsidies from the Soviet Union and from other Eastern European countries to keep the Cuban economy afloat.

Cuba has committed its resources to supporting revolutionary movements, from Central America to Portuguese Africa. Although Cuba's resources remain limited and its people live an austere though adequate life, Cuba provides technical assistance to other countries in the areas of health, education, construction, sports, and various economic fields. Some of these activities are for profit, and Cuban state enterprises behave in part as if they were multinational firms. But much of the assistance is offered free of charge or on highly favorable terms as a means to advance Cuban policy goals.

Cuba deployed 36,000 troops to Angola in 1975–76 and half that number to Ethiopia in 1977–78 to intervene in wars that were, at best, remotely related to the national interests of this small Caribbean country. Its armed forces won those wars. Since 1975 Cuba has maintained an overseas military force that is larger, relative to its population, than that the United States kept in Vietnam at the peak of that war. As an old Cuban janitor said in January 1979, with obvious hyperbole but reflecting deep national pride: "We have done twice what the Yankees could not do once in Vietnam."[1]

Though the Cuban government has also been a factor in Central America's revolutions and in the wars leading to the collapse of Portugal's African empire, the Cuban role has been decisive only once—in Angola in 1975–76—and Cuba has rarely been the primary force behind revolution in other countries. It is true that the Cuban government has not always been deterred by the absence of a revolutionary movement and, occasionally, has attempted to create one—as in Ernesto "Che" Guevara's ill-fated expedition to Bolivia, which ended in his death and that of many of his comrades in October 1967. But most revolutionary movements that Cuba has supported have emerged from conditions in each society.

Like all governments that are active on the world stage, Cuba has had failures as well as successes. Its personnel have been expelled from countries as diverse as Augusto Pinochet's Chile and Siad Barre's Somalia, Pol Pot's Kampuchea and Edward Seaga's Jamaica. The ostracism of Cuba by most Latin American governments in the early 1960s was caused in part by successful U.S. policies, but it was also an understandable response to Cuba's support for those who sought to overthrow those governments. In 1980, the setbacks experienced by the Cuban government in its relations with other Latin American governments were second only to the debacle of the early 1960s. The problems that led to these overseas defeats for the Cuban government were primarily of its own making.

Nor is the Cuban government free of problems at home. One-tenth of Cuba's population has rendered a clear negative judgment on the government by emigrating, mostly to the United States. For these people, glories abroad did not make up for hardships at home. And there may be others who would leave if given the opportunity. Many within Cuba oppose the authoritarian political regime that revolutionary leaders have established; consequently, these people live on the margins of Cuban society. They oppose the absence of means for open, peaceful, political competition and the lack of rotation of top office holders; they oppose the curtailment of the flow of information, the sharp restrictions on freedom of association, and the abuses the state has committed against tens of thousands of Cubans in the name of the revolution. They also criticize the regime's poor economic growth performance, which was especially deplorable during the 1960s.

In spite of foreign policy reverses and domestic opposition, however, Cuba's is one of the twentieth century's authentic revolutions. At the moment of victory in January 1959, it had broad and deep support. Since then deep cleavages have fractured Cuban society and led many people to oppose the revolutionary regime, yet just as many—probably a majority—committed themselves to a historic transformation of Cuban politics, society, economics, and military affairs, and to an assertive new role for Cuba in the world. Over the long run, support for the regime has endured. The zeal of those whose sense of identity was redefined by the revolution continues to be extraordinary.[2]

No master plan has guided Cuba's leaders, but they have responded effectively to many international opportunities. "No master plan," of course, does not mean no guiding principles. Fidel Castro's central ideas and attitudes embody a deep hostility toward the U.S. government and toward many U.S. values; a belief that the direction of history can be perceived and that conscious revolutionaries can and ought to accelerate the rate of change; and a conviction that revolution in one country is impossible because the "imperialist enemy" is a world system that must be met with global struggle. Castro's ideas do not make him inevitably—or even first—a Marxist-Leninist, but his historical orientation is compatible with Marxism, and his bold, risky, voluntarist leadership is at home with Leninism. It is "the duty of revolutionaries to make the revolution," Castro believes, because it is historically right and appropriate to fight everywhere the enemy that fights revolutions everywhere.

Perhaps, however, as some have charged, Cuba does not have a foreign policy. Perhaps the Cuban construction workers who fought courageously in Grenada against U.S. and English-Caribbean forces in October 1983, along with the tens of thousands of Cubans posted overseas, serve not their own, their government's, and their country's goals, but those of the Soviet Union. Perhaps Fidel Castro merely takes orders from his Soviet bosses. At least partly in contrast with these claims, I will argue that there is, indeed, a specifically Cuban foreign policy.

In 1959, Fidel Castro's vision, ambition, and beliefs led him and his comrades to break with the United States. Their understanding of the past, and their analysis of the international system's structure at that juncture, led them to form a close alliance with the Soviet Union. The Cuban revolution could not have been achieved, nor its policies maintained, without the efforts and sacrifices of its leaders and most of the Cuban people, but it would have failed without massive Soviet military, political, and economic support.

Cuban-Soviet relations were jolted when the Soviets pulled their ballistic missiles out of Cuba in October 1962 without prior consultation with the

Cuban government and despite its opposition. Relations between the two governments deteriorated in the 1960s, reaching a crisis in 1968, when the Soviet Union looked for substantial changes in Cuban policies. Angry over many Cuban domestic and foreign policies, the USSR imposed sanctions on Cuba. Cuba backed down, and the hegemonic relationship was subsequently rebuilt.

Soviet hegemony over Cuba rests on Soviet power and on the demonstrated Soviet willingness to use it, as well as on Soviet assistance to Cuba, which increased enormously in the late 1970s and 1980s. But Soviet hegemony over Cuba does not stem merely from Soviet force or bribery. Rather, Cuban leaders gradually understood that, given the choices they made about relations with the United States, relations with the USSR were both useful and desirable. Cuba accepted Soviet hegemony because Cuban leaders came to value it.

Soviet hegemony has practical significance for Cuban foreign policy as well as for domestic affairs. Cuba does not oppose Soviet foreign policy, nor does it criticize the Soviet Union publicly: in exercising its autonomy, Cuba respects Soviet interests. Therefore, the ties between the two countries are much tighter than the hegemonic relations the United States often has with small countries. Soviet hegemony also means that Cuba has more resources to carry out its policies overseas than it could muster on its own.

Within the context of Soviet hegemony, Cuban foreign policy is very much its own. In subsequent chapters I will show that the Cuban government decided on its own to deploy troops in Angola in 1975; that Cuba led the USSR in fashioning policies toward Central America, inducing the Soviets to behave in ways they otherwise might not have behaved; that Cuba has served as a broker and an advocate for other governments, especially Grenada's, in their relations with the Soviet Union; and that the evidence of direct Soviet coercion of the Cuban government after 1968 is limited. Over all, there is little evidence that Cuba acts in international affairs simply at the bidding of the USSR. Fidel Castro's Cuba is no one's puppet.

That Cuba has a substantial margin of independence within the framework of Soviet hegemony need not reassure its adversaries, however. It means that Cuba acts against them for its own reasons and that Cuban policies are consistent with, even if not dictated by, the aims of the Soviet Union because the Cuban government wants it that way.

Another important factor in Cuban foreign policy is the government's mixture of revolutionary militancy and political pragmatism. Revolutionaries though they are, Cuban leaders are neither dogmatic nor stupid: they have learned from past mistakes. Cuba helped to sabotage the International

Sugar Agreement in 1961; in later years it cooperated in efforts to regulate the world sugar market. Cuba was on a collision course with Francisco Franco's regime in Spain in the early years of revolutionary rule in Cuba; beginning in 1963, Spain and Cuba reached an understanding that allowed a mutually profitable trade to develop, and twelve years later Cuba officially mourned Franco's death. Cuba has supported many revolutionary movements, but it has also bargained shrewdly with governments—even suspending assistance to revolutionary movements in order to advance other, more important goals.

The Cuban government has most often committed foreign policy blunders when it acted from anger rather than from analysis, as was the case in its relations with some Latin American governments as early as 1959 and as recently as 1981. But in the first half of the 1980s, Cuba showed remarkable patience and maturity in the face of several setbacks. It rebuilt its relations with several Latin American governments, despite earlier errors in dealing with them and the hostility of the Reagan administration. Cuba salvaged its relations with Angola and Mozambique in 1984, when it seemed as if the United States and South Africa had outwitted Cuba in southern Africa. As these examples show, Cuban foreign policy is more often the result of calculation than impulse.

Cuban pragmatism is also evident in the area of international economics. Both Fidel Castro and the regime he leads feel disdain for and skepticism about the operation of markets in Cuba. But beyond its borders, the Cuban government has been remarkably responsive to the marketplace, aggressive in its pursuit of profit, and innovative in finding ways to earn money—whether buying Soviet petroleum at subsidized prices and reselling it at market prices or earning hard currency by building roads in Libya's Sahara desert. Cuba has shifted its exports from market to market to find better prices. It has also developed its trade relations with most Western European countries, Canada, and Japan, relations that helped Cuba to withstand U.S. and Latin American sanctions in the early 1960s. In the 1980s Cuba urged Latin American countries to repudiate much of their debt to the multinational banks even as it negotiated to honor its own.

Cuba sees the U.S. government as its historic enemy, but this need not mean that no mutual understanding is possible. Castro and the Cuban government opposed the U.S.-Soviet understandings that settled the 1962 missile crisis, but by the mid-1970s Cuba had reversed its policy. Cuba, like the Soviet Union, made some concessions to the United States in the 1970s, in response to comparable, earlier U.S. decisions, in order to strengthen and broaden the understandings that govern their relations. These understandings have become a cornerstone of Cuban foreign policy. They serve the joint interests of the three governments to avoid war in the Caribbean.

The Cuban government has acted according to its own hierarchy of foreign policy goals. In descending order of importance, it has attempted to create and defend a revolutionary regime at home and to establish the relations abroad that will secure and protect that regime; to support revolutionary Marxist-Leninist regimes in the Third World; to establish relations with other existing governments that do not directly threaten its security; to support revolutionary movements, especially those that oppose the aims of the United States and of governments aligned with it; and, where possible, to promote its own economic relations with other countries, in line with its more important foreign policy goals.[3]

The Cuban government's most important goal is its own survival. It took the bold risk of breaking with the United States and even welcomed Soviet strategic weapons on Cuban soil. The survival and prosperity of a more conventional regime might have been assured at less cost through better relations with the United States. This revolutionary vision, hostile to the U.S. government, remains at the heart of Cuba's domestic and foreign policy. Once the revolution had won power at home, Cuba had to attempt to make the world safe for its revolution: the regime had to survive. The Soviet alliance became necessary for the consolidation of that regime. Thus Cuba's challenge to the USSR in 1968 was short-lived because it would have endangered the regime.

Next, Cuba gives high priority to its support for revolutionary governments in the Third World that are committed to Marxism-Leninism in some form. Cuba has even been willing to send its troops across the seas to support revolutionary regimes and movements and, in the process, advance its own political objectives. These actions have strengthened Cuban relations with the Soviet Union and Eastern Europe and have established important ties with the successor states of Portugal's African empire, but they have complicated Cuba's relations with much of Latin America, the United States, and Western Europe.

In search of autonomy under Soviet hegemony and of security and influence everywhere, Cuba has also sought good relations with many nonrevolutionary governments other than the United States. Cuba has cultivated relations with industrialized capitalist countries as a way around U.S. efforts in the early 1960s to isolate Cuba and as a way to diversify Cuban trade. Cuba has even evolved a preference for relations with existing governments over support for revolutionary movements that seek to overthrow these governments—so long as these governments do not directly threaten Cuba. Cuba's bargaining since the late 1960s to improve its relations with Latin American governments reflects a consistent foreign policy choice.

Cuba's preference for relations with existing governments, rather than revolutionary movements, stems from its pursuit of political objectives with economic benefits. But, when a choice must be made, Cuba consistently chooses politics over prosperity. It broke with the United States. It backed Algeria with troops during the 1963 war between Algeria and Morocco, even though Cuba had more extensive trade with Morocco. It condemned Egypt for its accord with Israel at Camp David in 1979, even though Cuba had good commercial relations with Egypt. It sided with Vietnam in its war against China, even though China's trade with Cuba was one of its most significant economic relations at the time.

The priority of political over economic considerations is also clear in Cuba's support for revolutionary movements that are fighting against governments antithetical to Cuban policies and closely aligned with the United States, such as those in El Salvador, Morocco, and Israel. It has backed such movements even at the cost of economic gain. This has been true not only in the early years of the revolution but also more recently, as in the case of Cuba's support for the Polisario guerrillas, which required the sacrifice of its trade with Morocco.

Finally, of course, Cuba seeks good economic relations, provided they do not contradict the primacy of politics for this revolutionary Marxist-Leninist regime.

Although Cuba's priorities had not yet been clarified in the first few years of revolutionary rule, its hierarchy of objectives was in place by the early 1970s. Cuban leaders seek to make a world safe for revolution in order to promote and safeguard their values, advance their interests, achieve their ambitions, and enhance their influence. Cuba is a small country, but it has the foreign policy of a big power.

The Formative Years

1

An era came to an end in Cuba on New Year's morning 1959, when President Fulgencio Batista, Cuba's preeminent political figure for a generation, fled the country. During his first period in power, from 1933 to 1944, support for Batista rested on a broad coalition of Communists and conservatives, but the regime installed after his second military coup on March 10, 1952, had a much narrower base. The collapse of this regime set the stage for the termination of U.S. power in Cuba and for a realignment of Cuban foreign policy. The nature of this change was shaped by factors within Cuba and in the international system, by the early crises in U.S.-Cuban relations, and by Fidel Castro's ideas and tactics.

U.S. Hegemony

The U.S. occupation of Cuba began with the defeat of Spain in 1898. In 1902 Cuba became formally independent, but as a U.S. protectorate in a relationship best categorized as imperialism—the indirect governance of a conditionally sovereign state. At U.S. insistence, Cuba's Constitution contained clauses first proposed by U.S. Senator Orville Platt, known collectively as the Platt Amendment, giving the United States the right to intervene in Cuba at its discretion. Though Cuba would retain sovereignty, the United States also required Cuba to cede the use of territory near Guantánamo for a U.S. naval base, which the United States has retained ever since. The United States occupied Cuba again between 1906 and 1909, landed troops in 1917, and interfered persistently in the routine conduct of Cuba's affairs. In 1934, the Platt Amendment was repealed with the consent of both governments, and imperialism yielded to hegemony.[1]

Imperialism and hegemony are variants of asymmetrical international regimes.[2] Whereas under imperialism, the United States sought to change Cuba, under hegemony, it sought to preserve order. If under imperialism the United States was concerned with the details of internal rule, under hegemony these details were important only if they threatened the structure of Cuba's political system. U.S. imperialism imposed policies on Cuba; U.S. hegemony resisted only certain Cuban policies. No troops were landed under hegemony, and no U.S. officials ran agencies of the Cuban government.[3] Under hegemony the United States exercised power and prevailed most of the time, but it also restrained its behavior as long as two fundamental rules were observed: Cuba was to be loyal to the United States in war and diplomacy, and the flow of goods and capital between the two countries was to be relatively free and unimpeded.

A stable hegemony requires that the client share gains with the dominant state in what some have called "associated dependent development."[4] For example, beginning in 1934, the United States lowered its tariffs on Cuban sugar, and the U.S. secretary of agriculture was authorized to determine the annual sugar requirements of the United States, to assign percentage quotas to various sugar-producing areas, and to pay a premium over the prevailing world price to assure deliveries and protect producers in the United States, its dependencies, and Cuba. The United States accepted higher sugar prices at least in part for the sake of long-term stability and growth in Cuba.[5]

The Cuban economy recovered from the great depression of the 1930s thanks, in large measure, to U.S. policies, but the same policies stunted other aspects of Cuban development. Cuba's reciprocal tariff concessions to the United States impeded the growth of manufacturing through import substitution, and U.S. limitations on refined sugar imports from Cuba prevented further growth of Cuba's key industry. The premium prices for Cuban sugar, while beneficial in many respects, tied Cuba closely to sugar and tied Cuban sugar closely to the United States.

With the shift from imperialism to hegemony came a decline in the importance of U.S. firms in Cuba. In 1927, U.S.-owned sugar mills produced 62.5 percent of Cuba's sugar; by 1958 they produced only 36.7 percent. In current U.S. dollars, direct private investment by U.S. firms in Cuba fell from $919 million in 1929 to $553 million in 1946, rising only to $1,001 million in 1958. In constant dollars, the 1958 level was still well below that of 1929.

As a result of the repeal of the Platt Amendment and of the subsequent decline of the importance of U.S. firms in Cuba, the appeal of nationalism subsided from its peak in the 1920s and 1930s. By the early 1950s both the Batista government and its opposition (including the Communist party) had deemphasized such appeals, and as late as April and May of 1960 no more than a tenth of the respondents to a nationwide poll of urban residents expressed nationalist or anti–United States attitudes.[6] Before the revolution,

Cubans were antagonistic neither to U.S.-owned firms nor to the U.S. government.

On the eve of the revolution, a stable hegemony had been consolidated—built on power, resting on close economic relations, and facilitated by the decline of the appeal of nationalism. Cubans had taken control of the sugar industry and the banking system, but U.S. firms still owned Cuba's public utilities and all three petroleum refineries, still controlled over one-third of Cuba's raw sugar output, and still accounted for over one-third of all bank loans and deposits. The United States purchased about two-thirds of Cuba's exports and supplied about three-quarters of its imports. Sugar exports made up about four-fifths of all Cuban exports. Exports and imports accounted for about two-thirds of Cuba's national income.[7] The United States still resisted basic changes in Cuban foreign policy and defended the endurance of capitalism in Cuba. Cuba's dependence on one country, the United States, and one crop, sugar, posed a problem for potential revolutionaries: no matter how benign the U.S. government might be, could a revolution be implemented under these circumstances?

The Rebellion, 1957–58

Fidel Castro led the revolution against Batista and against the United States, though his second target was not clear initially. Born in 1926, Castro was active in university student politics, which often included violent confrontations in the 1940s.[8] He learned that a small and disciplined group could use violence effectively against its opponents, even without a large following.

In 1947, Castro joined an expedition to overthrow Rafael Trujillo, the Dominican Republic's dictator (an expedition that was never launched). A year later, Castro was part of a delegation from the University of Havana's Federation of University Students to a meeting of Latin American university students in Bogotá, Colombia, organized jointly with Argentine university students supported by President Juan Perón. While Castro was in Bogotá, the Colombian Liberal party leader Jorge Gaitán was assassinated; riots broke out. Castro joined the revolt until it was crushed, then sought asylum in the Cuban embassy until he could return to Cuba.[9]

On July 26, 1953, he led a band that stormed the Cuban Army's Moncada barracks in the city of Santiago in Oriente province—hence the name the Twenty-sixth of July Movement. This group sought to overthrow the Batista government. The attack failed, however; Castro was captured and jailed. After being released under an amnesty granted by Batista in 1955,

Castro left Cuba to raise funds in the United States and to train in Mexico. He landed in eastern Cuba on December 2, 1956, aboard the yacht *Granma,* and hid in the Sierra Maestra mountains, where he continued to fight the Batista government.

Castro burst on the international scene on February 24, 1957, when Herbert Matthews published the first of a series of articles about him in the *New York Times.* Matthews portrayed Castro sympathetically, as something of a Robin Hood figure. However, as Matthews wrote later, "Nearly all the American journalists who went up received an exaggerated idea of the number of guerrillas."[10] On May 20, 1957, CBS News broadcast Castro's first public appeal to the United States to stop sending arms to the Batista government, the activity that would become the major point of contention between the U.S. government and the rebels. The rebellion's foreign policy had three goals: to reduce U.S. support for the Batista government; to obtain arms, ammunition, and funds; and to convince the United States and Latin American countries to put pressure on the Batista government.

U.S. military aid to the Cuban government stemmed from four treaties, signed in the context of the Cold War and predating Batista's rule, designed to promote the defense of the Western Hemisphere rather than to combat an internal rebellion.[11] Nevertheless, both Batista and the rebels saw the United States as a Batista ally. Given the constraints of the hegemonic relationship, the United States would intervene only if the structure of Cuba's political system was threatened. As the civil war intensified in Cuba in early 1958, the United States remained uninvolved militarily. In practical terms, this policy meant that the United States took actions that bolstered both sides in the civil war.

On the one hand, the U.S. government enforced the Neutrality Act. On February 4, thirty people were indicted in Miami for conspiring to undertake a military expedition against the Cuban government; on February 13, former Cuban President Carlos Prío was indicted on similar charges. On February 18, large quantities of arms for anti-Batista groups were seized near Houston, Texas. In late March, pro-Castro Cubans were arrested near Brownsville, Texas.[12]

On the other hand, the U.S. government withdrew military support for Batista. On March 14, 1958, the U.S. government suspended the shipment of 1,950 Garand rifles to the Batista government. U.S. Ambassador Earl Smith was instructed to tell Batista not to use U.S.-made supplies against the rebels.[13] In early April, Secretary of State John Foster Dulles explained that the United States had embargoed arms shipments to the Cuban government because it was using them "to conduct a civil war" in violation of

Article 2 of the 1952 military aid treaty, rather than for international defense.[14] The rebellion had achieved its first foreign policy victory. Because it is easier to block formal public sales to a government than to prevent clandestine shipments, U.S. neutrality favored the rebels.

Nonetheless, the U.S. government did not call back U.S. military advisers, who continued to work with the Cuban armed forces despite protests by anti-Batista forces that their presence violated the 1952 treaty.[15] Most important was the U.S. advice to the Cuban Air Force under a 1950 treaty.[16] The Cuban Air Force was less concerned with hemispheric defense than with bombing rebels in the mountains. Overall, U.S. policies weakened the Batista regime while incurring the wrath of the rebels.

Subsequent U.S. policies angered all sides in Cuba. In May 1958, two Cuban government transport planes landed at the U.S. naval base at Guantánamo. Their mission was to exchange three hundred small rockets delivered mistakenly by the United States before the arms embargo; one of the planes was refueled. The rebels claimed the Batista Air Force was using this U.S. base to wage civil war. Although the charge was untrue, the facts were unclear at the time. The rebels retaliated. On June 27, a group led by Fidel's brother, Raúl, kidnapped ten U.S. and two Canadian citizens from the Moa Bay Company mining plant, which was owned by the U.S. government; the next day, twenty-seven U.S. Navy personnel were also kidnapped. The U.S. consul in Santiago negotiated with the rebels for the release of the hostages—the first step toward U.S. recognition of the authority of rebel forces in eastern Cuba. On July 3, the U.S. government explained what had happened in Guantánamo and pledged not to participate in Cuba's civil war. In exchange, the rebels released the hostages.[17]

Conflicts continued, however. On July 28, as agreed by the two governments, the Cuban Army withdrew the garrison guarding the plant that supplied water to the U.S. base, and U.S. marines entered Cuban territory to protect the plant. Two days later Fidel Castro demanded their withdrawal. On August 1, the marines returned to their base and the Cuban garrison returned to the water plant. The U.S. government explained the change as an effort to avoid a clash with the rebels.[18] Then, on October 21, the rebels kidnapped two U.S. and seven Cuban citizens at the Texaco refinery in Santiago. Two days later the U.S. government demanded their release and the rebels complied.[19] Throughout these crises, Castro acted like a head of government, and the U.S. government often treated him as such.

In late 1958, U.S. policy changed. The U.S. Central Intelligence Agency (CIA) reported, for the first time, that "a Castro victory might not be in the best interests of the United States."[20] Suddenly, the structure of Cuban politics appeared to be threatened. The United States had to act. On December 9, William Pawley was dispatched on an unofficial mission to persuade Batista to resign in favor of a military junta that would be both anti-Batista and anti-Castro.[21] Following instructions from Washington, Ambassador Smith told Cuban Foreign Minister Gonzalo Güell "that the United States will no longer support the present government of Cuba and that my government believes that the President is losing effective control."[22]

The withdrawal of all U.S. support was too much for the Batista regime. The majority of Cubans had swung to the opposition, and the rebel forces were achieving important military victories. The Army collapsed; Batista fled. By design, courage, and luck, Fidel Castro's small force had won. The U.S. government had been unable to prevent a revolution that it had come to believe was contrary to its interests. Its policies had antagonized all factions in Cuba and failed to produce alternatives to Castro's victory.[23]

During the struggle to overthrow Batista, Castro had succeeded in securing some weapons from other countries, most notably Costa Rica.[24] Not all of Castro's attempts to influence foreign governments before his victory were successful, however. He could not prevent British weapons sales to Batista's government, for instance. Once the U.S. government had imposed the arms embargo, Batista turned to the United Kingdom. In 1958, the British government sold arms, ammunition, and seventeen Sea Fury aircraft, twelve of which had been delivered when Batista fell.[25] On October 17, after learning of the deal, Fidel Castro ordered an embargo on all British goods in rebel-held territory and authorized sabotage against British firms; he also announced that all British property in Cuba would be confiscated after his victory.[26]

Surprisingly, the Soviet Union played no role in the insurrection. As the rebellion intensified, Soviet interest in Cuba grew, but there were no Soviet actions to support it.[27] The Cuban Communist party kept its distance from Castro's forces until mid-1958.[28] In 1952, Batista had broken off the diplomatic relations he had established with the USSR during his first presidency in 1942, but that did not prevent Communist countries, primarily the Soviet Union, from buying Cuban exports during the 1950s (see Table 1.1).

Fidel Castro had built up much support for his rebellion in Cuba and abroad, and his actions contributed to major changes in U.S. policies (such as the arms embargo) as well as to more minor modifications (such as the limits on the role of the Guantánamo base). Although the U.S. government had not become Castro's adversary, it was not his ally, and its attempts to

Table 1.1   Cuban exports to Communist countries, 1955–1961

| | Country of export (millions of dollars) | | | |
Year	Soviet Union	Other European Communist countries	China	% of exports to Communist countries
1955	—	37.0[a]	—	6.2
1956	14.2	3.3	—	2.6
1957	42.0	2.1	—	5.5
1958	14.1	0.0	3.6	2.8
1959	12.9	0.1	0.1	2.2
1960	103.5	14.3	32.1	24.3
1961	300.9	65.6	91.6	73.3

Sources: Ministerio de Hacienda, *Comercio exterior, 1956, 1957* (Havana: P. Fernández y Cia., 1958); Ministerio de Comercio Exterior, *Comercio exterior, 1963* 1, no. 3 (Havana); Ministerio de Comercio Exterior, *Comercio exterior, 1964* 2, no. 3 (Havana); Comité Estatal de Estadísticas, *Anuario estadístico de Cuba, 1982* (Havana).

a. Includes exports to the Soviet Union.

install a new Cuban government in December 1958 were hostile to his interests. This experience helped to shape Castro's subsequent decision to turn to the Soviet Union for support.

The International System

By the end of the 1950s, the international system of alliances provided both opportunities and constraints for an ambitious leader. At one level, the international system was "bipolar": only the United States and the Soviet Union had the political, economic, and military capabilities, including nuclear weapons, to defeat any opponent except each other.[29] While the capabilities of the United States exceeded those of the USSR, alliance with the Soviet Union had become a plausible alternative for countries that broke with the United States. The Soviet Union supported other Communist states in Eastern Europe and east Asia and was expanding its relations with countries in Africa and Asia, notably with Egypt, India, and Indonesia. The United States and the Soviet Union headed their own alliance systems, and each country required loyalty of its allies. In the 1950s, the USSR sent its troops into Hungary to assert its supremacy in its sphere, while the United

States helped install new governments in Iran and Guatemala and landed troops in Lebanon.

The independent military capacity of other once powerful countries was in question. The United Kingdom, France, and Israel were unable to prevail against Egypt in 1956; France was also mired in a colonial war in Algeria. Germany and Japan were mere shadows of their former military might. These conditions made it difficult for a country not to be aligned with a superpower; they also made it possible for any country, no matter how small, to consider such alignment.

At another level, the international system was more complex than bipolarity implies. The concentration of power in the United States and the Soviet Union and the terrorizing effects of nuclear weapons led to a "nuclear stalemate" that moderated the superpowers' willingness to use those weapons. No matter how obstreperous the behavior of a small country's leader might be, a nuclear war was not likely because of the fear that it might escalate into a global nuclear conflict. At the same time, the economic recovery of Europe and Japan was opening up new opportunities for a small country to diversify its trade. The emergence of many newly independent states was eroding the earlier international hierarchy and creating new opportunities for leadership among these states, making neutrality or nonalignment—as well as influence—feasible. The bipolar international system was thus becoming polycentric. As the superpowers became more reluctant to use nuclear weapons, small states maneuvered in the interstices of the international system. If bipolarity made international alignment with either superpower possible for a small country, polycentrism made some independence from both superpowers equally possible.

For Cuba, U.S. hegemony had made it difficult to develop significant relations with other countries. At the time of the revolution, Cuba did not have close relations with most other Latin American countries. Yet the revolution's early survival was assisted by broader trends in U.S.–Latin American relations. In 1958, one vivid event, televised throughout the world, symbolized the state of inter-American relations: the assault on Vice President Richard Nixon by angry mobs in Peru and Venezuela. Political change was under way in Latin America; between 1956 and 1958, dictatorships ended in Argentina, Colombia, Peru, and Venezuela. The U.S. government, doubting the wisdom of its past policies, became more receptive to change. This was the context for Cuba's break with the United States and the prelude to its new foreign policy.

Although U.S. power in the Americas was more fragile than before, it remained overwhelmingly dominant. By 1962, the United States was able to use its power to enforce the cooperation of most Latin American governments in punishing and isolating Cuba. To redress the imbalance of power in the Americas, Cuba had to reach out for allies elsewhere in the world.

The Beginning of the U.S.-Cuban Conflict

"The revolution begins now," said Fidel Castro on January 2, 1959, as he marched from eastern Cuba to Havana.[30] The new Cuban leaders believed that their revolution had to break the deep-rooted U.S. hegemony, and that Cuba's internal structure and the structure of the international system both required and permitted such changes. They developed strongly nationalist and increasingly radical ideas, deceiving the United States and seducing the Soviet Union in order to consolidate their power.[31]

In January 1959, few could have suspected the future of the new regime. The new President, Manuel Urrutia, had been a judge. The Prime Minister, José Miró Cardona, was a leading lawyer. On January 28, 1959, Foreign Minister Roberto Agramonte outlined Cuba's new foreign policy. Cuba would be faithful to the Organization of American States (OAS) and to the United Nations. It would work with Venezuela to establish a "democratic bloc." Cuba would respect the right of political asylum while seeking to have "war criminals" from the Batista regime extradited to Cuba. It would not reestablish diplomatic relations with the Soviet Union.[32] The first Cabinet had a moderate cast, but only nine of the twenty-one original members were in office a year later. Fidel Castro replaced Miró Cardona as Prime Minister on February 16, 1959.

On January 7, the United States recognized the new government; Ambassador Smith resigned three days later. The new ambassador, Philip Bonsal, was an experienced career diplomat. After his first long meeting with Bonsal on March 5, Castro told the press: "Without any doubt the United States has sent a good Ambassador."[33] Castro's warmth was surprising in light of his later statements. The day before the Bonsal meeting, the Cuban government had taken over the Cuban Telephone Company, a subsidiary of International Telephone and Telegraph. Years later, Castro said that Bonsal had offended him at their first meeting by bringing up the takeover of the telephone company.[34] Bonsal, however, thought that the meeting had been cordial. His version was that "I did not believe that I, as American Ambassador, should take any official notice of the intervention. I received no instructions from Washington to do so." He did tell Castro, he later recalled, that "I had come to Cuba for the first time as a young trainee for the telephone company a couple of weeks prior to Castro's birth in August 1926."[35] This exchange is typical of U.S.-Cuban relations. The U.S. government sent a good, experienced ambassador, fluent in Spanish, who thought that he was sensitive to the concerns of Cuban leaders. Castro's reaction, characteristically, is ambiguous. He may have secretly taken offense; he may have resented references to the enduring U.S. presence in Cuba, and he may have knowingly deceived both the ambassador and the official Cuban newspaper about his reactions to the meeting. Or he may not have taken offense at all and later changed his views of the meeting to suit the politics of other times.

One major issue in U.S.-Cuban relations was aid. "All aid should be well received," Castro said on January 9, in reply to a question about possible U.S. offers of technical aid. But when he requested the withdrawal of all U.S. military advisers from Cuba,[36] the United States complied.[37] In February, Castro welcomed direct foreign investment in Cuban industry as long as provision was made for it to become "national capital" in time.[38] A month later, when asked about foreign sources of funding for industrialization, Castro said that "it could come from the United States, from England, from France, from Germany . . . It would seem that there is abundant capital in the world at this time because we have received many offers of loans and investments."[39]

On March 3, 1959, Castro accepted an invitation to address the Association of Newspaper Editors in Washington, D.C.—an invitation that had been extended before Castro had become Prime Minister. The U.S. government was split on how to handle the visit. President Eisenhower ruled out seeing Castro, but the State Department set the tone, and Bonsal offered the embassy's help with the trip.[40] On the day of Castro's departure, the ambassador stated: "I know that you join me in the confident expectation that this highly welcome informal visit . . . will help toward mutual understanding and will strengthen the ties of affection and solidarity between our two nations."[41] U.S. Assistant Secretary of State R. Richard Rubottom has said that "we expected, and were prepared, to be helpful, assuming any kind of response and request from Cuba to help alleviate the situation—because the treasury was depleted."[42]

On April 2, Castro reinforced the expectation that he would ask for U.S. aid. He referred to a Cuban mission to Washington that had had encouraging preliminary discussions about assistance from the United States and the International Monetary Fund (IMF), and he added: "We are going to initiate talks with all institutions concerned with credit and industrial development from all possible sources." To "obtain money in the United States as well as in Canada," Castro announced that he was taking Central Bank President Felipe Pazos as well as the economics and the finance ministers on the trip to the United States.[43]

On April 15, Castro landed in Washington. The following day U.S. Secretary of State Christian Herter gave a luncheon in his honor, and Castro met for three hours with Vice President Nixon. To the surprise of U.S. officials and his own delegation, Castro did not ask for aid. When a reporter asked him if he had done so, he replied, in English: "No. What happens is that here in the United States you are accustomed to see governments coming for money. No, I came for good relations. For good understanding, for good economical relations."[44] He instructed his top aides not to discuss economic assistance with U.S. officials.

Central Bank President Pazos later reported that U.S. officials were "more than willing, anxious, avid, desperate" to discuss aid. Rubottom went out of his way to bring up the subject and to arrange for meetings at the U.S. Treasury Department. The general manager of the IMF gave a luncheon; Pazos still laughs at how difficult it was not to appear to be requesting a loan from the IMF in response to many initiatives.[45]

No one knows why Castro changed his mind. It is clearly not true that Cuba turned toward Marxism-Leninism or toward the Soviet Union because the United States refused to provide economic aid, or that aid was offered but on terms that were unacceptable. The United States was almost pushing aid on Cuba; the terms were never discussed because Cuban officials prevented it.

Castro's trip, and preparations for it, appear to have provoked a crisis within his inner circle. The timing of the trip represented a deadline by which two key decisions had to be made. The first was announced on April 9: there would be no elections, although the program of the Twenty-sixth of July Movement had emphasized elections since its founding in 1953.[46] Second, as became clear in Washington, no aid would be requested from the United States. The revolution could not be carried out in partnership with the United States; the new regime would escape U.S. hegemony, would not ask for U.S. money, and would confront the United States and the market economy. The purpose of Castro's visit to the United States shifted from gaining money to gaining time. These decisions struck at the heart of Cuban politics, in which governments had traditionally sought legitimacy through elections, and prosperity and security through U.S. hegemony.

After leaving the United States Castro toured several Latin American countries and attended a meeting of the OAS Economic Council. He called on the United States to provide a $30 billion loan over ten years to promote economic development in Latin America. Cuba's official newspaper, *Revolución,* later explained that he had requested the $30 billion for "economic development for the entire continent, not for our country."[47] Though this was a puzzling request from someone who had just refused to discuss loans for Cuba, it signaled Castro's bid to represent to the United States the aspirations of Latin American countries.

In May 1959, Cuba promulgated an agrarian reform law, which called for the confiscation of large landed estates.[48] The U.S. government told those U.S. firms affected by the law that they would have to exhaust all remedies under Cuban law before the U.S. embassy would consider making representations on their behalf. In June the U.S. government told the Cuban government that it recognized Cuba's right to carry out the agrarian reform, provided "such taking will be accompanied by the payment of prompt, adequate, and effective compensation."[49] Cuba replied that it rejected the principle of "prompt, adequate, and effective compensation," even though the Constitution of 1940 and the revolutionary government's own Fundamental Law required it. The latter was amended retroactively to exempt the government from such requirements; compensation would be in the form of long-term bonds.[50]

Events moved swiftly. In June Castro dismissed five moderate ministers, including Agramonte, from the Cabinet. Also in June, the chief of the Revolutionary Air Force, Pedro Luiz Díaz Lanz, defected and accused the Cuban government of communism before the U.S. Senate Subcommittee on Internal Security. Subsequently, Castro forced the resignation of another anti-Communist, President Manuel Urrutia, who was replaced by Osvaldo Dorticós. In October and November 1959, Castro moved to centralize power under his leadership. He took direct control of the Twenty-sixth of July Movement's organizations among university students and labor, installing his hand-picked leaders (including some Communist party members) at the national labor federation. Raúl Castro was named minister of the armed forces. On October 21, Huber Matos, the military commander of Camagüey province, who had voiced concern about Communist influence within the government, was jailed for conspiring against the government.

On the day Matos was jailed, Díaz Lanz dropped leaflets on Havana. The next day, Castro denounced the U.S. government for sins ranging from giving asylum to Díaz Lanz to economic aggression against Cuba. In a fiery speech on October 26, Fidel Castro charged that Díaz Lanz had bombed Havana, and held the U.S. government responsible. (In fact, the Cuban National Police reported that there had been casualties in the incident, but that they had resulted from shooting on the ground.)[51] There had been no bombing. In his speech, Castro called on Cubans' dormant nationalist emotions:

> The nation is convinced as it has never before been convinced that it is upholding a just and good cause. The nation is convinced of our loyalty, the nation is convinced that from this struggle there can be no retreat for us and we shall not retreat. The nation knows that we shall not give up the fight until our bodies are laid to rest. The nation is conscious of its destiny, certain of its rights, proud of its history.[52]

The nation was probably bewildered. A leader it wildly supported was rallying it against the U.S. government, an enemy it did not know it had. In November, Castro forced the three leading non-Communists remaining in the Cabinet—Pazos, Manuel Ray, and Faustino Pérez—to resign.[53] Ernesto (Che) Guevara became president of the Central Bank. The stage was set for radicalization at home and realignment of alliances abroad.

The Establishment of Soviet-Cuban Relations

On October 16, 1959, just before Castro's government definitively turned away from the United States, Alexandr Alexeev met with Fidel Castro. Alexeev had arrived in Cuba on October 1, officially as a TASS correspondent. On October 12 he had met with Guevara, who at the time ran the powerful industrialization department of the National Institute for Agrarian Reform. Guevara told Alexeev that "the only way to achieve Cuba's full independence was to build a socialist society."[54]

Alexeev has reported that Castro was very hostile toward the United States well before the Díaz Lanz "bombing." Castro told Alexeev that because of Cuban weaknesses and U.S. aggression, he "had to weigh every step carefully." When Alexeev asked about Soviet-Cuban diplomatic relations, Castro replied that the time was not yet right, that the proper political conditions had to be created. Castro promised to put a stop to anti-Soviet propaganda and to work toward establishing formal relations. Without prompting, Alexeev has reported, Castro quoted Marx and Lenin as intellectual guides of his actions; Castro also suggested that Soviet Deputy Prime Minister Anastas Mikoyan visit Cuba. Soon thereafter, the date for Mikoyan's visit was set for February 1960.[55]

Thus the evidence clearly shows that Castro was not pushed into Soviet arms by the United States or by domestic conflicts.[56] Castro's first meeting with Alexeev preceded the Díaz Lanz incident and the Matos affair. Although U.S.-Cuban relations had not been good in the autumn of 1959, they had yet to deteriorate irreparably. Instead, Castro assessed the opportunities and constraints faced by Cuba and decided to approach the USSR. The international system permitted this move; his own political circumstances required it. Behind the scenes, he prepared for realignment with the Soviet Union and seduced the Soviets by quoting Marx and Lenin and by carrying out anti-U.S. revolutionary policies. He thus manipulated both domestic and international politics for his own ends.

The Soviets were surprised by Castro's overtures. Cuba had not even acknowledged the USSR's recognition of the new government in January 1959. When Alexeev first requested a Cuban visa in February 1959, he had received no answer for six months. (Castro later told him that the delay was deliberate, because "the time was not yet right for the arrival in Cuba of the representative of a Soviet state organization".) Alexeev reports that he was "stunned" when Castro quoted Marx and Lenin at their October 16 meeting "because at that time we could not even imagine that he knew Marxist theory." Few Soviets knew much about Cuba; most were skeptical of the revolutionaries' credentials because so many of them were "bourgeois liberals." In addition, Cuban trade with Communist countries, especially with the Soviet Union, was less extensive in 1959 than it had been under Batista in the 1950s (see Tables 1.1. and 1.2).[57]

In fact, as early as February 1959, Castro had said that "Cuba ought to sell [sugar] to whoever would buy, whether they are Russians or Chinese," a position he reiterated a month later. And first in August and then in Sep-

Table 1.2 Cuban imports from Communist countries, 1958–1961

| Year | Country of import (millions of dollars) | | | % of imports from Communist countries |
	Soviet Union	Other European Communist countries	China	
1958	0.0	2.0	0.0	0.3
1959	—	1.9[a]	—	0.3
1960	88.2	18.8	11.2	18.7
1961	288.8	90.8	97.5	70.2

Sources: Ministerio de Comercio Exterior, *Comercio exterior, 1963* 1, no. 3 (Havana): ibid., *1964* 2, no. 3 (Havana); Comité Estatal de Estadísticas, *Anuario estadístico de Cuba, 1982* (Havana).

a. Includes imports from the Soviet Union.

tember 1959, the Soviets had bought some Cuban sugar on the open international market, at prevailing prices. Both transactions had been reported on the front page of *Revolución*.[58]

The first Cuban-Soviet trade agreement was signed, at Castro's instigation, in January 1960. Negotiated by Guevara and Carlos Rafael Rodríguez, it called for the Soviets to purchase 100,000 tons of Cuban sugar. Rodríguez's involvement highlighted the mediating role he and other members of the prerevolutionary Cuban Communist party played in bringing together the Soviet Union and Castro's government.[59]

Mikoyan arrived in Havana on February 4, 1960, and was wined and dined by Castro and other Cuban leaders for two weeks.[60] The visit, and a treaty signed on February 13, publicized Cuba's new relations with the Soviets and consolidated Communist support of the regime. The USSR agreed to buy a million tons of sugar per year, at prevailing world market prices, for the next five years: about one-fifth of Cuba's sugar exports. (This was mostly barter: the Soviets would pay in convertible currency for only up to 20 percent of their imports from Cuba; the remainder would be paid for in merchandise.) The Soviet Union also agreed to lend Cuba $100 million dollars for economic development projects, at 2.5 percent interest repayable in merchandise over twelve years, and to sell petroleum to Cuba for less than prevailing market prices.[61]

Although Castro had hinted about his desire to purchase weapons from the Soviets as early as his speech on October 26, 1959, the first formal (and secret) Cuban request for weapons came in early April 1960. Military relations were formalized when Armed Forces Minister Raúl Castro visited Moscow in July 1960. The first Soviet tanks arrived in September 1960; military advisers, artillery, armored personnel carriers, and other war materiel followed by year's end.[62] Cuba also established comparable links with Eastern European countries, beginning with Poland in late March. By mid-June 1960, Bulgaria, Poland, and Czechoslovakia had signed various agreements in Havana. China purchased 130,000 tons of sugar and pledged to buy a half million tons in 1961.[63]

The Soviets remained surprised by Castro's actions. In the summer of 1960 Boris Ponomarev, head of the International Department of the Central Committee of the Communist party of the Soviet Union, still had doubts about Castro's sincerity.[64] Nonetheless, a new Cuban-Soviet relationship had been established, and it was soon extended to include Eastern Europe. Cuba took the initiative: first in delaying the establishment of formal relations until conditions were favorable and then in accelerating the Cuban-Soviet tie as a way to defend Cuba from the United States. The skill of the

Cuban leaders in dealing with the Soviets led to their first major international achievement.

The Break with the United States

The break with the United States did not come suddenly. It was the result of a series of overlapping conflicts that developed gradually and that focused on political, military and economic issues. Of the last, disputes over sugar and petroleum were especially significant.

A recurring topic in U.S.-Cuban relations had been the sugar quota, about which the revolutionary government seemed to be of two minds. In February 1959, Castro had thundered that Cuba would give up the sugar quota for the sake of its independence,[65] since the quota and the premium prices paid by the United States for Cuban sugar were keeping Cuba dependent on the United States. But some of Cuba's new leaders still preferred prosperity with dependence. In August 1959, when the U.S. Department of Agriculture (USDA) increased Cuba's sugar quota for the year, Cuba's trade minister, Raúl Cepero Bonilla, expressed the hope that the increase would be permanent (Cuba's sugar quota for the year was raised again in October).[66] By mid-November, however, the Cuban government reached a different consensus: "The system of quotas has served, quite simply, to limit exports to the United States."[67] Even so, on December 17 the USDA raised Cuba's basic sugar quota for 1960 to 3.12 million tons.[68]

As 1960 began, the U.S. government made a last effort to improve relations with Cuba. It reiterated its pledge of nonintervention and its intention to prevent illegal acts against Cuba. It recognized "the right of the Cuban government and people . . . to undertake those social, economic and political reforms which, with due regard for their obligations under international law, they may think desirable."[69] The U.S. chargé in Havana, Daniel Braddock, also asked Argentine Ambassador Julio Amoedo to mediate between the two countries. At first, Cuba appeared to respond positively.[70] In fact, Amoedo later reported that Cuba "accepted my efforts at mediation as a dilatory tactic to diminish tension between Cuba and the United States while awaiting Mikoyan's arrival. My efforts proceeded satisfactorily until the arrival of Mikoyan. From that moment on, the Castro regime virtually paralyzed the negotiations with various excuses and evasions which were designed to gain time until the Cuban-Soviet pact was signed on February 13."[71]

The Eisenhower administration had begun to consider a cut in the Cuban sugar quota in late 1959.[72] When this fact became public in February 1960, the Cuban government stated that negotiations with the United States would continue only if the U.S. government took no "unilateral measures" to undermine the negotiations or to harm the Cuban economy.[73] Cuba accused the United States of indifference to the negotiations, even though it was Cuba that had avoided negotiation for several months. On March 1, Eisenhower asked Congress to grant him the discretionary power to adjust the sugar quotas of foreign countries, which prompted *Revolución* to headline its report: "Economic Aggression against Cuba."[74]

On March 4, the Belgian ship *La Coubre,* loaded with arms and ammunition for the Cuban government, exploded in Havana harbor. At a funeral oration for those killed in the explosion, Castro called it sabotage and blamed the United States, though he admitted, "we do not have full proof."[75] Castro was finally ready to sever the link with the United States. President Eisenhower understood: "On March 17, 1960 . . . I ordered the CIA to begin to organize the training of Cuban exiles, mainly in Guatemala."[76]

As the U.S.-Cuban confrontation escalated, Castro announced his strategy: "For each economic aggression, adopt a revolutionary law."[77] Guevara explained why Cuban leaders were confident of success: "We knew that, sooner or later, this battle would have to be fought . . . The present distribution of power in the world is what has permitted Cuba to take steps to cross the line between a colonial and a non-colonial country."[78] President Dorticós further noted: "We knew that there were other countries ready to buy the sugar which could not be sold to the United States."[79] At last ideas, tactics, and the structure of the international system had joined to make the break possible.

On June 27 the Agriculture Committee of the U.S. House of Representatives approved an amendment to the pending Sugar Act granting the President the discretionary power to cut Cuba's quota. The next day, on the Cuban Cabinet's order, the Cuban Petroleum Institute (ICP) sent 20,000 barrels of Soviet crude oil for processing to the Texaco refinery, with 40 percent to be paid in cash and the rest on credit.[80] When Texaco refused, the ICP seized the refinery. On June 30, the ICP sent Soviet crude oil for refining to the Shell and Standard Oil refineries. Texaco and Standard Oil had been told by U.S. Secretary of the Treasury Robert Anderson that "a refusal to accede to the Cuban government's request would be in accord with the policy of the United States government toward Cuba and that the companies would not incur any penalties under American antitrust laws should they take a joint stand in this matter." The U.S. government sought British collaboration so that Shell would take the same stand.[81] Shell and

Standard Oil also refused to refine Soviet oil, and their refineries were seized on July 1.

The U.S. Congress approved the Sugar Act on July 3. On July 5, the Cuban Cabinet authorized the expropriation of all property in Cuba belonging to U.S. citizens or firms.[82] On July 6, President Eisenhower cut Cuba's sugar quota for the remainder of 1960 by 95 percent. On July 9, the Soviet Union announced that it would buy all the Cuban sugar that the United States refused to buy. Soviet Prime Minister Nikita Khrushchev wrote to Castro that, "in a figurative sense," Soviet missiles would defend Cuba if it were attacked by the United States.[83] Armed Forces Minister Raúl Castro went to Moscow. The resulting Cuban-Soviet communiqué stated: "The Soviet Union will use all means at its disposal to prevent an armed intervention by the United States against Cuba . . . The socialist countries . . . can fully take care of supplying Cuba . . . with all the necessary merchandise which is now denied to it by the United States and other capitalist states."[84]

In September, Fidel Castro met with Khrushchev at the United Nations in New York. Between August and October, the Cuban government expropriated all U.S. firms, followed by all privately owned sugar mills, banks, and large industries and all commercial real estate in Cuba. The enemy was not just the United States but also the structures of capitalism.[85] The U.S. government responded by prohibiting all exports to Cuba, except unsubsidized foodstuffs and medicines. In December, Eisenhower fixed Cuba's sugar quota for 1961 at zero. When, on January 1, 1961, Cuba restricted the personnel of the U.S. embassy in Havana to a maximum of eleven and gave the rest of the embassy staff forty-eight hours to leave the country, the United States broke off diplomatic relations.[86]

From this point on, conflict between the United States and Cuba spilled over to the military sphere. Cuba had learned in late 1960 that the CIA was training Cuban exiles to invade Cuba and attempt to overthrow the government. In February 1961, the Cuban government uncovered a plot, traced to the CIA, to assassinate Fidel Castro by having him smoke poisoned cigars.[87] (The CIA had begun plotting Castro's assassination in 1960; its often far-fetched plans involved the criminal underworld and poison pills.)[88]

In March 1961, the Cuban government acknowledged that hundreds of guerrillas were fighting to overthrow it.[89] On March 13, President John Kennedy announced an Alliance for Progress with Latin America to promote reform, economic growth, and democracy and to reduce the appeal of communism. On March 31, the U.S. Congress extended the President's authority to set Cuba's sugar quota at zero.

With the Cuban Air Force as a target, a group of Cuban exiles in B-26 planes attempted to bomb strategic points in Cuba on April 15. They succeeded only in alerting the government to the group's activities; thousands of suspected opponents still living in Cuba were arrested, destroying the underground overnight.[90] On April 17, Cuban exiles trained by the CIA in Nicaragua and Guatemala landed at the Bay of Pigs, and were defeated within seventy-two hours; most were captured.[91] The Cuban government's victory crushed both the internal and the external counterrevolution and humiliated the U.S. government. In resorting to assassination attempts and to a covert, proxy invasion, the U.S. government failed to appreciate both the support many Cubans gave their government and the extent of Soviet support. The Soviet commitment to Cuba increased during this crisis, but its limitations also became clear. On the day after the landing at the Bay of Pigs, the Soviet Union asked the U.S. government to halt the aggression: "We will extend to the Cuban people and its government all the necessary aid for the repulse of the armed attack on Cuba."[92] The Soviets would arm the Cubans but they would not commit Soviet troops.

Cuba's "Incompatibility" with the Americas

As early as 1959, the clash between Cuba and the United States had widened to include the rest of Latin America. During that year, expeditions left Cuba in attempts to overthrow the governments of Panama, Nicaragua, the Dominican Republic, and Haiti. The Cuban government acknowledged with pride its support for the attacks on the Nicaraguan and Dominican governments but denied responsibility for the other two. The institutions of the inter-American system were increasingly called upon to maintain peace. Most important for this purpose were the Meetings of Consultation of the Ministers of Foreign Affairs of the American Republics, which were held under the authority of the Inter-American Treaty for Reciprocal Assistance (the Rio Treaty).[93]

Cuba's own attitudes toward the OAS were ambivalent at best. On January 23, 1959, Fidel Castro had stated that "people have lost faith in the OAS . . . It serves no purpose at all."[94] Nonetheless, Cuba used the inter-American system effectively to protect itself in 1959. At the August meeting of the foreign ministers of the Rio Treaty member states, held to discuss threats to peace in the Caribbean from Cuba and from Rafael Trujillo's Dominican Republic, Cuba deflected attention from itself by inducing a discussion of economic issues and focusing criticism on the Trujillo regime.[95]

By 1960, however, Cuba had become skeptical about all organizations in which the United States was dominant. In February, Guevara announced that Cuba would not join the newly founded Inter-American Development Bank. In March, Cuba announced that it would no longer accept actions taken under the Rio Treaty. On November 14, it withdrew from the World Bank.[96]

In August 1960, as conflict grew between Cuba and the United States, the foreign ministers of the Rio Treaty member states met at San José, Costa Rica, where they unanimously passed the Declaration of San José. (Although Cuba was not mentioned by name, the Cuban delegation walked out before the vote was taken.) The declaration condemned "the intervention or the threat of intervention, even when conditional, by an extracontinental power in the affairs of the American Republics." It affirmed that "no American state may intervene for the purpose of imposing upon another American state its ideologies or its political, economic or social principles." And it reaffirmed that "the inter-American system is incompatible with any form of totalitarianism."[97]

Four days later, Castro responded with the Declaration of Havana, his first formal call for revolution in the hemisphere. This declaration also called for the expansion of Cuba's relations with the Soviet Union and Eastern Europe, and recognized the People's Republic of China and accepted its economic and military aid.[98]

At this juncture, Cuba still had much support in the hemisphere. Although Mexico voted for the San José Declaration, it appended a reservation stating that "in no way is [the declaration] a condemnation or a threat against Cuba."[99] The Venezuelan foreign minister refused to sign the San José Declaration and resigned his office. Demonstrations broke out throughout Latin America in support of Cuba. By mid-1961, however, the Dominican Republic, Haiti, Guatemala, Honduras, El Salvador, Nicaragua, Costa Rica, Paraguay, and Peru had all broken off diplomatic relations with Cuba. Venezuela, Panama, and Colombia soon followed. At the January 1962 meeting of the foreign ministers of Rio Treaty member states, Cuba was alone in voting against all nine resolutions that were approved. Among them were resolutions that "the principles of communism are incompatible with the principles of the inter-American system," and that the "present Government of Cuba, which has officially identified itself as a Marxist-Leninist government, is incompatible with the inter-American system" and was thereby suspended from participation in it. Other resolutions excluded Cuba from the Inter-American Defense Board and cut off military trade with Cuba.[100]

Following these decisions, the United States imposed a full trade embargo on Cuba on February 3, 1962. The U.S. Treasury Department froze Cuban assets in the United States and prevented Cuban use of U.S. banks. Cuba responded with the Second Declaration of Havana, more militant than the first, in support of international revolution. Within five days, Argentina broke off diplomatic relations with Cuba.

It was the 1962 missile crisis, however, that turned the tide against Cuba in Latin America. On October 23, 1962, the OAS unanimously called for the immediate dismantling and withdrawal of all Soviet missiles and other offensive weapons from Cuba and recommended that member states "take all measures individually and collectively, including the use of armed force," to achieve those aims.[101] Venezuela and Argentina sent warships toward Cuban waters; ten other Latin American countries helped the joint military effort. Mexican President Adolfo López Mateos firmly opposed the emplacement of Soviet missiles in Cuba.[102] Cuba's virtually indiscrimate support of revolution and its reckless behavior in alliance with the USSR had backfired.

The inter-American sanctions imposed on Cuba gave legitimacy to the unilateral attempts of the United States to isolate Cuba, weaken its economy, and bring down its government.[103] The U.S. government sought to enlist its allies and neutral countries in breaking all relations with Cuba, and restricted travel to Cuba. It prohibited U.S. aid to Cuba and to any country that furnished assistance to Cuba or that allowed its vessels to carry goods to or from Cuba, and it prohibited the docking in the United States of ships of third countries engaged in such traffic. It forbid U.S. citizens and firms or their foreign subsidiaries to trade or have any financial relations with Cuba, or to permit their vessels to trade with Cuba. These regulations even applied to U.S. citizens working for firms in other countries, to trade in products manufactured in third countries using Cuban materials, and to trade in products manufactured in other countries with U.S. materials.[104]

In the fall of 1963, the Venezuelan government found in its territory a large cache of weapons sent from Cuba to arm Venezuelan guerrillas, a finding confirmed by an OAS investigating committee. Meeting in July 1964, the foreign ministers of the Rio Treaty member states found that Cuba had committed "an aggression" against Venezuela and "an intervention" in its internal affairs. They imposed sanctions on Cuba, including a break in diplomatic relations and the suspension of all trade with Cuba (except in foodstuffs and medicines) and of all sea transportation to or from Cuba. Bolivia, Chile, Mexico, and Uruguay voted against the resolution.[105] All members stated complied with the vote soon thereafter; only Mexico refused to break with Cuba. Castro's response made the case for Cuban support of revolutions: "The people of Cuba consider themselves to have an equal right to help, with the resources that are available to them, the revolutionary movements in all countries that engage in such intervention in the internal affairs of our country."[106] All the Latin American governments but Mexico's were targets.

Cuba's diplomatic relations with Latin America were in a shambles. Cuban leaders had acted boldly, but their two key policies—support for revolutions and an alliance with the Soviet Union so close that strategic missiles were soon deployed in Cuba—caused them to squander the good will they had gained in the struggle against Batista and in their early months in power. Mexico maintained relations with Cuba, but they were more "correct" than warm. The Western Hemisphere as a whole was inhospitable, with the U.S. government especially hostile. In order to survive, the revolution had to turn to the Communist countries, to the non-Communist industrialized world, and to other parts of the Third World.

Fidel Castro's Ideas and Tactics

Looking back on the early history of the Cuban revolution, it is important to ask, Was Fidel Castro always a Communist, or did his ideas change over time? Did he manipulate and deceive his friends and foes? Especially significant in answering these questions are his attitudes toward nationalism, the United States, and Marxism-Leninism.

History Will Absolve Me, a wide-ranging document dating from 1953 that is Castro's major statement in the years before his victory, says little about nationalism. The five primary laws that Castro said the revolution would proclaim were not aimed at foreigners. State takeover of foreign-owned public utilities, the only "nationalist" plank, was mentioned only in a long list of secondary measures.[107] Instead, Castro's proposals stressed political change, legitimacy, and the purification of a corrupt government. His emphasis on nationalism, apparently moderate and subsidiary to begin with, changed over time, as his proposals switched from the expropriation of some foreign property to the prevention of U.S. intervention in Cuba.

In 1957 and 1958, Castro wanted to stop U.S. government shipments of weapons and munitions to the Batista government and to prevent a U.S. intervention that might keep him from power. As he attempted to build a broad-based coalition, his emphasis on demands for state takeover of public utilities faded, along with some of his more radical social and economic proposals. In an article appealing for support, published in the United States in the magazine *Coronet* in February 1958, Castro stated that he no

longer planned "the expropriation or nationalization of foreign investments." Instead, he said, "foreign investment will always be welcome and
secure" in Cuba.[108] Most dramatic was his reassuring broadcast to the
United States, in English, from the Sierra Maestra mountains. In it he
stated: "Not communism or Marxism is our idea. Our political philosophy
is representative democracy and social justice in a well-planned economy."[109]

This public posture clearly contrasted with Castro's private feelings. He
had long been hostile to the United States. He wrote from the mountains to
his closest companion, Celia Sánchez, on June 5, 1958: "Having seen the
rockets that exploded in Mario's house, I have sworn that the Americans
will pay very dearly for what they are doing. When this war is over, a much
longer and bigger war will begin for me: the war that I will make against
them. I realize that this will be my true destiny."[110]

Castro had few early links with Marxism-Leninism or with the Cuban
Communist party, although he read Marx, Engels, and Lenin in his days at
the university.[111] A few days before the Moncada barracks attacks, he had
visited the Communist party's bookstore and met an acquaintance, Flavio
Bravo, a Communist party member, who introduced him to Carlos Rafael
Rodríguez, a member of the party's Political Bureau and a former minister
under Batista during World War II, when the Communist party was part of
Batista's government. Rodríguez joined Castro in the Sierra Maestra mountains in July 1958—the first formal gesture of support from the Communist
party for the insurrection.[112]

Most of Castro's early associates, however, were not Communists. Only
one of the participants in the Moncada attack was a Communist party member—Fidel's younger brother, Raúl, who had been a member of the party's
youth wing but who had joined the attack despite party objections.[113] After
the Moncada attack failed, the party condemned it.[114] The only intellec-
tually self-conscious Communist who became a close associate of Fidel
Castro's during the guerrilla war was Guevara, whom he met in 1956 in
Mexico.[115] Though not a party member, Guevara was explicit about his
ideology: "I belong to those who believe that the solution of the world's
problems lies behind the so-called iron curtain, and I see this Movement as
one of the many inspired by the bourgeoisie's desire to free themselves from
the economic chains of imperialism."[116]

On December 2, 1961, for the first time, Castro proclaimed on Cuban
television: "I am a Marxist-Leninist, and I will be one until the day I die."[117]
He said he had had "prejudices" against communism and the Communist
party, and that "I could not call myself a full-fledged revolutionary" even

on January 1, 1959. He hinted that he had toned down his radicalism as early as the 1953 statement in an attempt to broaden his appeal. A few days later, he added, "we have never deceived anyone." He went on: "Were we full-fledged Marxist-Leninists? No, we were not full-fledged Marxist-Leninists." But, he said, he had taken ideas "from Marxism-Leninism in my formative period." And as for speaking of Marxism-Leninism in the mountains, "we called it something else, we did not broach this subject, we raised other questions that the people understood perfectly."[118] In January 1962, Castro added: "When we began this struggle, we already had some knowledge of and sympathy for Marxism. But we could not for this reason call ourselves Marxists . . . We were revolutionary apprentices."[119]

In an interview in 1965, Castro reflected on these issues: "I think that all radical revolutionaries . . . do not announce programs that might unite all their enemies on a single front . . . In the Moncada program we had declared that we were going to nationalize some North American businesses, such as the electric company and the telephone company, and naturally we were in the middle of a struggle where it was not at all practical to say exactly what we intended to do with those businesses." Moreover, "in these circumstances, to have said that our program was Marxist-Leninist or Communist would have awakened many prejudices."[120]

The context of the December 1961 and January 1962 speeches is important. With the U.S. government still putting strong pressure on Cuba, Soviet aid and protection had become essential for the survival of revolutionary rule. The more orthodox a Marxist-Leninist Castro could portray himself to have been and to be, the more secure Soviet help would be. Thus his repeated denial that he had been a full-fledged Marxist-Leninist before 1959 is credible.

"Nobody is born a revolutionary," Castro told Lee Lockwood in 1965. "A revolutionary is formed through a process. It is possible that there was some moment when I appeared less radical than I really was." When Lockwood asked Castro whether those who had supported his original program "later had the right to feel that they had been deceived," Castro replied, "I told no lies in the Moncada speech . . . That was how we thought at the moment . . .[but] we have even gone beyond that program and are carrying out a much more profound revolution."[121]

The ideas of a political leader can, do, and should change as history unfolds. There is nothing inherently sinister about the fact that Castro's ideas changed throughout the 1950s. His experiences in war and, after 1959, in power probably contributed to his radicalization (which continued in the 1960s and later decades). The point is that even as Castro deepened his revolutionary convictions, he was telling Cubans and the world the exact opposite. He was suggesting, at times explicitly—as in the *Coronet* article or on film—and most often by omission of earlier themes, that he was becoming less radical and less nationalist. He has acknowledged that he toned down his views as early as *History Will Absolve Me*. The further "toning down" between 1955 and 1958 was deliberately deceptive—a deception he justified as a necessary strategy to make the revolution possible.

The subsequent shifts in Cuba's international alignments and in the course of the revolution at home resulted from the interplay between the structure of domestic and international politics on the one hand and Castro's evolving ideas and style of leadership on the other. The enduring U.S. public and private presence in Cuba required a would-be revolutionary to anticipate how the U.S. government might react to major changes within Cuba. Castro had to ponder, too, the nature of the international system at the moment of the revolution and the usefulness of becoming a Marxist-Leninist to secure the kind of support he would need from the USSR. But beyond the domestic and international factors, and beyond ideology, leadership characterized by deception and manipulation also shaped the course of the revolution. This revolution was achieved, in part, because Castro successfully deceived his enemies, many of his supporters, and the U.S. government with regard to the intensity of his radicalism at home and his hostility to the United States. These were, in fact, his primary ideas. Deception, which he believed to be both right and useful, would in the future be used as a strategy and a tactic.

Castro's strategy to reshape Cuban history was brilliant. Convinced that the revolution was impossible under U.S. hegemony, and expecting the U.S. government to move in due course to snuff out his government, he undertook radical change at home and engineered a break with the United States. The decision to seek those goals also reflected the real evolution of his ideas and his vision of what he wanted Cuba to be under his leadership.

Castro faced several problems: how not to alarm the United States so soon that it would stop the revolution before its defense was organized; how to secure Soviet support, given the fact that he had not been a Communist party member and had had poor relations with the prerevolutionary party; how to maintain popular support among a people who had not supported the Communist party, who had been oriented toward and liked the United States, who were not strident nationalists, and for whom the Soviet Union was, at best, a remote abstraction. In solving these problems, he deceived the United States and many Cubans who had supported him, gave the Soviets an exaggerated impression of his Marxist-Leninist orientation, and maintained enormous popularity.[122] He did not consider his strategy immoral because it made his rule possible and secure. This independent, self-conscious, shrewdly analytical decision to practice carefully implemented deception is a paramount explanation for the success of Cuba's revolution at home and its realignment abroad.

Beginning in March 1960, the focus of explanation shifts. Once President Eisenhower authorized the overthrow of the Cuban government, the United States became unwilling to negotiate to contain the conflict between the two countries. Both governments then escalated the confrontation.

Cuban revolutionary policy had acquired a global dimension, and Cuba began to use the international system to redress the imbalance of power of the Americas. The Cuban strategy built a close, multifaceted relationship with the Soviet Union; it supported revolutionary movements and revolutionary states; it abandoned hostility to other nonrevolutionary states and substituted the gradual reconstruction of state-to-state relations; and it exploited conflicts between the United States and other countries, including U.S. allies. Thus Cuba's global foreign policy was born.

The Security Regime

2

On April 16, 1961—the eve of the landing at the Bay of Pigs—Prime Minister Fidel Castro announced for the first time that the revolution was "socialist"; he confirmed it more formally on May Day.[1] In December, he announced that he was a Marxist-Leninist. The Cuban state owned most of the means of production outside agriculture, as well as all utilities, transportation, banking, and foreign trade. Highly centralized rule was consistent with the Cuban leaders' ideas about power; it also enabled them to root out opposition at home in order to face the foreign enemy. Cuba's own resources, however, were not enough to fight the United States. Close cooperation with the Soviet Union was needed to provide protection and resources. But as 1962 began, the questions facing Cuba came sharply into focus. What limits might the United States seek to impose on Cuban-Soviet collaboration? And what would be the framework and content of that relationship as desired by Cuba, regardless of U.S. wishes?

The tripartite military relationship among Cuba, the USSR, and the United States grew out of the October 1962 missile crisis. In early fall 1962, Soviet ballistic missiles arrived in Cuba. When the U.S. government detected them, a conflict ensued that brought the United States and the USSR to the brink of nuclear war. The settlement of the crisis, in fact, resulted in a new degree of international stability. This settlement was later modified as the three countries faced new crises, and there came about a limited "security regime": the pattern of explicit and implicit understandings among international adversaries that aims to enhance the security of each party.[2] The security regime embodies practical rules to ensure that Soviet-Cuban collaboration will be limited to the forms the United States finds permissible in exchange for a U.S. pledge not to overthrow the Cuban government. It relies on direct U.S.-Soviet consultation, with little direct contact between the United States and Cuba. It also has been one of the building blocks of Cuban-Soviet relations, which are based on Cuba's acceptance of the necessity and utility of Soviet hegemony. This chapter focuses only on the nuclear or conventional military dimensions of the tripartite relationship; Cuban military activities in other countries and support for revolutionary movements are discussed in later chapters. One of the key limitations of the security regime is that it does not restrain Cuba's activities in those areas.

Coming to the Edge of Nuclear War

On July 26, 1962, Castro worried in public: "The only danger that our country faces is that of a direct invasion by the Yankee armed forces . . . the revolution must take steps to guarantee the effectiveness of the fight and of the response to any direct attack from the Yankee imperialists."[3]

This call to arms is puzzling. During the preceding months, the Cuban press had given no hint that a major international crisis was impending. The U.S.-Cuban struggle continued, but it stopped well short of the threshold of nuclear war. The United States was also beginning to find it difficult to increase its pressure on Cuba. For example, on February 3, 1962, the U.S. government prohibited all remaining trade between the United States and Cuba, but these measures amounted to a negligible additional burden on Cuba.[4]

In April 1962, the CIA had reactivated plans to assassinate Castro by reopening contacts with underworld figures and with assassins inside Cuba, who received poison pills, explosives, rifles, handguns, and other equipment. This activity continued into 1963; other assassination plots were underway until 1965. Although these plots posed serious threats to Castro's life, it is unclear whether the Cuban police learned in 1962 of this increase in CIA activity. It is more likely that the Cuban police assumed that the CIA effort had never flagged and was simply continuing in 1962.[5]

The Cuban and Soviet governments probably became alarmed in the spring of 1962 when they learned of meetings between President Kennedy and José Miró Cardona, who headed the organized Cuban exiles in the United States and who would have become Cuba's President if the April 1961 invasion had succeeded. His last meeting with Kennedy occurred on April 10, 1962, after which the Kennedy administration and the exiles gradually became estranged. The threat from the exiles should not be exaggerated as a factor in the escalation of the U.S.-Cuban conflict, even though Castro mentioned it later as a rationale for his 1962 policy. In fact, also on July 26, 1962, Castro boasted that his government no longer feared an invasion by exiles because it was confident that it could defeat them again.[6]

There was also no evidence that the United States planned to invade Cuba with conventional forces. Cuba may have had sufficient reasons to increase its level of military preparedness to repel attacks from the United States, but the record did not justify emplacing ballistic missiles in Cuba. Nevertheless, Cuban leaders believed that an invasion was likely—considering the great hostility in U:S.-Cuban relations—and justified the introduction of ballistic missiles as the only sure way to prevent a U.S. landing.

In part, this decision was probably influenced by the reassessment of Cuban-Soviet relations that took place after a severe political crisis in Cuba itself. In March 1962, Aníbal Escalante was dismissed as organization secretary of the Integrated Revolutionary Organizations, the embryonic new Communist party. Escalante had been a key leader of the prerevolutionary Communist party. Castro accused Escalante of seeking to enhance his power and that of old Communists at the expense of the new Communists, who had fought alongside Castro. Many other old Communists were expelled from the new party, even though they had been close to the USSR, helping the Soviets reassess the meaning of the Cuban revolution.[7] This internal upheaval in the party called for a clarification of Soviet-Cuban relations.

For these various reasons Cuba and the Soviet Union moved to improve their relations. The United States had tracked the arrival of Soviet military supplies in Cuba since 1960.[8] A lull in such shipments came during the first half of 1962, coinciding with the Escalante crisis. On July 2, Armed Forces Minister Raúl Castro left for Moscow. Cuba and the USSR agreed to deploy strategic weapons to Cuba.[9] Soviet weapons shipments resumed. Direct radio and telephone communications between Moscow and Havana were also established for the first time.[10] Cuban-Soviet relations became even more cordial in August, when Alexandr Alexeev became the Soviet ambassador to Cuba. *Revolución* printed his biography, portraying him as a backslapping, smiling man, a fluent Spanish speaker, and Soviet founder of the bilateral relationship.[11] On August 24, the U.S. State Department briefed the press about the arrival in Cuba of Soviet surface-to-air missiles (SAMs), other equipment, and between three thousand and five thousand Soviet personnel, many of whom were military technicians (though they did not appear to be organized in combat units).

On September 3—for the first time—Cuba and the USSR admitted that a new arms buildup was under way in Cuba.[12] On September 4, President Kennedy outlined acceptability in U.S. terms: "There is no evidence of any organized combat force in Cuba from any Soviet bloc country; of military bases provided to Russia; of a violation of the 1934 treaty relating to Guantánamo; of the presence of offensive ground-to-ground missiles; or of other offensive capability either in Cuban hands or under Soviet direction and guidance. Were it to be otherwise, the gravest issues would arise."[13] Kennedy was also under intense domestic pressure regarding Cuba as a result of the failure of the 1961 Bay of Pigs invasion and the upcoming U.S. congressional elections in November 1962.[14] On September 13, he clarified his administration's policy: "If at any time the communist buildup in Cuba were to endanger or interfere with our security . . . or if Cuba should ever . . . become an offensive military base of significant capacity for the Soviet Union, then this country will do whatever must be done to protect its own security and that of its allies."[15]

In September and October, Cuba received from the USSR offensive weapons capable of carrying nuclear bombs. Nuclear warheads were not identified and were perhaps never deployed in Cuba, although they probably would have been sent later; otherwise, the missile launchers would have been pointless.[16] The new weapons included medium-range ballistic missiles (MRBMs), intermediate-range ballistic missiles (IRBMs), and jet light bombers (IL-28s). According to Cuban and U.S. sources, the final total of MRBMs and IRMs was forty-two.[17] Cuba also received what were then the most advanced Soviet jet fighters, MiG-21s,[18] as well as additional SAMs, cruise missiles, and Komar guided-missile patrol boats. Cuba had been receiving older MiG aircraft since the end of 1961.[19] However, the first hard evidence of offensive missiles was found on October 14.[20] On October 22, Kennedy imposed a naval blockade of Cuba.

On October 23, Fidel Castro responded, giving the superpowers an eventual exit from the crisis: "If the United States were able to give Cuba effective and satisfactory guarantees with respect to our territorial integrity and were to cease in its subversive and counterrevolutionary activities against our people, Cuba would not need to strengthen her defenses."[21]

On October 28, Moscow Radio broadcast the text of Prime Minister Nikita Khrushchev's letter to Kennedy. In it he pledged that "the arms which you describe as offensive" would be dismantled and returned to the USSR.[22] The world thus stepped back from the possibility of nuclear war. For the United States, the key elements in the solution were summarized in Kennedy's letter to Khrushchev:

1. You would agree to remove these weapons systems from Cuba under appropriate United Nations observation and supervision; and undertake, with suitable safeguards, to halt the further introduction of such weapons into Cuba.

2. We, on our part, would agree—upon the establishment of adequate arrangements through the United Nations to ensure the carrying out and continuation of these commitments—(a) to remove promptly the quarantine measures now in effect and (b) to give assurances against an invasion of Cuba.[23]

There was, and has been ever since, ambiguity in the terms of the settlement. President Kennedy's statement on September 4 indicated that the United States did not require the withdrawal of the SAMs, their requisite radar equipment, the Komar-installed short-range surface-to-surface missiles, or the thousands of Soviet technical military advisers.[24] The United States did insist that the MRBMs and the IRBMs had to go. Thus the three issues still to be settled were the presence of the IL-28s, the presence of Soviet combat troops, and the procedure for carrying out inspections; these issues could be worked out only in the context of Cuban-Soviet relations.

Cuba, the Soviet Union, and Crisis Management

The details of the missile crisis and its resolution provide insight into how the Soviet Union and Cuba responded to a volatile situation and into how, together and separately, they made decisions about actions that should be taken. Four notable examples of the decision-making process are discussed below.

The Installation of Strategic Weapons
Considerable confusion exists about the origin of the suggestion that strategic weapons be sent to Cuba. The September 3, 1962, Cuban-Soviet communiqué on military relations is the only public document pertinent to the question of who took the initiative in the military buildup of the summer of 1962, although this document makes no reference to missiles. It states:

> There was an exchange of views concerning the threats against Cuba from the aggressive imperialist circles. Because of those threats, the Government of the Republic of Cuba has approached the Soviet Government requesting help in providing armaments and the necessary technical advisers to train Cuban military personnel. The Soviet government took this request into consideration, and an agreement concerning this problem was reached.[25]

Herbert Matthews reports that Fidel Castro gave him "three different" and "contradictory" explanations over time. Matthews's final impression was that "Khrushchev had put forward the idea and Fidel had jumped at it, with enthusiastic support from his brother and Che Guevara."[26] Hugh Thomas has recorded many of Castro's contradictory statements (though Thomas, too, leans to the view that the Soviets took the initiative). Thomas argues, however, that the formal request almost certainly came from Cuba, because that is how Cuba and the USSR generally behaved. Even if the idea originated with the Soviets, Castro was probably happy with it since he had welcomed so warmly Khrushchev's "figurative missiles" in July 1960.[27] Carlos Franqui (then editor of *Revolución*) and Soviet defector Arkady Shevchenko, a former close adviser to Soviet Foreign Minister Andrei Gromyko, agree as well: It was a Soviet initiative, to which Cuba responded enthusiastically.[28]

By 1984, Castro's story had become more consistent. Cuba discussed with the Soviets the seriousness of its security problem, he said, without specifically recommending the placement of nuclear weapons in Cuba. Cuba wanted clear guarantees against a conventional war, especially against a U.S. invasion. The Soviets, in response, proposed the placement of missiles in Cuba, and Cuba accepted "without any hesitation."[29]

My own judgment is that Cuba formally requested strategic weapons on its territory, and this is also the official position of the Soviet government and of the Cuban armed forces.[30] But the first suggestion that the missiles be sent to Cuba probably came from the Soviets, and Cuba no doubt consented eagerly, viewing the offer as an appropriate response to its previous, more general request for full guarantees of its security. There has never been any suggestion that the Cuban government was unwilling to accept the missiles or that the Soviets coerced it into compliance. The USSR made its decision for a mixture of reasons, ranging from protecting its Caribbean ally to gaining an advantage over the United States.[31]

The terms under which the Soviet missiles were deployed in Cuba were important. Cuba granted the USSR extraterritorial rights to set up strategic nuclear bases. Carlos Franqui claims to have seen the Cuban-Soviet agreement and states that it specified that "the Cuban land on which the missiles would be set up would be Russian property."[32] In addition, as Castro explained on November 1 when referring to the missiles:

> The strategic weapons were not the property of Cuba. In the agreements on account of which they were sent to our country to strengthen our defenses in the face of threats of attack, it was agreed that these strategic weapons would remain under the command of Soviet personnel and would continue to be property of the Soviet state. Therefore, when the Soviet government decided to withdraw those weapons that belonged to them, we respected that decision.[33]

The Shooting Down of a U.S. Reconnaissance Plane

The Soviet and Cuban governments clearly differed in terms of their willingness to engage in war. Castro felt that, for a small country such as Cuba, there was little difference between conventional and nuclear war. "Conventional weapons with the employment of masses of airplanes are equivalent to the use of atomic weapons," he stated. Conventional attack by the United States on Cuba "would cost us millions of lives," Castro said, because the prolonged resistance of the entire population would result in a great many casualties.[34] Therefore, crossing the nuclear threshold was less significant for him than for the Soviets.

Castro's willingness to risk war bears on three conflicting versions of what happened at the peak of the missile crisis. A U.S. U-2 reconnaissance plane was shot down over Cuba on October 27, 1962, killing the pilot. This, the only armed attack and the only casualty during the crisis, could have triggered war.

The most common explanation of this event is that the plane was shot down by Cuban-operated SAMs.[35] Most, perhaps all, of the SAMs had been transferred to Cuban ownership. Castro's many references to his intention to shoot down any intruding aircraft are consistent with the explanation that the Cuban armed forces already had this capability. The official view of Cuba's Air Force and Anti-Aircraft Defense (DAAFAR) is that its forces shot down the U-2; a monument marks the place and preserves the remnants of the plane.[36] But DAAFAR probably could not have done this on its own; an independent Cuban SAM force was not even created until March 1963 because, though Cuba had the necessary technicians, it did not have the requisite engineers.[37]

The explanation that the Cubans shot down the plane is consistent with Castro's forthright statement in 1974: "The order to shoot at aircraft was given by us. We had the control over the anti-aircraft guns . . . Of course, at that time there was no Cuban personnel that could operate these ground-to-air missiles. They were Soviet specialists. But the order to the anti-aircraft to open fire was given by the Cuban side."[38]

Franqui has proposed a second version: Castro was visiting one of the Soviet bases when a U.S. U-2 reconnaissance airplane appeared on the screen. He asked how the base would protect itself if it were an attack plane. When he was shown the button to launch a ground-to-air missile, he pushed it, and the Soviet missile brought down the U-2 plane.[39] This explanation cannot be verified; Franqui does not say that he saw Castro do it.

Castro gave Tad Szulc a third version in 1984. Consistent with Franqui's story, Castro said that the U-2 was shot down by a Soviet SAM. But, in contrast with the other explanations, Castro told Szulc: "It's still a mystery how it happened. We had no jurisdiction and control over Soviet anti-aircraft missile batteries. We couldn't have fired against the U-2. But a Russian there, the battery commander, fired."[40] Castro implies that no Soviet-Cuban coordination occurred, that Cuba had no SAMs capable of shooting down the U-2, and that Cuba was not responsible for the incident.

In fact, Cuba did own SAMs in 1962; it is not clear how many SAMs in Cuba, if any, were Soviet-owned. Cuban officers were assigned to the Cuban-owned SAMs but, as Castro later explained, Cuba lacked trained personnel to operate the SAMs for another two years. When Castro was asked in July 1964 whether Cuba had full control over its anti-aircraft equipment, he replied: "The learning process with these weapons has been proceeding slowly."[41] Not until January 1965 could Castro boast, "It is in Cuba's hands to make a decision if the circumstances compel us."[42]

Khrushchev's letter to Kennedy on October 27, 1962, muddles matters further: "The weapons on Cuba, that you have mentioned and which, as you say, alarm you, are in the hands of Soviet officers," he wrote. "Therefore, any accidental use of them whatsoever to the detriment of the United States of America is excluded."[43] Minutes after this letter was issued in Moscow, the U-2 was shot down over Cuba.[44] Khrushchev's reference to the "hands of Soviet officers" skirts the question of ownership. It is consistent with the view that Cuba did not have full autonomy in the operation of its own SAMs in 1962, but it is not clear whether Khrushchev was referring only to offensive strategic weapons, intending to exclude the Cuban-owned SAMs from this reassurance.

During the 1962 crisis, Castro clearly suggested that Cuba was able to shoot down the U-2, and he seemingly took responsibility for the incident. Castro wrote to United Nations Secretary-General U Thant on November 15, 1962, concerning U.S. steps to inspect Cuban territory by air through the U-2s: "We wish to give warning that . . . any war plane which violates the sovereignty of Cuba by invading our air space can only do so at the risk of being destroyed."[45]

The contradiction between Castro's statements in 1974 and 1984 may be more apparent than real. Although Cuba had no jurisdiction or control over Soviet-owned missile batteries, it did have jurisdiction over its own. Cubans alone could not have fired the SAMs; a Soviet officer probably had to take operational responsibility for doing so, but Castro may nonetheless have given an order that was executed by a Soviet officer. Even if Castro's 1984 version is correct—and Cuba was not responsible for the shooting—the action was consistent with his reiterated intention to have such planes shot down and with his reasoning about the lack of significant differences between nuclear and conventional war. The incident furthered Castro's goal: hindering a settlement between the United States and the Soviet Union that would require the removal of the ballistic missiles from Cuba.

Most SAMs, perhaps all, were already owned by Cuba, though Cuba did not have the necessary trained specialists nor full operational autonomy over the SAMs. It therefore seems credible that Cuba and the USSR share responsibility for shooting down the U-2, and that Castro gave the order executed by Soviet specialists working with DAAFAR.[46] Fortunately, Kennedy postponed retaliation for this incident so long that it was never needed.[47]

The Removal of Strategic Weapons

Although the Soviets retained command and ownership of all the ballistic missiles stationed in Cuba, their decision to withdraw the weapons without consulting Cuba still came as a shock. Franqui learned of the Soviet decision from the wire services. He called Castro, who knew nothing. Castro was furious and reportedly began cursing.[48] Three years later, Castro explained his reaction in an interview: "We were . . . advocates of keeping the missiles in Cuba. Furthermore, the possibility that the Soviet Union would withdraw them as an alternative had never entered our minds." He agreed with an interviewer who characterized Khrushchev's behavior toward Cuba during the missile crisis as "highhanded."[49] In 1984, Castro still described himself as having been "very irritated" that an agreement had been reached without consulting him.[50] "We disagreed," Castro added in 1985, "because the decision was made without consulting us. That is the crux of the problem."[51]

Immediately, Castro formulated a strategy to advance his government's interests even at the risk of impeding the implementation of the U.S.-Soviet agreement.[52] On October 28, the same day the USSR agreed to remove the missiles, Castro went on television to say that Cuba would accept the settlement only if the following five points were also included:

Cessation of the economic blockade and of all the commercial and economic measures being carried out by the United States against our country throughout the world.

Cessation of all subversive activities, of the dropping and landing of weapons and explosives by air and sea, of the organization of invasions by mercenaries, and of the infiltration of spies and saboteurs . . . carried on from the territory of the United States and certain accomplice countries.

Cessation of the piratical attacks being carried out from bases in the United States and Puerto Rico.

Cessation of all violations of our air space and territorial waters by United States aircraft and warships.

Withdrawal from the naval base at Guantánamo and return of the Cuban territory occupied by the United States.[53]

In spite of Cuba's new conditions, the Soviets began to dismantle the missile installations.[54] Three days later, Castro told the Cuban people that the government would reject on-site international inspection even if its five points were accepted. Castro noted his "unhappiness" because "some differences arose during the evolution of the crisis between the Soviet and Cuban governments." But he also emphasized that he had "confidence" in the Soviets, who had been "good and generous" toward Cuba.[55]

Besides the ballistic missiles, the United States insisted on the removal of the IL-28s. Unlike the missiles, these aircraft had been donated by the Soviets to the Cubans, as was also the case with the MiGs and most or all of the SAMs. The Soviets affirmed that they did not intend to provide the Cuban IL-28s with the capability to deliver nuclear weapons, and they insisted that the planes could not be withdrawn without Cuban authorization. They said that the bombers were still physically under Soviet control, although the Soviets were obligated to transfer them to the Cubans.[56]

Revolución summarized the Cuban-Soviet differences on its front page by quoting Khrushchev: "We believed in Kennedy's word. The Cubans tell us that they do not."[57] The Cubans also told the Soviets that they would not accept on-site inspection and would not agree to the withdrawal of the IL-28s.[58] Carlos Lechuga, Cuban ambassador to the United Nations, said publicly that the IL-28s belonged to Cuba, that a transfer of ownership had occurred, and that their status was no different from that of other Soviet-supplied military aircraft that Cuba owned.[59]

A breakthrough came on November 12, when Soviet Deputy Prime Minister Anastas Mikoyan (in Havana from the second of November to the twenty-sixth) publicly endorsed Cuba's five points as a "program for peace" in the long run, but did not endorse substituting it for the inspection agreed to in the U.S.-Soviet settlement.[60] A week later, Cuba caved in. Castro wrote U Thant that the IL-28s were "antiquated equipment," adding that the planes were Soviet property—thus, "if the Soviet government considers [it] desirable for the smooth conduct of the negotiations and the solution of the crisis to withdraw these planes," then Cuba "will not object." He reiterated his promise to shoot down any U.S. planes that intruded into Cuban air space without authorization, and he continued to refuse to accept on-site inspection.[61] On December 12, Khrushchev reported to the Supreme Soviet that the IL-28s had been removed. He endorsed Cuba's five points as a "long term" solution to the crisis in the Caribbean.[62]

In 1963, Cuba relented slightly on its no-inspection policy. It would allow on-site international inspection provided its five points were implemented and the inspection included a "system of multiple verification in the countries of the Caribbean region, including the corresponding parts of the United States."[63] This new demand, reasonable for Cuba to make, was utterly unacceptable to the United States.

The Soviet Troops in Cuba

The final issue to be settled among the three countries was the presence of Soviet military personnel in Cuba. The U.S. government estimated that 17,000 Soviet troops and technicians were in Cuba at the peak of the crisis, including 4 combat groups. Private U.S. military experts put the number at 25,000.[64] Both figures are underestimates. Castro said later that "there were more than 40,000 Soviet soldiers in Cuba" at the height of the crisis and added that, in his view, "Kennedy was not concerned about the 2,000 or 3,000 Soviet military personnel left behind."[65]

The Soviets wanted to withdraw most of their troops; they were no longer needed for the operation or protection of strategic weapons. The Cuban government wanted a continued Soviet military presence, perhaps as insurance that some Soviets would die if Cuba were attacked.[66] This rationale applies to the presence of U.S. armed forces in Western Europe: it makes it more difficult to separate a superpower's fate from that of its allies.

Only Soviet military personnel whose work was directly linked to the missiles left; the Kennedy administration tacitly but unhappily agreed that some Soviet military staff would remain to train the Cuban armed forces. "The truth is that we did not think small numbers of Soviet ground forces in Cuba were a serious matter," wrote the President's Special Assistant for National Security Affairs, McGeorge Bundy, years later.[67] Kennedy administration officials repeatedly noted the continued presence of Soviet troops in Cuba throughout 1963. The Soviets made no promises not to introduce other military trainers or combat troops into Cuba in the future.[68] What constituted "training" was not specified; it could even include joint training maneuvers between a Soviet combat unit in Cuba and some units of the Cuban armed forces.

Toward a Limited Security Regime

The settlement of the 1962 crisis established the foundations for a limited security regime between the United States and the USSR and, grudgingly, between the United States and Cuba. These mutual understandings began with the pursuit of short-run self-interest: The superpowers wanted to avoid nuclear war. But at the heart of the enduring relationship among these countries has been the successful deterrence of U.S. aggression by the USSR and

Cuba. Given the size and training level of Cuba's armed forces and the Soviet alliance, successive U.S. governments have decided that the costs of invading Cuba in the absence of a world war are too high.

Gradually, a set of norms, rules, and procedures have also developed that are consistent with the notion of security regime formation. It remains an informal regime; there has never been a formal written agreement. What are often called the "understandings" take this form: You understand that I understand that I expect you to be committed to a certain course of action and not to another. The essence of the 1962 bargain is that each superpower stopped doing what the other found most objectionable. The joint gain was the avoidance of nuclear war.

The United States compelled the removal of Soviet strategic weapons from Cuba, and the Soviets promised not to reintroduce them; the USSR allowed U.S. verification of the Soviet withdrawal. The settlement recognized U.S. nuclear exclusivity in the Americas—a technological updating of the Monroe Doctrine, keeping outside powers from establishing a nuclear weapons presence in the hemisphere. The Soviet Union, humiliated before the world, nonetheless gained a conditional promise from the United States not to invade Cuba. That sole Soviet gain was undermined, however, by Cuban policy, and the arrangement defined in 1962 did not, in fact, go into effect at that time.

On November 20, 1962, President Kennedy noted that Cuba had not agreed to on-site inspection. Consequently, the United States would continue "to pursue its own means of checking on military activities in Cuba." The President pledged that the United States would "not, of course, abandon the political, economic and other efforts of this hemisphere to halt subversion from Cuba nor our purpose and hope that the Cuban people shall some day be truly free. But these policies are very different from any intent to launch a military invasion of the island." The President specified that "important parts of the understanding of October 27 and 28 remained to be carried out"—above all, the need for "adequate verification and safeguards." The President did not say that the United States would invade Cuba if these conditions were not met, but he left it clear that U.S. compliance with the settlement depended on adequate inspection.[69] By the same token, the failure to carry out fully the terms of the understandings also meant that the Soviets were not prohibited from introducing nuclear weapons delivery systems in Cuba, a subject that would resurface in 1970.

In a 1982 retrospective on the crisis, Secretary of State Dean Rusk, Secretary of Defense Robert McNamara, Under Secretary of State George Ball, Deputy Secretary of Defense Roswell Gilpatrick, White House Counselor Theodore Sorensen, and McGeorge Bundy said that the U.S. assurance not to invade Cuba did not "ever become a formal commitment of the U.S. Government."[70]

The Soviets tried to put the best face on a bad situation. Khrushchev told the Supreme Soviet that the "United States gave before the world a public statement not to attack the Cuban Republic and to restrain their allies from doing so. Both Cuba and the Soviet Union have reached satisfaction." He made no reference to any conditions attached to the statement.[71] The Cubans were not fooled, however. Cuban Ambassador Lechuga told U Thant that there was no "effective agreement" because the U.S. government's "mere promise not to invade Cuba . . . has never been given formal shape."[72]

The 1962 settlement left some other issues unresolved that would later haunt the parties. The United States disliked the continued presence of Soviet troops in Cuba, but it did not make their withdrawal a part of the settlement, nor did it seek a pledge that no combat troops would be introduced in the future. Moreover, there was no mention of naval bases to service Soviet strategic weapons-bearing submarines, although that might be considered within the "spirit" of the 1962 settlement.

It was agreed in 1962 that the United States would tolerate Cuba's own military might below the threshold of strategic weapons. Thus the United States insisted on the withdrawal of the IL-28 bombers, but not on the withdrawal of MiG-21 jet fighters or other MiGs. Nor did the United States insist on the dismantling of the SAMs or on other disarmament measures in Cuba. Indeed, there might not have been a major crisis in 1962 if Cuba had received only non-nuclear weapons; Kennedy had accepted this level of militarization before the October crisis. On November 20, Kennedy also made it clear that the United States opposed Cuban support for revolutionary movements abroad and would counter such Cuban policies. But the President said that such Cuban behavior would not in itself be enough to nullify the no-invasion pledge, which depended only on adequate inspection.

Much retrospective analysis has focused on the merits of the missile crisis settlement. One objection is that it allowed the Cuban government to consolidate its authority; that was explicit in the bargain. Another criticism is that its terms have been broken. As President Ronald Reagan put it in his radio address of December 14, 1985: "What are we to do about Cuba's willful disregard of the 1962 Kennedy-Khrushchev understanding of which President Kennedy said, 'If Cuba is not used for the export of aggressive communist purposes, there will be peace in the Caribbean?'"[73] This objection has been spelled out by the National Bipartisan Commission on Central America, chaired by Henry Kissinger:

The euphoria surrounding the resolution of the Cuban missile crisis in [1962] seemed to open the prospect that the Cuban revolution would at least be confined to its home territory . . . This was more than an expectation. It was a declared policy objective of the United States. Obviously it has not been achieved. The problem has been that it was eroded incrementally. This often made it difficult to see the erosion clearly and, as a practical matter, made it even more difficult to halt at any given point. The increases in the Cuban threat were always so gradual that to stop them would have required making a major issue of what was, at the time, only a small change. The total effect of such small changes, however, has been . . . an enormously increased military power and capacity for aggression concentrated on the island of Cuba, and the projection of that threat into Central America (as well as into Africa and the Middle East).[74]

This and Reagan's statements contain several inaccurate assertions: Both suggest that the 1962 settlement included a restraint on Cuban support for revolution elsewhere and that Cuba's projection of military power overseas was banned in 1962. The Kissinger commission also falsely suggests that the increase of Cuba's military power was forbidden. Furthermore, it is incorrect to imply that such Cuban behavior is an erosion of the 1962 settlement.

From a U.S. perspective, and with hindsight, perhaps the U.S. government should have attempted to prohibit Cuba's support for revolutionary movements and to limit Cuba's buildup of non-nuclear weapons. It would have required great foresight, however, to have imagined in 1962 that Cuba would eventually deploy troops overseas. The problem with these criticisms is that they ignore two central facts. First, in 1962 the world was close to nuclear war; insistence on secondary issues would have carried the risk of crossing the nuclear threshold, thus sacrificing fundamental goals for the sake of worthy but less vital interests. Second, the USSR had only limited control over Cuba, which was willing to risk war even over the existing terms of the settlement. Had the United States attempted to impose greater restraints on Cuba, the likelihood of war would have increased. Even today, the 1962 settlement passes two tests of history: It made sense then, and it makes sense now, even if it is, of course, not the answer to all problems in relations among the United States, the Soviet Union, and Cuba.

Implementing the Security Regime

Although the 1962 crisis did not actually establish a security regime, it set the stage for one: Each government took some steps to accommodate the security concerns of the other two. The Soviets withdrew their strategic weapons. The United States gave a conditional pledge not to invade Cuba, which it fulfilled. And Cuba, in consenting to the removal of the IL-28s that it owned so briefly, acquiesced in the deal, under protest.· During the next quarter-century, each government took steps that strained or violated the spirit of the 1962 settlement, but each also took steps to strengthen it. All three have made unilateral, unreciprocated concessions as time has passed.

U.S. Policies toward Cuba

Until 1970, the United States was responsible both for actions that undermined the 1962 settlement and for steps that promoted it. In the aftermath of the 1962 crisis, the U.S. government disbanded Operation Mongoose, the goal of which had been to promote an internal revolt in Cuba. But in June 1963, President Kennedy approved a new program of sabotage against Cuba "to nourish a spirit of resistance and disaffection."[75] Simultaneously, however, the administration began to explore accommodation with Cuba. Ambassador William Atwood, a special adviser to the U.S. delegation to the United Nations, conducted discussions in New York with the Cuban ambassador to the United Nations. One intermediary was French journalist Jean Daniel, who met with Kennedy and subsequently with Castro in Havana.[76]

The confusion of U.S.-Cuban relations was epitomized on November 22, 1963, when Daniel met with Castro to convey informally Kennedy's thinking about improving bilateral relations. That same day, Kennedy was assassinated, and a CIA agent gave a poison pen to a high official of the Cuban government (whose code name was AM/LASH) to be used to assassinate Castro.[77] It remains unclear at what level the CIA assassination plots were authorized during the Kennedy and Johnson administrations, although top CIA officers believed they had presidential authority.[78] The Cuban government knew that such plots were under way. In any case, the CIA continued to support AM/LASH in an attempt to have Castro assassinated until mid-1965, when the relationship was ended.[79] AM/LASH was probably Rolando Cubelas, a commandant of the university students' Revolutionary Directorate in the war against Batista and later a key Castro ally. In February 1966, Cubelas and six others were arrested for plotting with the CIA to assassinate Castro with U.S.-made weapons.[80]

U.S.-Cuban relations during these years remained troubled, in part because Cuba did not recognize a gradual shift in U.S. policy. In April 1964, President Lyndon Johnson discontinued authorization for CIA-controlled sabotage raids against Cuba; thus he formally (but secretly) abandoned the goal of overthrowing Castro, although the last CIA contact with a potential assassin took place in mid-1965.[81] Because Cuban exiles continued their efforts at sabotage and assassination on their own, because they had been linked in the past with the CIA, and because the Johnson administration did not communicate its policy change to Cuba, it was impossible for the Cuban government to perceive the difference. Yet the United States began to behave as if it had made a nonaggression pledge to Cuba, not just a pledge that there would be no invasion. Thus U.S. policy shifted from undermining the 1962 settlement to taking unilateral, unreciprocated steps to reinforce it.

The United States changed its formal position, without securing any reciprocal concessions from the USSR or Cuba, on August 7, 1970. At the end of July, the Soviets sought a statement from the Nixon administration concerning the status of the 1962 settlement. National Security Adviser Henry Kissinger ascertained from the State Department that there had been no formal agreement, either orally or in writing, although the exchanges were "sufficiently lengthy and detailed to constitute mutual assurances." Kissinger summarized the key points for Nixon. "However," he stated, "the agreement was never explicitly completed because the Soviets did not agree to an acceptable verification system (because of Castro's opposition) and we never made a formal non-invasion pledge." Kissinger also noted that the Soviets had removed their missiles and had not reintroduced them, and that the United States had not invaded Cuba.[82]

On behalf of President Nixon, Kissinger communicated to the USSR a reformulation of the security regime. The United States defined the understandings "as prohibiting the emplacement of any offensive weapons of any kind or any offensive delivery system on Cuban territory. We reaffirmed that in return we would not use military force to bring about a change in the governmental structure of Cuba."[83] The U.S. government had thus dropped the question of on-site inspection, even though Kissinger knew that this had been a sticking point. A security regime that had never gone into effect for that very reason was now being "reaffirmed." No concession was sought or extracted from the Soviets, much less from the Cubans. No mention was made of aircraft of any type, or of Soviet troops in Cuba.[84] To be sure, Kissinger's reformulation of the terms of the settlement rested also on the significant improvement since 1962 of U.S. technical surveillance through satellites and spy planes, so that on-site inspection was no longer so important. But the United States was giving up a political claim for reciprocal Soviet or Cuban concessions.

Then, the plot thickened. After deteriorating during the 1960s, Soviet-Cuban military relations improved. In July 1969, a Soviet flotilla visited

Cuba for the first time. In early 1970, Amed Forces Minister Raúl Castro spent several weeks in the USSR. And on September 16, 1970, a U.S. U-2 plane discovered evidence that new naval facilities were being built at Cuba's Cienfuegos harbor.[85] On October 5, the Soviet government "reaffirmed" the 1962 understanding and stated that it was not doing anything in Cienfuegos to contravene that settlement. Soviet Ambassador Anatoly Dobrynin told Kissinger that "while he could not make an agreement that Soviet subs would never call at Cuban ports, he was prepared on behalf of his government to affirm that ballistic missile submarines would never call there in an operational capacity." According to Kissinger, Dobrynin asserted that the Soviets did not have and would not build a military naval facility in Cuba, and that they considered all exchanges with the United States since August 1970 to be amendments to the 1962 understandings.[86] The Soviets stopped their construction activities in Cienfuegos; the Soviet news agency TASS reiterated publicly that the USSR was not building a submarine base in Cuba.

The Soviet "challenge" to the United States in 1970 was, in fact, modest. On the eve of the U.S. discovery that naval facilities were being built at Cienfuegos harbor, there was no Soviet submarine in that harbor. No full-scale base was ever built, and there was no floating drydock in Cienfuegos.[87] Nevertheless, the 1970 amendments to the 1962 understandings were useful. Once again, each side stopped doing what the other found objectionable. In October, the United States obtained a clarification of the 1962 settlement, banning submarines carrying ballistic missiles from operating out of facilities in Cuba. In August, the United States established the precedent of nonreciprocal concessions when it dropped the requirement for on-site inspection. The Soviets and the Cubans gained a "reaffirmation" of the previously unconsummated 1962 understanding. They also gained U.S. toleration of Soviet naval visits to Cuba, begun in 1969, as long as these remained below the specified threshold. President Reagan reaffirmed this Soviet right in 1981.[88] The Cuban Navy has had its own base at Cienfuegos since before the revolution; nothing in the amendment prevents the Soviets from assisting in the development of that base. Thus, in 1970, all gained and no side lost anything of consequence.

Soviet and Cuban Policies toward the United States
The Soviet and Cuban governments bore the responsibility for the 1962 and 1970 crises. In the early 1970s, Soviet naval visits to Cuba were stepped up, undermining the 1970 amendments. The Soviets also tested the limits of the 1970 amendments by sending different types of submarines, eventu-

ally including some carrying ballistic missiles to various Cuban ports.[89] Access to Cuban ports enabled the Soviets to continue employing older, diesel-powered submarines, which generally cannot remain out on patrol for long periods. But Soviet naval deployments have never amounted to a full-scale base of operations in Cuba.[90]

Soviet activities since 1970 have remained well within the boundaries of the 1970 understanding and in line with Dobrynin's statement to Kissinger. They pose no serious threat to U.S. security. They include reconnaissance missions to identify Western naval ships and to collect intelligence on Western ships and aircraft.[91] Cuba also benefits because its navy trains with the Soviet navy through joint maneuvers contributing, albeit modestly, to their joint defense.[92] These maneuvers have continued in the 1980s.[93]

After 1970, the next major event affecting security relations among the United States, the Soviet Union, and Cuba was a unilateral step by Cuba. At the first congress of the Cuban Communist party in December 1975, Fidel Castro recalled how difficult it was initially to "understand fully the value" of the 1962 settlement, but he now solemnly acknowledged its worth; thanks to it, the threat of U.S. invasion had receded.[94]

Just as, in 1970, the United States had unilaterally dropped a condition that had prevented the establishment of the security regime, Castro did the same in 1975 by making no mention of the "five points" Cuba had insisted on in 1962—although he stopped short of saying that Cuba felt bound by the understandings. In 1975, Cuba wanted to support the USSR but, with thousands of Cuban troops engaged in war in Angola, it may also have wanted to reassure the United States. Whatever its motives, Cuba sought no reciprocal U.S. concession, and it got none.

The willingness of the Soviets and the Cubans to behave moderately within the evolving security regime was tested in 1978–79. In November 1978, the United States discovered the arrival of MiG-23 fighter bombers in Cuba, the first major qualitative upgrading of Cuba's Air Force since 1962. The United States invoked the 1962 understanding and was reassured by the Soviets that the planes lacked strategic weapons (although some versions of this plane can carry them), consistent with the Soviets' view of their 1962 commitments, which they were prepared to honor. This was the same distinction as that drawn in 1962 between the IL-28s, which had to be removed, and the MiGs, which were permitted to stay.[95]

During the 1978 incident, the Cubans and the Soviets reassured the United States, and Armed Forces Minister Raúl Castro gave praise: "There is a difference between the Carter administration and its predecessors." He saw a new "realism that led to some positive steps." More in sorrow than in anger, he commented on the "deep contradictions" in the Carter administration's policies toward Cuba, including the "threat of creating a crisis" because of the discovery of the MiG-23s, which, he said, had actually arrived in Cuba about a year earlier, when Cuba's engagement in the Horn of Africa was at its peak.[96] To end the secrecy about the new planes, Cuba began to display them in public.[97] In communicating with the U.S. government, the Soviets went beyond reassurances of compliance with the 1962 understandings. Dobrynin told the U.S. government that it was "free to make a public statement about the non-nuclear capability of the aircraft, but that we should not imply that the Soviets had agreed not to increase the number of MiG-23s that could be supplied to Cuba."[98]

More difficult to handle was the U.S. discovery in 1979 of a Soviet ground force unit in Cuba. By the late 1960s the United States had lost track of the residual Soviet troop presence in Cuba. The Soviet brigade was found as a result of stepped-up U.S. intelligence on Soviet activities after the fall of the Shah of Iran. This rediscovery surprised and troubled the United States because it surfaced in the midst of U.S. Senate debate about the strategic arms limitation treaty (SALT II). The incident of the "Soviet brigade" was one factor in the failure of the U.S. Senate to ratify that treaty. The finding evolved into a crisis, above all, because of domestic political considerations in the United States. Eventually, the reconstruction of the intelligence data in late 1979 suggested that there had been a continuous Soviet troop presence in Cuba. The Soviets were surprised, too, that they were pressed to change their policy when they were doing nothing differently.[99]

President Castro reassured the United States: "You call it a brigade and we call it a training center . . . set up at the end of the 1962 October crisis." He stressed accurately that it was "within the spirit of the October agreements . . . within the status quo established as a consequence of the spirit of the October crisis . . . We have no nuclear weapons, we have no strategic weapons . . . There has been absolutely no change in the functions or the size of that installation."[100]

Castro's moderate response allowed the Soviets to be moderate too and gave the Carter administration a way out. The earlier understandings were amended yet again. In effect, the Soviets agreed for the first time not to introduce combat troops into Cuba in the future, nor to turn the existing unit into a self-sufficient combat force. Also for the first time, the mutual understandings were extended to cover conventional forces. The Soviets were conscious that these changes went well beyond the 1962 or 1970 understandings. They were making a unilateral concession. In return, they gained little: renewed official U.S. acceptance, dating back to 1962, of a continued Soviet military ground force presence in Cuba.[101]

President Castro's comments on the Soviet brigade, however, revealed a new set of problems. He confirmed that Cuba had received MiG-23s, which it owned and operated, and that Cuba had recently received its first diesel-powered submarine. In contrast to earlier arrangements, Soviet personnel in the unit that concerned the United States were expected "to work with us . . . subordinated to our armed forces" in "training and maneuvers."[102] Thus whereas in 1962, the Soviets had reassured the United States that the weapons in Cuba were still in Soviet hands, in 1979, Cuba was reassuring the United States that it had not installed a Soviet base because Cuba owned, operated, and directed all the activities at issue. While at one level this was preferable for the United States, it also meant that Cuba's own military capabilities were becoming a U.S. security concern.

In 1979, Castro identified an emerging problem. Despite his acknowledgment in 1975 of the worth of the 1962 settlement, and despite Cuban consent to the withdrawal of the IL-28s in 1962, he said, "we are not bound by that agreement because . . . we were not a party to it."[103] He was right: Cuba was not a party to the understandings in the same way that the United States and the Soviet Union were. New problems within the security regime could not be addressed by the United States and the USSR alone, since Cuba's growing military capability was beginning to affect U.S. security directly. Thus the new U.S. security concerns with regard to Cuba stemmed, ironically, from U.S. and Soviet decisions not to consult Cuba in 1962. Those decisions set the precedent of handling security matters concerning Cuba through the U.S.-Soviet channel, leaving the Soviets to deal with Cuba. Within two decades, the procedure that had allowed the United States to humiliate Castro in 1962 had become a disadvantage of the settlement and an impediment to the resolution of future conflicts.

The Reagan Years

The security regime was confirmed by President Reagan. Secretary of State Alexander Haig proposed in 1981 to bring "the overwhelming economic strength and political influence of the United States, together with the reality of its military power, to bear on Cuba" to deal with the problems of revolution in El Salvador "at its source." Instead, Haig reported, "Reagan, despite some sentiment among his advisers to do otherwise, decided to abide strictly by the understandings on the status of Cuba reached by the U.S. and the USSR in the aftermath of the Cuban missile crisis."[104]

Reagan's policies toward Cuba have shown much ambivalence. On December 14, 1984, Reagan forcefully called attention to the violations that, as he perceived it, the Soviets and the Cubans had committed against the 1962 understandings and asked rhetorically what should be done about them.[105] Ironically, on the same day, his government signed a migration agreement with Cuba whose terms required the U.S. government to defend Cuba's human rights record (so that those who had been found "excludable" under U.S. immigration law could be returned to Cuba) and to agree that Cubans entering the United States in the future would be considered normal immigrants, not "refugees" fleeing from Communist persecution. In short, the most conservative U.S. President to have dealt with Castro's Cuba chose, like the others, to abide by the terms of the security regime, however flawed he considered them, as preferable to the alternatives.

The Security Regime: Principles, Rules, and Procedures

Since 1962, a trilateral, limited security regime has emerged among the United States, the Soviet Union, and, more ambiguously, Cuba. It originated from each country's acting in its own self-interest and from the threat of war in 1962, and was strengthened by the successful Cuban-Soviet deterrence of U.S. actions. Although the regime has been plagued by crises resulting from ambiguities in the understandings themselves, each crisis has also been resolved according to the same principle: Each side should avoid, or should cease to do, what the other finds most objectionable. Each crisis has also defined ever more specific rules about the type of military collaboration the United States will tolerate between the USSR and Cuba. Each crisis has relied on the same procedures for its resolution: high-level communications between the USSR and the United States in the context of Cuban actions. It is difficult to understand, for example, why the Soviets made a concession in 1979 if one does not take into account the change in Cuba's attitude toward the 1962 settlement in the intervening years and, thus, its change of behavior in 1979.

The U.S.-Soviet-Cuban security regime has several key features.[106] The regime is desired by the two superpowers and, since 1975, by Cuba. In 1970, 1978, and 1979, each party took care to avoid humiliating the others and to avoid making threats of war. The three parties, believing that the understandings advance mutual security, have used them as a basis for fresh negotiations. The understandings reflect norms of prudence and the underlying balance of power, but the parties have gone beyond mere power relations to strengthen the barriers against armed conflict through the arrangements that now characterize the security regime. Had the regime not been developed, the crises in 1970, 1978, and 1979 might have been more contentious. By the 1970s, the Soviet Union had reached strategic parity with the United States: In contrast to its 1962 situation, the USSR no longer had a compelling reason to back down. Nor did Cuba fear a U.S. invasion during the Carter presidency. That both backed down is best explained by the existence of the security regime. Neither side has sought expansion of its power within the limits of the understandings; rather, their goals have become moderate.

Competition within the scope of the understandings is now focused on the specification of rules, not on a wider conflict. All parties see war as very costly; that was the reason to pull back in 1962, and it is also why the United States moved from informal to formal observance of the no-invasion pledge and why the Soviets and the Cubans, too, have been conciliatory. The increase in Cuba's military capability in the 1970s made the security regime more stable by increasing the costs to the United States of nonobservance. With Soviet backing, Cuba successfully deterred a U.S. attack. But the continued increase in that capability poses new problems for the trilateral regime.

Thus far, precedents have been binding within the context of the limited understandings. They have been alluded to, applied, and refined. The three states have not discarded the principles, rules, or procedures established in the initial settlement as their interests and capabilities have changed; understandably, however, all have sought to amend them to fit new circumstances. And although immediate self-interest remains paramount, the unilateral and, at times, nonreciprocal concessions made by all three parties suggest that they have a complex vision of their long term interests, one that requires the regime's preservation.

The fact is all three countries have gained from these understandings, as their conceptions of security have converged over time. Cuba came to value the security regime as promoting its own survival and to define its interests as consistent with those of the Soviet Union and the United States. Cuba stopped pressing the USSR to contradict the understandings, and began to act in ways that made the resolution of conflicts more likely. The Soviets, in turn, felt that their initial decision in 1962 was justified: the survival of their Cuban ally was ensured.

From the U.S. point of view, the trilateral regime updates the Monroe Doctrine for the nuclear age. With regard to Cuba, in contrast to all other theaters of war, the Soviet Union has recognized the strategic supremacy of the United States and pledged not to challenge it. In 1979, the USSR even accepted limitations on the deployment of its conventional forces. Thus it may be surprising that most of the disaffection with the security regime is felt by the United States. This dissatisfaction results from focusing on the security regime's limitations and losing sight of its accomplishments.

The trilateral security regime has always involved restrictions on U.S. behavior. The understandings commit the United States not to invade Cuba. Although U.S. conservatives find this restriction unacceptable, its consequence—a guarantee of Cuba's security—defines the regime itself: those who oppose that feature must prepare to declare war. Moreover, the understandings do not, nor were they ever designed to, prevent the increase of Cuban military power, the deployment of Cuban troops in other countries, and Cuban support for revolutionary movements. These limitations of the understandings have been present since their origin; the 1962 settlement never addressed the issues of Cuba's own power or its activities in other countries. These issues deserve attention, but as part of the broader foreign policies of the parties. A valuable international arrangement need not be abandoned just because it has not solved all problems of legitimate interest to the three countries.

A New Agenda

New issues have arisen in the military relations among the three countries since the late 1970s; in particular, both Cuban and U.S. military capabilities and doctrine have changed in ways that threaten the other's security interests. But these interests can be addressed within the context of the existing trilateral understandings, provided both countries deal directly with each other.

U.S. military doctrine has evolved, in recent years, with great concern about the ability of North Atlantic Treaty Organization (NATO) countries to fight a general conventional war in Europe. One approach holds that increasing NATO conventional war capability would reduce U.S. need to use nuclear weapons, and this strategy has bipartisan support as a means to arms control. But U.S. and other NATO forces in Europe would, under such a policy, have to be resupplied from the United States during a prolonged conventional war, and many of these reinforcements would have to come from ports in the Gulf of Mexico. Under these circumstances, Cuban or Soviet military attacks in the Straits of Florida would imperil U.S. and NATO strategy.[107]

Also since the late 1970s, Cuban military capabilities have vastly improved. The successful Cuban interventions in Angola and Ethiopia in the period 1975–1978 led to an accelerated modernization of Cuban weapons inventories. Cuba needed more up-to-date equipment to do the job; the Soviets rewarded Cuba's good military performance with weapons. The deterioration of U.S.-Cuban relations as a result of Cuba's intervention in the Ethiopian-Somali war in 1978 gave greater urgency to the Cuban military buildup. Two aspects of this buildup may affect U.S. ability to resupply troops in Europe in the case of general conventional war: the introduction of MiG-23 fighter bombers and of diesel-powered submarines in Cuba.[108] The MiG-23s were far beyond Cuba's previous capabilities; and the submarines, though old models, can cause much damage in war, as did German submarines in the Caribbean and the Gulf of Mexico during World War II.

Were a European war to break out, one tactic could be a direct U.S. strike in Cuba to destroy the aircraft; intensive antisubmarine warfare would follow. Because air strikes might be incomplete and antisubmarine warfare is difficult and slow, an invasion of Cuba might be required. The United States, remember, would already be fighting a general war against the Soviet Union in Europe. Even a successful U.S. attack on Cuba short of invasion would significantly delay and impair the resupply of Europe, leading to many U.S. casualties and a drain of U.S. assets.

The more seriously one takes this scenario, the more sense it makes to amend the trilateral security regime in the following way: Cuba should agree, with Soviet consent, to remain outside a war between NATO and the Warsaw Pact countries. Cuba could demonstrate its adherence to this policy by keeping its submarines above water in designated ports and its aircraft on the ground. The United States, too, could keep its aircraft on the ground at bases in southern Florida and Guantánamo. Movement of aircraft by either party would require advance notice.

Such an amendment to the trilateral regime would serve both Cuban and U.S. interests because war would be prevented between them. Both sides would require an explicit amendment to the understandings because they could not assume that the previous understandings would continue to hold once war had broken out between the United States and the Soviet Union. Even in the absence of war, such an amendment would serve their joint interests because it would establish procedures to address the arrival of even more modern Soviet military supplies in the years to come.

The amendment would serve Cuba's primary security concerns in two ways. First, the new understanding would ensure Cuba's survival in the event of a general war. Second, even if no such war were to take place, the understanding in itself would accord Cuba the recognition of sovereign equality it has long sought from the United States. It would engage the United States in a process of negotiation that would reduce the likelihood of bilateral conflict, even in the absence of a European war. The proposal would even serve some Soviet interests; its ally would not be destroyed if war broke out in Europe, and Soviet forces in Cuba could continue to monitor U.S. war movements.

For the United States, the understanding would make it possible to fight more effectively in the event of war; even in the absence of war, it would allow the United States to plan and deploy its resources more effectively. The process of negotiation with Cuba might also curtail other Cuban foreign policy behavior to which the United States objects. Moreover, since Castro is known to be least predictable when decisions need to be made quickly and under great pressure (see Chapter 9), as would be the case if war broke out in Europe in the absence of prior understandings, the amendment would serve the interests of all by providing a framework conducive to more rational behavior on Castro's part.

Is it reasonable to expect that Cuba would not automatically fight on the Soviet side in the case of a war in Europe? Yes, for current Cuban policy already decouples Soviet and Cuban fortunes in war. Cuba is not a member of the Warsaw Pact. And at a moment of tense Cuban-Soviet relations in December 1984, the Cuban Communist party's Central Committee reported to the Cuban people its "decision and . . . strategy to resist through our own forces" in the case of a U.S. attack. This was possible "thanks to Soviet assistance," but the report conveyed the clear impression that the Soviet and Cuban governments had agreed that no Soviet troops would defend Cuba if the United States attacked.[109] If the USSR is exempt from going to war to defend Cuba, why should Cuba not be exempt from going to war to defend the USSR?

On its own, the Cuban government has taken some steps to build trust between the United States and Cuba. As noted above, the Cuban government makes public information about its MiG-23s and its submarines, thereby helping U.S. intelligence. Cuban leaders have also made reassuring statements about Cuba's willingness to abide by the terms of the security regime even if Cuba does not consider itself to be a full participant.

After the Chernobyl nuclear power plant accident in the USSR in April 1986, at the request of Florida Congressman Michael Belirakis, Cuba made public some information about the safety features of the two nuclear power reactors being built with Soviet assistance near Cienfuegos; Castro also offered to exchange more information with the United States about the safety of their respective nuclear power plants (for years Cuba has been supplying technical information on its nuclear energy program to the International Atomic Energy Agency). Following this Cuban step, in September

1986 the USSR agreed to give the United States technical information on the safety features of the two nuclear reactors being built near Cienfuegos.[110] And in 1988 Cuba and the United States began to negotiate to allow a U.S. nuclear plant safety team to inspect the Cienfuegos facility while a comparable Cuban team would inspect a U.S. nuclear plant.[111]

On another point at issue between the two countries, in 1984 Cuba further modified its views on what unilateral U.S. inspection measures it would accept. U.S.-Cuban negotiations over immigration and the repatriation of 2,746 Cubans then in the United States, begun in July 1984, were suspended by Cuba in August because of the direct flight of a U.S. SR71 reconnaissance plane over Cuba. Castro told the *Washington Post:* "Practically all the data the United States wants to get about Cuba they can get through satellites . . . and through the flights around Cuba." The flights directly over Cuba remained unacceptable, Castro said, but he signaled for the first time that flights around Cuba would be allowed.[112] The United States replied that the overflight was unrelated to the immigration negotiations, which resumed and resulted in an agreement in December 1984. Although the Cubans believe that the number of reconnaissance flights around Cuba increased from 8 during the Carter administration to 120 during Reagan's first term, they also believe that the frequency of flights directly over Cuba remained unchanged from the Carter to the Reagan administrations.

In fact, by the late 1970s Cuba had told the U.S. government in private that it understood that the United States had the technical means of verifying Cuban and Soviet activities by means of planes and satellites—a process to which Cuba did not object because it could not stop them. But Cuba continued to object to direct overflights. The significance of Castro's interviews in 1985 was that they made public Cuba's conditional acceptance of U.S. surveillance.[113]

The behavior of both governments, as well as Castro's statements, indicate that Cuba and the United States are now closer to agreement on one of the central issues of 1962: U.S. inspection of military activity in Cuba. The Reagan administration has not been willing to cancel direct reconnaissance flights over Cuba, but it has behaved with restraint. Cuba, in turn, has accepted flights around Cuba and satellite surveillance. The Central Committee even recognized that Cuba's national security required that "Pentagon and CIA strategists should know that we are strong in every respect"— such knowledge, they believed, would deter a U.S. attack.[114] Though Cuba had balked at U.S. inspection in 1962, in 1984 it came to acknowledge that its own security depended on it.

If the two governments address each other directly on old and new matters that affect their joint security, building on and going beyond the norms, rules, and procedures of the trilateral understandings begun in 1962, a safer world may result, to the benefit of all. The value of the trilateral security regime has been well tested. During the second half of the 1980s, for the first time since 1962, the future evolution of that regime rests mainly in the hands of the U.S. and Cuban governments.

Cuba's Challenge to the Soviet Union in the 1960s

3

Cuba has always existed in a hegemonic relationship with a superpower, either the United States or the Soviet Union. During the first thirty years of revolutionary rule, Soviet hegemony over Cuba was constructed gradually, painfully, and at great cost; in the end, however, the relationship was successfully established to the benefit of both governments. The end of U.S. hegemony over Cuba in 1959–60 did not quickly lead to easy relations between Cuba and the USSR. Instead, friction permeated the first decade of Cuban-Soviet relations. Only since the end of the 1960s has Cuba become one of the USSR's closest allies, a relationship that has deepened since the mid-1970s.

Hegemony in Cuban-Soviet Relations

Hegemony is a form of an international regime, combining structural and ideological components. The distribution of power is so asymmetrical in a hegemonic relationship that the dominant state ordinarily prevails over the client in virtually all areas at issue. The dominant state resists and seeks to reverse policies that it considers adverse to its interests. However, coercion is a brittle and unstable basis on which to fashion hegemony. Most dominant states also pursue policies that are helpful to the client, and they have clothed their power in an ideology that promotes their claim to serve the common good. As discussed in this book, the notion of hegemony includes both the dominant state's disproportionate power and its acceptance by the client as legitimate and beneficial to both. Hegemony also implies that the client has some autonomy and that the dominant state restrains its behavior. Hegemony is in part imposed, but only in part; in order to be stable, hegemony depends too on its being wanted by the client.

Cuba had greatly loosened the bonds of U.S. hegemony before the revolution; public conflicts developed frequently between the U.S. and Cuban governments. U.S. hegemony was manifested through the actions of U.S.

firms and citizens, which penetrated Cuban society and economy. The Soviet Union, by contrast, does not have direct foreign investments in Cuba. Its hegemony is exercised over the Cuban government and, through the government, over the Cuban economy and society. Although the manifestations of U.S. and Soviet hegemony within Cuba have differed, the two hegemonic relationships have shown greater similarities internationally. Even so, U.S. hegemony over Cuba before the revolution had become less restrictive, while Soviet hegemony after the revolution tightened during the 1960s and into the 1970s and 1980s.[1]

Hegemony is a variable, not a constant. A situation based originally on power alone might evolve toward true hegemony, as in the cases of U.S.-German relations after 1945, U.S.-Cuban relations between 1902 and 1958, and Cuban-Soviet relations after 1968. Moreover, hegemonic relations may be "loose" or "tight." In a loose hegemony, such as that which characterizes U.S. relations with Western Europe, Canada, Japan, and prerevolutionary Cuba, serious foreign policy disputes may arise in public. The United States exercises its dominance over a few important security and economic issues while permitting conflicts in other areas.

In a tight hegemony, in contrast, serious disputes may arise between the client and the dominant state but not be aired in public. Nor does the client undertake policies in opposition to the dominant state's defined interests. A tight hegemony does not end autonomy, though it makes the exercise of autonomy more difficult. The USSR exercises such a tight hegemony over Cuba; it is characterized by the asymmetrical concentration of power in Soviet hands, the shared ideology that justifies Cuban subordination to Soviet foreign policy, the institutionalized coordination of policies through centralized bureaucracies to provide benefits for both countries, Cuba's commitment not to criticize the USSR publicly or oppose its foreign policy in practice, and, nonetheless, Cuba's retention of considerable autonomy in the formulation and implementation of foreign policy. Despite these restrictions on its actions, a tight hegemony does not render Cuba a mere puppet of, nor a proxy for, the Soviet Union.

Because Cuba had sought even greater autonomy from the Soviets in the 1960s, the two countries came to open conflict in 1967–68, when the USSR had to coerce Cuba into recognizing Soviet hegemony. Once this conflict was weathered, the two countries' relations evolved toward greater consensus and greater Cuban acceptance of the legitimacy of Soviet hegemony, as evidenced by the minimal foreign policy differences between the two countries since 1970—and in no case has Cuba opposed major Soviet interests.

At key moments, moreover, especially after 1970, Cuba came to exercise its autonomy from the USSR by leading the Soviets on foreign policy issues, although it remained mindful of and behaved consistently with Soviet interests. By taking a position in the vanguard, it succeeded in modifying Soviet behavior toward Third World revolutionary situations. At the same time, Cuba supported Soviet foreign policies, often acting in partnership with the Soviets. For these reasons, Cuba's policies presented a worrisome challenge to its adversaries.

In short, Cuba's current relations with the Soviet Union differ from the relations that both superpowers have with their European clients. Cuban leaders are much more likely than Eastern Europeans to "want" Soviet hegemony. Cuba lacks the troubled history of war and other conflicts that bedevil Soviet relations with Eastern Europe, and Cuba is not physically occupied by Soviet troops. Compared to the much looser relations between the United States and Western European countries, the Cuban-Soviet link is a very tight bear hug.

Cuban-Soviet Relations, 1962–1968

Cuba's revolutionary government did not come to power on the backs of Soviet tanks, unlike the governments of every other Communist country closely tied to the USSR as a full member of the Warsaw Pact. Indeed, Fidel Castro is the only long-time leader of a Soviet ally who came to power denying he was a Communist. Thus the establishment of Soviet hegemony necessarily followed an unusual pattern. Between 1960 and 1962, Cuba's overtures to the USSR culminated in the stationing of Soviet strategic weapons in Cuba, but the settlement of the 1962 missile crisis strained Soviet-Cuban relations and delayed Cuban acceptance of Soviet hegemony. The resulting period of difficult relations—economic, political, and military—lasted through 1968, when Cuba differed publicly with the USSR over important issues.

Economic Relations
The Cuban revolution could not have survived at home without Soviet economic assistance, nor could it pursue its far-flung foreign policy today without Soviet aid. This economic dependence on the Soviets remains a key constraint on Cuban policies as well as a powerful instrument for their implementation. The nature of the assistance is complex. No dollar figure captures its many dimensions (nor is such a figure calculable), but the scope of the support can be suggested.

The Soviet Union and other socialist countries rescued Cuba from economic strangulation in 1960, when U.S. economic pressures failed to over-throw the Cuban government, primarily because of the Soviet decision to back Cuba. By 1965, the USSR accounted for 47 percent of Cuba's exports and for nearly 50 percent of its imports, while the Council for Mutual Economic Assistance (CMEA) countries, which included the USSR and its Eastern European allies, accounted for 61 percent of both imports and exports.[2] Cuba came to depend also on Soviet subsidies, notably in the form of preset prices for sugar, Cuba's main export. The Cuban-Soviet economic treaty of 1960 called for Soviet purchases of Cuban sugar at prevailing world market prices, with the Soviets paying for only one-fifth in convertible currency and the rest through barter trade. In 1961 and 1962, the Soviets agreed to pay higher than market prices (4.09 cents per pound versus 2.7 to 2.8 cents per pound of sugar sold on the world market).[3]

Largely because of a sharp decline in Cuban sugar production and exports, the world price of sugar skyrocketed early in 1963, with the result that the Soviets were then paying less than the prevailing world market price. On April 27, 1963, Fidel Castro arrived in the USSR for the first time and was greeted with great fanfare by Soviet leaders. During the thirty-seven day visit, Castro and the Soviets explored a range of subjects, from the countries' differences during the 1962 missile crisis to the emerging problem of sugar prices. The world price of sugar had risen to 8 cents a pound in the London market (about double the Soviet price), averaging well over 10 cents a pound during Castro's visit.[4] The two countries signed a new agreement, according to which the Soviets agreed to pay 6.11 cents per pound; they also released Cuba from the obligation—which Cuba had not been able to fulfill—to deliver a fixed quantity of sugar to the USSR. During 1963, the world market price for sugar averaged 8.34 cents, over a third above the price set by the Soviets.[5] In explaining this agreement to the Cuban people, Castro emphasized Soviet "generosity" in increasing the price it paid to Cuba. In fact, however, Cuba was selling its sugar in 1963 at higher prices on the world market, and the share of Cuban sugar exported to the USSR fell from 41.2 percent in 1962 to 27.8 percent in 1963.[6] (Total Cuban exports to the Soviet Union fell from 42.3 percent in 1962 to 30.2 percent in 1963.)[7]

Upon his return to Cuba, Castro also announced a change in Cuban economic development strategy. Since 1959, Cuba had emphasized rapid industrialization even at the expense of sugar production. For a time, Cuban leaders thought of sugar cane itself as the curse of history; therefore, sugar cane cultivation was neglected and at times curtailed. This strategy backfired, as the drop in sugar production deprived Cuba of the foreign exchange it needed to import machinery and equipment for industrialization. As a result of the Cuban government's policies and of the continuing U.S. economic offensive, a severe economic crisis ensued. Strict rationing was imposed in 1962 (and, though eased, persists in the late 1980s).

In June 1963, Castro announced that Cuba would again emphasize sugar production, forgoing rapid industrialization. In January 1964, he committed Cuba to produce 10 million tons of sugar in 1970.[8] Although the renewed emphasis on sugar production was sensible, Castro had chosen an outlandish production target—about double the "normal" sugar output of the 1950s—compared with a 1963 output of only 3.8 million tons. The new policy of increasing sugar production was also bound to contribute to a worldwide oversupply of sugar and, therefore, to depress world sugar prices.

Much sounder was Cuba's new policy with regard to the price paid by the Soviets for sugar. Cuba understood that the high free market prices of 1963 were aberrant. A prudent policy would forgo high short-term gains for more modest, but more reliable, prices from the USSR over the long run. In January 1964, Castro returned to the Soviet Union to sign a new treaty on the sugar trade. The Soviets agreed to buy 24 million tons of Cuban sugar between 1965 and 1970 at the set price of 6.11 cents per pound. The purpose of the treaty was to "eliminate the influence that the fluctuations in the world market price of sugar have on the economy" of Cuba and "to create a more solid base for planning the economic development of Cuba in the long run."[9] The new treaty ended the Soviet obligation, defined in the 1960 treaty, to pay for one-fifth of its sugar purchases in convertible currency; this change further limited Cuba's economic options, linking it more closely to the Soviet economy. But the most sensitive issue remained: The fixed Soviet price for sugar was once again about half the prevailing world market price. Castro explained, "We insisted on the establishment of a fixed price and a long term agreement covering the sale of our sugar. This was much more convenient for us than receiving high prices now, for instance, during this year, of say eight or nine cents per pound . . . we had to have in mind what would happen when the price of sugar dropped to three cents per pound."[10]

This proved to be a statesmanlike and farsighted decision. Although still high in 1964, the world price of sugar dropped sharply for the rest of the decade. Between 1965 and 1970, the average world market price never exceeded 3.7 cents per pound; in 1966, 1967, and 1968, it ranged between 1.8 and 1.9 cents per pound. The price paid by the Soviets, therefore, was at least two to three times more than the prevailing world market price for the duration of the treaty; this amounted to a massive and, at last, a generous Soviet subsidy to the Cuban economy. Most U.S. and Soviet scholars agree that, from 1960 to 1967, the amount of this subsidy ranged from $730.1 to $736 million (but see Appendix B).[11] From 1960 to 1971, the cumulative Soviet sugar price premium amounted to $1,202 million dollars.[12] This premium amounted to an outright grant: it did not have to be repaid and did not carry interest, nor did the Soviets control how Cuba would use the transferred resources. Although the Soviet-Cuban trade in sugar proved to be good for Cuba in the long run, the need for Cuba to accept a price lower than that which prevailed in the world market in 1963 and 1964 probably added to the strains in the two countries' relations.

From 1960 to 1964, in addition to the sugar subsidies, the Soviets also provided Cuba with loans to promote economic development worth $459 million, at interest rates of 2 to 2.5 percent, repayable in ten to twelve years.[13] During the 1960s, these loans helped Cuba to build or improve over 160 major industrial enterprises, including the modernization of 114 sugar mills. The pace of Soviet support for economic development accelerated in the early 1970s; by the end of 1974 the enterprises built or modernized by the USSR accounted for 10 percent of Cuba's gross industrial product. To further these projects, 4,500 Cubans were trained in the Soviet Union through 1971, and thousands of Soviet specialists worked in Cuba.[14]

Soon another loan program, also bearing low interest rates, was needed to finance Cuba's trade deficits with the USSR. While Cuba showed surpluses in its trade with the Soviets in 1960 and 1961 (about 64 million pesos combined), massive annual trade deficits began in 1962, never below 100 million pesos per year, and amounted to 3,637 million pesos from 1962 to 1974.[15] The lowest bilateral trade deficit occurred in 1965, and even that represented over 14 percent of the total trade turnover (exports plus imports) between Cuba and the USSR in that year. The size of the trade deficit increased during the late 1960s.

Some of the terms under which Soviet-Cuban trade was conducted contributed to strains between the two governments. When Ernesto (Che) Guevara, Cuba's minister of industries, addressed the Second Economic Seminar of the Organization of Afro-Asian Solidarity, held in Algiers in February 1965, he argued that the "development of countries now starting out on the road to liberation should be paid for by the socialist countries." He explicitly rejected the common Soviet view of "developing mutually beneficial trade based on prices rigged against underdeveloped countries." With socialist countries trading at prevailing world market prices in many products—and, except for the Soviets and the Chinese, purchasing Cuban sugar at those prices—Guevara stated, "We must agree that the socialist countries are, in a way, accomplices of imperialist exploitation . . . The socialist countries have the moral duty of liquidating their tacit complicity with the exploiting countries of the West." Although Guevara acknowledged the premium prices paid by the Soviets and the Chinese for Cuban sugar, he said, "this is only a beginning; the real task consists of fixing prices that will permit development."[16]

In 1965, Cuban officials complained that the price of Soviet exports to Cuba had risen to offset the premium on sugar; Cuba's purchasing power had not in fact improved. As a result, a joint Cuban-Soviet board was established to work out import prices.[17] Problems may also have arisen because the price of machinery and equipment for CMEA countries in the 1960s was about 30 percent higher than the level indicated by world market prices (even taking into account the normal lag in the adjustment of CMEA prices to the world market).[18] The National Bank of Cuba, disregarding that time lag, is reported to have found in a 1965 study that the price of goods imported by Cuba from the USSR exceeded world market prices for the same goods by 50 percent.[19] A comparison of premium prices paid by the Soviets for Cuban sugar and of premium prices paid by the Cubans for Soviet machinery and equipment shows that Cuba subsidized the USSR more than the latter subsidized Cuba in 1960, 1964, and 1965 (although Cuba came out ahead for the entire period 1960–1964). The renegotiation of machinery and equipment prices in 1965, and increased Soviet sugar subsidies relative to the world market price of sugar since then, put Cuba well ahead in this exchange during the second half of the 1960s.[20]

The hard bargaining required to place Cuban-Soviet trade relations on terms favorable to Cuba may have soured the relationship overall. Although the negotiations worked to Cuba's advantage, Guevara's harsh rhetoric must have hurt the Soviets. Cuban-Soviet political relations deteriorated sharply at the very moment when economic relations became more satisfactory for Cuba. This is but one of many cases in modern Cuban history when good economic relations alone have failed to prevent a deterioration in overall relations, and when the quality of political relations has proved more significant than the quality of economic relations.

Political and Military Relations
On September 28, 1963, Castro broke publicly with the Soviet Union over a legacy of the 1962 missile crisis: the Nuclear Test Ban Treaty. He announced that, given U.S. hostility toward his regime and given Cuba's unique geographic and historical situation, Cuba would not sign the treaty.

Castro took care in wording his rejection to avoid any implication that Cuba was siding with China (then vying for leadership of the Communist world) against the USSR. An example indicates how he particularized the decision:

> We are in a very concrete situation: the enemy is there, at ninety miles, harassing us, blockading us . . . Our line is to struggle against this enemy and it is, besides, our own line. Cuba has her own line which corresponds to the concrete situations in which the history of the Cuban revolution is molded and to the specific conditions of the place in the world where this happens: in the neighborhood of Yankee imperialism.[21]

On October 7, Cuba's ambassador to the United Nations, Carlos Lechuga, announced that Cuba would not sign a treaty declaring Latin America free of nuclear weapons (a Mexican initiative, with U.S. and Soviet support) unless the treaty also prohibited nuclear weapons in the Panama Canal Zone (then occupied by the United States), Puerto Rico, and all U.S. bases in the Western Hemisphere outside the mainland United States, and unless the Guantánamo naval base was returned to Cuba.[22]

In addition to these international issues, Cuban domestic affairs indicated growing tensions with the Soviets. Factional disputes within Cuba imperiled the USSR's staunchest allies within the Castro regime. In March 1964 Marcos Rodríguez, a member of the prerevolutionary Communist party (PSP), went on trial on charges of informing for Batista's police. During the month-long trial, the behavior of the old party was also examined. Many prominent members of the PSP took the stand to defend themselves and the party. Rodríguez was finally convicted and executed; several former PSP leaders were demoted from government positions after the trial. It was the second time in two years that PSP members' loyalty to the revolution had been questioned.[23]

Perhaps because of its concern over the far more serious Chinese challenge to its leadership among Communist states and movements, the Soviet Union was patient with Cuba over these differences and, on the surface at least, amicable relations continued.[24] On February 18, 1965, the USSR granted Cuba a credit of 167 million pesos to cover the bilateral trade deficit expected for the year. Seven days later—just after Guevara's charges in Algiers about Soviet collusion with capitalism—Raúl Castro went to Moscow to attend the meeting of Communist parties. The meeting was boycotted by China, which finalized the split in the international Communist movement. Cuba, which had not responded to previous invitations to attend meetings of Moscow-oriented Communist parties in March and June 1964, at last did so, siding with the Soviets against the Chinese. On March 13, Fidel Castro warned the Chinese that "division in the face of the enemy was never a correct strategy, never a revolutionary strategy."[25]

Rapid deterioration of Sino-Cuban relations followed, along with momentary improvement in Soviet-Cuban relations. By mid-1965, China was flooding Cuba with its own propaganda, aimed especially at military officers. After Cuba protested in September, China sent another 58,041 propaganda magazines. In November, China also announced that it would buy only 600,000 tons of Cuban sugar in 1966 (compared with 800,000 in 1965) and that it would sell Cuba only 135,000 tons of rice in 1966 (compared with 285,000 in 1964 and 281,800 in 1965).[26] China refused to grant Cuba new credits and insisted that bilateral trade be balanced.[27] On January 2, 1966, in his opening address to the Tricontinental Conference, gathered in Havana to promote the worldwide unity of revolutionary forces, Fidel Castro denounced the Chinese government. Mutual recriminations intensified; Cuba accused China of siding with the United States against Cuba and accused the Chinese leadership of senility.[28]

Cuba was vulnerable to restrictions on imports of rice, a staple for most Cubans. In 1959, Cuba produced about half of the rice it consumed and imported the rest.[29] Rice production then fell steadily from a high of 307,000 tons in 1960 to a low of 49,000 tons in 1965.[30] In 1965, China accounted for more than 14 percent of Cuba's imports and exports, ranking second to the USSR in importance for Cuban trade. Indeed, China alone was more important than all of Eastern Europe (not including the USSR) for Cuban trade. China also made a loan to Cuba to finance the bilateral trade deficit of 22.8 million pesos in 1965. (Notwithstanding their bad political relations after 1965, China still bought almost 8 percent of Cuban exports and supplied almost 6 percent of Cuban imports in 1970. By 1970, however, the bilateral trade was balanced, so that China did not need to provide new trade credits.)[31]

Cuba's assertion of its independence in the realm of foreign policy resumed in 1966, when it sharpened its attacks on the USSR and its allies for placing trade with Latin American countries whose governments were Cuba's enemies ahead of solidarity with Cuba. On July 26, 1966, Castro denounced trade between Communist countries and Chile (whose President was the Christian Democrat Eduardo Frei): "It is our duty to warn the socialist countries against Frei's hypocrisy . . . Cubans have every right to feel injured by any country that offers technical and economic aid to the Frei regime . . . Lamentably, countries in the socialist camp sometimes make mistakes. But it is not correct to place so much of the blame on them as on the pseudo-revolutionaries who advise and counsel them mistakenly."[32]

For some time—especially after the Tricontinental Conference—Cuba had pressed the USSR, other socialist countries, and the Moscow-oriented Communist parties of Latin America to support armed struggle as the necessary path to revolutionary victory. In a bitter polemic against the Yugoslav Communist party, for example, the Cuban Communist party's position was: "There is a multiplicity of experiences [on how to seize power] but not one of them does not support the need to use violent methods in the fight against imperialism . . . One cannot point to a single example of a victorious revolution which has failed to use, as a fundamental instrument, violence, insurrection, or the armed struggle."[33] Cuba's greetings to the USSR on the anniversary of the October Revolution were blunt: "The Cuban Revolution is Latin America's sequel to the October Revolution . . . Today our Party considers that these traditions oblige the communists of the majority of the countries of Latin America . . . to prepare and carry forward armed insurrection on behalf of national liberation . . . Those who remain on the sidelines will cease to be communists."[34]

The Cuban government was deeply distressed, not only by Soviet policy toward the rest of Latin America but also by the weak Soviet response toward the assertion of U.S. power. In 1965, more than twenty thousand U.S. troops intervened in the Dominican Republic to "prevent another Cuba"; U.S. combat troops were introduced in the Vietnam War, and the bombing of North Vietnam intensified. From Cuba's perspective, the Soviet response to U.S. attack on a Soviet ally was unacceptably mild in each case, raising questions about Soviet commitment to Cuba's defense. Cuba itself gave unqualified public support to the government of North Vietnam and to the Viet Cong fighting against the Saigon government.

Cuba saw itself as the new Mecca of revolution in the Americas and as a more faithful defender of international revolutionary interests than the Soviet Union. According to Cuban leaders, the test of a true Communist, especially in Latin America, was agreement in thought and action with Cuba. On March 13, 1967, Cuba broke with its former allies in the Venezuelan Communist party, which it accused of betraying the cause of revolution in Venezuela by abandoning the armed struggle. Cuba also strained its relations with most other Moscow-oriented Communist parties in Latin America. Castro declared, "This Revolution will follow its own line. This Revolution will never be anybody's satellite or yes man. It will never ask anybody's permission to maintain its own position either in matters of ideology or on domestic or foreign affairs."[35]

In the summer of 1967 Armed Forces Minister Raúl Castro sketched the Cuban military's position. Referring to reports of a conversation between President Lyndon Johnson and Prime Minister Aleksei Kosygin in which Johnson had asked that the Soviets dissuade Cuba from supporting other revolutionary movements, Raúl Castro asserted that Cuban-Soviet relations were based on "mutual respect and absolute independence." He added, "We have no boss; our people have no master."[36] Fidel Castro carried the thought a step further: "We must say realistically that we are thousands of miles away from any country that can give us any kind of help and, in case of invasion here, we must get used to the idea that we are going to fight alone."[37]

On August 10, Fidel Castro "condemned" economic and technical assistance from socialist states to non-Communist Latin American countries, especially Venezuela and Colombia.[38] Cuba also became the only Communist country not allied with China that did not send its top leader to the fiftieth anniversary celebration of the October Revolution; the head of the Cuban delegation was the minister of public health, who did not speak in public.[39] Conflict between the two governments had been building for some time; the most serious crisis in Cuban-Soviet relations was about to explode.[40]

In short, Cuba publicly took issue with the USSR and its allies on several points: Soviet willingness to place "state" interests ahead of support for (often small) revolutionary movements; Soviet skepticism that Communist parties should always be committed to armed struggle; the less than militant Soviet response to the U.S. attack on North Vietnam; the Soviet expectation that the USSR be respected as the leader of the international Communist movement on all issues; and, above all, Cuba's claim to be the true revolutionary Communist vanguard of Latin America.

In addition, the Cuban government pursued a radical social and economic strategy at home, one deeply at odds with the more orthodox Soviet approach to development. Cuba believed that it could march headlong into "communism" faster and with greater conviction than the Old World's geriatric socialist states. But the Cuban government's record at home left much to be desired. In carrying out its unorthodox approach to development, Cuba discontinued its use of financial instruments. Its economy, billed as centrally planned, had no budget, no plan, no auditing, not even financial statistics to determine costs. An avowedly Marxist-Leninist state, Cuba barely had a functioning Communist party and had never held a party congress, and its Central Committee met rarely. This presumed democratic regime had a make-shift Constitution, had held no nationwide elections since it had come to power, and had no legislative assemblies. This vanguard proletarian regime had allowed the decay of the organized labor movement, in effect replacing it with the small "advanced workers' movement." Workers were asked to "volunteer" to work overtime without pay; wages were paid without regard to quality of work, effort, or hardship.

During 1968, the Cuban regime launched a "revolutionary offensive," under which it closed bars and expropriated all remaining nonagricultural businesses in private hands (barber shops, hot dog stands, and the like). The regime wanted to create a "new man" and to transform the country's culture. Presumed deviants were rounded up for forced labor. Some twenty thousand political prisoners languished in jail a decade after the revolution. Tens of thousands left for the United States every year. And although the armed forces took charge of much of the sugar harvest and supervised much of the rest of the economy, the 1970 sugar harvest fell short of the targeted production of 10 million tons (8.5 million tons were produced). Radicalism at home and abroad had placed increasing pressures on the Cuban government.

The Crisis of 1968

Unlike the 1962 missile crisis, the Cuban-Soviet crisis of 1968 was not a conflict over a particular issue. Instead, tension between the USSR and Cuba, which had been building throughout the 1960s, came to a head over a number of related issues and events. The focal point was the Cuban leadership's trial of a good many former members of the PSP—the so-called microfaction—on charges of conspiring with Soviet and Eastern European officials to undermine the policies of the Cuban government and Communist party.

The first signs of tension were evident early in the year. During a speech marking the anniversary of revolutionary victory on January 2, 1968, Fidel Castro announced a slowdown of Soviet petroleum deliveries to Cuba and the concurrent intensification of oil rationing. Cuba was very vulnerable to petroleum sanctions. In 1958, it produced only 1.8 percent of the crude petroleum it needed; in 1967, when it produced a slightly higher 2.3 percent, the USSR supplied 99.3 percent of all Cuban petroleum imports.[41]

Soviet oil exports in earlier years had increased to match the increase in Cuban oil consumption; when Soviet supplies had nonetheless fallen short of demand (as at the end of 1966), Cuba had been allowed to borrow from the next year's allotment. In 1967, however, Cuban oil consumption increased 8 percent while Soviet oil supplies increased only 2 percent, well below the average 5.5 percent annual increase between 1964 and 1967. At the end of 1967, when Cuban oil supplies again fell short, Cuba requested that it be allowed to borrow from its 1968 expected oil supplies. As part of a new policy to punish the Cuban government until it changed its behavior toward the USSR and its allies, the Soviets granted only 64.2 percent of the requested fuel oil and 54.1 percent of the requested gas oil (though they granted 106.5 percent of the requested gasoline). Consequently, some petroleum for the Cuban armed forces had to be diverted for civilian use. Castro praised the Soviet effort but noted that the USSR could no longer supply Cuba as in the past.[42]

That line held only briefly. The next month, *Granma* (since 1965 Cuba's official newspaper) published without comment two articles from the Soviet press. Both noted record Soviet petroleum production in 1967, an improvement of oil technology, a reduction in the costs of oil production, and an expectation of continued increases in oil production in 1968.[43] The Soviet press also reported and cheered increased Soviet exports (including oil products) to Brazil, Chile, and Colombia, all of which Cuba considered its archenemies.[44]

Within days of the announcement of the oil import reductions, another problem surfaced as Cuba inaugurated an international cultural congress. The congress had five working commissions headed by twenty presidents, of whom five were Cubans; none, however, was from the Soviet Union or Eastern Europe (although a Soviet delegation participated in the congress).[45] At the congress Castro asserted that "there are ideas espoused in the name of Marxism that are, in fact, fossils." Conscious of his ideological heresies, Castro stated his "hope, of course, that we will not be 'excommunicated' for expressing these thoughts."[46]

At the end of the month the Cuban Communist party announced that a "microfaction" had been discovered in its midst, led by Aníbal Escalante, who had been at the vortex of the 1962 crisis and who was supported by many old-timers from the PSP.[47] The charges against Escalante and his associates were presented by the Cuban Communist party's second secretary, Armed Forces Minister Raúl Castro, to a three-day emergency meeting of the party's Central Committee. The investigation had been conducted by the Interior Ministry. Led by the Castro brothers, the Central Committee dismissed two of its members and nine others from the party.

"Microfactionists" were identified within the party, the armed forces, the Interior Ministry, the labor federation, some state enterprises, and intellectual circles. Forty-three of these people were arrested. Accused of crimes of opinion and association, thirty-five of them were convicted and imprisoned at a subsequent trial. These dissidents had opposed the government's radical domestic and international policies. In the eyes of the Cuban leaders, the dissidents were dangerous because their views were shared to some extent by many other party members not directly associated with Escalante. Above all, the Cuban leaders feared links among these Cuban government officials and party members, the USSR, and Eastern European governments and Communist parties.

Raúl Castro charged the microfactionists with having criticized Cuban policy during the 1962 missile crisis and with having praised Soviet policy instead. He also charged them with, more recently, "copying and distributing articles from Latin American leaders . . . in frank disagreement with our policies, many of which came from the TASS and Novosti agencies." Some had also met with the staff member of the Central Committee of the Communist party of Czechoslovakia, Frantisek Kriegel, who was in charge of Czech-Cuban relations; with East German technical advisers working in Cuba; with the consul and the commercial attaché of the East German embassy in Havana; with several Soviet advisers to the Cuban Interior Ministry; with the second secretary of the Soviet embassy in Havana; and with many journalists from the Soviet Union, East Germany, and Czechoslovakia.[48]

Raúl Castro also reported on his conversation with the chief of the Soviet advisers to the Interior Ministry, who had insinuated that he "should arrest" Deputy Interior Minister Manuel Piñeiro for not having reported sooner to the Soviets that some Soviet advisers had met with some of Escalante's associates. Instead, Raúl Castro had "warned" the chief Soviet adviser against "meddling in some of our internal affairs." He also reported the words of the second secretary of the Soviet embassy in Havana, Rudolf Shliapnikov (who was presumably bugged), who had joked about how delays in Soviet oil deliveries could put pressure on Cuba. Shliapnikov had also supposedly told some Cuban labor leaders that the Cuban revolution "was basically led by the bourgeoisie and the petty bourgeoisie" and that Cuba's "conditions were ripe for another Hungary."[49]

Whereas Raúl Castro exempted most Soviet and East European advisers from the charge of conspiring against the Cuban revolution, Minister Carlos Rafael Rodríguez did not. "It is no longer possible," he said to the assembled Central Committee members, "to allow a situation where many officials from government and party organizations from the socialist countries work against the Cuban Revolution even here in this country."[50]

The Cuban Communist party's Central Committee also approved the decision of the party's Political Bureau not to send a delegation to the Budapest meeting of Communist parties, sponsored by the USSR in opposition to China and its allies and attended by representatives of sixty-three Communist parties.[51] The Cuban party's Central Committee let it be known that its decision to boycott the meeting was a protest against the Soviet decision to slow down the delivery of petroleum to Cuba, requiring the imposition of further drastic measures to conserve petroleum supplies.[52]

There was also a symbolic message. The Cuban press announced the discovery of the microfaction and its links to the Soviet and Eastern European governments and parties on January 28, the anniversary of the birth of José Martí, Cuba's national hero, who died in 1895 fighting for independence. *Granma*'s front page featured the following words under a picture of Martí: "Have today's revolutionaries fulfilled Martí's mandate? . . . We have fulfilled and exceeded it because, besides having the Fatherland, we have no master."[53]

As a result of the escalating tensions between the two countries, the USSR suspended shipments of military supplies to Cuba in 1968.[54] In February, the Cuban Foreign Ministry denied a report in *Le Monde* that Cuba might purchase weapons from the United Kingdom. The reasons given were that the British probably did not wish to sell weapons to Cuba and that Cuba did not have the foreign exchange to buy them; the ministry did not say, however, that it would be wrong in principle to buy weapons from a NATO country.[55]

The USSR also suspended its technical assistance to Cuba. Cuba's radical domestic policies had made it vulnerable to this pressure. In 1967, Cuba had discontinued the degree-granting university program in accounting and suspended the teaching of the political economy of socialism; it also cut enrollment in economics courses at the University of Havana from 4,818 in 1964–65 to 1,338 in 1969–70. Consequently, Cuba depended all the more on foreign economists. Yet, as two Cuban economists wrote after the fact, "at the same time as this process occurred, foreign technical assistance was virtually frozen, as was the pre- and post-graduate training of faculty in other socialist countries."[56]

"Great is the task that faces us," Fidel Castro told the Cuban people in March 1968. "Let us struggle bravely . . . to minimize our dependence on everything from abroad. Let us fight as hard as possible, because we have known the bitterness of having to depend to a considerable extent on what we can get from abroad and have seen how this can be turned into a weapon . . . against our country. Let us fight for the greatest independence possible, whatever the price."[57] Despite this resolve, Cuba could not resist much longer the combined impact of U.S., Soviet, and Chinese economic sanctions. On August 23, Castro went on national television to discuss military intervention by the Soviets and the Warsaw Pact countries in Czechoslovakia. He began by noting that "some of the things we are about to say are in some cases in conflict with the emotions of many." He continued, "We accept the bitter necessity that required sending those troops into Czechoslovakia."[58]

Castro's speech also complained about the insufficient commitment of Eastern European countries to the cause of socialism. He was hard on Czechoslovakia—not a very courageous stand when that country was under invasion. Yet his criticisms of the Czechs reflected wider criticisms of all Warsaw Pact countries. Castro charged that the Czechs had sold World War II–era weapons to Cuba at a high price, which Cuba was still paying. They also "sold old junk with obsolete technology." Discussing the Czechs' deviation from the true principles of socialism, Castro asked whether the Soviet intervention "might mean that the Soviet Union will also stop . . . those policies that have been depending on the prevalence of the market and the beneficial effects of market prices." He reiterated that Cuba supported guerrilla movements, not what he called the "right wing" leaders of the Communist parties of Venezuela, Guatemala, and Bolivia, whom he considered responsible for "treason" to the cause of Latin American revolution. Castro criticized the constant harping on peace in the socialist countries, "which contributes to the disappearance of the spirit of struggle, to the weakening of peoples' ability to face risks and sacrifices." He asserted the impossibility of improved relations between socialists and imperialists. And he asked "whether Vietnam, Korea, and Cuba are integral parts of the socialist camp from which they cannot be wrested by the imperialists." In short, he asked, "will Warsaw Pact divisions be sent to Cuba if the Yankee imperialists attack our country?"[59]

Despite Castro's criticisms of Eastern European governments, this speech was the turning point in Cuban-Soviet relations. Castro had swallowed hard and endorsed the exercise of power by a big country over a little one. The invasion gave Cuba an opportunity to demonstrate its loyalty to the USSR in crisis; in turn Cuba called on the Soviets to pledge anew to defend socialism, not only on their borders but also in the faraway Caribbean.

In a 1975 report to the first congress of the Cuban Communist party, Castro argued that "the starting point of Cuba's foreign policy . . . is the subordi-

nation of Cuban positions to the international needs of the struggle for socialism and for the national liberation of peoples."[60] He spoke at length
about the Soviet contribution to the Cuban revolution and about Cuba's
gratitude and loyalty to the Soviet Union. The congress ratified Castro's
position with regard to the Soviets and repeated his statement in its resolution on foreign policy.[61] Gone forever were the criticisms of Soviet foreign
policies and the public assertions of Cuban independence from the USSR.

The Soviet Union had exercised its hegemonic power in 1968, making it
clear that it would no longer tolerate public Cuban criticism while it subsidized the Cuban economy. Although Soviet power is at the heart of its
hegemony over Cuba, direct Soviet pressure on Cuba was never very great
because Cuba finally got the message. But Cuban-Soviet relations evolved
as a result of the 1968 crisis in a way that goes beyond the effects of Soviet
power. At long last, Cuban leaders came to appreciate that the USSR really
had rescued the Cuban revolution in the early 1960s, and that it continued
to make Cuba economically viable. They came to understand the Soviets'
remarkable patience with Cuba's domestic and international policies of the
late 1960s, many of which failed and were eventually repudiated by the
Cuban government itself. Cuba also came to align itself more closely with
Soviet foreign policy.

Cuban leaders slowly realized that a centrally planned economy requires
planning, budgets, wages linked to the quality and quantity of work, and
other "orthodox" economic measures that the Soviets and East Europeans
employed. The first Cuban five-year plan went into effect in 1976: overtime
pay was again linked to overtime work; management reforms were implemented. The Communist party developed as well. A new Constitution went
into effect in 1976; nationwide direct local elections and indirect provincial
and national elections were held for new national, provincial, and munici-
pal assemblies.

Thus a profound ideological change occurred in Cuba, especially after
the disastrous failure of the sugar harvest to reach the targeted 10 million
tons in 1970. This change stemmed from Cuban learning as well as from
Soviet coercion. The Cuban government at last accepted a tight Soviet
hegemony. Cuba would no longer criticize the Soviet Union in public, even
when it disagreed with it in private. And Cuba would undertake policies on
its own to strengthen this newly desired hegemony.

The Reestablishment of Soviet Hegemony

4

The events of 1968 ended Cuba's dissidence and began the reestablishment of Soviet hegemony over Cuba, with much less discord than formerly. Fidel Castro had not been publicly humiliated during the conflict, nor had his government been insulted. Shrewd Soviet patience and just the right amount of force had turned the tide of events in Cuba.

The next turning point in Cuban-Soviet relations occurred in 1975 when Cuba deployed troops in Africa, pursuing its own interests but acting in close collaboration with the Soviets. This international activity strengthened Cuba's links with the Soviet Union and, because of Cuba's still-faltering economy, increased the economic costs of Cuban policy to the USSR. The benefits to the Soviet alliance of Cuba's new political and military activities overseas were manifold. Because the economic costs were so high, however, Eastern European countries were asked to share the burden.

The Soviet Union rebuilt its hegemony over Cuba on the basis of consensus rather than mere asymmetry of power, and shared the costs of supporting Cuba with other members of the Council for Mutual Economic Assistance (CMEA). Cuba received so many economic incentives that it became easier for the Cuban government to consent to Soviet hegemony than to contest it. Gradually, this Soviet policy helped to persuade the Cuban government that its relationship with the USSR was intrinsically desirable. Closeness between the two countries increased in a number of areas, especially military relations, the organization of the Cuban bureaucracy, and economic relations, which are the subjects of this chapter.

This improvement did not mean that Cuba had no reservations concerning the acceptance of Soviet hegemony. Problems recurred, especially in 1984 and in 1987. Soviet power remained at the core of Soviet-Cuban relations and although it permitted Cuba a margin of autonomy, the USSR imposed clear limits on Cuban foreign policy. Cuba could exercise its autonomy consistently with Soviet interests; it could not criticize the Soviets in public as it had done in the 1960s, nor oppose them in practice.[1]

Military Relations

Military relations between Cuba and the USSR improved soon after the resolution of the 1968 crisis. In early 1969, the Soviets resumed regular shipments of military materiel to Cuba. These weapons deliveries had been free of charge since mid-1962, when the USSR canceled the part of Cuba's debt that had been incurred through weapons purchases; Cuba was not charged for Soviet weapons thereafter.[2] In July 1969, a Soviet Navy flotilla paid its first visit to Cuba. In November 1969, Soviet Defense Minister Marshall Andrei Grechko visited Cuba; in April 1970 Armed Forces Minister Raúl Castro spent five weeks in the USSR. Soviet long-range reconnaissance aircraft began to travel to Cuba on a regular basis.[3]

Just as military relations were the catalyst for improved overall Soviet-Cuban relations in 1969, so the Soviet-Cuban military link helped deepen the two countries' ties after 1975. Cuba acquired Soviet-made MiG-23 aircraft and submarines in the late 1970s and early 1980s, and acknowledged the presence of Soviet military personnel associated with the Cuban military's "training and maneuvers"—what the U.S. government has called a combat brigade. In 1979, Castro said that between two thousand and three thousand Soviet military personnel were in Cuba (the same number as remained in 1962) and that they were "subordinated to our Armed Forces." He added that there were "Soviet [military] personnel in practically all [Cuban military] installations" (see Chapter 2).[4]

At the height of the Angolan War in 1975, Cuba began a military buildup. In December, Castro reported that over the next five years the USSR would supply the Cuban armed forces "with a considerable amount of even more modern combat arms, characterized by higher firepower, greater maneuverability, and greater automation components," on top of those weapons delivered since 1962 whose value he estimated at "several thousand million pesos."[5] In 1978, at about the time of the Cuban and Soviet entry into the war in Ethiopia, the two countries' military high commands began to plan for war jointly, even though Cuba remained outside the Warsaw Pact.[6] The same year marked the arrival of MiG-23 aircraft, MI-8 helicopters, and antitank weapons in Cuba.[7]

The continuous Cuban buildup of the late 1970s had been planned in the absence of overt, hostile U.S. actions. The same was true of a new buildup planned for the early 1980s. Although Cuba has at times suggested that it obtained Soviet weapons in response to Reagan administration hostility, the main effect of U.S. actions was to speed up deliveries of weapons that had already been scheduled. The Soviets delivered five years' worth of weapons in 1981–82, virtually doubling Cuba's military capabilities.[8] In addition, from 1982 through 1984, Cuba received about the same quantity of weapons as it did during 1981. The Soviet decision in 1984 to limit the scope of military commitment to Cuba was accompanied by a decision to increase Cuba's weapons supplies so that Cuba could defend itself.[9] Cuba does not manufacture sophisticated weapons; it began manufacturing light weapons only in the early 1980s.[10] Over the long run, therefore, the USSR and Cuba grew closer in their military relations in the 1970s and early 1980s, though the Soviets also made clear in 1984 the outer limits of their pledge of military support to Cuba. These trends coincided with their increased joint military activity in third countries (see Chapter 6).

In 1985, the U.S. government estimated that a Soviet combat brigade of 2,500 troops and a total of 7,000 Soviet military personnel were in Cuba (along with up to 8,000 Soviet civilians). The U.S. government also calculated that more than half the Soviet military equipment delivered to Cuba between 1960 and 1984, measured in terms of its value, arrived between 1981 and 1984. Periodic Soviet naval deployments to Cuba continued; through 1984, there had been twenty-four instances since such deployments began in 1969. Soviet BEAR naval reconnaissance and antisubmarine aircraft had also been deployed to Cuba fifty times through 1984. The U.S. government has reported that the Soviets operate three separate facilities dedicated to signals intelligence at the Lourdes complex, near Havana; these activities target primarily U.S. commercial satellites.[11] Clearly, military issues have had a very high priority in Cuban-Soviet relations.

Reorganizing Cuba's Bureaucracy

The reconstruction of Soviet hegemony after the 1968 crisis encompassed many other areas as well, including cultural relations. On April 22, 1969, Cuba established the Cuban-Soviet Friendship Association, the Soviet counterpart of which had been established years earlier.[12] The only surprise was that this organization—designed to promote relations in such fields as literature, music and dance, the plastic arts, and film—had not been established earlier.

After the 1970 sugar harvest debacle, the Soviets gave special attention to restructuring the organizations that managed Cuban-Soviet economic relations. The Soviets encouraged Cuba to adopt government agencies and policies modeled on theirs. At first, the Soviets may have pressured Cuba to accept these new bureaucratic methods; eventually, the Cubans realized that these methods were needed for the smooth functioning of Cuban-Soviet relations. Soviet and Eastern European bureaucratic forms were reproduced in Cuba and utilized in Cuba's dealings with those countries, to link Cuba to its allies in regular, predictable ways and to improve Cuba's economic efficiency and reduce its need for subsidies. Cuba accepted this reorganization both because it made sense and because the Soviets were insistent. At the same time, Cuba could afford the reduction of subsidies from the Soviets because the world price of sugar rose by over 300 percent from 1970 to 1974. This reduction in its dependence on subsidies also increased Cuba's leverage and autonomy.

One key step was the establishment in December 1970 of the Cuban-Soviet Joint Commission for Economic, Scientific, and Technical Collaboration, which held its first meeting in September 1971.[13] Chaired by Carlos Rafael Rodríguez, it became the mechanism for reordering bilateral economic relations. In June 1972, Fidel Castro traveled to the USSR to negotiate Cuba's entry into the CMEA, which voted to admit Cuba as a full member in July 1972.[14] As with the cultural developments described above, the only surprise is that membership had not come sooner.

Cuba's Economic Relations with the USSR

As we have seen, Soviet support for the Cuban economy has been crucial for the Cuban government's survival. Soviet resources have bolstered Cuba's domestic economy and freed other resources, enabling the Cuban government to conduct a vigorous policy abroad. At the same time, Soviet economic assistance has made it easier for Cuba to accept Soviet hegemony at the cost of limiting, to a degree, Cuba's freedom of action.[15] After the 1968 crisis, Cuba's economic relations with the Soviets had to be adjusted and expanded. In 1976, the signing of new economic agreements to contain the effects of declining world sugar prices and to reward Cuba for its victory in the war in Angola generated new, massive subsidies. This policy continued in the 1980s, though the Soviets sought at times to curtail the high costs of subsidizing Cuba's economy.

1970–1975

In December 1972, Castro traveled to the USSR to celebrate the fiftieth anniversary of its founding and to sign several major agreements: Cuba's payment of principal and interest owed to the USSR from loans dated 1960 to the end of 1972 was postponed until January 1, 1986. No additional interest would accrue on this debt between 1973 and 1985. Beginning in 1986, payments would stretch out for another twenty-five years. The origi-

nal credits had ten-to-twelve year repayment periods; this agreement length-
ened them to forty-seven to fifty-one years. The USSR, in addition, granted
new interest-free credits to cover Cuba's expected bilateral trade deficits
over the next three years, with the principal repaid beginning in 1986. The
Soviets also agreed to supply technicians to work in Cuba and to receive
Cubans for training in the USSR. Moreover, the Soviet Union granted credits worth 300 million rubles, bearing interest, to be repaid beginning in
January 1976, to finance large-scale economic development projects, which
the agreement identified, ending the hiatus in Soviet support for Cuban
development projects. The Soviets also agreed to subsidize the price of
Cuban nickel exports, raising the price per ton 35 to 40 percent above prevailing world market prices, and to build a new nickel refining plant at
Punta Gorda. Finally, the Soviets agreed to double for 1973 the price they
paid for Cuban sugar (see Table 4.1).[16]

These agreements were generous, but they required few new net transfers
of funds from the USSR to Cuba. The major component was the postponement of Cuba's outstanding debt. The Soviet sugar price agreement—
which seems an important new commitment of funds by the Soviets—
mainly adjusted the Soviet price to the rapidly rising world sugar price.
Whereas Soviet sugar subsidies had been significant in the late 1960s, the
situation had changed dramatically by December 1972. The world price of
sugar began to rise in the late 1960s, exceeding the price the Soviets paid
to Cuba by late 1971, and it remained higher in 1972. The world price again
outstripped the Soviet price throughout 1974; the Soviet price overtook the
world price again only in the spring of 1975.[17]

Therefore, the Soviets provided no significant sugar price subsidies from
1971 through 1975. Other Soviet concessions in December 1972 were
made easier because the cost of subsidizing Cuban sugar had temporarily
disappeared. Thanks to the high price of sugar, the Cuban economy boomed
in the early 1970s, making up in part for the great economic losses of the
1960s. Moreover, the high sugar prices and the reduced need for Soviet
subsidies gave Cuba a margin of autonomy. It could thus accept more easily
the organizational restructuring sought by the Soviets and the greater integration of its economy with that of the USSR and the CMEA, both of which
also improved Cuba's own economic efficiency.

Cuba exercised its economic autonomy by shifting its trade away from
the USSR when world sugar prices were high. As a result, Cuba earned
enough foreign exchange in convertible currency to be able to import more
goods form non-Communist countries—a trend that had already begun in
1963. In 1970, when Cuba had a lot of sugar to export and when the Soviet

Table 4.1 Sugar prices, 1958–1985

Year	World price (U.S. cents per pound)	Soviet price (U.S. cents per pound)	Soviet price (Cuban cents per pound)
1958	3	3	3
1961	3	4	—
1962	3	4	—
1963	8	6	—
1964	6	6	—
1965	2	6	6
1968	2	6	—
1970	4	6	6
1972	7	6	—
1973	9	12	—
1974	30	20	—
1975	20	26	22
1976	12	27	—
1977	8	27	22
1978	8	37	27
1979	10	37	27
1980	28	47	34
1981	17	35	28
1982	8	39	28
1983	9	46	40
1984	5	44	39
1985	4	49	45

Sources: World and Soviet prices (U.S. cents per pound) from José Luis Rodríguez, "Las relaciones económicas Cuba-URSS, 1960–1985," *Revista del CIEM: Temas de la economía mundial,* no. 17 (1986): 25. Soviet price (Cuban cents per pound) computed from Table 4.2.

Note: All prices are annual averages. Prices are not adjusted for inflation. The "Soviet price" is the price the USSR actually paid to Cuba.

price for sugar exceeded the world price by more than 50 percent, Cuba sent 50 percent of its exports to the USSR. By 1972, when world sugar prices were rising rapidly, that proportion fell to 29 percent. Similarly, in 1970, CMEA countries took 65 percent of Cuba's exports; in 1972, when Cuba joined the CMEA, they accounted for only 45 percent, as Cuba shifted sugar sales from the CMEA to the rest of the world market to take advantage of higher prices. These higher prices also had an effect on Cuba's imports from CMEA countries. In 1972, the CMEA supplied 60 percent of Cuban imports; in 1975, it supplied only 48 percent because Cuba used its convertible currency to import more goods from the West.[18] Therefore, Cuba's first three years of membership in the CMEA were marked by economic separation from, rather than integration with, its presumed preferred trading partners.

This Cuban behavior presented some problems for its Communist partners, but, on balance, it was not contrary to Soviet or CMEA interests. They, too, benefited from the reduction in the cost of supporting the Cuban economy. In this as in other cases, even under a tight hegemony, Cuba's exercise of its autonomy since 1970 has not been opposed to Soviet interests.

The period 1971–1975 was marked by the paradox of integration between Cuba and its Communist allies in organizational matters and divergence between them in matters of trade. None of the partners—Cuba, the USSR, or Eastern European countries—wanted to increase Cuban dependence on Soviet bloc trade, much less subsidies. But the Soviet bloc governments wanted to remodel Cuba's economy to end the risky policies of the late 1960s; they wanted Cuba to be reliable, not costly. In turn, at the very moment when it enjoyed its greatest external economic autonomy, Cuba recognized its continued need for Soviet and East European aid and accepted Soviet recommendations on organizational and even domestic economic policy issues because they made sense. It was no longer Soviet coercion over Cuba that forced this acceptance; instead, the ideologies and policies of the two governments gradually converged. Soviet hegemony became Cuba's insurance for the future.

1975–1980

The years 1974 through 1976 were a watershed for Soviet-Cuban relations. Looking back early in the 1980s, Cuban Vice President Carlos Rafael Rodríguez observed that "Cuba had taken fifteen years to establish close PB [Political Bureau] to PB relations" with the Soviets.[19] Soviet party General Secretary Leonid Brezhnev's visit to Cuba in 1974 was the political breakthrough. On the military side, in 1975 Cuba sent 36,000 troops to Angola; on the economic side, the world price of sugar continued to drop. Cuba deserved rewards for its military accomplishments; it needed help to face the decline of the world sugar price.

In April 1976, as part of a broad trade agreement, Cuba and the USSR agreed that the average price paid by the Soviets for Cuban sugar in 1975 would henceforth be the minimum Soviet price.[20] The date is significant. By that time, as was not the case at the time of the agreements of 1963–64, the world market price had fallen; the agreement to maintain the 1975 price was, therefore, a substantial Soviet commitment to subsidize Cuban sugar. Moreover, the agreement was signed just as Cuba succeeded in forcing South Africa to withdraw its troops from Angola.

The 1976 agreement stipulated that prices for Cuban exports would be based on a sliding scale keyed in part to the average price of Cuban exports (basically sugar, nickel, and citrus fruits) in the world market over the past five years, and in part to the five-year average of selected Cuban imports from the USSR (especially petroleum).[21] It was also contemplated that these averages would be adjusted annually to protect both parties in the event the formula worked badly. Cuba expected that the 1976 agreement would freeze its "terms of trade"—the amount of imports a country can buy with its exports—with the USSR.[22]

As a result of this agreement and of trends in world sugar prices after 1975, Cuba's economic dependency on the USSR began to deepen. The Soviet price for Cuban sugar, fixed at the very high 1975 level, did not follow the world price's downward trend for the remainder of the 1970s. Therefore, beginning in 1976, Soviet sugar subsidies to Cuba (compared with the real world market price) became massive, far exceeding the subsidy levels of the 1960s. (The data discussed in this section and the next can be found in Tables 4.1 and 4.2; see technical notes in Appendix B). Even when world sugar prices rose again in 1980, the Soviet sugar subsidy remained enormous.

Under the 1976 agreement, the USSR also subsidized Cuba through petroleum prices; the price for Soviet petroleum sold to Cuba rose much more slowly than the world price. Cuba estimated that its average payment for Soviet petroleum between 1976 and 1980 was 70 pesos per ton, compared with a prevailing price of 200 pesos per ton.[23] The high Soviet sugar and petroleum subsidies in the late 1970s changed the bilateral trade balance. Although Cuba had had trade deficits with the USSR every year from 1966 through 1975 (worth about 2.5 billion pesos cumulatively, with repayment postponed to 1986), Cuban trade surpluses appeared in 1975–1978. The agreement worked well enough for Cuba during the late 1970s because the five-year price scale still reflected the rising sugar prices of the early 1970s. Cuba's terms of trade with the Soviets deteriorated little in the late 1970s.

The higher Soviet price after 1975 stimulated the diversion of Cuba's sugar exports to the USSR. Until 1975, the Soviet share of Cuban exports had oscillated around 45 percent. From the early to the late 1970s, the Soviet share of Cuban exports jumped by about 20 percentage points. Because Cuban-Soviet trade is largely on a barter basis (not in currencies that are readily convertible into other international currencies), Cuban imports

Table 4.2 Cuban-Soviet trade relations, 1958–1986

	1958	1965	1970	1975
Cuban exports to USSR (percent)	2	47	50	56
Cuban imports from USSR (percent)	0	49	53	40
Cuban balance of trade with USSR (millions of pesos)	14	−106	−162	412
Cuban price for Soviet petroleum (pesos per ton)	—	—	18	39
Soviet price for Cuban sugar (pesos per ton)	71	134	131	482
Cuban terms of trade, for sugar and oil, with USSR (1975 = 100)	—	—	59	100
Cuban sugar exports to USSR (percent, by value)	3	57	52	58
Index of Cuban export prices to USSR (1975 = 100)	—	28	33	100
Index of Cuban import prices from USSR (1975 = 100)	—	—	57	100
Cuban terms of trade with USSR (1975 = 100)	—	—	57	100
Soviet subsidy for Cuban sugar (millions of pesos)	−2	95	134	−261
Soviet subsidy for Cuban sugar as percent of GSP	—	—	—	−2
Soviet subsidy for Cuban trade deficit as percent of GSP	—	—	—	−3

of Soviet products rose as well. The Soviet share of Cuban imports, which had fallen somewhat from the late 1960s to the early 1970s, rose by over 15 percentage points.[24] The barter nature of Cuban-Soviet trade meant that Cuba was less able to select its trade partners. In effect, Cuba's use of Soviet subsidies and loans was tied to its purchase of imports from the USSR—this inflexibility limited the usefulness of the Soviet subsidy to Cuba.

In preparing the 1976–1980 five-year plan, Cuban officials had foreseen that the world price of sugar would fall from the 1974 and 1975 levels, but they did not anticipate how far it would fall (they thought that the average world market price for 1976–1980 would be $0.15 per pound).[25] Because of the gap between plan and reality, that plan had to be set aside. The policy

1977	1978	1979	1980	1981	1982	1983	1984	1985	1986
71	73	68	56	56	67	70	72	75	74
54	65	68	63	63	68	68	66	67	70
208	168	− 143	− 650	− 876	− 455	− 364	− 830	− 937	− 1,380
51	66	75	83	103	126	147	174	193	—
490	599	589	743	605	625	873	868	987	862
77	73	63	72	48	40	48	40	41	—
77	80	76	62	59	73	76	77	82	82
101	123	121	149	131	133	180	179	202	180
113	127	130	145	168	198	222	252	273	—
90	97	93	103	78	67	81	71	74	—
891	1,852	1,708	976	1,031	2,011	2,590	2,763	3,360	2,856
6	11	10	6	5	9	11	11	12	11
− 1	− 1	1	4	4	2	1	3	3	5

Sources: Comité Estatal de Estadísticas, *Anuario estadístico de Cuba, 1982, 1983, 1984, 1985, 1986* (Havana).

Note: All pesos are in current prices. All prices were recorded as actually having been paid. The global social product (GSP) is Cuba's widest measure of aggregate production. Technical explanations in Appendix B.

of Soviet price subsidies best explains why the Cuban economy did not collapse during that period and, indeed, why it prospered at all.

The 1980s
The 1976 agreement contained the seeds of future trouble. Because world sugar prices fell in the late 1970s while oil prices rose, the 1976 agreement also required that Cuba receive a lower price for sugar from the Soviets in the early 1980s, and pay more for oil. The Soviets may not, in fact, have intended to freeze the terms of trade; their intention in 1976 was to help Cuba in the near and intermediate future, not necessarily forever. Soviet prices had been variable since the 1976 agreement because annual price adjustments were made on both political and commercial grounds. In the

late 1970s, when Cuba had trade surpluses with the Soviets, prices were adjusted annually to reduce their magnitude; that technique worked to Cuba's favor in the early 1980s, when adjustments were made to reduce Cuban trade deficits.[26]

Indeed, not all went well in Soviet-Cuban economic relations. The price paid by Cuba for Soviet oil increased in the late 1970s, and the price the Soviets paid for Cuban sugar even fell slightly in 1978–1979. These factors contributed to Cuba's economic recession of late 1979 and early 1980 and to the exodus of over 125,000 Cubans from Mariel harbor in 1980. In 1980 and 1981, moreover, the by now familiar Cuban trade behavior was repeated: When the world market price rose, Cuba diverted sugar exports from the Soviet market to market-economy countries to obtain foreign exchange in hard currencies. Whereas 76 percent of Cuban sugar exports went to the USSR in 1979, that percentage dropped to 59 in 1981, despite a billion pesos' worth of Soviet subsidies.

The price the Soviets paid for Cuban sugar fell decisively in 1981 just as the price of oil rose sharply. Because of the peso's devaluation relative to the dollar, Cuba's dollar-equivalent earnings fell more. The combination contributed to Cuba's 1982 economic crisis; it had to request a rescheduling of its hard-currency debts because it lacked convertible currency to pay interest and principal owed to private international banks. The Soviet sugar price rebounded strongly in 1983, was cut again in 1984, rose to an all-time high in 1985, and in 1986 it fell back to the 1984 level.

Although the Soviet sugar price fell from 1980 to 1981 and again from 1983 to 1984, the Soviet subsidy for Cuban sugar rose in both instances because the world market price fell faster than did the Soviet price. From Cuba's perspective, these apparent increases in the Soviet sugar subsidy were illusory; Cuba got less for each pound of sugar from both the USSR and market-economy countries. Nonetheless, these numbers show again the importance of Soviet trade to Cuba. Even as they paid less for sugar, the Soviets twice cushioned the impact of worldwide price deflation.

Despite continuing subsidies in the form of preferential sugar, nickel, and oil prices, the overall trade situation for Cuba deteriorated after 1980, when the price of Cuban imports from the USSR rose faster than the price of Cuban exports to the USSR. Measured as terms of trade, Cuban exports bought only 74 percent as much from the USSR in 1985 as in 1975. In particular, Soviet-Cuban terms of trade for sugar and oil, which had worked to Cuba's advantage until 1975, deteriorated sharply after 1980. In 1985 Cuban sugar bought only 41 percent as much Soviet oil as it did in 1975.

Castro chose not to publicize Cuba's generally worsened terms of trade with the Soviet Union in the 1980s; in fact, he spoke as if it had not occurred. In October 1981, when Soviet sugar prices had dropped and the buying power of Cuban exports had fallen to 78 percent of the 1975 level, Castro said: "If the products . . . of the Soviet Union increase in price, sugar, nickel and other products increase in price."[27] Speaking at the end of 1984, Castro was equally wrong in implying that the overall Cuban-Soviet terms of trade had remained frozen at the 1975 level. He said: "[Our] prices are protected against the variations of the prices of the merchandise that we import from the socialist area because, either the value of our sugar grows to the extent that the value of the imports we receive from that area grows, or the price of our sugar remains constant . . . and the price of the merchandise we import from the socialist area remains constant."[28] In fact, by 1984, Cuba had lost over a quarter of the purchasing power of its exports to the USSR; its terms of trade for sugar and oil worsened even more. These circumstances were the background to the Cuban-Soviet dispute during 1984–85 (to be examined in a later section).

As a result of these trends, a Cuban trade deficit with the Soviets reappeared in 1979 and grew in the early 1980s, exacerbating Cuba's 1982 international economic crisis. The Soviets provided loans at low interest rates to cover these bilateral trade deficits. According to the Cuban central bank, "the typical USSR trade credit contemplates, in all cases, no cash payment [Cuba pays in goods] and a 12-year repayment period at an annual interest rate which in no case exceeds 4 percent." (Soviet credits for development projects have usually been repayable over twenty-five years and have borne a 2 percent interest rate).[29] But unlike price subsidies, which work as hidden grants that never have to be repaid and bear no interest, loans must be repaid with interest.[30] And yet, because the terms were basically still very favorable to Cuba, the Soviet share of Cuban exports rose in the 1980s, after a dip in 1980–81; the Soviet share of Cuban exports and imports in the 1980s was very high by historical standards. Together, the sugar price subsidy and the trade deficit subsidy rose to about a tenth of Cuba's global social product (GSP)—Cuba's widest measure of aggregate production—in the late 1970s; this figure rose to 16 percent in 1986.

If the same method of determining prices in Cuban-Soviet trade continues, however, then Soviet prices for Cuban sugar will fall by the end of the 1980s, reflecting the declining world sugar prices of the early to mid-1980s. Soviet oil prices will also decline, but not as much as sugar prices, with a net result that the buying power of Cuban exports will deteriorate further, and Cuba's trade deficit with the USSR will grow (unless, on political grounds, the Soviets step outside the established pricing formulas to subsidize the Cuban economy even more).

These changes in trade policy have affected bilateral financial relations.

According to Castro, not only were payments on Cuba's debt to the Soviets postponed in 1972 but "the debt has been postponed more than once . . . Every time we have proposed a five-, ten-, or fifteen-year postponement and without interest, this has been conceded [by the Soviets] without any difficulty."[31] In the mid-1980s, Cuba was in urgent need of such financial assistance. The trends in Cuban-Soviet trade were discouraging; Cuba's general international trade performance remained weak; Cuba had serious problems in repaying its convertible currency debt; and repayment of the pre-1972 Cuban debt to the Soviets, postponed by a 1972 agreement, came due on January 1, 1986. By early 1985, the moratorium on the repayment of this debt's principal and interest had been extended at least to 1990. Although Cuba has been making some payments on the debts incurred to the USSR since 1973, these also appear to have been rescheduled over time. In March 1987, the Cuban government estimated that its debt to the socialist countries was worth about $10 billion dollars.[32]

The Soviets supported Cuban economic growth, not just by providing subsidies and loans to finance Cuba's trade deficits but also by financing development projects. By 1978, more than a tenth of Cuba's industrial production came from enterprises built with Soviet help, including about a third of the electric power-generating capacity and almost all of the steel production.[33] In 1983, Castro summarized the major economic projects in the country. One, the Las Camariocas nickel plant, was a joint project with other CMEA countries. All other major industrial projects under way had been financed through long-term Soviet development loans: a petroleum refinery and a nuclear energy plant in Cienfuegos, an electric power plant east of the city of Havana, and the Punta Gorda nickel processing plant.[34] Altogether, three hundred major economic projects were under construction with Soviet help in Cuba in 1983.[35]

During the 1980s Soviet petroleum has taken on new significance in the Cuban economy. The policy behind Cuban-Soviet trade in petroleum was changed in 1981 as a result of the Soviet desire to provide incentives for Cuban energy conservation and to help Cuba meet its convertible currency debt service obligations. As in the past, both governments decide in advance on an estimate of Cuba's crude oil needs for a given year. Under the new agreement, however, whatever crude oil Cuba saves from that amount can be resold in the world market for hard currency. The actual shipments of resold crude oil are handled by the USSR, which then pays Cuba, thus saving the cost of shipping the oil from Soviet ports to the Caribbean Sea and back to Rotterdam. Cuba buys the crude oil in rubles, orders Soviet traders to sell it in convertible currency, and then receives these funds.[36]

From 1981 through 1985, such oil reexports yielded Cuba over 1.9 billion pesos in convertible currency. Beginning in 1983, the value in convertible currency of Cuba's oil reexports exceeded that of sugar exports. In 1985, the former were worth three times more than the latter.[37]

In recent years, Soviet policies of support to the Cuban economy have oscillated between two poles. At times, as in 1981, 1984, and 1986, the Soviets shifted from support through the price system (amounting to outright grants) to support through low-interest loans. If sustained, this policy should reduce the Soviets' real cost of supporting Cuba while providing incentives to improve Cuba's international trade efficiency. At other times, as in 1983 and 1985, Cuba has convinced the Soviets to increase subsidies through the price system so that Cuba does not depend as much on loans to cover its large trade deficits with the USSR. The tone of Cuban-Soviet relations depends on the choices made between these policies.

Soviet economic aid has increasingly affected Cuba's performance. After an outstanding recovery in the early 1970s, the Cuban economy slowed down during the second half of the 1970s, though it continued to grow. It then slid into recession in late 1979 and the first half of 1980.[38] Since 1980, Castro said in February 1986, the GSP—the widest measure of Cuba's economic health—had grown at an average annual rate of 7.3 percent.[39]

Nonetheless, Castro's blistering criticism of Cuba's economic performance at the Third Party Congress suggests it is very unlikely that the economy achieved the officially reported growth rate.[40] The discrepancy between reported and probable rates is clearest in estimates for 1981 and 1982. A discussion by Central Planning Board President Humberto Pérez suggests that real growth for 1981 (in 1980 prices) might have been 6 percent—a good recovery from the serious recession of 1979–80.[41] In contrast, Cuba officially reported 16 percent growth in the GSP for 1981 (in constant prices),[42] even though physical output was growing more slowly than GSP, and Soviet sugar prices fell sharply. One reason for this discrepancy is the big jump in Cuban wholesale prices that went into effect on January 1, 1981, and in retail prices, which were also raised later in 1981. Despite claims to have applied appropriate price deflation, Cuba's statistical system probably did not calculate accurately the GSP for 1981 in constant prices.[43] Nor are the reports of 3.9 percent GSP growth for 1982 consistent with Cuba's need to reschedule its convertible currency debts due that year in the wake of changes in Soviet sugar and oil prices. Although the Cuban government may overstate growth rates for the early 1980s, economic performance was positive on average from 1981 to 1985, outpacing the economic growth of most Latin American countries for the first time since

1960. This good performance is explained to a large degree by Soviet and other CMEA support.

The Castro government's third decade in power featured a much greater economic dependency on the Soviets, a renewed trade deficit, worsening terms of trade, and an economy increasingly unable to stand on its own in the world. Yet, despite the occasionally severe disputes in Cuban-Soviet economic relations, including some that stemmed from changes in Soviet economic policies toward Cuba begun in 1980, the economic support from the USSR has made consolidated revolutionary rule possible in Cuba. No effort to measure rubles or pesos can come close to measuring the importance of Soviet support. This dependency does not prevent Cuba from pursuing its own programs, but it curtails the scope of Cuba's possible divergence from Soviet policies.

Cuba's Economic Relations with the CMEA

The cost of supporting the Cuban economy led both Cuba and the Soviet Union to involve the other European members of the CMEA—East Germany, Czechoslovakia, Poland, Hungary, Rumania, and Bulgaria—in sharing that burden.[44] The other CMEA members had come to Cuba's rescue in 1960 by granting development credits, at 2.5 percent interest, repayable in eight to twelve years. In the early 1960s, the Eastern Europeans also financed Cuba's trade deficits with them. In 1964 that amount exceeded 130 million pesos, equivalent to the amount of the Cuban trade deficit financed by the USSR. Earlier in that decade, the amount of Eastern European financing of Cuba's trade deficit had not exceeded 15 percent of the amount financed by the Soviets.[45] This steep rise in financing may have shocked the Eastern Europeans into cutting back.

The Eastern European countries brought their trade with Cuba into balance in 1965, thus ending the need to finance Cuba's trade deficits (Tables 4.2 and 4.3; see Table 4.3 for data discussed throughout this section). That change may explain the harsh language used about Eastern European countries by Cuban Minister of Industries Guevara in the mid-1960s, and by Fidel Castro in 1968. Trade by CMEA countries (excluding the USSR) with Cuba remained mostly balanced through 1974. In fact, in the early 1970s—thanks to higher sugar prices—Cuba ran large trade surpluses that may have been used to repay Eastern European aid of the early 1960s. As already indicated, Cuba's 1972 entry into the CMEA was followed by a further decline in Cuba-CMEA trade.

The CMEA countries increased the prices they paid for sugar in the early 1970s to match the increase in the world price. But their prices remained well below the price paid for Cuban sugar by the USSR and by Cuba's main market-economy partners; in 1975, the prices paid by Japan and Spain were 60 percent higher than those paid by the Eastern Europeans. In effect, then, in 1975 Cuba gave a sugar price subsidy to CMEA countries (not counting the USSR) that exceeded 94 million pesos. Rich in foreign exchange in convertible currency, Cuba bought almost twice as much from West Germany as from East Germany that year.

The principle of "fraternal relations" called for something better. In June 1976, following the signing of the key trade agreement between Cuba and the USSR, the CMEA granted Cuba the benefits from its Comprehensive Program—subsidized financing of economic development projects, as had been granted years earlier to Mongolia—in recognition of Cuba's relative economic underdevelopment within the CMEA and as a way to promote its development.[46] The CMEA agreed to pay more for Cuban sugar than world market prices; price trends would be based, as in the Soviet case, on five-year average prices, with annual adjustments. Begun in 1977, the CMEA sugar subsidy (not counting the Soviet subsidy) peaked at 322 million pesos in 1984, falling to 246 million pesos in 1986. In addition, CMEA countries have financed Cuba's trade deficits with them. These two forms of assistance generated subsidies equal to 1 percent of the Cuban GSP through 1981, rising to 3 percent between 1982 and 1985.

The Soviet Union has consistently paid higher prices than other CMEA countries (except for Hungary in 1981). All Eastern European countries have at some point cut the sugar price paid to Cuba, and only the price paid by Czechoslovakia remained stable for as long as three years (1977–1979). The CMEA agreement provides only a general framework for prices; Cuba negotiates specific prices every year with each country.[47]

The July 1976 CMEA agreement went beyond setting a formula for the price of sugar. The CMEA countries also agreed, in principle, to many measures to promote Cuba's development.[48] In fact, the benefits of CMEA membership to Cuba have been slow to materialize until recently.[49] For example, on the day Cuba joined the CMEA, its representative, Carlos Rafael Rodríguez, proposed the joint construction of new nickel-producing plants in Cuba. An agreement was not signed until 1975; construction of the Las Camariocas nickel plant, the CMEA's first industrial project in Cuba, did not begin until July 1983. Rodríguez has argued for the need to "speed up the process of collective discussion for similar projects." Cuban scholars express frustration with the CMEA's slow and complex procedures. And, despite the CMEA's backing of Las Camariocas, Castro candidly noted that "the fundamental participation [in the project] is the USSR's."[50]

This was not the only problem. Since joining the CMEA in 1972, Cuba

Table 4.3 Cuban trade with CMEA countries, 1965–1986

	1965	1970	1975	1977
Cuban exports to CMEA countries, excluding USSR (percent)	15	14	8	9
Cuban imports from CMEA countries, excluding USSR (percent)	11	10	8	11
Cuban exports to all CMEA countries (percent)	61	65	64	80
Cuban imports from all CMEA countries (percent)	61	63	48	64
Cuban balance of trade with CMEA countries, excluding USSR (millions of pesos)	4	14	−23	−99
Cuban balance of trade with all CMEA countries (millions of pesos)	−102	−148	389	108
East German price for Cuban sugar (pesos per ton)	136	124	359	357
Bulgarian price for Cuban sugar (pesos per ton)	112	110	355	372
Czech price for Cuban sugar (pesos per ton)	134	132	356	355
Hungarian price for Cuban sugar (pesos per ton)	—	100	379	378
Rumanian price for Cuban sugar (pesos per ton)	—	104	357	355
CMEA (excluding USSR) subsidy for Cuban sugar (millions of pesos)	19	30	−94	66
CMEA (excluding USSR) subsidy for Cuban sugar plus subsidy for Cuban trade deficit as percent of GSP	—	—	−1	1

has asked the Eastern European countries to stop producing sugar from beets and, instead, to import more cane sugar from Cuba. In 1984, Rodrí-guez acknowledged the failure of this policy, even though "of the socialist countries, we are the most efficient producer."[51] Nonetheless, there were some accomplishments. In July 1981, a CMEA agreement committed the USSR, East Germany, and Bulgaria to provide 470.5 million pesos to modernize Cuba's sugar industry through 1985 and an additional 330 million pesos through 1990. Cuba was to specialize in the manufacture of sugar mills, including parts, for export; produce its own components; and supplement them with imports from the USSR, East Germany, and Czechoslovakia. The CMEA agreed that Cuba would be its leading supplier of sugar outside Eastern Europe. Sugar imports from Cuba in 1983 represented 24 percent of consumption for the USSR, just under a third for East Germany

1978	1979	1980	1981	1982	1983	1984	1985	1986
9	10	10	13	11	11	13	11	13
11	11	13	14	16	16	14	13	12
81	78	66	69	78	82	85	86	87
76	80	75	77	84	84	80	81	82
−104	−52	−183	−147	−357	−338	−260	−377	−235
64	−196	−833	−1,023	−811	−702	−1,090	−1,314	−1,615
363	362	423	485	500	498	505	500	548
396	414	423	474	500	513	446	415	401
355	355	431	362	444	522	499	505	508
399	399	537	657	591	—	—	—	—
—	—	—	—	—	—	—	—	—
134	148	31	139	231	281	322	309	246
1	1	1	1	3	3	2	3	2

Sources: Comité Estatal de Estadísticas, *Anuario estadístico de Cuba, 1982, 1983, 1984, 1985, 1986* (Havana).
Note: See Table 4.2.

and Rumania, a sixth for Czechoslovakia, three-quarters for Bulgaria, and nothing for Hungary and Poland, which were self-sufficient.[52]

In the area of citrus fruit production, in July 1981 the CMEA countries agreed that Cuba should be their main supplier. CMEA investments to develop Cuban citrus fruit production would amount to over 300 million pesos through 1985 and an additional 295 million pesos through 1990. Some of these investments would be in the form of convertible currency so that Cuba could buy equipment from market-economy countries.[53] Nonetheless, in 1984 Rodríguez reported that the citrus exports program had "fallen behind schedule," even though the CMEA countries also agreed in 1981 to pay "preferential prices for our citrus fruit that are higher than world market prices" and had committed themselves to purchase most of the citrus fruits Cuba produced.[54]

In these three major areas of the Cuban economy—nickel, sugar, and citrus fruits—the story is the same. The CMEA has been painfully slow in carrying out development projects, resulting in high opportunity costs for Cuba. The burden of keeping the Cuban economy afloat has been shared by the CMEA, but this support was modest during the decade after Cuba joined the organization. The June 1985 CMEA summit declaration registered disappointment that not all members were sharing the costs fairly, and noted that "the CMEA membership as a whole should contribute to speed up the development" of the three least-developed members—Mongolia, Vietnam, and Cuba.[55]

CMEA's financing of Cuban development projects deserves comment. The Las Camariocas project is expected to produce 30,000 tons of nickel per year. Cuba will sell 15,000 tons to market-economy countries; the remainder will go to CMEA countries as payment in kind for the plant, proportionate to the size of each country's investment, for twelve years (CMEA charges 2 percent interest). In anticipation of these payments, the USSR more than doubled the price it paid for Cuban nickel beginning in 1981, thereby making Cuba's repayment terms even easier.[56] Financing terms differ between the CMEA-backed Las Camariocas nickel project and the Soviet-backed Punta Gorda nickel project. The Soviets require that Cuba deliver half of its nickel output for six years; the CMEA requires it for twelve years.[57] Repayment in kind applies also to CMEA investments in sugar and citrus fruits.[58]

Over the years some tensions have arisen over other issues between Cuba and its CMEA partners. Cuba did not wish to be a mere producer of raw materials. Although it exported some new, nontraditional products to market-economy countries in the early 1980s, it was able to add "very few new export items" to its CMEA sales in those years, according to Fidel Castro. When Cuba launched a drive to increase exports in 1985, its exports to market-economy countries increased twice as fast as exports to socialist countries.[59] One point of contention was Cuba's desire to include its electronics and computer industries in the CMEA export agreements, which commit CMEA members to buy preferentially from each other. Cuba began exporting alphanumeric displays to the Soviet Union in the early to mid-1980s; these items became part of a Cuban agreement with the CMEA in 1984. In 1986, Cuba obtained authorization and financing from the CMEA to produce computer keyboards for export. However, minicomputers, which Cuba has been producing since 1970, were not included in a CMEA program until 1988, when Czechoslovakia agreed to buy some.[60]

A second problem stemmed from the CMEA's policies toward Latin

American countries that were not members of the CMEA—the subject of a dispute harking back to the differences between Cuba and the Eastern Europeans in the 1960s. For example, in 1982 a Cuban scholar criticized CMEA loans to Latin American countries under military rule, claiming that CMEA loans "should have political significance." She wrote, "The fact that the largest loans have been given to countries such as Brazil, Argentina, and Bolivia leads to the conclusion that there has not been a process of analysis and coordination to shape appropriate choices, especially when the final goal is to strengthen the struggle for political and economic independence and to weaken the actions of imperialism in the region."[61]

Moreover, the degree of preferential treatment for Cuba in CMEA financing of development projects, as compared with terms for other countries, has been quite modest. For instance, the CMEA's terms for financing the Las Camariocas nickel plant included repayment over twelve years at 2 percent interest. At roughly the same time, Brazil built a hydroelectric project in Bahia using Soviet and other equipment; the financing included a substantial loan from the Soviet Bank of Foreign Trade, repayable over fourteen years at 3.5 percent interest. Just as Cuba paid in nickel for its plant, the Soviets agreed to buy Brazilian coffee for an amount equal to the value of the Soviet generators.[62] The CMEA's preferential treatment of Cuba over Brazil was therefore slight. Overall, CMEA policy toward contracts with Third World countries is to amortize loans over eight to fifteen years and to charge interest between 2.5 and 3.5 percent; usually arrangements are made for payments in goods or in nonconvertible national currency for the purchase of products in the contracting country.[63] Thus Cuba's net gain from CMEA membership in terms of financing for development projects is limited.

Nonetheless, by the mid-1980s the benefits to Cuba of CMEA membership had gradually materialized, first in preferential sugar prices and more recently in major investments by the CMEA in the production of sugar, nickel, and citrus fruits under financing terms that were, indeed, favorable for Cuba.

In addition to the joint CMEA programs, Cuba has made many bilateral agreements with CMEA members besides the USSR. The East Germans, for example, have built new cement plants in Nuevitas and Cienfuegos and the Czechs in Sancti Spíritus, and the Rumanians modernized the plant in Santiago de Cuba.[64] East Germany alone sold about fifty "turn-key" industrial plants to Cuba over twenty years and financed the Cuban purchases.[65] These are not gifts; Cuba paid for these projects, although on preferential terms.

As part of its growing CMEA relations in the 1980s, Cuba agreed to supply labor to several countries while receiving many advisers from these countries. By early 1984, over 12,000 Cubans were employed as "guest workers" in East Germany, Czechoslovakia, and Hungary. In January 1987, the first Cuban guest workers arrived in Siberia to work in construction and forestry projects.[66]

The Eastern Europeans took the initiative in proposing guest worker programs. The pioneering agreement was signed between Cuba and East Germany in 1978. In July of that year, the first Cubans arrived, on two-year contracts, to train as skilled workers; 851 returned to Cuba in 1980, but another 300 reenrolled for another two-year contract. In East Germany, Cuban guest workers are regular factory employees. About 2,000 Cuban workers were in East Germany until 1980; the number rose to 5,386 by 1982 and to 6,328 by early 1984.[67]

Although guest worker agreements are mutually beneficial, problems have arisen. Some Cubans have difficulty acclimating to their new living conditions in East Germany. Most Cuban workers do not know the German language when they arrive. Some are homesick, others dislike the climate. A fair number have trouble with some East German customs. One Cuban official said that "the Germans' quiet, reserved manner bothered" many Cubans and "being punctual and conscientious was not always easy" for them. Some Cubans had an easier adjustment because they fell in love. But the Cuban government has discouraged the immigration of Cubans' East German spouses because it fears that they will find it difficult to adjust.[68] Such circumstances may have prevented a more rapid increase in the transfer of Cuban workers to Eastern Europe. In mid-1982, the level proposed for 1985 was 20,000 workers, whereas only about 12,000 Cubans were actually working there in 1985.[69]

In order to protect the interests of Cuban workers in Europe, the Cuban Confederation of Labor (CTC) signed agreements with its counterparts; the CTC has its own personnel in Eastern Europe, although these Cuban workers are formally represented by the unions where they work. Cubans receive the same salary as Europeans for the work they do. A small portion of each worker's salary is remitted to the Cuban government, apparently as a Cuban foreign exchange tax. In the short term, Cuba benefits from these remittances to the government and to relatives. Later, after the workers return, Cuba will benefit from their new skills and their more disciplined work habits.[70]

Cubans work in Eastern Europe as a result of contracts signed by governments, not just, as in Western Europe, as the result of individual decisions to migrate. The contracts protect the Cubans from unfair discrimination, but they also limit their freedom. Cuban guest workers are discouraged from bringing their families to Eastern Europe or returning with a spouse. Skills may be learned by guest workers under any circumstances, but the Cuban program is designed to bring the workers home, not to settle them permanently in Europe. Remittances are a feature of all guest worker situations, perhaps less so in the Cuban case. Guest workers generally respond to labor shortages in Europe and work at jobs that Europeans no longer want, but Cuban guest workers are formally incorporated into a program to upgrade their skills.

More generally, training for Cuban citizens has been an important feature of Cuba's relations with the USSR and Eastern Europe. As early as 1960, Cuba sent 1,000 young people for professional study in the Soviet Union. In 1977–78, 2,584 Cubans were studying in Soviet institutions of higher education, a number that rose to 6,978 in 1986–87; the number of Cuban students in other CMEA countries was 488 in 1977–78 and 558 in 1986–87.[71] By the end of 1984, 9,102 Cubans were studying in 52 Soviet cities: 7,000 in universities, 1,333 at secondary school levels, and 769 in postgraduate programs.[72]

Many specialists from the Soviet bloc have also worked in Cuba's civilian economy in recent years. Of the 1,714 foreign advisers of Cuba's Ministry for Basic Industry in 1984, 87 percent were Soviets. The number of Soviet advisers was expected to more than double to 3,460 in 1985.[73]

Although the presence of CMEA advisers is no doubt valuable, some Cuban officials have stressed the need for greater Cuban self-reliance. For example, in 1972 Minister of Education José Ramón Fernández commented on aid from East Germany, Bulgaria, Hungary, Czechoslovakia, and, especially, the USSR, stating "that we did not want them to do our job for us but that they would teach our specialists . . . Their help is valuable, we appreciate it a lot, but we have to carry out our own struggle and we have to design the plans and programs for our own situation to provide solutions for the country's needs."[74]

Cuba's dependence on its Soviet and CMEA allies to provide its people with training and advisers—a source of some tension in the 1960s—has contributed to generally good relations since the 1970s, although problems remain. In the future, the gradual development of closer relations between Cubans and Europeans in the workplace may deepen Cuba's links with CMEA countries.

Cuba's Economic Dependency on the Soviet Bloc

Cuba remains vulnerable to international pressure, as Cuban authors have noted. Díaz Vázquez, for example, has "categorically asserted" that Cuba's "dependency on foreign trade . . . has been deepened as a consequence of the entire process of economic reorganization" in the 1970s, with the result that "the external sector is the Cuban economy's strategic element."[75] Imports are more important to Cuba's economy than in the past, while the bulk of Cuba's industry specializes in the final assembly of manufactured products and thus depends on foreign supplies;[76] this pattern is typical of industrialization by means of substituting for imports, which is common in other countries.

There is a continuing debate about whether Cuba is more dependent on foreign trade than it was before 1959. Arguing for the view that Cuba is less dependent, Claes Brundenius has accurately noted that many trade comparisons are "distorted" because they include subsidies in the form of preferential prices from the Soviet Union and other socialist countries that rose sharply after 1975. He has also argued correctly that Cuba has introduced new export products, and that a process of industrialization through import substitution in areas of the economy other than sugar has been under way since the 1970s. Yet, in a broader perspective, the subsidies from the USSR and other CMEA countries are central facts in the Cuban economy. Cuba's dependency on other countries has intensified since 1975 because of this indivisible mixture of trade and financial subsidies. The "distortions," as Brundenius calls the effects of the subsidies, are real—and the Cuban economy depends on them. Therefore, the calculations and cautions of Carmelo Mesa-Lago are apt. He finds little change in Cuba's degree of dependency—in the importance of trade for the Cuban economy, the importance of sugar in Cuban exports, or in the extent to which Cuban trade has been concentrated on a single partner. Crude sugar made up 80 percent of Cuban exports (excluding Cuban reexports of Soviet petroleum) in 1986—a figure that, though high, is fairly typical for both pre- and post-revolutionary periods.[77] Mesa-Lago has also warned that one must choose carefully the time frame of any such comparison. There have been moments—as in the early to mid-1970s, on which a study by William LeoGrande focused—when it seemed as if a permanent reduction in dependency had occurred, only to be reversed in later years.[78]

Although Cuba's capacity to manufacture many of the products that it consumes has increased greatly since the 1960s, Cuba remains remarkably dependent on foreigners. The key difference between the 1980s and the

1950s is that Cuba has come to depend so much on subsidies and other financial assistance, especially from the USSR. Cuba's need for such subsidies shows no signs of abating. Cuban dependence on the Soviets declined briefly in the early 1970s, but it has increased markedly again since 1975. Trade figures show the same story. The Soviet share of Cuban trade rose greatly after 1975. In the 1980s, the CMEA's share (excluding the USSR) of Cuban trade returned to the high level of the early 1960s, with the added feature of massive price and trade deficit subsidies. Furthermore, CMEA countries including the USSR accounted for 80 to 87 percent of Cuban exports and imports between 1982 and 1986 (see Tables 4.2 and 4.3).[79]

This dependency on international trading and financing partners has several noteworthy features. One has been discussed by LeoGrande: "When the Cuban economy is prospering . . . indicators record a rise in dependency."[80] This is true because a boom in sugar exports leads paradoxically to both prosperity and dependency—a phenomenon that illustrates what has been called in other contexts "associated dependent development."[81] This link between prosperity and dependency suggests that Cuba is still vulnerable to sugar price fluctuations over the long term.

A second feature of Cuba's international dependency—its economic integration with CMEA countries—has progressed enough by the 1980s that LeoGrande's once accurate statement that "the Cuban economy does not respond to exigencies of the Soviet economy" needs to be revised.[82] Until the late 1970s, periods of economic prosperity in Cuba were associated mostly with the price of sugar in market-economy countries. Mesa-Lago and Jorge Pérez-López, for example, have shown a close relationship between world sugar prices and Cuba's GSP from 1962 to 1981, both measured in current prices, with a one-year time lag.[83] The situation had become more complex by the late 1970s, however. In 1979, Castro was already explaining Cuba's severe economic difficulties in terms of the Soviet inability to supply Cuba with the imports it needed.[84] In the early 1980s, as Cuba became more dependent on the Soviets, both the performance of the Soviet economy and the trends in world sugar prices became the key factors affecting Cuban economic performance. Let us focus on four examples, in each case assuming that international economic changes affect Cuba after a lag of one year.

First, in 1981, the growth of the Soviet economy slowed markedly;[85] the USSR cut its sugar price, and the Cuban-Soviet terms of trade turned sharply against Cuba. Given the simultaneous drop in the world sugar price, Cuba's economic problems in 1982 were predictable. Second, though world sugar prices increased only 2 percent in 1983,[86] in 1984 Cuba's GSP grew by 7.3 percent in constant prices (by the somewhat overstated official data), probably because Soviet and other CMEA economies recovered in 1983,[87] and because the USSR in 1983 increased the sugar price it paid Cuba 40 percent while it increased the oil price paid by Cuba only 17 percent. As a result, Cuba's terms of trade in 1983 improved 20 percent after three successive years of decline. The Cuban economy began to recover in late 1983 and continued to grow in 1984. Third, considering that the world as well as the Soviet, Czech, and Bulgarian sugar prices fell in 1984, it is not surprising that the Cuban economy's growth rate in 1985 was one-third slower than in 1984. Fourth, in 1986—though world sugar prices increased from 4 to 6 cents a pound—the USSR cut the price it paid for Cuban sugar by 12.7 percent; in 1987, for the first time ever, the Cuban government reported an economic recession, with GSP falling 3.5 percent (in constant prices).[88] Thus the "rhythm" of the Cuban economy may still reflect in part the effects of world sugar prices, but now it may also be affected by the "exigencies" of the Soviet economy. At times, as in 1984 and in 1987, this new factor may be more important than the trend in the world price of sugar. If this is the case, the nature but not the fact of Cuba's vulnerability to the international economy has changed.

The impact on Cuba of events in the USSR and other CMEA countries has gone beyond the increasing synchronization of their economies. As already noted, organizations and procedures from the older socialist countries were reproduced in Cuba. Consistent with the Eastern European experience, in the 1970s Cuba stopped emphasizing policies aimed at furthering the equal distribution of income.[89] The president of the Central Planning Board justified unequal distribution of income during the transition to socialism as follows: "There should be goods and services in the market that can only be bought by those who earn more . . . [and who] make a greater contribution to society."[90] Moreover, Soviet and CMEA investments in Cuba favored "heavy" industry, just as they did in their own countries, and favored increases in investment rather than consumption. Under CMEA pressure in December 1984 (as will be discussed), Cuba reshaped its economic strategy, further sacrificing consumption in favor of investment.[91]

Soviet hegemony over Cuba is apparent in Cuba's response to trends in the Soviet system. The conscious implementation of the Soviet economic model in Cuba resulted in the adoption of new, more orthodox ideas, structures, and policies.[92] These were one product of hegemonic relations and one outcome of Cuba's dependency on the Soviet bloc. If capitalism generates dependency or interdependency through the market, socialism generates dependency through power and ideology.[93]

A key source of Cuba's continuing dependency is its economy's poor international performance. This fact accounted for the government's December 1984 decision to redesign its economy to emphasize better performance in international trade. Despite the good rate of economic growth reported for 1984, Cuba fell short on its commitments to CMEA countries to export agreed-upon quantities of its key products—sugar, nickel, and citrus fruits; production of the last two actually declined. Moreover, Cuban growth in 1984 depended on increased imports.[94] Thus "associated dependent development" works this way in Cuba: the more domestic economic growth in all areas, not just sugar, the greater Cuba's dependency on international trade.

Cuba's poor international economic performance has two important political consequences. Cuban economist José Luis Rodríguez has noted, in his thoughtful study of CMEA prices,

> an objective contradiction between the need to ensure, through the price system, increased equality in the development levels of the socialist countries . . . and the need for prices to provide incentives to promote higher levels of economic development. In this sense, the problems of the less developed [CMEA] countries can only be solved outside the price system . . . the reduction of the gap in the development levels of the socialist countries would be incompatible with the economic laws that have to govern relations among CMEA members. Therefore, the existence of "political prices" is justified in the dealings with the less developed [CMEA] countries.[95]

Castro called attention to the other consequence of Cuba's poor international economic record. He said in 1985 that the vast Soviet support "created a mentality among us. Everything had been solved, everything was ensured, and no one ever asked: would exports increase?" He noted that Cuba's resources for growth have come from its own people—"and fundamentally from the Soviet Union."[96]

Thus, against its best interests, Cuba by the mid-1980s had worked itself into an international economic cocoon that restricted the scope of its trade. The CMEA's pursuit of economically sound policies was at odds with Cuba's interests; Cuba had to depend on CMEA political decisions for its economic well-being. At the same time, Cuba's dependent "mentality" helped to make its decision makers less conscious of the need to improve international economic performance and even more dependent on the political decisions of the CMEA. This two-pronged dependency curtailed Cuba's autonomy. Cuba's new economic goal, set in December 1984, was to become more efficient in international economic transactions and to export more, honoring commitments to socialist countries and also selling more to capitalist countries,[97] a recipe for efficient growth but also for greater dependence on international trade.

Cuba had limited the scope of its international economic activity in part as a result of its government's 1981 decision to acquire from the socialist countries most of the goods that had been acquired in the convertible currency market.[98] The party's Central Committee reaffirmed this decision in 1983, calling for the "replacement of imports from capitalist countries with imports from socialist countries" and for "preference in developing trade with the socialist camp."[99] This was in many ways a rational policy. The CMEA preferential prices for Cuban exports presupposed a Cuban disposition to import from CMEA countries. Cuba could be sure that the CMEA would not cut off supplies under U.S. pressure. Sales of Cuban nickel to Western Europe, for example, have been made much more difficult by U.S. regulations that forbid the import of products whose Cuban nickel content exceeds 20 percent of the total. Cuban scholars report that Japan, Spain, and the United Kingdom (which had supplied transportation equipment to Cuba) seemed, especially in the early 1980s, reluctant to service the equipment, to supply spare parts, or to maintain regular deliveries as a result of U.S. pressure.[100] For these reasons, the Cuban government believed that Cuba's economic security was best served by diverting trade toward CMEA countries.

In making this shift, however, Cuba went too far and failed to anticipate the negative consequences. Isolated even further, Cuba became objectively dependent as a result of its acceptance of CMEA political decisions. Unaccustomed to the rigors of competition and quality standards in the international market, more reliant on barter trade and less reliant on convertible currency transactions, Cuba became more psychologically dependent on CMEA countries. In this way Cuba imposed on itself a spiraling and deepening self-blockade. It remains to be seen whether Cuba can regain the capacity to stand on its own in the international economy.

Cuba's Acceptance of Soviet Hegemony

Since the 1968 crisis in Cuban-Soviet relations, Cuba has aligned its foreign policy with that of the USSR. Three events illustrate Cuba's loyalty and its consent to Soviet hegemony.

The first occurred in 1973 at the Nonaligned Movement summit in Algiers, at which Castro excoriated the USSR's critics within the movement. He denounced "the theory of two imperialisms"—those of the United States and the Soviet Union—which he said was held even by some "from supposedly revolutionary positions" and which appeared "in certain political and economic documents drafted for this Conference." He eloquently defended Soviet contributions to Cuba's security and development, concluding with a phrase that others have interpreted as advocating a natural alliance between the Third World and the USSR: "Any estrangement from the socialist camp means weakening and exposing ourselves to the mercy of the still-powerful forces of imperialism."[101]

Cuba's second affirmation of Soviet hegemony came in 1980, when the stakes were higher. The Soviets' invasion of Afghanistan in December 1979 had been condemned by most countries, including most members of the Nonaligned Movement, in a United Nations General Assembly vote. Cuba had become the head of the Nonaligned Movement the previous September but had voted with the Soviets on Afghanistan. Castro explained the reasons for Cuba's vote: "We were not going to be on the side of the United States. Simply that."[102] As a result, Cuba lost its bid to be elected a member of the United Nations Security Council, which would ordinarily have been a foregone conclusion for the Nonaligned Movement's leader.

Cuba's stand on Afghanistan reflected its new ideological and policy consensus with the Soviets. There is no evidence of the kind of Soviet pressure that preceded Cuba's endorsement of the 1968 Soviet invasion of Czechoslovakia. In contrast to its actions in the 1960s, Cuba stopped well short of opposing Soviet interests. In the choice between the Nonaligned Movement and the USSR, there was no doubt: Cuba was a Communist country first and foremost, under Soviet hegemony. That self-definition placed an enduring limit on its autonomy.

The third event that allowed Cuba to affirm its stand with the Soviets was the boycott of the 1984 Los Angeles Olympics. Cuba was one of the last countries to join the Soviet boycott, well after all other CMEA members (Rumania excepted). Even though Cuba had a good chance to excel in the Olympics and was in the midst of a dispute with the USSR, it eventually sided with its ally. The Cuban press insisted that the "decision was not influenced"; instead, "it was a question of solidarity" with the Soviets and the Eastern Europeans.[103]

The narrowing of Cuban-Soviet foreign policy differences even led Cuba to break with its own policy precedents. For example, Cuba did not follow the Soviet lead in severing diplomatic relations with Israel in 1967, but it did so in 1973—the only time since 1960 that Cuba has taken the initiative in breaking off diplomatic relations with another country.[104]

In the 1970s Cuba still diverged from the Soviet Union on a few foreign policy issues, though these have little practical significance. Unlike the

USSR, Cuba is not a party to the nuclear nonproliferation treaty. In addition, in 1978 the Soviets broke with Cuba over the conditions for supporting the creation of a denuclearized zone in Latin America. Although Cuba would not change its policy in opposition to the zone until the United States agreed to return the Guantánamo naval base to Cuba and agreed not to deploy nuclear weapons in Puerto Rico and U.S. facilities in Panama, at Mexico's request the Soviets signed a protocol committing themselves to respect such a zone.[105] Similarly, Cuba has sided with the Third World rather than with the USSR on some issues in the complex negotiations over the Law of the Seas.[106]

Vice President Rodríguez has articulated his government's views on the relationship between hegemony and autonomy. Cuba's "unbreakable alliance" with the USSR is "a permanent element in our international policy," he has said, adding, this "does not necessarily mean that we coincide absolutely in our views on each of the problems of international life, for Cuba and the Soviet Union operate in different geographic regions and are at very different stages of economic development."[107] In 1981 Rodríguez stated that Cuba remains ready to "subordinate always its national interests to the interests of socialism," but clarified that this does not imply "subordination of our foreign policy every day . . . to that of other socialist states." Stating that Cuba has "its own goals and its own interests," he finds a "great coincidence between Soviet and Cuban foreign policies." Rodríguez explained that this similarity in foreign policy stemmed from the two countries' "common condition as socialist states" and from their pursuit of "identical historical objectives." The differences in their historical circumstances have led, however, to "different perspectives on their relations with capitalist countries."[108] This formulation justifies ideologically the acceptance of Soviet hegemony, but it also insists on the expression of some Cuban autonomy.

The Strains of Change, 1983–1987

On October 20, 1983, Cuba was elected head of the CMEA Executive Committee for the first time; Vice President Carlos Rafael Rodríguez announced that the next CMEA Council would meet in Havana in May 1984. Six days later, U.S. and English Caribbean forces landed in Grenada. Because of the differing Cuban, Soviet, and Eastern European responses to the invasion, Cuba's relations with the USSR and other CMEA countries worsened sharply. Cubans died fighting the invasion, while the Soviets and the Eastern Europeans limited themselves to verbal protests (see Chapter 6).

Soviet inaction over Grenada was the first of a series of events over the next fifteen months that signaled Soviet intention to cut back on support for Cuban domestic and foreign policies. The nature of this crisis differed from that of 1968. In 1984 the Soviets did not attempt to change the composition of the Cuban leadership, not even to change the main outlines of Cuban foreign policy. But the USSR wanted Cuba to become more prudent in its use of military and economic resources so that the costs to the USSR from Cuban foreign and domestic policies would not climb. In particular, the Soviets reduced military support for Cuba, as events in Grenada made clear, and narrowed the extent and nature of their support for the Cuban economy.

Cuba's economic relations with the Soviet bloc continued to deteriorate in 1984. While prices paid for Cuban sugar by the Soviets, the Bulgarians, and the Czechs fell from 1983 to 1984, they fell less rapidly than the world sugar price. Therefore, the opportunity cost of Cuban sugar subsidies borne by the USSR and other CMEA countries increased by 7 percent and 15 percent, respectively, even though Cuba received fewer funds from sugar sales than it had in the previous year. Moreover, the good record of economic growth in Cuba in 1984 was generated in part by an increase in imports. In addition, the price Cuba paid for Soviet petroleum increased 18 percent from 1983 to 1984. The Soviet subsidy to Cuba, expressed as a percent of the GSP, reached its highest level yet (Tables 4.1, 4.2, and 4.3). These results angered all concerned.

These Soviet and Eastern European policy changes pressured Cuba to alter its own economic policies in order to depend less on subsidies from its allies. The reduction of Soviet and Eastern European prices for Cuban sugar and the increase in the price paid by Cuba for Soviet petroleum had the effect of more than doubling Cuba's trade deficit with the USSR from 1983 to 1984. It also forced Cuba to import less from the other CMEA countries. Though these trade deficits were covered by Soviet and Eastern European loans, Cuba was obligated to repay the loans with interest. In order to avoid these loan costs and the further deterioration of its terms of trade, Cuba had to export more and import less. Of course, Cuba also sought to persuade the Soviets and the CMEA to reemphasize the policy of virtual grants of aid through highly subsidized prices for Cuban sugar and other products—and that, unlike loans, did not have to be repaid.

As relations worsened, the meeting of the CMEA Council, scheduled for May, was postponed until June 1984 and shifted from Havana to Moscow. Castro did not attend; instead, Rodríguez represented Cuba. Cuba was the only CMEA member not represented by its head of government or head of state.[109] Relations were sufficiently repaired by October 1984 for the CMEA Council to meet in Havana—the council's first meeting in Cuba.

Nonetheless, Soviet and CMEA pressure on Cuba continued. Castro had to admit that a general problem of the "persistence of substantial delays in the delivery of merchandise" from the CMEA included Cuba. After citing weather, sabotage, and constraints on resources as contributing factors, he acknowledged "deficiencies in our own plans [because] Cuba's exports to the member countries, albeit increasing in all cases, are not meeting the obligations assumed in the trade agreements."[110] In December Castro stated the enduring reason for this problem: Whenever choices had to be made, sugar "deliveries to the socialist area have been reduced in order to send them to the hard currency area." He affirmed that this long-standing practice "must be totally eradicated."[111] The Soviets and the Eastern Europeans evidently demanded that Cuba give priority to its export agreements with them as a way to reduce Cuba's trade deficits, even if Cuba had to reduce domestic consumption. To respond to these concerns and to preempt further pressure, Castro launched a major reorganization of the Cuban economy in the weeks that followed. In July 1985 he dismissed the architect of Cuba's past economic policies, Central Planning Board President Humberto Pérez.

Another source of discord in Cuban-Soviet relations in late 1984 was a Soviet decision to cut back on its military commitment to the defense of Cuba itself (not just of Cuban forces overseas). In December 1984 the Cuban Communist party's Central Committee had to tell the Cuban people that, if invaded, Cuba could not depend on Soviet military participation. Cuba's only "strategy [would be] to resist by means of our own forces," said the Central Committee statement.[112]

When the Soviet leader Konstantin Chernenko died in early 1985, Fidel Castro was alone among Communist leaders in office in not attending his funeral. The official reasons for Castro's absence were that just before Chernenko's death he had gone without sleep for two nights working hard at the Cuban Women's Federation Congress and that General Raúl Castro, who headed the Cuban delegation to the funeral, knew better the new Soviet leader, Mikhail Gorbachev.[113] Even if these reasons were true, the fact that Chernenko's year in office had been the worst in Cuban-Soviet relations since 1968 was probably more significant.

Both Gorbachev and Castro sought to start their relationship on a good note. In 1985, Cuba met 99 percent of its export obligations to CMEA countries. As a reward, the price that the Soviets paid for Cuban sugar jumped by 13.7 percent from 1984 to 1985. Because world sugar prices fell during the same period, the Soviet subsidy to Cuba through the sugar prices grew by 21.6 percent. In 1985 Soviet-Cuban collaboration also increased in Angola (see Chapter 6). In early 1986 Castro attended the Soviet party congress in Moscow and met at length with Gorbachev; Castro was given the place of honor as the first foreign speaker at the congress. On his return to Moscow in November, Castro was awarded the Order of Lenin for the third time, for his sixtieth birthday.[114]

Other strains appeared in Cuban-Soviet relations, however. In April 1986 Castro launched a process that he called "rectification." Castro decided to back off from reliance on market forces and motivations as an instrument to promote economic development; for example, though Cuban peasants had been allowed to sell some of their products in a free market since 1980, such sales were prohibited again in 1986. Many other changes were made in policies and personnel to emphasize the need to work for the benefit of the homeland rather than merely for oneself.

Whereas in the 1960s (as we have seen) Castro pursued radical policies at home and abroad, including sharp criticism of what he saw as Soviet backsliding toward capitalist practices, in the late 1980s he was careful to emphasize his continued loyalty to the Soviet Union in foreign policy. He also refrained from criticizing Gorbachev's domestic reforms explicitly. But Castro's general critique of the reliance on market forces and motivations— features that were at the heart of Gorbachev's reforms and of similar changes in China and in Eastern Europe—complicated Cuban relations with the USSR. In partial compensation, Castro, other Cuban officials, and the mass media focused on some commonalities between Gorbachev's reforms and Castro's rectification, such as the punishment of corrupt officials.

In 1986 economic strains resurfaced in Cuban-Soviet relations. The Soviets wanted to cut their costs in Cuba—and they cut the price they paid for Cuban sugar by 12.6 percent. Cuba's trade deficit with the USSR increased 47 percent from 1985 to 1986. Also in 1986 the value of Cuban exports fell, with the value of exports to socialist countries falling more than the value of exports to market-economy countries. In January 1987 Castro announced that Soviet prices for Cuban products would not rise that year because Soviet oil exports had suffered from the drop in world oil prices.[115] As noted earlier, in 1987 the Cuban economy slid into the first officially recognized recession.

The Cuban press began to put some ideological pressure on the Soviets, quoting Guevara's admonitions that socialist countries ought to pay preferential prices above those prevailing in the world market.[116] In June 1987 a high-level conference in Moscow addressed serious problems in the management of Soviet aid to Cuba, Vietnam, and Mongolia, focusing on the great delays in the completion of tasks.[117] The Soviets wanted the Cubans to meet their trade obligations.

Another consequence of Gorbachev's reforms in the USSR was a greater public openness (*glasnost*). Soviet debates with regard to Cuba became public. In August 1987 Vladislav Chirkov wrote that Cuban development had been "less rapid than we would have liked." Cuban labor productivity was "still very low"; production capacity was "underused"; and "a third of all enterprises operate at a loss." Chirkov noted that Cuba had a "big debt to the socialist countries," adding that "one can well imagine how heavily this weighs morally on the Cubans." Chirkov reported Cuba's acknowledgment of its "failure to make full use of the plant, equipment, and other material resources received from the USSR," of its "delays in installing imported equipment, [the] lack of technological discipline on the part of Cuban personnel, and the inadequate use of specialists trained in the USSR." Chirkov stated that the Soviets and the CMEA were also partly responsible for these shortcomings. Although Chirkov affirmed that the Soviets "will not abandon" Cuba, he reported on the doubts of some in the USSR concerning whether the U.S. military threat to Cuba was real or exaggerated.[118]

The Cuban government was furious. Using sharp language, Vice President Rodríguez responded. He took offense at Chirkov's giving "particular prominence to those negative aspects of the Cuban economy" without sufficient emphasis on Cuba's achievements and on U.S. threats to Cuba. Rodríguez also reminded "specialists from socialist countries" who advocated Soviet use of market prices to pay for imported Cuban sugar that "by paying these preferential prices the Soviet Union and other socialist countries" demonstrate "the different nature of socialism and its superiority."[119]

Pravda's correspondent in Havana also challenged Chirkov's lack of emphasis on Cuban successes and chided him for suggesting that Cuba was a "bankrupt begging for alms."[120] Soviet writers began to discuss other topics concerning Cuba, for example, the relationship between Cuba and Colombia's M-19 insurgency (see Chapter 5).[121] Clearly, in 1987 Cuba was the topic of much debate within the Soviet Union.

For the November 1987 anniversary of the Russian Revolution, Castro traveled to Moscow to clear the air. Once again he was the most honored foreign guest; he spoke at length with Gorbachev. Castro's comments on the trip were enthusiastic, as were those of other high-ranking Cuban officials.[122] In essence, the USSR pledged that the prices to be used in Cuban-Soviet trade would be set according to political criteria. The USSR's central state budget would subsidize Soviet state firms that incur losses as a result of their trade with Cuban state firms. Cuba would thus be protected against adverse effects from the introduction of market reforms in the USSR. In January 1988 the Cuban and Soviet foreign trade ministers emphasized that, in 1987, "both sides met their commitments to deliver" goods, and they "stressed the high degree of cooperation and understanding which prevails in keeping with the ties of friendship, affection, and respect."[123]

In short, Cuban-Soviet relations are changing in the late 1980s. Although Cuban foreign policy remains fully under Soviet hegemony, the strains in strictly bilateral relations that first appeared in late 1983 have recurred; the two countries' divergent domestic policies have also complicated their relations. On the one hand, Cuba received fewer economic benefits from the USSR in 1986 and 1987. On the other hand, the Cuban government is slowly beginning to learn that Gorbachev seems prepared to ease Soviet control over its allies in order to permit greater diversity in domestic politics and economics.[124] This does not make Cuban-Soviet relations simpler, but the strains are far from signaling a break.

The USSR has successfully rebuilt a mutually acceptable hegemony over Cuba after its display of power in 1968. Throughout the 1970s and 1980s, without further coercion, Cuban leaders have professed their loyalty, gratitude, and support for the USSR, and they have recognized the importance of Soviet military and economic support. Cuba has come to respond to the "exigencies" of the Soviet economy as it has adopted many ideas, organizations, and policies parallel to those of the USSR.

Cuban-Soviet economic, political, and military relations grew closer after 1975. To reward Cuban military achievement in Angola, and to rescue the Cuban economy from the collapse of the world sugar price in early 1976, the Soviets launched a massive, comprehensive aid program while enlisting other CMEA governments in supporting Cuba. In the truest sense, the Soviet bloc's support for Cuba is invaluable, for the Cuban government could not have survived nor undertaken its many endeavors abroad without that support.

Soviet hegemony over Cuba was built on the asymmetry of power, enforced through Soviet coercion in 1968, facilitated by the Cuban economy's inability to compete internationally, and refined through the increasing ideological and policy consensus between the two governments over foreign policy.[125] Public disagreements over foreign policy issues have virtually disappeared: Cuba does not oppose Soviet interests; it exercises its autonomy mindful of, and consistent with, those interests. At crucial times, as with the Soviet invasion of Afghanistan, Cuba has adopted policies at great cost to its own interests. There is no evidence of Soviet coercion in these more recent cases. And even over domestic Soviet policies at odds with Cuba's own, Cuba is circumspect in its criticism of the USSR. The tight Soviet hegemony thus places real and significant limits on Cuba's autonomy.

Problems remain within the hegemonic system. Some stem from the snail's pace of the CMEA support procedures. Others derive from the slower growth of the Soviet and other Eastern European economies in the 1980s. More serious still is the frustrating weakness and vulnerability of Cuba's economy, which remains incapable of competing in international markets on its own. The Cuban economy's dependency on the Soviet bloc has restricted Cuba's political autonomy. Cuba depends increasingly on the good will of the CMEA, largely because it has chosen to shelter its economy from the rigors of international competition. Thus Cuba's rational and conscious pursuit of economic security in the early 1980s came at the cost of autonomy and efficiency.

Perhaps the most serious problem facing Cuba is that Cubans still have not come to grips with their relations with the USSR. In interviews, Cuban officials and academics give no evidence of hidden hostility to the Soviets and indicate no special wish to break out of their embrace. They do seem to consider their relations with the USSR as intrinsically desirable. Yet, even the most articulate Cuban officials and scholars have difficulty describing the relationship. In lengthy, generally friendly, and detailed interviews conducted in March 1985, the subject of Cuban-Soviet relations was the only topic that elicited a rash of "no comments," even in response to simple questions. Perhaps the best explanation came late one night from a friend, who said that Cubans did not like to hear themselves described as anyone's puppets.

If the ideological legitimation of Cuban-Soviet relations is to endure, it requires a more effective articulation of its nature, its limitations, and its decision makers' beliefs about the historic worth of the alliance. The Cuban government represents an authentic, indigenous revolution, proud of its defiance of the United States, one whose leaders did not come to power on the backs of the Soviet Army, yet one that has depended in the past—and will in the future—on the USSR. It remains the formidable task of that government to explain its relations with its premier ally to the world and, above all, to its own people.

Support for Revolutionary Movements

5

Cuba stands ready to act boldly and assist other revolutionaries to seize power. Its level of support for revolutionary movements has varied over time, but Cuba has been more consistent than the Soviet Union, the People's Republic of China, and other Communist states. Cuban support for revolutionary movements—an important element and a consistent defining feature of Cuban foreign policy since January 1959—has occurred for both strategic and ideological reasons. Ideology explains the continuity in Cuban support for foreign revolutions; strategy accounts for Cuba's choices of movements to support. Cuba's leaders believe this policy will advance their values and effectively promote Cuba's interests, and those of its friends, in punishing its foes.

Because of this subject's sensitivity, my discussion of Cuban support for revolutionary movements is based exclusively on published Cuban sources, published statements by Cuba's revolutionary allies, and my own interviews (see Appendix A). It has not been possible to establish a complete account of Cuban support for revolutionary movements or to determine precisely the nature and amount of support for particular movements at given times. Nor can all allegations of Cuban support for revolution be corroborated following this approach. That does not imply that such allegations are false; quite the contrary, they provide a necessary guide to Cuban behavior in this area. The restrictions I have imposed in this book on what constitutes "evidence" of Cuban support for revolution should enhance its credibility. At a minimum, this chapter represents information to which the Cuban government admits.

Support for revolution has had a high priority in Cuban foreign policy, but not the top priority. More important has been ensuring the survival of revolutionary rule through relations with the Soviet Union, and state-to-state relations that serve important political goals. Support for revolutions has also been used to ensure the Cuban government's survival; relations have been improved and consolidated with some governments to whom Cuba has given immunity from its subversive efforts. In specific cases, Cuba has curtailed its support for revolutionary movements to serve these higher foreign policy ends.

Support for revolutionary movements has had other benefits for Cuba. It has been an instrument of Cuba's foreign policy against its adversaries, those countries alienated by Cuba's early and nearly indiscriminate support for revolutions. By the mid-1960s Cuba had learned to use this tool more effectively and, in general, Cuba's enemies have been deterred. Its support for revolution has also increased the cost to the United States of hostility to Cuba. Cuba's policy of supporting revolutionary movements has given it an independent capacity to influence the USSR, sometimes leading Soviet policy and at other times providing useful support that incurs Soviet gratitude. Support for revolution has, moreover, been a positive act in itself from the Cuban government's perspective, helping to create friendly governments and therefore to make a world safer for Cuba's brand of socialism.

Although Cuba's support throughout the 1960s for anticolonialist revolutionary movements continued during the early 1970s, Cuba supported revolutionary movements in the Americas less often in the early 1970s than before because it bargained effectively to expand its state-to-state relations for the first time since 1960. The result was a relative displacement during these years of Cuba's support for revolution from Latin America to Africa and Indochina. With the collapse of the Portuguese empire, the U.S. defeat in Indochina, and the Zimbabwe settlement, revolutionary movements gained power. In late 1977 Cuba reactivated its support for revolutionaries in Nicaragua, subsequently doing the same for guerrillas in El Salvador and Guatemala—all of whom were fighting governments that had not made peace with Cuba.

The support of revolutionary movements, in Cuba's view, is an effective means to combat the United States and its allies throughout the world. In a lawless world where Cuba's main enemy—the U.S. government—has attempted to subvert the Cuban government itself, has contributed to the overthrow of Salvador Allende in Chile, and supports those who have sought to overthrow Nicaragua's Sandinista government, the Cuban government believes that it has rights comparable to those of the United States. It is the duty of Cuban revolutionaries to support revolution wherever possible for the sake of their ideological beliefs and of their own security. They perceive the United States as a subversive power whose counterrevolutionary efforts match in intensity Cuba's support of revolution and whose resources are vast compared with Cuba's. Although U.S. actions were not the cause of this Cuban policy—the Castro government's support for revolution began before the U.S. government's attacks on Cuba—U.S. practices soon became an additional reason to pursue the policy.

Cuba's Decision-Making Rules: Whom to Support When?

Cuban foreign policy decisions about providing support for revolutionary movements are guided by four rules. The first commits the Cuban government to the active support of revolutionary movements in other countries but is subject to the three other rules. The second requires that precedence be given to state-to-state relations so that such movements will not be supported if Cuban security would be seriously threatened by such support. The third states that Cuban support for a revolutionary movement, once begun, will be sacrificed as part of a bargain to advance Cuba's other political goals. The fourth rule requires that Cuba's role in the vanguard of revolutionary movements be recognized.

Cuba's decisions about proper international revolutionary behavior are governed by its commitment to certain norms in an ends-dominated ethical system. The morality of an act depends on whether it advances or retards the achievement of revolutionary goals, and the ethics of the use of violence depend on its purpose. This ethic does not automatically exclude as immoral any type of target or tactic. However, it protects many noncombatants from the use of violence, whether arbitrary or for personal gain, and prudence protects nonelite noncombatants from much harm. It is thus not true that, in the Cuban view, "anything goes" in a revolution.

An ends-dominated ethic requires political centralization for enforcement. It also justifies the use of many kinds of force, including war itself, strategic deception about the tactics and the ultimate ends of the revolutionary leaders, kidnapping, and sabotage under certain circumstances. It tolerates (but discourages) political assassination. Cuban leaders developed this ethical system during their own revolutionary struggle in the 1950s. An ends-dominated ethical system widens the scope of military targets and actions but also provides some restraints for the protection of the innocent. Such an ethic is not a sufficient guide for a revolutionary government. It must be supplemented by rules that refine decision making.

The Rule of Internationalism

The first rule governing this aspect of foreign policy is that Cuba supports revolutions in other countries. The rule of "internationalism" (to use the

Cuban government's term) is derived from the experience of Cuba's own revolutionaries—above all, Fidel Castro—from their personal background, revolutionary struggle, and experience in power both before and after relations deteriorated with the United States and were established with the Soviet Union.

This policy is captured eloquently in a passage of the Second Declaration of Havana, read by Castro on February 4, 1962, before a mass meeting, in response to the decision of the Organization of American States (OAS) to suspend Cuba from active membership: "It is the duty of every revolutionary to make the revolution. In America and in the world, it is known that the revolution will be victorious, but it is improper revolutionary behavior to sit at one's doorstep waiting for the corpse of imperialism to pass by."[1] This statement, which presents the ideological basis of Cuban support for international revolution, also points out the difference between Cuba and many Moscow-oriented Communist parties which insist that revolutionaries ought to wait for favorable "objective conditions" before reaching for power.

On January 15, 1966, in his closing speech at the Havana Tricontinental Conference to support revolutions in Africa, Asia, and Latin America, Castro went further. "The imperialists," he said, "are everywhere in the world. And for Cuban revolutionaries the battleground against imperialism encompasses the whole world . . . And so our people understand . . . that the enemy is one and the same, the same one who attacks our shores and our territory, the same one who attacks everyone else. And so we say and proclaim that the revolutionary movement in every corner of the world can count on Cuban combat fighters."[2]

In 1982 Ramiro Valdés, interior minister and Political Bureau member, explained the roots of the Cuban policy: "Where did we Cubans learn internationalism? It did not come mainly from theory nor from books . . . No. We learned to be internationalists by living life and with our own blood." He added that although "the revolution was not made in Cuba based on a calculation of the aid that we might receive from abroad . . . our own forces, sufficient to overthrow the tyranny and to conquer power, would not have been able to overcome the brutal assault of Yankee imperialism" without internationalist assistance.[3] Cuba's internationalism thus resulted more from the revolutionary government's initial weakness than from the revolutionary war itself.

Moreover, support for internationalism had been a part of the lives of key Cuban leaders. Fidel Castro took part in the riots in Bogotá in 1948 and was trained to invade the Dominican Republic. Argentine-born Ernesto

(Che) Guevara worked in Guatemala in the early 1950s. The Cuban leaders began to support revolutionary movements in 1959, before Cuba had even established relations with the USSR and before the U.S. government had committed hostile acts.

The duty to support revolution is compatible with Marxism-Leninism, though it does not necessarily rise from it. The Cuban government's evolving ideology has provided a means for the leadership to interpret reality; it serves as a lens through which to see the world or as a framework within which to evaluate the evidence. The ideology of the Cuban leaders also has descriptive and prescriptive content, especially the belief in the march of peoples toward revolution. For these reasons, support for revolution has become an intrinsic component of Cuban foreign policy; it is not peripheral, or accidental, or purely reactive to hostile policies of the United States and its allies.

The Rule of Precedence

The second rule governing this aspect of Cuban foreign policy is that support for revolution is subordinate to a higher value: the Cuban government's survival. State-to-state relations that enhance Cuba's security have precedence over support for revolution. Cuba will not initiate support for revolutionary movements fighting against a government that has good political relations with Cuba. This decision-making rule emerged in response to the near-total breakdown of Cuba's diplomatic relations with other countries in the early 1960s—a breakdown that occurred, in large part, because Cuba had not observed this rule at the outset and had supported revolutionary movements against a wide range of governments.

In 1959 Cuban leaders began to articulate elements of this rule. On April 24 about eighty insurgents, mostly Cubans, acting apparently without the sponsorship of the Cuban government, landed in Panama in an attempt to overthrow that country's government. Fidel Castro, traveling throughout the continent, commented: "It has been a vexatious incident . . , and inopportune. It is vexatious for us that our fellow citizens have engaged in an act that constitutes a denial of the principles which we have been defending publicly for the sake of the security of our sovereignty and the future of the revolution . . . Precisely when we were representing Cuba overseas, we have been placed in an unpleasant situation." He then identified two tactical principles: first, "Cubans do not have the right to intervene in a country where there is no evident tyranny or despotism," and second, Cuba must follow a policy of nonintervention for its own protection. "To break the principle of nonintervention is for us . . . a real double-edged sword," Castro said. "How can we sacrifice that principle that serves as a guarantee of our sovereignty?" Cuba sent two army officers to work with Panama to terminate the invasion, and placed one of its navy's frigates at Panama's disposal.[4]

To Castro, the invasion of Panama by these Cubans was wrong, not because such activities are always wrong, but because of its context. It came at an inopportune time, embarrassing him. But it also led to a preliminary definition of the new government's policy. First, state-to-state relations should take precedence over support of revolution; invasions would not be launched against governments that respected Cuban sovereignty or under conditions that might threaten Cuban security. Second, those planning invasions must take into account the domestic political conditions of the target state. The "Panama rule" was the forerunner of the rule of precedence.

Such "freelance" invasionary forces were not uncommon in the early days of Cuba's revolutionary government. On the eve of Castro's mid-March trip, the Cuban Navy had stopped an expedition from Cuba against François Duvalier's government in Haiti.[5] While Castro was still in South America, on May 7, 1959, the Cuban government captured twenty-two men who were about to leave Cuba to invade Somoza's Nicaragua. Commander of the Revolution Camilo Cienfuegos thundered: "With what you have done, you have betrayed Cuba, endangering the security of the nation."[6]

By June 1959 Cuba had sorted out its position on foreign revolutionary movements. The Cuban government sponsored expeditions against the Dominican Republic and Nicaragua, both of which cited Cuba as the source before the OAS. Cuba refused to cooperate with the OAS investigation of Nicaragua's allegations. In addition, Cuba's ambassador to the United Nations acknowledged Cuban support for the Dominican rebels. *Revolución* praised the new Cuban foreign policy as not being "encased in the old molds of international law."[7] The Dominican case met the test of the Panama rule: unconventional warfare against an old-fashioned dictator, Rafael Trujillo, who was himself trying to overthrow Castro. In the case of Nicaragua, the Somoza family had been a target for revolutionaries well before the Cuban revolution.

Cuba's rapid diplomatic isolation in the early 1960s—largely as a result of its support for Latin American revolutionary movements—required it to revise the Panama rule and to adopt the narrower rule of the precedence of state-to-state relations. The new version plays down the significance of the internal structure of a regime, giving priority to the first part of the Panama rule alone: Regimes, even if they are right-wing and authoritarian, need not be opposed if their policies toward Cuba advance important Cuban goals.

Good examples are the uninterrupted relations between Cuba and Mexico, between Cuba and most states in Africa, Asia, and the West Indies, and especially between Cuba and the Franco regime in Spain. The 1963 Spanish-Cuban bilateral trade agreement was an important and profitable turning point for Cuba, given the country's isolation from most market economies at that time; in the 1960s, Spain was Cuba's main non-Communist trade partner. Franco also resisted pressures on his government to break political and economic relations with Cuba. In exchange, Cuba did not support the overthrow of Franco's government—a policy made easier by the fact that there was no active revolutionary struggle against it.[8]

Since Franco's death, the Spanish government at times has charged that Cuba gave some support to the Basque terrorist organization ETA. Cuba denied this charge, but the Spanish government believes that Cuba did provide such support until Spanish protests forced Cuba to return to the rule of precedence.[9] In the early 1980s, Spain asked Cuba to give asylum to six ETA members expelled from France. Cuba did so, despite Castro's misgivings because, as he later added, "we want to be neither accomplices nor jailers of ETA members, nor to meddle in Spain's internal affairs." Castro noted that ETA had sought official contacts with the Cuban Communist party but that these had been denied.[10] On the whole, the rule of precedence worked effectively in Cuban-Spanish relations.

Another result of the revision of the Panama rule was to make Cuban intervention in other countries' internal affairs easier if their governments broke with Cuba. Liberal democratic regimes would not be exempt from Cuban support of revolution. The Cuban government sought to overthrow the Venezuelan government, beginning early in the 1960s when the two countries still had diplomatic relations. In May 1967 the Cuban Communist party's Central Committee publicly admitted that three Cubans had joined with Venezuelans in a landing party. After attempting to show that none was a Cuban official, the Central Committee added: "But there is no question here of our being interested in evading any responsibility whatsoever . . . nor does the Cuban Revolution ask permission or forgiveness in order to carry out its duties of solidarity with all revolutionary forces of the world, including Venezuelan revolutionaries. Revolutionary acts are justified by the very existence of imperialism."[11]

The nature of the target regime had come to matter less in the decision to support revolution; its relations with Cuba and the United States mattered most. Cuba did not require hostility between a third government and the U.S. government; it did require that the third government not support U.S. policies toward Cuba. Thus Spain (even with U.S. military bases) and Mexico have been immune from Cuban support for revolutionary activity; but Venezuela (a showcase of the U.S.-sponsored Alliance for Progress) became a target. A decade after Franco's death, Castro still remembered him fondly: "Franco did not behave badly, we have to recognize it. Despite the pressures on him, he did not break diplomatic and trade relations with us . . . That Galician knew how to do things. Good heavens, he did behave well."[12]

The Rule of Bargaining

Because Cuba had no diplomatic relations with most governments of the Americas in the 1960s, and did support revolutions against several of those governments, the rule of precedence was often inapplicable. To improve the Cuban government's chances for survival, Cuba developed another rule to guide foreign policy: support for revolution could be used for bargaining. Cuba would suspend its ongoing support for revolutionary movements, begun before the rule of precedence had been formulated, in return for a suspension of hostilities against Cuba and other benefits. Like the rule of precedence, the rule of bargaining gives priority to state-to-state relations, and both ordinarily prevail over the rule of internationalism. Unlike the rule of precedence, the rule of bargaining operates in the context of prior active Cuban support for revolutionary movements and of Cuba's search for specific advantages.

In 1964 Castro explained Cuba's position on aid to revolutionary movements: "We will help in the manner we deem most convenient, depending on the circumstances and considering what [other governments] do with regard to us."[13] He told Richard Eder that Cuba would withhold material support from Latin American revolutionaries if the United States and its Latin American allies would cease their material support for subversive activities against Cuba. That is, if other governments respected the Cuban government, it would reciprocate; Cuba would abide by the same international norms that others followed with regard to Cuba.[14]

Cuba used this type of bargaining successfully to reestablish diplomatic and economic relations with many Latin American governments against which, years before, it had supported guerrilla movements. Changes in the policies of the governments of Chile, Peru, and Venezuela opened the door to such bargaining. Chile's Frei government took the initiative in reestablishing economic relations with Cuba in 1969. The military government that came to power in Peru late in 1968 set a new foreign policy course that was much more independent of the United States; Cuba responded in March 1969 by sending a delegation headed by Carlos Rafael Rodríguez to a meeting in Lima of the United Nations Economic Commission for Latin America. The Peruvians treated the Cuban delegation with great courtesy; Rodríguez publicly praised the military government's expropriation policies. Relations developed further when, in May 1970, Cuba sent relief aid to Peru in the wake of a massive earthquake.[15] Rafael Caldera's new government, installed in Venezuela in 1969, adopted a foreign policy of "ideological pluralism" and a domestic policy of reconciliation with and amnesty toward guerrillas. Eventually Cuba reestablished full relations with these and other Latin American governments.[16]

These changes in Cuban policy made sense in light of most guerrilla movements' defeat in South America by the end of the 1960s, and after Guevara's death in Bolivia in October 1967. However, defeat alone had not prevented Cuba from supporting revolution in the past, nor would lack of success deter it in the future. Local conditions are a factor in shaping Cuba's decision to support insurgencies, but not a sufficient explanation.

Cuban policy changes were consistent not only with the changing local situation but also with Soviet preferences in Latin America. If Soviet preferences were the main motivation, however, Cuba would not have behaved as it had in the mid-1960s. Cuba's support for revolution, and the Soviet reluctance to commit resources in a similar manner, had been a major reason for the disputes between them. Nor did Soviet pressure in 1968, and Cuba's acceptance of the Soviet invasion of Czechoslovakia, explain Cuba's policy changes in the crucial year 1969. In June 1969 Carlos Rafael Rodríguez headed Cuba's delegation to the Moscow conference of Communist parties; he was one of the top Cuban leaders with a high interest in improving Cuban-Soviet relations. Yet, he still emphasized disagreements between Cuba and other Communist governments and parties on the issue of support for revolutionary movements.[17]

Castro, updating the rule of bargaining in 1975, said: "We live in a world where respect for international norms is a must, and we have always been willing to respect them. But those who have tried to export counterrevolution will never have the right to demand that we respect international norms." In such cases, Castro stated, Cubans demonstrated "our solidarity" with revolutionary movements "since we were not bound by any norms." Cuba fought enemy governments by supporting insurgents trying to overthrow them. But Castro held out the possibility of a bargain: "We have observed international norms and are willing to go on observing them, as those who also respect them will discover."[18] The maintenance of Cuban-Argentine relations even after the 1976 military coup in Argentina is a good example of bargaining at work. Mutually beneficial commercial relations led Cuba to suspend support for revolutionary movements in Argentina and to give priority to formal relations with the Argentine government.[19]

To protect themselves, many South American governments learned to make use of this Cuban rule. One of the more public statements about bargaining was made in September 1986 by Brazilian Foreign Minister Abreu Sodré, as he explained the conditions that led Brazil to reestablish diplomatic relations with Cuba the previous June. Faced with the charge that Cuba would send guerrilla trainers disguised as diplomats to its new embassy in Brasilia, Sodré said: "The talks that we had were not public, but they were tough." The Cubans, he added, "know that they will have no space for such activities."[20]

Bargaining was also applied in the context of U.S.-Cuban relations in early 1973 to reach a formal agreement concerning hijacking, which ended an epidemic of air piracy.[21] Cuba agreed not to support hijackers, and the United States pledged not to support hijackings of Cuban vessels. The Cuban government may also have believed that hijacking violated its own norms: Hijacking threatened nonelite noncombatants and did not increase support for a revolutionary cause. Most hijackers—clearly not revolutionaries—embarrassed the Cuban government. Cuba's ends-dominated ethic did not embrace using innocents as means for unrevolutionary ends. Cuba continued to honor the hijacking agreement even after it gave formal notice to terminate the pact in 1976.

Bargaining was also at work in Cuba's policies toward Central America in the early 1980s, when Cuba called attention to U.S. support for those who sought to overthrow Nicaragua's Sandinista government. Although in Cuba's view, the United States had no right to challenge Cuban support of revolutionaries in El Salvador (given U.S. actions in Nicaragua), Cuba offered to bargain over El Salvador. In February 1982, Castro endorsed and went beyond the initiative of Mexican President José López Portillo, aimed at cooling off disputes between the United States, Nicaragua, and Cuba. Castro stated that Cuba was "willing to work in the search for negotiated political solutions to the problems of El Salvador, Central America, the whole region"[22] in order to improve its own security and probably that of Nicaragua. Jesús Montané, a member of the party's Secretariat in charge of international relations and an alternate member of the Political Bureau, said in Havana in April 1982: "We cannot always advance as swiftly as we would like . . . alongside our determination and solidarity with the popular and revolutionary movement, which we have never denied, we must be ready to offer our willingness to negotiate."[23] Castro reiterated his position on El Salvador in mid-1983: "If there is an agreement that everyone stop supporting, in one way or another, the revolutionaries just as much as those who are oppressing the country, we are ready to accept such a formula." He emphasized the need for "mutual concessions," leading to "an honorable agreement that both parties accept similar commitments."[24]

In the case of Colombia, however, Cuba went back on the rule of bargaining, lowering the expected priority of state-to-state relations even after the Cuban and Colombian governments had made peace. In the 1960s Cuba had supported guerrillas in Colombia. In the 1970s it suspended that support, and in 1975 it reestablished diplomatic relations with the Colombian government. In 1980 Cuba again supported a revolutionary movement (this time the M-19 Movement) that sought to overthrow the Colombian government. As a result, in 1981 Colombia again ended relations with Cuba.

Cuba has denied Colombian allegations that it supplied weapons to the M-19; it also denied any connection with the entry of weapons into Colombia and with the M-19's landing on the Colombian coast in 1980. Although the Cuban statements implied that it did not share the M-19's ideology, Cuba did not deny assisting the M-19 short of supplying them with weapons or giving logistical support and advice before their landing.[25] In interviews in Havana in March 1985, Cuban officials acknowledged that Cuba had good enough relations with the M-19 to know in advance about the movement's plans to invade Colombia, leaving from Panama. But they also said that Cuba warned the M-19 against taking such a step. As if justifying Cuban support for the M-19, these officials emphasized the Colombian government's hostile policies toward Cuba at the time and its close cooperation with the United States.

Colombia had sought to undermine the Nonaligned Movement's Havana Summit throughout 1979 and helped to block Cuba's election to the United Nations Security Council later that year. Anger at Colombia's government was probably the main factor in Cuba's retreat from the rule of bargaining in this case. As one thoughtful interviewee put it, Cuban officials did not pay much attention to Colombian and U.S. allegations of Cuban support for M-19 guerrillas because of the bad state of Cuban-Colombian relations, even though "ordinarily, the behavior would be different because such acts affect Cuba's global credibility, which implies not acting in this manner [supporting revolutionary movements] in the case of countries with which we have diplomatic relations."[26] This is a clear statement of the rule of bargaining.

Another explanation for Cuba's actions in Colombia may be that the policy was a mistake. The year 1980 was very difficult domestically for Cuba.[27] The decision to support the M-19 might not have occurred in less strained times. Cuba's actions were not coordinated with those of the Soviet and Eastern European governments, which had been cultivating trade relations with Colombia.[28] In any event, Cuban support for the M-19 broke the rule of bargaining. Despite this incident, Cuba has generally observed the rule since 1969.

Cuban relations with the Colombian government began to improve again after Belisario Betancur became President in 1982. By 1986 the M-19 was internally divided. In November 1986, Cuba announced its willingness to renew diplomatic relations with President Virgilio Barco's new government in Colombia.[29]

The Vanguard Rule

Cuba expects to be recognized as a leader of international revolutionaries because it believes it has the correct strategy for victory. In general, it does not support revolutionary movements that do not defer to Cuba; it has even been willing to split a revolutionary movement. In 1967 Castro denounced the "capitulators" and "defeatists" who led the Venezuelan Communist party and who, Castro claimed, had given up on the armed struggle as the path to power. He stated Cuba's claim to a position in the vanguard of revolutionary struggles—and its effect on Cuban foreign policy—in this way:

> Our stand regarding Communist parties will be based on strictly revolutionary principles. The parties that have a line without hesitations and capitulationism, the parties that in our opinion have a consistent revolutionary line, will receive our support in all circumstances; but the parties that entrench themselves behind the name of Communists or Marxists and believe themselves to have a monopoly on revolutionary sentiment—what they really monopolize is reformism—will not be treated by us as revolutionary parties. And if in any country those who call themselves Communists do not know how to fulfill their duty, we will support those who, without calling themselves Communists, conduct themselves like real Communists in action and in struggle.[30]

Months later, after Guevara's death in Bolivia, Castro denounced the Bolivian Communist party, especially its secretary-general, Mario Monje, for betraying the guerrillas.[31] By the fall of 1968, Cuba had publicly attacked the Moscow-affiliated Communist parties of Guatemala, Bolivia, Venezuela, Peru, Colombia, and Nicaragua.[32] Carlos Fonseca Amador, a founder of Nicaragua's Sandinista Front for National Liberation (FSLN), published in Havana a denunciation of the Nicaraguan Communist party as Somoza's collaborators.[33] Cuban publications noted with approval "the splitting-off of the radical revolutionary Communist sectors from the traditional party apparatus and policy that has taken place in Venezuela, Colombia and more recently Guatemala on the issue of the leading of the people's war."[34]

That split also occurred in El Salvador, where the Communist party published Guevara's Bolivian diary and Castro's introduction to it with a commentary of its own. According to the commentary, the fact that "over the past eight years dozens of groups have failed in their attempts to successfully create and develop guerrilla forces . . . permits us to disagree with the opinions of Comrade Fidel Castro in his prologue to the Diary of Che, in which he condemns all those who concluded that Che was mistaken." In response, some Salvadoran Communist party members who supported armed struggle as the way to power left to form their own movement.[35]

Cuba even denounced revolutionaries engaged in armed struggle who did not accept its leadership. In 1966, Castro attacked Guatemala's Yon Sosa and the Thirteenth of November Revolutionary Movement as Trotskyites while approving another Guatemalan revolutionary movement, led by Luis Turcios Lima. Although Cuba's relations with Yon Sosa subsequently improved, Cuba's attack on both the Communist party and Yon Sosa's forces seriously hurt the prospects for revolution in Guatemala.[36]

The vanguard rule was also at work in Cuba's relations with African revolutionaries. For example, from 1963 to 1968 Cuba strongly supported the revolutionary activities of Pierre Mulele, who was fighting to overthrow President Joseph Mobutu's government in the Congo (later renamed Zaire). But when in September 1968 Mulele gave up the armed struggle and accepted Mobutu's offer of amnesty, Cuba denounced Mulele as a "traitor." In Africa as in Latin America, Cuba demanded unswerving commitment to armed struggle even when the cause seemed lost.[37]

In the 1970s, Cuba changed its policies toward the traditional Communist parties of Latin America when they recognized Cuba's position in the vanguard. In exchange, Cuba broke with some of the same guerrilla movements it had supported before, such as Douglas Bravo's Armed Forces of National Liberation in Venezuela, which Cuba once endorsed over the Venezuelan Communist party.[38] In June 1975, the Communist parties of Latin America and the Caribbean gathered in Havana to acknowledge Cuba's leadership in exchange for Cuba's recognition that armed struggle was only one path among many toward power, and one to be tried only as a last resort. All the Communist parties that Cuba had denounced only a half-dozen years earlier signed the accord. The FSLN was not represented nor was it mentioned in this declaration; neither was El Salvador. There was thus no hint of the revolutionary experience that awaited Central America.[39] Cuba thus compromised on several points about the proper path to power for the sake of receiving the allegiance of the Communist parties. This was a necessary precondition for the unified Communist support that was given to Central American revolutionary movements in the years that followed.

Cuba's newly recognized vanguard role helped it lead some of these cautious Communist parties toward the path of armed struggle in late 1977, when Cuban foreign policy again came to emphasize support for revolutionary movements. As Cuba's official report to the 1980 Scientific Anti-Imperialist Conference stated, "At the end of 1977, the people's revolutionary movement, which had been hard hit by imperialism in the preceding years, showed signs of recovery. Mass struggle and revolutionary action became stronger and more visible in Central America and in . . . Bolivia, Peru and Colombia." The Sandinista victory in Nicaragua "revived the efficacy and viability of armed struggle as a decisive means for seizing power when all other ways are closed off." The Sandinista victory depended on creating a "broad, mass-based social force . . . under the political leadership of the Sandinista front." Moreover, "the revolutionary victory was not only a political victory but also—and this was decisive—a military triumph." In short, "the victory was won because the masses fought; their strategy was correct; a trained military force defeated the National Guard; and all anti-dictatorial sectors, from the grass roots on up through the vanguard leadership, the FSLN, were united."[40]

Castro himself was more forthright: "What do the experiences of Guatemala, El Salvador, Chile and Bolivia teach us? That there is only one path: revolution. That there is only one way: revolutionary armed struggle."[41] Cuban support for the formerly cautious Salvadoran Communist party came only after the party had confessed its past mistake of failing to begin the armed struggle sooner. The party's general-secretary, Schafik Jorge Handal, discussed "the Communist Party of El Salvador's errors" with the Cuban press.[42] The honor and memory of Guevara had been vindicated at last.

In general, the Cuban government has abided by its four rules to govern decisions about support for revolutionary movements. This stability in the conceptual framework guiding Cuban foreign policy has helped the leadership revise specific policies in response to changing circumstances. The main change in this aspect of Cuban foreign policy has been the growth in the scope and effectiveness of Cuban support for revolution. Supporting revolution has evolved from a regional to a worldwide policy.

Comrades in Struggle

Cuba refined the categories of allies it would support as its policy encompassed the globe. It has supported four types of revolutionary movements—which I will call quasi-states, anticolonialist movements, worthwhile revolutionary movements, and untrustworthy movements. Cuban policy toward these groups is shaped by three factors: the degree of overt international approval of particular revolutionary movements; the ideological kinship between Cuba and a given revolutionary movement; and the requirement that revolutionary movements acknowledge Cuba's leadership. Where international approval is high, ideological kinship close, and Cuba's leadership accepted, Cuban support is considerable. The outstanding example is Cuban support for the Popular Movement for the Liberation of Angola in 1975, when it faced the South African invasion of Angola. Where international approval is low, ideological kinship distant, and Cuba's position in the vanguard not accepted, Cuban involvement tends to be limited, brief, and narrowly designed to serve Cuban ends. This set of circumstances characterized Cuban support for the former Katanga (Shaba) gendarmes in Angola in their opposition to Zaire's government.

The Quasi-States

Cuba has openly and formally treated four revolutionary movements as states: the Provisional Revolutionary Government of South Vietnam before 1975, the South West Africa People's Organization (SWAPO), the Palestine Liberation Organization (PLO), and the Democratic Saharawi Arab Republic (RASD), represented by the Polisario movement, which is fighting for the independence of the former Spanish Sahara from Morocco. Cuba considers them the legitimate and sole representatives of the peoples of Vietnam, Namibia, Palestine, and the former Spanish western Sahara, respectively. In 1965 Cuba was the first government to recognize the Provisional Revolutionary Government of South Vietnam and the first to send an ambassador to the "liberated" zones. During the war in Vietnam, Cuba sent medical teams and food, and in 1965 it sent ten thousand tons of sugar.[43]

Much Cuban assistance to these movements has been overt. Cuba stresses that the quasi-states have received broad recognition from the international community. The RASD, SWAPO, and PLO are full members of the Nonaligned Movement. All have extensive support in United Nations organizations. Cuba's rules of precedence and bargaining are inapplicable in these cases because Cuba considers South Africa, Israel, and Morocco illegal occupying powers; they also have little to offer Cuba. The quasi-states have armies in combat and are ideologically compatible with Cuba. Although Cuba recognized only one quasi-state in the late 1960s, it acknowledged three in the early 1980s. Revolutionary movements in South Africa and Puerto Rico could eventually qualify as quasi-states. Prudence, the limited strength of the combatants, and the nature of the local situation, however, restrain Cuban support in these cases.

Because Polisario has controlled parts of the former Spanish Sahara, Cuba has been able to include the RASD in its routine foreign aid program at least since early 1979. In 1980, Cuba established diplomatic relations with the RASD and sent a twelve-person medical brigade to work in the Sahara, as if that were no different from sending Cubans to assist any other state,[44] notwithstanding Morocco's rule over most of the western Sahara's population centers and phosphate mines.

The Sahara has been visited officially by at least two members of the Political Bureau of Cuba's Communist party. Mohammed Abdelazis, head of the RASD and Polisario secretary-general, has been received in Cuba as a head of state to request "all your support and aid in every field, particularly toward the achievement of victory." The RASD resident ambassador in Havana is a member of the Polisario Political Bureau. The RASD defense minister has visited Cuba to discuss "questions of mutual interest" with Armed Forces Minister Raúl Castro. The RASD has acknowledged that some of its leading professional cadres are being trained in Algeria, Libya, and Cuba. Cuba also reported that it had 552 young Saharawi students in the Isle of Youth by late 1982 and 569 in 1984 (altogether in Cuba, there were perhaps over 1,000 students). In 1984 most of the RASD's medical doctors were Cubans or Cuban-trained Saharawis. It is not clear whether Cuba has provided military training to Polisario guerrillas but, in the words of a well-informed interviewee in 1985, that would be "normal" for relations of this type. There were no Cuban troops in the Sahara.[45]

The wide international recognition of the RASD facilitates Cuba's support. Cuba, in turn, has helped the RASD both at the Havana Nonaligned Summit in 1979, presided over by Fidel Castro, and in the United Nations General Assembly, which in 1979 recognized the Sahara's right to independence, and Polisario as the representative of the people of the Sahara, urging Morocco to "terminate its occupation." By 1983, the RASD had been recognized as independent by fifty-six states, including twenty-six in Africa and thirteen in Latin America and the Caribbean. Cuba refers to Morocco as a foreign power occupying a part of the Sahara.[46]

Cuban aid to Polisario and the RASD also makes it clear that the maintenance of good relations with Cuba requires continuing attention by others. Speaking before the United Nations General Assembly in 1979, Castro noted that Morocco had maintained diplomatic and trade relations with Cuba at the very moment when U.S. economic policies against Cuba were at their peak effectiveness in the early 1960s. Then, in the mid-1970s Morocco occupied the Sahara; in 1977 Morocco deployed its troops to Zaire's Shaba province to help Zaire repel an invasion by Shaba exiles believed to have Cuban backing; and in 1978 Morocco again deployed its troops to Shaba to help Zaire hold the province after French and Belgian troops had defeated yet another invasion by alleged Cuban-backed Shaba exiles. In response to these Moroccan decisions, Cuba decided to support the Polisario movement.[47] This change in Cuban policy illustrates the primacy that Cuba usually accords to politics over economics.[48]

In contrast to Cuba, the Soviet Union is officially neutral on the western Sahara question. It does not recognize the RASD as a state; no formal party relations exist between the Polisario and the Soviet Communist party; and there is no evidence of Soviet military support for Polisario. The USSR's phosphate trade agreement with Morocco, still in force, is the largest commercial deal that it has ever concluded with a Third World country.[49] Phosphate sales to the USSR have enabled the Moroccan government to partially finance the costs of the war against the RASD. Support for the RASD is an example of a Cuban policy that comes close to opposing Soviet policy on a significant issue.

SWAPO is a full member of the Nonaligned Movement, but it has had little success in gaining formal recognition as a state, despite broad international support for Namibia's independence. Cuba treats SWAPO as a quasi-state, recognizing it as the only legitimate representative of the Namibian people. However, SWAPO's representation in Cuba is before the Communist party only—not before the Cuban government. Although SWAPO participates as a state in meetings of representatives from African countries in Cuba, Cuba does not always invite it to other formal state occasions.[50] Cuba favors "increased support for the armed struggle . . . led by SWAPO" against South Africa. Sam Nujoma, SWAPO's leader, has thanked Cuba for "its concrete material assistance," which normally means military aid, and for "political and diplomatic support."[51] Cuba began to train Namibian students openly in early 1978; there were 600 in Cuba in 1979 and in 1983, rising to 1,275 by 1987.[52] Together with Angola, Cuba has conditioned the withdrawal of its troops from southern Angola on the withdrawal of South African forces from Namibia. But Angola and Cuba have proposed that the partial withdrawal of Cuban troops might begin before all South African troops have left Namibia as part of a process leading to Namibia's independence.[53]

Cuba recognizes the PLO as the only legitimate representative of the Palestinian people. The PLO has an embassy and resident diplomatic personnel in Havana, and it was a member of the Coordinating Bureau of the Non-aligned Movement during Castro's chairmanship.[54] Cuban relations with the PLO were slow to develop, however. In 1968, the Cuban-sponsored secretariat of the Organization for Solidarity of the Peoples of Africa, Asia, and Latin America (OSPAAL) issued an "appeal to the socialist countries and revolutionary parties and forces now in power . . . to give the necessary military assistance to the revolutionary organizations of the Palestinian people, which as Al Fatah, the Organization for the Liberation of Palestine, the Popular Front for the Liberation of Palestine and others, lead and develop the revolutionary armed struggle."[55] Nevertheless, though the USSR and most of its close allies broke off diplomatic relations with Israel after the 1967 Arab-Israeli war, Cuba did not do so until September 1973. Not until Yasser Arafat's visit to Cuba in November 1974 was an agreement reached to open a PLO office—later raised to the rank of embassy—in Cuba. Only then could Arafat quote Castro as saying that the Palestinian revolution can count on Cuba, its support, and its aid.[56] Since then, Palestinians have been trained at Cuba's "Nico López" center, its top school for party leadership cadres.[57]

The Anticolonialist Movements
As a result of the Cuban leaders' belief that colonial rule may always be opposed by revolutionaries, Cuba has supported many anticolonialist movements. These movements have also received substantial international approval, though less than the quasi-states; embassies were not established in Cuba.

Beginning in 1959, Cuba enthusiastically supported revolution in Algeria against the French and gave strong backing to the Algerian Provisional Government, which was the first revolutionary movement Cuba treated informally as a quasi-state.[58] Cuban relations with the United Kingdom, France, and even Portugal, remained important, however; the rule of the precedence of state-to-state relations applied to their home territories, even when Cuba supported revolutionary movements in their colonies. Despite the decline in Cuban support for some revolutionary movements in Latin America in the early 1970s, Cuban support for anticolonialist movements did not decline during those years. With the virtual completion of decolonization, of course, the need for and significance of this type of Cuban support had declined by the 1980s.

The extent of Cuban support for the Popular Movement for the Liberation of Angola (MPLA)—the prime example of a Cuban-backed anticolonial movement—was spectacular. The MPLA first requested and received Cuban assistance in transporting weapons in the spring of 1975. At least as early as August 1975, some Cuban advisers, led by General Raúl Díaz Argüelles, had arrived. In late September, the first Cuban ships, carrying no fewer than 480 military personnel, some civilians, 25 mortar and anti-aircraft batteries, 115 vehicles, communications equipment, and medical supplies, sailed from Cuba; they arrived in Angola in early October. This Cuban support was in part a response to prior South African moves into Angola. Because the Cubans were soon engaged in combat, South Africa became alarmed and intervened more massively in Angola in mid-October 1975. In response, Cuba committed more forces. Flying on Cuban civilian aircraft, 650 special troops of the Ministry of the Interior arrived in Angola on November 8, three days before independence.[59] Altogether, no fewer than 1,100 Cuban military personnel and an undetermined number of civilians were in Angola before independence.

Troops from Guinea and Guinea-Bissau fought alongside MPLA and Cuban troops. Soviet weapons were sent directly to Angola for MPLA and Cuban use. The Soviets had supplied weapons to the MPLA years earlier, suspended such shipments from 1972 to 1974, and resumed them in late 1974, but the main increase in Soviet weapons supplies occurred in 1975 after November 10. By December 1975, the Soviets were also transporting Cuban troops.[60] War raged until the withdrawal of South African troops from Angola in March 1976.

Cuba's ties with the MPLA began in the early 1960s. The MPLA had been endorsed by the 1966 Havana Tricontinental Conference. By 1968, the Havana-based OSPAAL secretariat included the MPLA's Paulo Jorge (later Angolan foreign minister). Many MPLA leaders studied in Cuba beginning in the 1960s, including some who later became members of the MPLA Central Committee and ministers of the Angolan government. Cuba had been training MPLA "revolutionary and military cadres" since 1965, according to Political Bureau member Armando Hart. Political Bureau member Jorge Risquet has noted that "Fidel sent Che [Guevara] in early 1965 to meet with the MPLA leadership . . . in Brazzaville. He offered revolutionary Cuba's solidarity to Agostinho Neto . . . Soon after, Cuban soldiers began arriving in Cabinda [Portuguese enclave north of Angola] to train the MPLA guerrilla front . . . At Comrade Neto's request, Cuba took charge of arming and training a guerrilla column which was to cross Zaire" into Angola. At this time, Cuba trained and armed over one hundred MPLA guerrillas. (At times Cuba also supported Jonas Savimbi's UNITA (National Union for the Total Independence of Angola), also fighting against the Portuguese, with training and military assistance. By 1974, however, UNITA and the MPLA were fighting each other; since then Cuba has backed only the MPLA).[61]

Why did Cuba send troops to Angola? Cuba has emphasized its long-standing ties with the MPLA and the ideological—even racial—affinity of the Cuban and Angolan movements and peoples. MPLA leader Agostinho Neto's views on race and ideology were consistent with those of Cuban leaders. Neto opposed a racial war against the whites and welcomed whites and people of mixed race in the struggle against the Portuguese;[62] this position made it easier for the MPLA to welcome white, mixed race, and black troops from Cuba. Marxist-Leninist in orientation and committed to the armed struggle, the MPLA had long been considered a worthy candidate for Cuban support.

The apparent imminence of Angolan independence probably convinced the Cuban government that it was the time to act, while the South African invasion of Angola made it politically easier for Cuba to obtain quick international support and more difficult for the United States and its allies to object. Cuba and South Africa thus engaged in a classic action and reaction escalation of the conflict. Moreover, in April 1975, Saigon had fallen to the Communists; the United States seemed humiliated and unlikely to intervene in Angola. Hence Cuba's decision to intervene in Angola was risky but international factors made it less reckless than it might have been. Cuba took action to confirm its place in the international system, to demonstrate its autonomy from the Soviets (while acting consistently with Soviet interests in helping to create a Marxist state in Angola), to defy the United States, and to turn back South Africa's thrust and gain black Africa's applause. No other step has been so significant in catapulting Cuba onto the world stage; both international system and ideological factors combined to allow a bold display of Cuba's power.[63]

A consensus has emerged that Cuba's decision to send troops to Angola was its own. Ricardo Alarcón, Cuba's deputy minister for foreign relations, has stated: "The decision to send troops to Angola was taken exclusively and autonomously by the Cuban government at the request of only one government—the government of Angola." General Vernon Walters, in 1975 deputy director of central intelligence, said in 1985: "I believe that . . . Castro was pursuing his own aims—which happened to be, in large part, convergent with those of Moscow."[64] And Arkady N. Shevchenko, a Soviet defector and formerly high Soviet Foreign Ministry official, has said: "[Deputy Foreign Minister Vasily] Kuznetsov told me that the idea for the large-scale military operation had originated in Havana, not Moscow."[65]

To be sure, Cuba's decision, as Walters noted, was consistent with Soviet interests, but it was nonetheless a remarkable contribution from the junior to the senior partner in the Cuban-Soviet alliance. Cuba's decision to act in Angola—and its success—gave Cuba much leverage with the Soviets; it was the impetus for the decisions by the USSR and other CMEA countries in mid-1976 to increase dramatically their help to Cuba. It also established Cuba's position in the vanguard of Communist states. Henceforth, when Cuba pledged its support for a movement or a government, others would listen.

Cuba also strongly supported the African Party for the Independence of Guinea-Bissau and Cape Verde (PAIGC). As its founder, Amilcar Cabral, explained, some PAIGC radio broadcasts came from Cuba. At Cabral's request, Cuba also sent weapons, medicines, other supplies, and provided training for PAIGC cadres. Jose Bernardo Vieira, who became general-secretary of the PAIGC and president of the Council of the Revolution in Guinea-Bissau, received a year of training in Cuba. Cuba also sent fighters. Cuban Interior Minister Ramiro Valdés explained that the PAIGC was "one of the first African liberation movements we established links with . . . shortly after the triumph of our revolution . . . Cuban fighters went to make their modest and disinterested contribution to the Guinea-Bissau patriots." One such fighter, Pedro Rodríguez Peralta, was captured by the Portuguese as he fought, according to Fidel Castro, "side by side with the Guinea-Bissau patriots." The Portuguese eventually released Rodríguez Peralta, who was rewarded in 1975 with membership in the Cuban party's Central Committee.[66] Many Cubans fought in Guinea-Bissau and in some other African countries, too.[67] (In contrast, Mozambique's FRELIMO—Front for Mozambique's Liberation—received little Cuban backing).[68]

Cuba treats the African National Congress (ANC), which is fighting against the government of South Africa, as an anticolonialist movement. Discussing the military equipment used by its guerrillas, ANC leaders have said: "We have no intentions of hiding the fact that we are supported by the socialist community: the Soviet Union, Cuba, the German Democratic Republic and all the other socialist countries." Moreover, the ANC has sent many students to these countries. Cuba routinely reports the presence of South African students in Cuba; someday it may treat the ANC as a quasi-state.[69] The limited international recognition accorded the ANC and its military weakness probably account for the fact that Cuba does not yet treat it as such.

Cuba also has supported Puerto Rican independence, mostly by raising the issue in the United Nations and in the Nonaligned Movement. In 1975, then President Osvaldo Dorticós stated, "Cuba unhesitatingly reaffirms its feelings of solidarity and ratifies in full its pledge of unlimited support to the Puerto Rican cause . . . Cuba does not consider the Puerto Rican cause and duty of solidarity as a matter of discussion between the United States and Cuba." Rather, Cuba "considers Puerto Rico to be a Latin American nation subjected to colonial domination and its relations, therefore, not an internal affair of the United States."[70] This same reasoning underlies Cuban support for the quasi-states; in Puerto Rico's case, the very low level of support for independence among Puerto Ricans and the divisions within the pro-independence movements constrain Cuba's support.

Cuba provided some arms to pro-independence Puerto Ricans in the late 1960s. In 1969 the OSPAAL secretariat called "upon all progressive forces to extend their solidary support" to both the embryonic Puerto Rican Communist party and the Armed Liberation Commandos, an urban guerrilla group that attacked U.S. firms.[71] By the late 1970s, however, Cuba had come to emphasize overt, legal solidarity in international organizations and eschewed violence in support of Puerto Rican independence, though Cuba probably retained links to Puerto Rican groups that still engaged in violence on behalf of independence.[72]

Cuba has not always been steadfast in its support of anticolonialist revolutionary movements. In the late 1960s the Eritreans' fight against the government of Ethiopia was defined as an anticolonialist struggle. The OSPAAL secretariat rejected the view that the Eritrean struggle was a separatist or religious war: "The revolution in Eritrea is part of the global anti-imperialist struggle."[73] But Cuba dropped its support for the Eritrean insurgency when it fought alongside the Ethiopian government against the Somali invasion in 1977–78. The rule of bargaining was thus applied to relations with Ethiopia. Cuba gained the alliance of the Ethiopian military government and sacrificed, in exchange, its support for the Eritrean rebellion.

With regard to French overseas territories in the Caribbean, Cuban actions have been constrained by the rule of precedence of state-to-state relations. Cuba has maintained generally cordial relations with the French government for the sake of politics, trade, finance, and technology. Nonetheless, Cuba hosted the first consultative meeting of anti-imperialist organizations of the Caribbean and Central America in June 1984, which called for the complete liberation of the remaining colonies.[74] Cuba emphasizes its relations with legal Communist parties in the Caribbean, which support autonomy more than independence, and eschews support for violent groups.[75] Another foreign policy rule, the rule of bargaining, was applied to Portugal after the 1974 revolution. Cuba attempted to safeguard Portuguese interests, even as it sent massive forces into Angola, in order to preserve the prospects of the Left within Portugal itself.[76]

"Worthwhile" Revolutionary Movements

Revolutionary movements that the Cuban government considers worthwhile generally have little international support outside Communist parties; at times, Cuba may be their only support. They are ideologically close to Cuba and accept its vanguard role. Such movements need not be Marxist-Leninist to receive Cuban support, though they often are. Despite loyalty to Cuba, these movements have had troubled relations with it. Cooperation has required virtually unqualified allegiance, much ideological affinity, a commitment to armed struggle and, at times—as in El Salvador in the 1980s—humility from a contrite Communist party. Cuba has at some point denounced many of those whom it had previously supported, or would eventually support, in Venezuela, El Salvador, Guatemala, Nicaragua, and whether "right-wing" orthodox Communist parties or "left-wing" deviationists. Because worthwhile revolutionary movements lack the international approval and support of quasi-states and anticolonialist movements, they have fewer alternative sources of training, money, or other resources. Their recognition of Cuba's vanguard role thus often determines how much assistance they get. Such movements have been sacrificed to the rule of bargaining when other states have dealt politically with Cuba rather than fight it militarily.

Because of the priority it gives to state-to-state relations, Cuba has not supported worthwhile revolutionary movements against the government of Mexico and of most independent African, Asian, or West Indian states.[77] As a result of bargaining, Cuba cut its support for insurgencies against Latin American governments that reestablished formal relations with Cuba (except for Colombia in 1980–81) and adopted a position more independent of U.S. foreign policy.

Cuba's first large-scale commitment of its own personnel to help a worthwhile revolutionary movement seize power in Africa occurred in the Congo (now Zaire). On April 25, 1965, Guevara left Cuba to fight against the government of Moise Tshombe, alongside the Congo's National Council of the Revolution. Guevara was joined by two hundred Cuban troops and a ship loaded with arms. He and the Cubans left the Congo in December 1965 at the request of the Congolese guerrillas, who were preparing for an armistice. A legacy of this expedition was the continued operation of a Cuban training camp for guerrillas in Brazzaville for the PAIGC and MPLA, among others.[78]

Guevara went to Bolivia next, in an attempt to create a revolution where none existed—the most extreme example of Cuba's commitment, literally, to "export" revolution. A small band of militant revolutionaries (so the theory went) would create the objective conditions for revolution. Two members of the Central Committee of the Cuban Communist party, Juan Acuña and Antonio Sánchez Díaz, accompanied Guevara and died with him in Bolivia in October 1967. Many Cubans as well as people of other nations accompanied them; others were training in Cuba for the struggle in Bolivia when Guevara was killed.[79] His death was the most severe setback to Cuba's policy of support for revolutions.

In more recent years, Central America—notably Nicaragua, El Salvador, and Guatemala—has been the focus of Cuba's support. Nicaragua's revolution was a broadly based national mutiny, which gained much international backing, against the Somoza family dynasty; in the end even the U.S. government helped to edge Anastasio Somoza out of power. Cuba played an important role in that revolution, although Cuban leaders have not discussed it. One of the founders of the FSLN, Tomás Borge, minister of the interior since revolutionary victory in 1979, has mentioned two of Cuba's contributions to the insurrection against Somoza: training and weapons. Borge "had spent over a year in Cuba, in a military school from which I graduated. This qualified me to train my fellow Sandinistas." Moreover, Borge said, during the insurrection "the President of Costa Rica . . . lent us valuable help by facilitating the delivery of some arms which Fidel Castro gave to our revolution."[80]

Cuba has publicly denied that Cuban civilian or military advisers have ever worked in El Salvador with the guerrillas. It has also denied that any of the weapons Cuba has received for its own use from the Soviet Union have been redistributed in Central America. But Cuba has not denied that it may have coordinated the acquisition and delivery of weapons from other countries to the Salvadoran guerrillas. Cuba has admitted that it helped train Salvadoran guerrillas. Castro acknowledged in late 1981 that Cuba had supplied weapons and ammunition to the Salvadoran guerrillas in late 1980 and early 1981 for their general offensive,[81] noting only that it had become more difficult for Cuba to continue to do so. He also said that his denial of U.S. allegations of Cuban support "did not imply a moral judgment over the facts imputed to us, nor the self-denial of the sacred right to help a fraternal people in a way that may be feasible. It would not be immoral nor damnable to help with weapons."[82]

In 1985 Cuba's official position changed. When asked about Cuban aid to guerrillas in El Salvador, Castro said: "I am not saying yes, I am not saying no. In practice, in reality, it is almost impossible . . . for military supplies to reach the revolutionaries in El Salvador." But he implied that Cuban weapons had, indeed, been sent to the Salvadoran guerrillas "a long time after that final offensive" in 1981.[83]

Cuba has also supported the Salvadoran insurgency in the United Nations, in the Nonaligned Movement, and among Communist countries. Radio Havana and Cuba's printing presses have served the Salvadoran revolution; Cuba has given money to the guerrillas, mostly through its "front organizations." In 1988, 200 wounded Salvadoran guerrillas were in Cuba for treatment. The main Salvadoran guerrilla organization, the Farabundo Martí National Liberation Front, which has a permanent mission in Havana, has acknowledged that "we couldn't possibly move ahead without the aid of the socialist camp, Cuba and Nicaragua."[84]

Cuba's leadership has also been acknowledged by the Salvadoran revolutionaries. As noted earlier, in 1980 the secretary-general of the Salvadoran Communist party, Schafik Handal, admitted publicly the party's earlier errors of strategy. Jaime Barrios, member of the Central Committee of the Salvadoran Communist party, "described the difficulties on the way traveled by the left-wing forces of his country toward unity and emphasized the Cuban Communists' contribution to bringing these forces closer together."[85] Cuban leaders mediated among the contending leftist forces split by Cuba's policies a decade earlier, when a wing of the Salvadoran Communist party seceded to begin the armed struggle over the opposition of the party leaders; all eventually came to accept Cuba's role in the vanguard.

In Guatemala as well, in the 1980s Cuba has promoted unity among the disparate guerrilla forces that Cuba helped to divide in the 1960s over the commitment to armed struggle. The Guatemalan guerrilla movement has a unified permanent mission in Havana. Guatemalan guerrillas have received political and military training in Cuba.[86]

In short, Cuba has supported revolutionary movements that it has deemed strategically and ideologically worthwhile in Latin America and in Africa. It has provided, at various times, personnel, weapons, funds, training, and other support. This type of revolutionary activity has been one of Cuba's most distinctive, controversial, independent, and enduring policies. Cuba has also been prepared, when appropriate, to suspend support for such movements if other, more important policy goals require it.

"Untrustworthy" Movements

"Untrustworthy" movements engage in armed struggle against incumbent governments, and may even espouse some socially radical programs, but are ideologically distant from Cuba or other more orthodox Marxist-Leninist movements and parties—for reasons that are arcane at times. They lack international approval and legitimacy. They do not accept Cuba's vanguard role. While such movements are easily sacrificed to the rules of precedence and bargaining, these rules need not prevent some Cuban aid, even though the recipients have only a modest claim to sustained support. Cuban support for these movements is narrowly instrumental. That is, Cuba provides assistance for specific purposes and for limited periods of time.

It is logical and prudent for Cuba to have contacts with movements that it does not trust, including small terrorist groups, in order to assess their goals and practices and perhaps to collaborate in the short term. This does not mean that Cuba will get involved with anyone and to any extent. On the contrary, self-limiting norms, rules, and policies make collaboration with untrustworthy movements recurring but not sustainable, frequent but not intense, and necessary but not desirable.

One example is the limited Cuban support for the Shaba exiles against the government of Zaire in the late 1970s. Once loyal to Moise Tshombe, these former police officers sought to make their home province of Shaba—formerly Katanga—an independent state. Although Cuba had fought against Tshombe's short-lived national government, collaboration between Cuba and the Shaba exiles was possible once the former police officers fled to Angola. The exiles invaded Zaire's Shaba from bases in Angola twice, first in early 1977 and then in early 1978. Cuba has said that it sent no doctors, intelligence officers, troops, or advisers, and did not supply weapons or provide training for this specific invasion. (Some Cuban troops may have crossed briefly into Zaire without authorization, however). Castro commented on the view attributed to the U.S. government that "Cuba could have supplied and reorganized the Katangan force in Angola as early as 1975," saying, "There is some truth to this because, during the war in Angola, the Kantangans fought on the side of the MPLA . . . and they fought alongside us on a few fronts . . . This was late 1975 and early 1976." He continued, "After the war, we refused and avoided every form of commitment to and collaboration with the Katangans . . . We did not want the Katangans to become the source of conflict between Zaire and Angola." He also explained that Cuba had only "political reasons for not having supported the Katangans," not moral or legal reasons. "We are simply opposed to this type of operation by the Katangans." In 1977 he said, "The Katangans' operations created a complicated situation" and forced Cuba to stop its troop withdrawal from Angola. In February 1978 Castro admitted that his government had unsuccessfully attempted to persuade the Angolan government to prevent the second invasion of Shaba.[87]

The collaboration between Cuba and the Shaba exiles was limited to the 1975–76 war against their common enemy, Zaire's government. Further Cuban support of the exiles would have threatened Cuba's good relations with other African states that feared Cuban subversion. Cuba, said Castro in 1978, was "opposed to conflicts among the peoples of Black Africa" and, except for Cuban support for revolutionaries in Zimbabwe, Namibia, and South Africa (and in the Congo in the 1960s), "we do not interfere in the internal affairs of any African country regardless of what kind of government" it has. This is an example of the application of the rule of the precedence of state-to-state relations.[88] For strategic and ideological reasons, a movement such as that of Katanga, which did not accept Cuba's vanguard role, was not to be supported on a continuing basis.

A second, more controversial example of Cuban support for untrustworthy movements is Cuba's relationship with drug traffickers—a by-product of its relations with the Colombian guerrilla group M-19. On November 15, 1982, a federal grand jury in Florida indicted 14 people, including the chief of the Cuban Navy, the president of Cuba's Institute for Friendship with Peoples, the former Cuban ambassador, and the former Cuban minister-counselor to Colombia, on charges of drug trafficking. Jaime Guillot Lara, a Colombian citizen, was one of those indicted, on charges that he paid Cuba for protection and assistance in the drug business and helped ferry weapons to the M-19, beginning in August 1980. Most of the 14 were subsequently convicted. Contrary to the view at times expressed in the United States that Cuba is a major center for drug trafficking, the U.S. government's charges against Cuban officials are narrower.

The central charge is that Cuba's connections with drug traffickers help to arm guerrilla movements. But Francis Mullen, administrator of the U.S. Drug Enforcement Administration, has testified that "only a very small portion" of illicit drugs "pass through Cuba. If Cuba were completely neutralized as a transit point, the effect on drug availability in the United States would be minimal." Mullen has further stated that "Cuba is not open to any and all smugglers . . . The Cubans apparently deal only with those drug smugglers they trust or those who can provide some benefit or service to Cuba such as smuggling weapons, illustrated in the Guillot investigation." Mullen acknowledged that "an individual caught trafficking in Cuba, through Cuba, or in Cuban waters, normally does receive a severe penalty" from the Cuban government—provided, in Mullen's view, that the government itself is uninvolved.[89]

The Cuban government has indignantly denied that it has aided drug smugglers. It has reported that from 1970 to 1982, when the indictment against Guillot and the 4 Cuban officials was issued, it captured 36 ships and 21 planes engaged in drug trafficking through Cuban air space or waters, and arrested 230 traffickers, most of whom were U.S. or Colombian citizens. Cuba claims that it intensified its drug interdiction efforts during 1981 and 1982. It reports that its agents have captured and destroyed hundreds of thousands of tons of drugs. In 1978, Cuba signed a search-and-rescue agreement with the U.S. Coast Guard, which also led to some cooperation on drug interdiction; the U.S. government acknowledged Cuban cooperation under that agreement, until in response to the Florida indictment Cuba suspended the agreement in 1982. Cuba has also challenged the veracity of the witnesses in the Guillot case, who were offered immunity from prosecution and whose testimony was at times contradictory.[90]

Castro has acknowledged that Robert Vesco, a U.S. fugitive from justice who is reputedly deeply engaged in drug trafficking, has been to Cuba and has received medical treatment there. Castro insisted, however, that Cuba did not join Vesco in his business endeavors.[91]

Cuba has made no public acknowledgment of its relations with the M-19 and its drug trafficker allies. In an interview in Havana in March 1985, a thoughtful official who had investigated the matter reported that—in the ordinary conduct of their diplomatic and political work at the offices, homes, and clubs of leading Colombians, including high-ranking political figures—Cuban officials dealing with Colombian affairs met persons who turned out to be drug traffickers. The interviewee claimed, however, that the Cubans did not know this at the time. High Cuban officials, including Cuba's ambassador to Colombia, knew Jaime Guillot Lara. Guillot and other drug traffickers had many dealings with Cuban officials who were seeking to promote legal trade between Cuba and Colombia. When in 1982 the U.S. government identified Guillot as a drug trafficker and sought his extradition (Guillot was in Mexico at the time), the Cuban government officially intervened to protect him. (Guillot escaped and has not yet been found). By that time, Cuba knew that Guillot had bought and delivered weapons for the M-19. Cuba claims to have acted only to protect Guillot from "political persecution"; although Cuban officials recognized that Guillot was engaged in drug trafficking, they insisted that this was not the "origin" of his relations with Cuba. The interviewee affirmed strongly that no Cuban official named in the indictment was involved in the drug trade.

We can conclude that Cuba has been involved with persons engaged in illegal international activities, some of which involved drugs and others, weapons. Cuba's principal interest has been in the political and military significance of the activities. At times Cuba has protected major drug traffickers while aware of their involvement in the drug trade. Some Cuban officials, acting independently, may have become involved in the drug trade. This interpretation of events is compatible with the positions of both the U.S. and the Cuban governments: Cuba did deal with persons engaged in drug trafficking because of its interest in their simultaneous involvement in weapons traffic and in legal trade, even if the Cuban government might not have been directly involved in the drug business. And this interpretation fits what we know about Cuba's continuing relations with "untrustworthy" movements. It is also an example of an irresponsible policy on the part of a government that claims to be building a better society.

The Significance of Cuban Support for Revolution

How significant, in the end, is Cuban support for revolution? Several answers to that question are possible. The first answer—that Cuban support has been unsuccessful—focuses on revolutionary movements that owe their existence almost wholly to Cuba. Guevara's failed Bolivian gamble in 1967 is the purest Cuban-originated insurrection. Although the Venezuelan insurgency of the early 1960s had important indigenous roots, the endurance of small guerrilla bands as late as 1967–68 was primarily the result of continued Cuban support; this movement failed too. Similar cases range from the Dominican Republic in 1959 to Colombia in 1980–81. These failures illustrate Cuba's willingness to support some revolutionary movements even when, objectively, there is no local revolutionary situation that might warrant support.

A second answer focuses on the net difference Cuban support makes in the survival of indigenous revolutionary movements. Cuba's impact is at times important, though typically secondary. For example, Cuban support for the Nicaraguan revolution before 1979 and the guerrillas in El Salvador in the early 1980s was substantial. Cuba was the guiding symbol for the Sandinistas and their most important supplier of weapons in the crucial closing months of the Nicaraguan revolution. But the Cuban role still took second place to indigenous factors, which explain the most about the origins and evolution of the Nicaraguan and Salvadoran civil wars. The suspension of Cuban support for Salvadoran guerrillas would probably not end that insurgency, but it would weaken it.[92] Cuba also played a secondary role in the victory of the PAIGC. Only in Angola in 1975, when the MPLA won control of the government, was the Cuban contribution decisive.

A third answer to the question about the significance of Cuban support varies depending on whether Cuba has been associated with victory or defeat. In Latin America, except in Nicaragua, Cuba has been associated primarily with defeat; in the former Portuguese colonies of Africa and in Indochina, it has been associated with victory. The association, however, does not explain those outcomes. Portugal gave up the defense of its empire after its own revolution in 1974; the outcome in Indochina had little to do with Cuba. As noted above, the Cuban role was decisive only in Angola. No other victory depended so much on Cuban support; the others would probably have occurred without that support. Cuba can attribute few victories to its own efforts over thirty years of exertion. It is simply difficult to export revolution.

A last answer compares Cuba's effort with its own resources. By this standard, Cuba's commitment to revolution is astounding: It has sent military personnel, weapons, money, doctors, and nurses, and has provided military and political training as well as the services of Radio Havana and Cuban printing presses. No longer is any institution in Cuba exempt from the duty to support the revolution overseas.

Explaining Cuban Support for Revolution

Some would argue that the pattern of Cuban support for revolution is best explained as a response to domestic constraints, to conditions in target countries, and to Soviet and U.S. policies. None of these factors sufficiently explains the shifts in Cuban support for revolution. But the last three have played a role in the evolution of Cuban support for revolution.

Domestic economic constraints have had little effect on the pattern of Cuban support for revolution. For example, Cuba has increased this support for revolutions in the Caribbean and Central America during periods of good economic performance (such as 1959 and 1978), during periods of severe economic crisis (such as the early and late 1960s and 1979–80), and during periods of intermediate economic performance (such as the mid-1960s). Cuba has supported revolutionary movements in Africa with little interruption since the early 1960s. Its peak commitments, as in the Congo in 1965 and Angola in 1975, were made under different domestic economic circumstances; the economy was coming out of a deep recession in the first case and out of a boom in the second. Thus a deteriorating domestic economy in itself is unlikely to force Cuba to cut its support for revolutionary movements. Two of the periods of greatest Cuban support for such movements—in the late 1960s and in 1979–80—were also times of deteriorating domestic economic performance.

Cuban support for revolutionary movements is affected but not determined by local conditions. The local situation obviously affects the possibility of victory: Strong, indigenous insurgent forces are more likely to win.

But Cuba has also supported revolution when the prospects for victory have been poor. Cuban support for worthwhile revolutionary movements in Central and South America in the 1960s, for example, cannot be explained by the prospects for victory, and Cuba has continued to support guerrilla efforts even when victory was extremely unlikely, as in Venezuela in 1967–68. Cuba has also created insurgencies where none existed, as in Bolivia in 1967–68. If local conditions were to explain the pattern of Cuban support, Cuba should have cut off support for many Latin American guerrillas much sooner in the 1960s. Moreover, its support for untrustworthy movements throughout the years, as in the case of the M-19 in 1980–81, is clearly unrelated to their prospects for victory.

Similarly, equally repressive policies existed in both Argentina and Chile in the 1970s; local conditions do not account for the differences in Cuban policies toward those two countries. Cuba had good trade relations with Argentina but continued to support the overthrow of the Chilean government. The difference is that whereas Argentina was willing to bargain with Cuba, Chile was not. Cuba's decision to increase its support for revolution in Nicaragua in 1977, and later in El Salvador and Guatemala, was made easier not only by changing local conditions but also by the fact that those governments had never bargained with Cuba to prevent its support of local insurgencies.

Despite the fact that local conditions do not fully explain the pattern of Cuban support, it is likely that persistent defeat would lead Cuba to look for alternative policies, as probably took place in 1969. In that year the main change in the environment for Cuban policies was the willingness of three Latin American governments—Chile, Peru, and Venezuela—to change their policies toward Cuba. Thus the change in local revolutionary prospects was a contributing factor but not the decisive one.

The Soviet Union has had little impact on the pattern of Cuban support for revolution, despite Cuba's great economic and military dependency. The burst of Cuban support for revolutionary movements in 1959 cannot be attributed to the USSR. It is difficult to ascertain the Soviet view of all Cuban efforts in 1967–68, but we do know the USSR had been distressed about Guevara's adventurism and Cuba's condemnation of the leadership of Moscow-affiliated Communist parties.[93] In the 1960s, Cuba began its support for many revolutionary movements, support that has lasted into the 1980s; Cuba's ties with these movements today cannot be explained as the outcome of Soviet influence over Cuba. As cases in point, Cuba allied itself with the Sandinistas when the latter were denouncing the old-line Nicaraguan Communists; Cuba supported Guatemalan guerrillas in the late 1960s when they were denouncing that country's Moscow-affiliated Communist party; and Cuba began supporting the MPLA when Cuban-Soviet relations were less close than they later became.

The decline in Cuban support for revolutionary activity in Latin America in 1969 was consistent with Soviet preferences, and the decline in Cuban attacks on Moscow-oriented Communist parties was probably a condition of increased Soviet support for Cuba, evident in the 1970s. But Cuba did not match the caution of the Soviets, or cut off assistance to revolutionary movements in Africa; indeed, Cuba retained stronger ties to the MPLA in Angola than did the USSR. The pattern of Cuban behavior in 1969 is better explained as a response to new opportunities for bargaining with Latin American governments than as caving in to the Soviet Union; where such opportunities for bargaining did not exist, as in white-ruled Africa and in Indochina, Cuban policy did not change.

Since the early 1970s, there has been an increasing convergence of Soviet and Cuban views. Of the two governments, the USSR's has changed the most. Some Soviet-affiliated Communist parties have also changed course; for instance, the Guatemalan Party of Labor, has changed its views on the need for the armed struggle at least four times! Over the past thirty years, Cuba has maintained greater consistency than the Soviet Union in support of revolutionary movements. Even in recent years, Cuba is the leader on Central American and Caribbean matters within the Soviet-Cuban alliance. As a Cuban scholar has argued, "Cuba inserted in that alliance a specific conception about the revolutionary struggle."[94] Cuba, then, acts autonomously in these revolutionary situations but neither challenges nor opposes Soviet interests and policy.[95]

In 1982 Castro described these relations as follows: "One of the great lies that the imperialists use concerning Central America is their attempt to impute the revolutions in this area to the Soviet Union . . . The Soviets did not know even one of the present leaders of Nicaragua . . . during the period of revolutionary struggle." Castro went on to say that "the same holds true for El Salvador," where—"with the exception of the Communist party," which was "not one of the major groups—the Soviet Union did not know the leaders of these revolutionary organizations and had no contact with them. The same goes for Guatemala." In contrast, Castro said, Cuban leaders knew the Central American revolutionary leaders very well.[96]

Cuba plainly operates within the boundaries of Soviet hegemony. Its government could not have remained in power without Soviet aid; Cuba has not acted in opposition to Soviet interests and policies since the 1970s; and it could not have carried out its effective assistance to the MPLA in 1975–

76 without Soviet help. Indeed, Soviet aid and protection have permitted Cuba to conduct its foreign policy even when, at times, it was at odds with the USSR. But Cuba has retained enough autonomy that, beginning in the 1970s, it helped to shift Soviet policy toward greater support for revolutions. It would be a far simpler world if Cuba were a mere Soviet puppet. In fact, it is Cuba's radicalizing leadership in the context of Soviet hegemony that makes Cuba's international behavior so significant.

The United States has played a lasting though quite general role in Cuban support for revolution, even if the origin of Cuba's policy precedes U.S.-Cuban hostilities. The United States has been the ultimate target of Cuba's strategy of revolutionary support, the enemy to be fought by the creation of more Vietnams. At the same time, the evolution of U.S. policy has not greatly affected the pattern of Cuban activity. Cuba has supported revolutionary movements both when the United States has been conciliatory (as in 1975–1977) and when the United States has been hostile (as at most other times). The beginning of Cuban support for revolutions in 1959 had little to do with U.S. policies, although the acceleration of Cuban support in the early 1960s was part of Cuba's strategy of struggle against the United States and its allies. Nevertheless, as the United States relegated Cuban matters to secondary importance (when U.S. attention turned to Vietnam) in the mid- and late 1960s, Cuban commitment to the support of revolution reached its height.

Cuba's deemphasis of support for revolution against Latin American governments after 1969 was a response to changes in the policies of those governments, well in advance of conciliatory U.S. policies. In addition, the U.S. government's efforts at conciliation in 1975 were stopped by Cuba's intervention late that year in the Angolan Civil War, and by a conference held in Havana to support Puerto Rican independence. Conciliatory efforts by the United States in 1977 were halted by Cuba's entry into the war in the Horn of Africa; Cuba's support for Salvadoran revolutionaries increased in 1979–80 despite the Carter administration's efforts to conciliate Sandinista Nicaragua. Cuban support for revolution in Central America continued in the 1980s despite the hostile policies of the Reagan administration. Thus there is no systematic relationship between U.S. policies and changes in Cuba's support for revolution.

The U.S. government could bargain with Cuba, although this approach is difficult because U.S. interests go beyond purely bilateral relations. No other policies have worked for the United States—not economic pressure and sanctions, not threats and actual invasion, not bluff and bluster. Cuba has continued to support revolutions. But bargaining has worked on narrower issues (such as hijacking and immigration) and might work on Central American and Angolan issues. U.S.-Cuban bargaining on discrete issues in various parts of the world would take effort and patience, with no guarantee of success, nor would a bargain be feasible if the United States asked Cuba to abandon the rule of internationalism altogether, rather than in particular cases. But this may be the only way for the U.S. government to moderate Cuba's international revolutionary behavior.

Cuba's government has sought to make the world safer for revolution. This is consistent with Cuban leaders' beliefs that the march of history is headed toward revolution, that such support enhances their own and Cuba's international influence, that it gives Cuba leverage with its Communist allies, and that it is a prime weapon in the struggle against the U.S. government. Cuban support for revolutionary movements is neither indiscriminate nor perpetual but, rather, is part of a strategy to defend Cuba's own interests and to advance its radical ideology.

Support for
Revolutionary States

$$\boxed{6}$$

To make a world safer for revolution, Cuba developed a policy of collaboration with many Third World states that it deemed "revolutionary." Although this policy had its roots in the early years of revolutionary rule in Cuba, it blossomed in the 1970s, when more revolutionary states sought Cuban support, when the collapse of the Portuguese empire in 1974 led to five successor states (all politically close to Cuba), and when the role of the United States in the international system seemed to weaken in the wake of its defeat in Vietnam. In these circumstances, Cuba projected its power overseas more easily; it also had more to offer revolutionary states. The explanation for the remarkable overseas spread of the Cuban revolution, therefore, lies in factors both outside and intrinsic to Cuba.

In addition, Cuba's support for revolutionary states stemmed from ideological and strategic factors. Its leaders believed that Cuba was right to assist its friends in power in other lands, in part to repay the solidarity from which they had benefited when facing the United States. But this policy was also one more way to combat the historical enemy, the U.S. government, to break out of the isolation the United States had tried to impose on Cuba, and to generate international influence and support, thereby enhancing the security and power of the Cuban government.

The consolidation of Soviet hegemony over Cuba permitted the closer coordination of Cuban and Soviet policies in the Third World--including, at times, joint assistance programs. The USSR provided a shield for some of Cuba's riskier ventures, while Soviet subsidies for the Cuban economy after 1975 enabled Cuba to project its power overseas. If Cuba's support for revolutionary movements stems ordinarily from its own conceptions of international relations (with some degree of independence from the Soviet Union), Cuba's support for revolutionary states is more complex. At times, Cuba took the initiative in its alliance with the Soviets; at other times, it played the role of a supportive client state following the USSR's lead and bolstering its policies. This does not mean that Cuba had no interests of its own; rather, a major explanation for the fact, timing, and manner of some of these Cuban engagements overseas is to be found in Moscow rather than in Havana. Thus Cuban support for revolutionary states encompasses the full spectrum of its foreign policies: from the commercial to the militant, from the autonomous to the contingent.

These important aspects of Cuban foreign policy are evident in three key cases. One is Cuba's continued support for Angola's MPLA (Popular Movement for the Liberation of Angola) government against internal insurgents and South African incursions—an extension of Cuba's support of the MPLA before Angola's 1975 independence. The second is Cuban-Soviet joint assistance to the Ethiopian government in repelling Somalia's invasion of the Ogaden region in 1977–78. The third is Cuba's support for Grenada's revolutionary government between March 1979, when it came to power, and its overthrow in October 1983. Each instance illustrates the scope and complexity of Cuban assistance and of Cuba's relations with the USSR; each is discussed in detail. This chapter then concludes with an overview of Cuba's aid to Third World countries, with special attention to Nicaragua.

What Cuba Had to Offer

The international spread of the Cuban revolution is in some ways similar to the spread of large multinational business firms. Several concepts from scholarly studies of multinational firms are suggestive. The home market environment of such a firm must encourage the development of innovations, and these must eventually be demanded abroad.[1] There also must be some imperfection in international markets in goods or labor, so that international trade does not meet this need. Certain firms may acquire disproportionate market power in imperfect markets, developing into oligopolies. Policies in the host and home countries are often designed to strengthen, regulate, and occasionally, curb such oligopolies.

Firms often develop market power through product differentiation, brand names, and special marketing skills. The mere possession of an innovation, or of other special assets, does not in itself give a firm great advantage. The asset must be an integral part of the firm rather than sold to a foreign producer. These assets are often intangible, stemming from the work of scientists, from certain managerial skills, or from the existence of fundamental values that are shared by members of an organization. The capacity to develop internationally powerful organizations is not limited to particular countries. Finally, it must be profitable for the firm to act outside the home country.

This description of the operations of multinational firms can be applied to aspects of Cuban foreign policy. The Cuban government's key innovation was its development of the only military establishment in the Third World willing and able to engage in combat far from home, with professional skill and efficacy, even for purposes remote from or unrelated to the direct defense of the home country. Its troops were generally loyal, although there have been desertions, especially after Cuba's combat troops entered the Angolan War in 1975. On the whole, however, the Cuban armed forces are militarily and politically reliable and thus attractive to foreign allies. Their broad-scale international involvement dates from the 1970s; only then did their professionalism reach a high enough level to enable them to enter combat overseas.[2] The availability of reliable troops willing to engage in combat overseas was valuable because the deployment of Cubans made it possible for revolutionary governments in the Third World to face internal or external threats without requesting deployment of Soviet troops.

Cuba's demography was favorable to international military activism. No fewer than a third of all Cubans are black, making their presence more acceptable in Africa and easier for the Cuban government to justify.[3] During the 1960s Cuba also experienced a baby boom, which increased the number of men of prime draft age during the next decade. In 1974, on the eve of the Angolan War, about 390,000 Cuban males were aged between fifteen and nineteen; in 1978, as war raged in Ethiopia, about 518,000 Cuban males fell into that age cohort. In 1985, the number was about 596,000.[4]

Cuba has made innovations in nonmilitary areas as well. It now exports services, especially in education (including physical education and sports), health, and construction. The fishing fleet has grown. By the early 1980s, its sugar industry exported parts and services. Cuba's overseas civilian personnel were also loyal. Their loyalty stems from Cuba's strict command and control procedures, from careful selection of personnel, from economic and career incentives to personnel serving overseas, and from the deep commitment and enthusiasm that many Cubans serving overseas feel for their country's own revolution.

Educational improvements in Cuba shaped its international activism. In the 1953 census 23.6 percent of the population, aged ten and over, was illiterate; the illiteracy rate was probably about 21 percent in 1958 and fell to 12.9 percent in 1970. In the 1981 census, the illiteracy rate for the population between the ages of ten and forty-nine was 1.9 percent; if the entire population were included, this figure would probably be 4 to 5 percent. The proportion of Cuba's population aged six and over that had attained at least a sixth-grade education was 11 percent in 1953, 15.5 percent in 1970, and

40.8 percent in 1981. Moreover, Cuba's capacity to send highly qualified personnel overseas in the 1960s had been limited but, thanks to both population growth and educational change, the supply of persons with university education reached 288,000 in 1981—more than five times larger than in 1953.[5]

The supply of teachers for overseas work also rose. Cuba's pupil-teacher ratio in the public primary schools (including preschool) fell from 31:1 in 1965–66 to 14.5:1 in 1985–86, as a result both of a near doubling of the supply of primary school teachers and of a drop in the number of babies born per year in the 1970s. Primary school enrollment peaked in 1975–76, then dropped 40 percent by 1985–86, while the supply of primary school teachers remained unchanged.[6] By the end of the 1970s Cuba thus had a surplus of primary school teachers, who have since been retrained or employed in teaching foreigners in Cuba or abroad. Nonetheless, Cuba's educational performance in the 1960s was not as good as some believed. Its "special marketing skills" created the impression that education had improved more and sooner than was actually the case.

Cuba also committed substantial resources to develop physical education and sports programs.[7] Cuban athletes have won many Olympic gold medals in boxing and track. Whereas Cuba never won more than thirty medals in any of the Pan American Games held in the 1950s, it has never won fewer than a hundred medals per game held since 1971; by the 1980s it ranked second to the United States. These successes gave Cuba international prestige and influence.

In the area of public health, a substantial emigration of medical doctors occurred between 1960 and 1962. Despite a crash training program, the number of doctors was the same in 1965 as in 1958; it fell to 6,152 in 1970. The disorganization of Cuban life in the late 1960s took its toll on public health. Yet again Cuba's "special marketing skills" created the impression overseas that the health of the average Cuban had improved. Public health did begin to improve, finally, in the 1970s. The stock of medical doctors reached 22,910 in 1985 and the supply of nurses and nurses' auxiliaries increased 3.5 times the 1970 figure—to 42,109 in 1985.[8] The Cuban government emphasized broad public health measures, preventive medicine, and government funding for health services in order to provide access to health care to all Cubans regardless of personal income.

Fishing has been another successful area of the Cuban economy. From 1958 to 1978, the fishing catch increased tenfold and the fishing fleet was modernized. Shipyards expanded, and Cuba developed the capacity to build large ships.[9] Because a great deal of fishing occurs in international waters, Cuba had to make arrangements with other governments.

In contrast, Cuba's performance in the construction sector at home is uneven. Although there has been considerable military and public construction, the construction and maintenance of housing has been one of the Cuban government's signal failures.[10] Cuba's decision to send construction workers overseas may in part explain its inability to meet its own population's housing needs. Cuba also began to export cement in the 1970s, even though it did not yet meet its own cement consumption needs, on the expectation that the income from cement exports would buy needed imports and would open a market for further exports in the future, a theory that turned out to be true, but at the expense of those in Cuba who still had no adequate shelter.[11]

Cuba's "product specialization" in the international market was in labor-intensive activities by troops, doctors, teachers, construction workers, and other personnel. Beginning in the 1970s Cuba delivered both its citizens' services and their political loyalty. With very few exceptions, the subsidized Cuban economy cannot provide capital to other countries. Cuba's "products"—the services of its people—cannot be exported unless Cuban agencies and state firms deploy Cubans to foreign countries. Thus a political agreement is also required to locate Cuban personnel in another country, making its activities worrisome to its adversaries and rewarding to its allies.

Oligopolistic businesses often invest overseas for competitive reasons; when one invests, others follow. Cuba belongs to a small international oligopoly, competing to supply military, political, and other resources to Third World countries. That oligopoly includes primarily the major powers; Cuba is the only country of its size, scale, and degree of underdevelopment in the club. Cuba's international activity promotes its "brand name," Marxism-Leninism, and it relates best to other affiliates of the same "brand name." The efficacy of these Cuban policies increased in the 1970s as Cuba itself became more loyal to the "brand name" and to the "trademark holder," the Soviet Union.

Cuba's support for revolutionary states has been profitable. The USSR responded to Cuba's actions in Angola by increasing markedly its subsidies to Cuba. At the same time, Cuba gained leverage over the United States, the Soviet Union, and other countries. Cuba began to play a large role in international affairs; it became influential the world over. Since 1978, moreover, Cuba has begun, literally, to make a profit as its civilian state firms began to charge market rates for the services they performed in some Third World countries, especially those rich in oil resources.[12]

In short, the factors within Cuba explain much about its capability for international engagement, the timing of its decisions to deploy personnel overseas after 1970, and the nature of its involvement. The existence of such a capability did not require Cuba to use it, however. Therefore, one must look at its actual international activities to understand its relations with revolutionary states.

The Great Allies: Angola and Ethiopia

Cuban Assistance to the MPLA

Cuba's first commitment to independent Angola was the continued deployment of its troops to ensure the MPLA's victory in the Angolan Civil War and, in March 1976, South Africa's retreat from Angola. A key factor is the context for Cuba's help: The MPLA asked for Cuban assistance at a time when the international system seemed to have changed. The United States had been defeated in Vietnam, for example; U.S. domestic opinion was strongly opposed to new military engagements in the Third World. The opportunity to project Cuban influence abroad, and even to impress the Soviets, seemed irresistible.

Equally important were factors within Cuba. Cuba first deployed troops because doing so was its best tool for supporting the MPLA. At the peak of the 1975–76 war, Cuba had 36,000 troops in Angola commanded by Division General Abelardo Colomé.[13] In relation to Cuba's population of 9.4 million, these troops were the equivalent of a U.S. deployment of over 800,000 troops, more than the United States had in Vietnam at the peak of that war.[14] In contrast, Cuba's civilian presence in Angola in July 1976 still numbered only in the hundreds, though it rose a year later to 3,500.[15] Cuba's "profits" from its troop deployment were spectacular: Its forces halted South Africa's advance; Cuba became a major presence in Africa's international politics; and Cuba was rewarded by the Soviet Union, whose interests it had also advanced.

In the late 1980s Cuba's troops had not yet gone home. Angola's government faced a continued, serious insurgency from Jonas Savimbi's UNITA (National Union for the Total Independence of Angola) in southern Angola as well as recurrent South African incursions into, and occasional occupation of, southern Angola. The support Savimbi received from the South African government had contradictory effects. It helped UNITA to fight the Angolan government, but it also justified the continued Cuban presence in the eyes of many Africans. Cuban troops in Angola primarily protect towns and installations; they engage in combat with South Africa's or Savimbi's forces only sporadically. (Only 10,000 Cuban troops had been injured or killed, or were missing in Angola from 1975 to 1986, according to Brigade General Rafael del Pino, who defected from Cuba in 1987.) Angola and

Cuba have agreed that all Cuban troops will withdraw upon Angola's request. In late 1984 Cuba had about 10,000 troops posted in the capital city of Luanda, in the northernmost oil-producing province of Cabinda (where they guard Gulf Oil's installations), and in other central and northern Angolan provinces. Another 20,000 Cuban troops were posted in southern Angola. At that time, Cuban-Soviet relations were somewhat strained; the USSR had curtailed its economic support and had even put some limits on its military commitment to Cuba. Then Angola and Cuba proposed the gradual withdrawal of Cuban troops in southern Angola on condition that South Africa withdraw from Angola and grant Namibia's independence.[16] The negotiations did not succeed. Subsequently, Soviet relations with Cuba and Angola improved. In mid-1985 the Luanda government launched its largest offensive of the ten-year war against Savimbi, to no avail. In late 1985 the U.S. government began to assist Savimbi, after a decade's interruption in such aid.[17]

The level of fighting intensified but the war remained stalemated. In late 1986, there were more than 40,000 Cuban military and civilian personnel in Angola (up to that time, more than 200,000 Cubans had served in Angola). The 1984 Angolan-Cuban offer of a partial Cuban troop withdrawal had left the fate of Cuban troops in northern Angola open to separate negotiation. In September 1986 Castro hardened Cuba's position when he said that Cuba was willing to keep troops in northern Angola until the apartheid regime was dismantled in South Africa, but he did not renege on the promise to withdraw all troops if Angola requested it.[18]

In fact, in July 1987—again at a time of strain in Cuban-Soviet relations, marked by curtailed Soviet economic support for Cuba—talks began anew between Angola and the United States. Cuba and Angola modified their 1984 proposal, agreeing to a Cuban troop withdrawal from southern Angola "in shorter periods and larger groups" and to a fixed schedule for the withdrawal of Cuban troops from northern Angola. Moreover, a Cuban delegation (led by Political Bureau member Jorge Risquet) began to participate actively in these negotiations. Because of intensified Cuban and South African participation in the Angolan War in late 1987, the negotiations proceeded slowly. But in May 1988 the first direct talks were held (in London), involving officials from Angola, Cuba, South Africa, and the United States; in August, they agreed to a cease fire.[19]

The size of Cuba's military presence in Angola has varied over the years. As the civil and international war over Angola appeared to end in 1976, Cuba and Angola agreed to the gradual withdrawal of Cuban forces. This process was interrupted in 1977, when former Zairean police officers invaded their home province of Katanga (Shaba) from bases in Angola; Moroccan troops were deployed to help Zaire repel the invasion. Although a partial Cuban troop withdrawal resumed later that year, it was interrupted again by a second Shaba invasion in mid-1978; French, Belgian, Moroccan, and Senegalese troops came to Zaire's defense. Later in 1978 Angola and Zaire agreed not to support those forces trying to overthrow their respective governments. A third partial withdrawal began in 1979 to be interrupted in August 1981, when South African forces occupied a large portion of southern Angola. But Cuba's troop presence in Angola never fell below 18,000. After 1980, Cuba steadily increased its military presence in Angola in response mainly to South African incursions.[20]

The nature of Cuba's military presence in Angola was more complex than this summary suggests. The line between Cuban civilians and military personnel was blurred. Castro said of Cuban construction workers in Angola, "We must be workers and soldiers at the same time. We will build the bridges and we will defend the construction of these bridges." In 1986, he even joked about "our brave so-called civilian cooperation personnel."[21] This duality of roles is consistent with Cuba's tradition of a "civic soldier," whereby citizens are expected to be proficient at both military and civilian tasks.[22]

The civilian component of Cuba's relations with Angola has also been important and has helped Cuba to diversify its international activities. Angola has become a market for Cuba's nontraditional exports, as a result of a trade agreement of May 5, 1981. Cuba has kept up its obligations, but Angola often did not meet its own export targets to Cuba because of wartime disruptions; thus Cuba's trade balance with Angola has been favorable.[23] Cuba's exports to Angola are those typical of a newly industrializing country. Its industrial development is superior to Angola's, and indeed to that of most of Cuba's African trade partners. Consequently, Cuba's African engagements generate a demand for Cuban manufactured exports that is atypical of Cuban exports overall, giving Cuba experience with the international marketing of nontraditional products.

In other ways Cuba is also in the position of an "advanced" country in relation to Angola. At independence, Angolan adult literacy rates were estimated at 15 to 20 percent; the public health situation was also very poor.[24] Angola was one of the first countries to receive Cuban educational aid. Twelve Cuban teachers arrived in 1976; there were 40 in 1977 and 800 in 1978. Thereafter, two groups of Cuban teachers were organized to provide a steady supply to sixteen of Angola's eighteen provinces. From 1978 through 1983 more than 4,000 Cuban teachers served in Angola. Many were primary school teachers working to raise literacy standards; secondary school and university teachers taught scientific subjects. In 1977, only about 1,750 of the 25,000 Angolan primary school teachers were actually trained to teach.[25] Cuban teachers face a linguistic barrier, however. Even sympathetic outside observers have reported that Cuban teachers do not know Portuguese well; some Cuban teachers cannot write Portuguese competently, so the students must correct the teachers' spelling.[26] In addition to sending teachers, Cuba also brings young Angolans to study in Cuba, especially at the Isle of Youth. The first 226 arrived in 1976; that number reached 2,644 in 1979. It fell to 2,116 in 1981 but rose again in 1983 and to more than 4,000 in 1987. Many of these Angolans are teachers, of whom 2,800 had been trained in Cuba by the end of 1983.[27]

Cuba's medical assistance to Angola began during the 1975 war. In 1981, 335 Cuban doctors, 12 dentists, 174 nurses, 157 medical technicians, and 8 support personnel worked in Angola, for a total of 686 in sixteen provinces; in 1980 there had been 255 medical personnel, only 53 of them doctors. Cuban health personnel saw about one million patients each year in 1980–81.[28]

Hundreds of Cuban construction workers also arrived in Angola in 1977. At first, Cuba donated their services.[29] By the early 1980s Cuba had deployed 2,400 construction workers to Angola, who worked mainly in Luanda building bridges, housing, schools, and other projects; Cuba began to charge Angola for these projects at commercial rates. Cuba's Caribe Union of Construction Enterprises (UNECA) also signed regular commercial contracts with Angola.[30]

Cuba charged Angola commercial rates for construction projects and for other civilian services it supplied. Thus some Cuban state enterprises behaved in fact, not just metaphorically, as multinational firms owned by the Cuban government, and Cuban relations with Angola were profitable both politically and economically. Little of Cuba's civilian aid to Angola took the form of grants. Angola paid in convertible currency (from its oil revenues) for services rendered in construction and health; Cuban services in education were paid for half in convertible currency and half in other currencies or in kind.[31]

Cuba competed with privately owned multinational firms in these areas by underselling them. Although Cuba charged commercial rates for the services of its personnel, they were not high. In U.S. dollars per month, the rate for an adviser to a minister was $1,300 and for a medical doctor with eight years of experience, $1,100; other rates were lower. Angola bore additional costs for housing and other supplies for Cuban personnel. The

Cuban government received the income from the Angolan government, while Cuban personnel received the equivalent of their Cuban salary from the Cuban government and a small additional stipend from the Angolan government. The difference between the sums that Angola paid and the salaries of Cuban personnel amounted to a substantial profit for Cuba. The competitive rates gave Cuba business but also helped Angola, which spent less than it would have under a contract with a private firm. As Angola's military and economic situation deteriorated in 1984–85, Cuba shifted many of its civilian projects back to a grant basis, which will continue until Angola's economy recovers. One result of this decision was a reduction in the level of Cuban civilian assistance to Angola; for example, by 1987 the number of Cuban construction workers in Angola had fallen to 1,700. Military services have remained on a quasi-grant basis: Cuba does not charge Angola for the salaries of military personnel. However, Angola provides all lodging, food, and similar supplies. In addition, it pays Cuban soldiers a small monthly stipend and it pays Cuban officers a more substantial stipend (the amount rises according to military rank).[32]

Despite generally good relations between Cuba and Angola, there have been differences. As discussed in Chapter 5, the Shaba exiles' invasion of Zaire from Angola, strained Angolian-Cuban relations. In late February 1978 Cuba's chief representative in Angola, Jorge Risquet, asked President Agostinho Neto to curtail the activities of the Shaba exiles in Angola so that no incident would be provoked that might require more Cuban troops in Angola at a time when Cuban troops were fighting in the Horn of Africa. Nonetheless, the Shaba invasion went forward. Cuba was faced with an Angolan ally that it could not control.[33]

The extreme pressures of war in early 1984 also strained Cuban-Angolan relations. In 1982 Cuba and Angola had coordinated their policies concerning the linkage between Namibia's independence from South Africa and the withdrawal of Cuban forces from southern Angola.[34] On February 16, 1984, Angola and South Africa reached an agreement calling for the withdrawal of South African troops from Angola, establishing procedures to continue talks and monitor these agreements, and pledging some Angolan restraint over SWAPO guerrillas fighting South Africa.[35] There is no evidence of prior Cuban-Angolan coordination on this agreement; the Cuban press did not refer to it for a month. The Cuban government was reportedly angry that Angola had not consulted Cuba. In March, Angola's President and defense minister traveled to Cuba; the Cuban-Angolan communiqué noted that "Angola has kept the Government of Cuba informed in detail of the talks *now* under way with South Africa and the USA."[36] Cuban-Angolan coordination improved by October 1984, when Angola made a detailed proposal, with Cuba's public support, for the gradual withdrawal of Cuban forces from southern Angola, linked to Namibia's independence.[37] In 1985 Cuban officials insisted that Cuban-Angolan relations were good but recognized their past differences.[38] The limits of Cuban influence in Angola had become clearer.

Soviet-Cuban Collaboration in Angola and Ethiopia

One consistent theme in interviews I conducted in Havana in March 1985 was the major difference in the nature and degree of Soviet-Cuban coordination in sending Cuban troops to Angola in 1975 and to Ethiopia in late 1977. William LeoGrande has argued, "In Ethiopia, Cuban-Soviet cooperation emerged earlier and was far more extensive."[39] One of the best-informed people I interviewed in Cuba brought up and praised LeoGrande's work, specifically agreeing that an "effective collaboration" and a "coordinated plan" existed between the USSR and Cuba with regard to the initial decision in Ethiopia, but not in Angola.

A high Cuban government official contrasted the longstanding relations between Cuba and the MPLA with the more recent relations between Cuba and Ethiopia. He said that one reason why "it may be true" that there was a closer Cuban-Soviet link in Ethiopia is that much more sophisticated military equipment was needed to help Ethiopia in the war with Somalia than was the case in Angola. Another high Cuban official commented that Ethiopia's top leader, Mengistu Haile Mariam, established military relations with the USSR before he did so with Cuba. In the 1975 war in Angola, Cuban forces began arriving before the bulk of Soviet weapons (though the MPLA had earlier received some Soviet weapons to fight against the Portuguese). This Cuban official argued that the Soviet and Cuban decisions to intervene in Ethiopia were made independently, although he agreed that their implementation was "closely coordinated"; he said that Cuban troops operated much Soviet-supplied equipment and had the responsibility for training Ethiopian soldiers.[40]

Gabriel Garcia Márquez's account of Cuba's 1975 intervention in Angola, which was based on direct access to Fidel Castro and other high Cuban officials, stresses that, at the outset, Cuban troops were transported in Cuban merchant ships and in old civilian airplanes, not in Soviet transports.[41] There are no such Cuban claims about the transportation of Cuban troops to Ethiopia. But it should be noted that in Angola the Soviets sent a great many weapons, that Soviet transports began to be used for Cuban troops in late 1975, and that general Soviet military protection for Cuba was permanently decisive.

Nevertheless, there is no evidence that the Soviets coerced the Cubans into sending troops to Ethiopia or that the Cubans did so reluctanctly after the Ethiopians had contacted them. A former very high Ethiopian official described the early, quick enthusiasm of Cuban officials for the Ethiopian revolution as developing soon after contacts were established; in contrast, he said, the Soviets were more cautious, even though they preceded the Cubans in their alliance with the Ethiopian government. The Cubans even coached the Ethiopians on how to deal with the Soviets, counseling patience when the Soviets did not step in at once to replace military and other support cut off by the United States. He further recalled Castro's personal effort in 1977 to mediate between Somalia and Ethiopia (shuttling by air between the two countries) and Castro's anger at the intransigence of Somalia's President Siad Barre. Cuba had had very close military and civilian relations with Somalia. After Castro's attempt at mediation failed, Cuba went to war on Ethiopia's side against its former Somali ally. In the judgment of the former Ethiopian official, "the Cubans were equal partners, not mere followers, motivated by idealism and ideology and their diplomatic failure with Somalia."[42]

Hence, both a high degree of Soviet-Cuban coordination in Ethiopia and Soviet leadership played roles in that war. Cuba's behavior in the Horn of Africa approximates that of a supportive client. To advance its standing in Moscow, Cuba joined the Soviet Union in supporting Ethiopia at war. In contrast, Cuba's role in Angola was more autonomous, leading the Soviets beyond what they might have done by themselves. Nevertheless, in the Ethiopian case, Cuba's margin of autonomy was still considerable and its actions uncoerced; its decision to support Ethiopia, once made, was more enthusiastic and more rapidly implemented than that of the Soviets. These cases illustrate the mixture of hegemony and autonomy in Cuban-Soviet relations and also show that Cuba advanced Soviet interests even when it pursued its own. As time passed, initial Cuban-Soviet differences over Angola narrowed. Although the Soviet military was less prominent in Angola than in Ethiopia, it has remained in both countries. Cuban-Soviet-Angolan coordination has improved and become routinized through a regular series of trilateral consultations.[43]

Beginning in 1977, other differences over Angola emerged between Cuba and the USSR. In May 1977 Nito Alves staged a major coup attempt against Neto's government. Alves apparently believed that he had Soviet support for the coup, although the Soviets did not intervene actively on his behalf. Cuban troops in Angola quickly supported Neto and helped him put down the coup, while Cuba's ambassador to Angola was recalled and replaced immediately after the coup, suggesting either a coolness toward Neto or organizational disarray.[44]

During interviews in 1985 and 1986 in Havana, disagreements between Cuba and the Soviet Union with regard to the Alves coup attempt were played down, although the interviewees confirmed that differences had arisen in the Cuban and Soviet responses to the coup attempt. One person noted that Alves was an "adventurer" and the type of political leader about whom the Soviets are quite skeptical. He and others also emphasized that the Soviets are ordinarily slow and cautious in such crises, while the Cubans are quick to respond. This is a plausible description of the May 1977 events in Angola. This account also suggests that Cuba's willingness to back its allies in domestic disputes in other countries is greater than that of the USSR. The Soviets may be more reluctant and thus may be less reliable allies than the Cubans.

The continuing differences in Soviet and Cuban behavior toward Angola are also reflected in data published by the U.S. government on the presence of Cubans, Soviets, and other Eastern Europeans in Angola. In 1981, 67 percent more Cubans held civilian jobs in Angola than did citizens of the USSR and Eastern European countries combined. In the military sphere, the Cuban presence was fourteen times greater than the combined total of the Soviet bloc.[45] Cuba retains its leading position in its alliance with the Soviet Union as both countries carry out their policies toward Angola.

Cuba and Ethiopia

Despite the important differences between the degree of Cuban-Soviet coordination of policy in Angola and in Ethiopia, there were also important similarities between Cuba's interventions in both countries. In both cases Cuba responded to requests from local allies and contributed combat troops and military support services. In both cases general Soviet support existed. The results of both interventions were politically profitable for Cuba. In both cases Cuba was able to assure African countries that its commitment was confined to a specific task. The war against Somalia to retain the Ogaden region for Ethiopia, for example, "was fought not to invade another country," said Castro. Rather, it was "a defensive war to protect territory invaded by foreign aggressors." At the peak of the war, Cuba deployed pilots, tank crews, artillery personnel, and armored infantry in Ethiopia.[46] It claimed to uphold the policy of the Organization of African Unity so that the boundaries inherited from colonial powers would be preserved. In both

Angola and the Horn of Africa the United States was constrained by African opposition to Cuba's enemy; the United States found it difficult to side with South Africa's incursion into Angola or with Somalia's irredentist invasion of Ethiopia. Thus, factors specific to the situations in southern and in eastern Africa help to explain Cuba's success.

Cuba's support for Ethiopia was complicated by the Eritrean revolution seeking independence from Ethiopia. In his April 1978 trip to Cuba, Mengistu asked for Cuban support to fight the Eritrean rebels. As noted in Chapter 5, Cuba once supported the Eritreans. In March 1975, Castro spoke of Eritrea's "national liberation movement," regretting a "situation in which two causes of progressive trends are confronting each other." The Cuban-Ethiopian communiqué of April 1978 did not mention Eritrea, although it denounced "imperialism and its reactionary allies" that "encourage secessionism."[47] In the fall of 1979 Mengistu visited Cuba again and referred in public to Cuban-Ethiopian military collaboration against the threats to Ethiopia's revolution. Armed Forces Minister Raúl Castro's reply made no reference to Eritrea, only to the Ogaden. He spoke of Cuba's combat deeds in the past, not in the future, and he emphasized the Soviet commitment to defend Ethiopia.[48] In March 1985 a high Cuban government official put it simply: "The Eritrean problem is Ethiopia's, not Cuba's."[49] The 1976 military treaty between Cuba and Angola committed Cuba to defend Angola against foreign attack and also to "organize and train [Angola's] armed forces . . . for the struggle against sabotage and counterrevolution."[50] Cuba made no such commitment to Ethiopia. Moreover, Cuba has failed to persuade the Mengistu government to negotiate with the Eritreans.[51] Although Cuba has sacrificed the Eritreans to its support of Mengistu's government, Cuba's past relations with the Eritreans set a limit on the extent of that support and, as a consequence, limited the extent of Cuban influence on Ethiopia's government.

Nonetheless, the posting of Cuban troops on the Ogaden facing Somali forces freed Ethiopian troops to fight the Eritreans. Cuban military training of the Ethiopian military was also useful in Eritrea. Thus Cuba provided at least indirect military support to Ethiopia against Cuba's former revolutionary allies in Eritrea.[52]

By late 1983 the Ogaden was under Ethiopian control even though Eritrea was not, and even though other insurgencies had broken out. Cuba judged that it had fulfilled its mission; Ethiopia may also have wanted to save on the cost of supplying the Cuban forces. The reaction of the rest of Africa to the Cuban presence was also a factor. A cutback of Cuba's troop level in Ethiopia in 1984 was necessary to calm the fears of some Africans about Cuban intentions on the continent, whereas Cuba's presence in Angola, where it faces South Africa, has always been accepted more easily. Cuba reduced its troops in Ethiopia from about 10,000 in 1982 to perhaps 3,000 in 1985.[53] Cuba maintained this level of military support for the Ethiopian government in the late 1980s.

The extent of Cuba's commitment to nonmilitary programs in Ethiopia can be compared with similar commitments in Angola. Ethiopia's population in the late 1970s was about five times larger than Angola's; the real gross national product of both was comparable. Ethiopia is thus much bigger and much poorer.[54] In 1979, 1,211 Ethiopians, aged eight to sixteen, came to study at the Isle of Youth; this was fewer than the number of Angolans in Cuba. The number of Ethiopians at the Isle of Youth reached 2,300 in late 1982—about the same as the number of Angolans. The total number of Ethiopians studying in Cuba fell from about 3,200 in 1982 to 2,763 in 1983.[55] In the area of health care, the first 32 Cuban health personnel, including doctors, had arrived in Ethiopia in 1977. In late 1984, there were 234 (of whom 130 were doctors and dentists)—less than half the number in Angola.[56] In Ethiopia, Cuba's most important construction project was a cement plant that, when finished in 1984, tripled Ethiopia's cement output. The Cuban construction workers were directed by East German technicians, and East Germany also financed the project. In contrast, Cuba's construction projects in Angola were wholly its own.[57] Cuba also sent teachers to Ethiopia (in 1983 they worked in thirteen of Ethiopia's fourteen provinces), but the language problems were more serious than in Angola. As in Angola, Cuban trade agreements with Ethiopia promoted nontraditional Cuban exports. In the early 1980s, Cuba agreed to export agricultural tools, equipment for irrigation, and other such products to Ethiopia.[58]

In 1977, Cuba intervened in Angola's internal affairs to defend Neto's government against a coup attempt. In Ethiopia, Cuba at one point undermined Mengistu's government. The All-Ethiopian Socialist Movement (also known as Meison) was formed early in 1976 as a civilian political party providing critical support to the military leadership. It fell into disfavor, however; Mengistu banned it in August 1977. Concerned about the lack of a civilian party, the Cuban ambassador to Ethiopia, José Pérez Novoa, with the support of the embassy of South Yemen, helped to bring an exiled Meison leader into Ethiopia: this leader was arrested at once. The top leaders of the trade union organization were also arrested for links to Meison, and Ethiopia expelled the Cuban ambassador and the Cuban political counselor.[59] Cuban officials claim that the ambassador made a mistake and that his actions were not part of Cuba's policy, which was to promote the unity of all revolutionary forces, not to weaken Mengistu. They argue that Mengistu understood how the incident happened after the two governments discussed it. Pérez Novoa was appointed ambassador to India in 1981.[60]

In spite of all of these factors, it would be a mistake to think that Cuban-Ethiopian relations are poor. Cuban officials emphasize their enthusiasm for the Ethiopian revolution and the good relations between the governments.[61] Indeed, Cuba's assistance to Ethiopia is second only to its aid to Angola. Moreover, Cuba supported Ethiopia's military government even at the cost of considerable embarrassment, in fighting its former Somali and Eritrean comrades.

Common to both cases is the pattern of Cuban assistance. Cuba helps the most in areas where it has made innovations: military operations, but also health and education. In addition, Cuba has responded to U.S. "oligopoly competition" by providing specific "products" that are ideologically well defined and consistent. Cuba's aid is, in a sense, retained within its own organization: it sends people and services, not cash. The Ethiopian case also demonstrates Cuba's ability to begin and to end decisively a specific military task.

On balance, these two major interventions strengthened Cuban relations with the Soviet Union and Eastern Europe and turned Cuba into a major force on the African continent. But these events also show a wide range of behavior in Cuban-Soviet relations. Cuba led in Angola and followed in Ethiopia. Soviet-Cuban differences often persist even within their joint interventions. Although they do not jeopardize the alliance, these differences demonstrate Cuba's autonomy under Soviet hegemony. Cuban policy remains its own even when it depends on the USSR for general support, because Cuba retains the right to refuse support in particular instances and exercises its right to lead the Soviets.

Cuban Activities in Grenada

The relations between Cuba and the People's Revolutionary Government of Grenada—from the successful coup of the New Jewel Movement (NJM) on March 13, 1979, until its overthrow on October 25, 1983, by U.S. and English-Caribbean forces—can be assessed thanks to the declassification of documents captured by the U.S. armed forces in Grenada, corroborated in part by Cuban officials.

There is no evidence that Cuba had a direct role bringing the NJM to power in March 1979, although the NJM had had normal relations with the Cuban Communist party, and Prime Minister Maurice Bishop had spent time in Cuba.[62] After the coup, however, Cuba quickly supported the new NJM government, and diplomatic relations were established. By September 1979 Cuba said publicly it had sent twelve medical doctors to Grenada and was training Grenadan fisherman, providing technical aid to develop Grenada's hydraulic resources and its agriculture and to build roads, and granting scholarships to Grenadans for study in Cuba.[63]

In April 1979 Grenada also received secretly more than 3,000 rifles, other light weapons, and ample ammunition from Cuba. Given Grenada's population of about 100,000, this gave the new government an impressive arsenal. Because Cuba did not manufacture AK-47 rifles and other military materiel, its transfer of weapons to Grenada was probably cleared with the USSR. The first weapons from the Soviets arrived in June 1981.[64] More Soviet weapons arrived between 1981 and 1983, turning Grenada into the eastern Caribbean's premier military power.

By mid-1980 Cuba's medical staff had seen nearly half of Grenada's population; Cuban doctors tripled Grenada's own stock of physicians. Soon Cuban assistance spread to the areas of education, communication, and sports, and to the building of a major international airport, a project begun in late 1979. The design of the airport was standard for civilian tourist airports in the eastern Caribbean (of course, Soviet or Cuban military planes could have used it in emergencies). In contrast to its projects in Angola, Cuba donated all this construction work. It also made other donations, including ten fishing boats. By March 1982 Cuban-Grenadan agreements on 137 different topics were formalized, rising to 193 by the end of the year.[65]

Military collaboration also increased. The secret treaty governing relations for 1982–1984 called for the permanent stationing on Grenada of twenty-seven Cuban military specialists, to be supplemented as needed. Cuba also granted scholarships for military training in Cuba. This document gives the fullest picture of Cuba's military help to a favored ally. According to its terms, Grenada would supply the following to Cuban military personnel: fresh foodstuffs, medicines, individual medical care, chauffeurs, cooks, laundry and maid service, office equipment, water, electricity, telephones, maintenance of buildings and furniture, means of transportation (including fuel, lubricants, maintenance, and repair), armaments and ammunition from Grenada's own stocks, and a stipend for the "personal expenses" of every Cuban military specialist "equivalent to 30 U.S. dollars." For its part, Cuba pledged to supply the requisite military specialists, the personnel and the material means to build housing and office space for them, dried foodstuffs and clothing, as well as job-related materials for these military specialists, and "the salary in Cuba of the military personnel."[66]

Cuba as Grenada's Broker

Beyond the formal agreements, Cuba's key contribution to Grenada was to serve as a leader and as a broker with Communist countries. As Grenada's ambassador to the Soviet Union wrote, the Soviets were "very careful, and for us sometimes maddingly slow, in making up their minds about who [*sic*] to support. They have decided to support us for two main reasons. Cuba has strongly championed our cause," and the Soviets were impressed with the Grenadan government's policies.[67]

Cuba's leadership and brokerage roles derived in part from Grenada's poor communication with the rest of the world. Cuba was the point for transshipment of goods stipulated in Grenada's military and other agreements with the USSR, Vietnam, and Czechoslovakia.[68] At times Cuba coached Grenada on how to bargain with the Soviets, just as it had earlier coached the Ethiopians. For example, on November 1982 the Cuban and Grenadan ministers of communications discussed how to develop Grenada's links to the Intersputnik satellite system. A record of the meeting stated: "So it was proposed by the Cuban side that a specialist . . . advise on the discussions with the Soviets. This point was fully agreed by the Grenadian [*sic*] side. Cuba also manifested that it is ready to help . . . also in the technical conversations with the Soviet Union until Grenada has the prepared personnel."[69]

Cuba's leadership role had wider implications. Cuba provided guidance for Grenadan and other Caribbean delegates attending an international meeting in Libya in 1982. With Grenada's help, it was easier for Cuba to rally other Caribbean delegations to its views and to cool off support for Libya's policies.[70] Grenada also helped Cuba with the Socialist International—an association of the world's Social Democratic parties—of which the NJM (but not the Cuban Communist party) was a member. The Cuban Communist party, thanks to and along with the NJM, met in secret to exchange information and design joint policies with Socialist International members such as Chile's Radical Party, the Jamaican People's National Party, and El Salvador's Nationalist Revolutionary Movement.[71]

Nothing in the declassified documents suggests that Grenada was supporting revolutionary movements to overthrow the neighboring governments in the English-, French-, or Dutch-speaking Caribbean, probably because it did not wish to provoke them or the United States. The NJM had excellent relations with Communist and other radical parties in the Caribbean, but these were not very different from good relations among kindred Social Democratic or Christian Democratic parties.[72] Moreover, the NJM emphasized good state-to-state relations in the eastern Caribbean. It limited its support for insurgencies to rebels far from Grenada, donating $50,000 to SWAPO's struggle against South Africa and working with Cuba and others to support the Salvadoran guerrillas.[73] Grenada followed Cuba's lead in keeping some distance from movements it considered untrustworthy. For instance, it gave no response to a request from Colombia's M-19 guerrillas "to develop best possible links."[74]

The NJM government, in short, relied heavily on Cuba; both benefited. The minutes of meetings of the NJM Political Bureau are filled with casual proposals to request Cuban help, which the members clearly expected to receive; NJM leaders also expected Cuba to brief them on issues coming up at international meetings. Cuba does not seem to have lorded it over Grenada. Quite the contrary, the NJM continuously asked Cuba for help and behaved willingly as Cuba's own client. Grenada found Cuban hegemony desirable and used it to make contact with a more distant and cautious Soviet Union. The documents are clear on two key points: The Grenadans thought the Cubans acted autonomously, not as Soviet proxies, and they thought the support of the Cubans was essential if the Soviets were to be persuaded to make (albeit reluctantly) commitments to Grenada.

Grenada's Break with Cuba and the End of NJM Rule
There were problems in Cuban-Grenadan relations, some of which may be typical of Cuba's ties with other countries with which it has generally good relations. Interactions between individual Cubans and Grenadans were, at times, not good, especially at the airport project—the centerpiece of Cuban aid to Grenada. By 1981 some Grenadan workers were distrustful of Cuba's intentions in building the airport. There was continuous friction between Cuban and Grenadan workers in 1982. The latter felt that they were not getting enough recognition for their own work. Some conflicts stemmed from disputes between male Cuban and Grenadan workers over their relations with Grenadan women. Religious differences also cropped up, with Cubans viewed as atheists by the more religious Grenadans. The language differences added to the difficulties. In August 1983 the NJM Political Bureau observed "a rise in anti-Cuban sentiment" among the Grenadan airport workers and concluded that "Cubans [were] not fully understanding [of] Grenadian [*sic*] customs."[75]

Other problems stemmed from both countries' underdevelopment. These are some of many instances of shared incompetence: A group of high-ranking Grenadan officials en route to the USSR was housed in awful conditions during their stay in Havana; although 60 percent of the spare parts Cuba had agreed to deliver for Grenada's fishing industry had arrived by April 1982, some boxes had not yet been opened and a number could not be found at all; by September 1982 only two of the ten fishing boats that Cuba had begun donating in 1979 were still working: as late as August 1983 Grenada's use of Cuban aid in the fishing industry was so ineffective that Cuba considered repatriating its personnel.[76]

There were also problems of communication between the governments. Grenada's embassy in Havana did not function well, although the ambassador, Leon Cornwall, was a member of the NJM Central Committee. Communications were ordinarily handled through Cubans in Grenada and, occasionally, when Grenadan leaders visited Cuba. As Cornwall told his comrades, "The party forgets that there is an Embassy in Cuba."[77] Cornwall at times had difficulty in arranging to meet with Cuban officials on instructions from his government.[78] Another problem resulted from the Grenadan embassy's nonpayment of bills to the Cuban state enterprise that services embassies. When no payments had been made for some time, the embassy's electricity, telephone, and telex services were cut off, as was the Grenadan ambassador's home telephone service. The NJM Political Bureau was furious. Cuba's view was that Cornwall lived extravagantly and that the Grenadans should have paid or discussed the problem; it was Cuban policy to cut off services to embassies for nonpayment.[79]

The most serious problem was Cuba's lack of awareness of trends within Grenada and the NJM. On October 13, 1983, Bishop was overthrown by a group led by Finance Minister Bernard Coard and Commander in Chief of the Armed Forces General Hudson Austin. Bishop and three other former Cabinet members were executed on October 19. Castro said that Bishop had "very close and affectionate links with our party's leadership" but that "Coard's group never had such relations nor such intimacy and trust with us. Actually we did not even know that group existed." Although Bishop had been in Cuba a few days before he was deposed, he did not tell the Cuban leaders about the NJM's internal problems. On October 15 Castro wrote the NJM Central Committee to express his disapproval of the coup.[80]

The events in Grenada should not have come as a complete surprise to Cuba, however. Manuel Piñeiro, head of the Americas Department of the Cuban Communist party's Central Committee, had told Cornwall in the summer 1983 on the basis of reports from Cuban personnel in Grenada that the quality of NJM government and party work was deteriorating. Cubans in Grenada raised the matter with members of the NJM Central Committee.[81] The Americas Department knew that the NJM had no more than eighty members when it took power in March 1979 and, five years later, only about two hundred members and candidate-members. In the apt phrase of the deputy chief of the Americas Department, the NJM was not a party but a "secret lodge."[82] But the depth of Cuba's ignorance of the opposition to Bishop remains astonishing. Cuba did not even know that Coard had left the NJM Political Bureau under pressure in 1982, a year before he led the coup against Bishop, until the U.S. government declassified the captured documents.[83]

Cuba's commitment to Bishop and its lack of knowledge about events in Grenada led it to refrain from full support of the Coard-Austin government while it signaled that it would honor existing agreements. On October 15, Castro wrote to the NJM that Cuba regarded Bishop as the "central figure" of the Grenadan revolution but that it would now "pay the strictest attention to the principle of not interfering in the slightest in the internal affairs of Grenada, fulfilling the promises made in the field of cooperation. Our promises are not to men. They are to the peoples and to principles."[84] The new NJM leaders believed that the "deep personal friendship between Fidel and Maurice . . .[had] caused the Cuban leadership to take a *personal* and not a *class* approach to the developments in Grenada." They also thought that it was "clear that the Cubans' position creates an atmosphere for speedy imperialist intervention."[85]

On October 21 the Organization of Eastern Caribbean States met in Barbados to request U.S. and British intervention in Grenada. The next day, the Caribbean Common Market (CARICOM) met in Trinidad and agreed to sever diplomatic and economic relations with Grenada's new government. The NJM appealed to Cuba. Castro replied on October 23, stating that Cuba would not send reinforcements if only the Caribbean states invaded Grenada: "Jamaica, Saint Lucia, and Barbados have no forces to invade Grenada and, in that case, they [the Grenadan armed forces] could defeat them with their own forces without greater difficulties." Moreover, Castro said, "Cuba cannot send reinforcements . . . because of the overwhelming U.S. air and naval superiority in the area." Given Bishop's death and other problems in Grenada, Castro said, "the unfortunate developments in Grenada render the useless sacrifice entailed in the dispatching of such reinforcements in a struggle against the United States morally impossible before our people and the world." In the face of an approaching U.S. naval task force, however, Cuba would keep its personnel in Grenada "as a matter of our country's honor, morality, and dignity." Cubans in Grenada would defend their positions if the United States invaded, Castro said, but owing to "the limited number of those forces, it is impossible to assign them any other mission." He instructed all Cubans in Grenada to remain under Cuban command.[86]

On October 25, U.S. troops and forces from Jamaica, Barbados, St. Lucia, Antigua-Barbuda, St. Vincent and the Grenadines, and Dominica invaded Grenada, overthrowing its government. At the time 784 Cubans were in Grenada, including 636 construction workers and 64 military personnel from the Armed Forces and Interior Ministries (12 of whom had arrived the day before). Eighteen people (including spouses and children) were housed in the Cuban embassy. The remainder came from 13 other Cuban agencies, the two largest contingents being in public health (17) and education (12). Many Cubans fought courageously; 24 died and many were injured. Although 92 percent of the Cubans on Grenada were performing civilian tasks, most were trained as reservists, consistent with the Cuban "civic soldier" tradition.[87] Their struggle was testimony to their loyalty to the Cuban government and to the capacity of Cuba's reserve training program to instill fighting skills.

The quality of Cuban officership, however, was poor. Colonel Pedro Tortoló, commander of Cuban forces in Grenada, arrived on the eve of the invasion. He described his own behavior in an interview later in Cuba, where he was at first received as a hero. Tortoló said that he expected only a U.S. rescue mission (a number of U.S. citizens, mostly medical students, were in Grenada at the time): "I never thought they were going to launch an invasion." He was asleep when the attack began. He had not issued weapons to all Cuban construction workers, nor had he issued enough ammunition to those who got weapons. Therefore, "the U.S. troops captured several of our comrades who had run out of ammunition along with another group that was unarmed." In the end, Tortoló and most other Cuban officers surrendered, as did most Cubans on Grenada.[88]

A key factor in Cuba's response to the U.S. intervention in Grenada was the need to impress the United States with Cuba's commitment to, and capacity for, combat in the event that the United States were to attack Cuba. For this reason, Cuban personnel had been ordered not to withdraw from Grenada as the United States prepared to attack even though, in the Cuban government's judgment, Grenada's government was "practically indefensible." Withdrawal would be a "dishonor and could stimulate aggression not only in Grenada but also in Cuba and elsewhere." Once the battle for Grenada began, the Cubans in Grenada were ordered not to surrender. The fact that they did posed a serious problem for the Cuban military. To set an example, Tortoló and the other officers serving in Grenada were eventually demoted to punish conduct unbecoming an officer. Nonetheless, the Cuban armed forces pointed to the reservists' fight against U.S. forces: "It has been demonstrated that one can fight against the best troops and that one need not be afraid."[89]

In 1975 the Cuban military had not been deterred from the Angolan War by the lack of military transport facilities. In 1983, however, their absence was one of Castro's reasons for not sending reinforcements to Grenada and for his view that the same constraint would apply if Nicaragua were invaded.[90] But the real difference between the two situations was not transportation; rather, it was the direct involvement of the U.S. armed forces in Grenada (and conceivably in the future in Nicaragua), but not in Angola in 1975 or in Ethiopia in 1977. In the Caribbean, where the United States seeks to exercise primacy, the scope for bold Cuban military actions was more limited than in Africa.

Cuba's involvement in Grenada also differed from other Cuban endeavors because the construction of the new international airport became its central project, dwarfing the size of its military, health, and education activities. Nonetheless, these four areas of activity accounted for most of Cuba's presence.

If the Angolan and Ethiopian cases had shown the limits of Cuban influence over its allies, the Grenadan case showed Cuba's inability to obtain intelligence—even to learn that its best friend, Maurice Bishop, was about to lose his job and his life. The Grenadan case also shows best Cuba's leadership and brokerage roles with regard to the Soviet Union and Eastern Europe. Cuba worked to engage initially reluctant allies in Grenada; thus its defeat was painful, for it was so plainly a Cuban project. Lack of knowledge about Grenada, lack of influence within the country, and lack of power to prevent local and international events the Cuban government opposed are the hallmarks of Cuba's four-year love affair with a revolution that committed suicide in Grenada.

Was the Anti-Bishop Coup also Anti-Cuban?
Although some have speculated that the anti-Bishop coup was also anti-Cuban and pro-Soviet,[91] it is not likely that the Soviets were actively involved in planning the coup. Cuba needed to use its influence to involve the Soviets in Grenada. In late 1982, the Grenadan ambassador in Moscow reported that, for the Soviets, the "very distant" Caribbean was "quite frankly, not one of their priority areas." He concluded, "we have to work

on the Soviets for some considerable time before we reach the stage of relationship that, for example, we have with the Cubans."[92] Only in 1980 did the Soviets begin to provide substantial military and economic aid; by 1983 they supplied a huge arsenal to Grenada, though their economic aid was more modest.[93] In short, the Soviets were cautious and slow, though probably no more so than they have been in Angola, Ethiopia, and Nicaragua.

Some members of the Coard-Austin group may have had anti-Cuban feelings. For example, Central Committee member Leon Cornwall, former ambassador to Cuba, brought up his problems serving in Cuba during the factional debates, although he never linked his attitude toward Bishop to his attitude toward Cuba.[94] General Austin had served as construction minister and was aware of the problems between Cuban and Grenadan workers at the airport. He also carried the NJM's protest to Cuba when services were cut off to Grenada's embassy in Havana. Still, Austin was proud of the airport project and was also proud of and satisfied with Cuban-Grenadan military relations.[95] Coard told the NJM Central Committee in September 1983 that "he had personally raised a number of times with the Cuban comrades the need for advisers in party building, organisation and ideological work . . . However, there has not been a positive response so far."[96] These remarks suggest that he wanted more Cuban aid.

The Soviets had reason to be upset with a visit Bishop made to the United States in June 1983. Cuba helped Bishop to arrange that trip, but Grenada did not tell the Soviets about the planned trip. When a high Soviet Foreign Ministry official asked the Grenadan ambassador after the fact for a briefing on Bishop's meeting with U.S. National Security Adviser William Clark, he was told, "the results are confidential." The Soviet official stressed that "it would have been courteous to inform them of the intention to visit."[97]

The Soviets knew Coard better than Bishop because Coard had traveled to either the Soviet Union or Eastern Europe every year since 1979,[98] and he was more self-consciously Marxist-Leninist than Bishop. At the time of Bishop's overthrow, the Soviet press did not defend Bishop, nor did it condemn the Coard-Austin faction; its own reporting of the coup was neutral (though the Soviet press published Cuba's defense of Bishop and Cuba's critique of the coup).[99] Soviet scholars who have written about this coup are divided between those who condemn it and those who appear neutral to Bishop and Coard.[100] As in the case of Alves's attempted coup against the Neto in Angola, the Soviets may have favored Coard over Bishop, but there is no evidence they did much about it.

In interviews conducted in March 1985, Cuban officials expressed their belief that the Soviets had not promoted or assisted Coard's coup, but one official interviewed did not discount the possibility that individual Soviet officials might have encouraged Coard. These Cuban officials believed that the Soviets were even less informed than the Cubans and just as surprised by events in Grenada. Although all the Cuban officials interviewed agreed that anti-Cuban sentiments arose within the NJM after Cuba disapproved of Bishop's overthrow, they were split on whether these feelings had existed before.[101]

No significant evidence presents itself of anti-Cuban feeling within the NJM before Castro reacted to Bishop's overthrow, or of an active Soviet role in the events that led up to or followed Bishop's overthrow (in spite of the Soviets' probable preference of Coard over Bishop). As in the case of the Alves coup attempt in Angola, however, differences in behavior between Cuba and the USSR are evident. Cuba condemned Bishop's overthrow and killing publicly and immediately; the Soviets did not. Cubans fought and died for the Grenadan revolution; the Soviets only protested the invasion. These differences show yet again the zone of autonomy that marks Cuban-Soviet relations and the difficulty both have in exercising influence abroad.

The Dimensions of Cuba's Support for Revolutionary States

The Scope of Cuba's Activities Abroad
By the end of 1986 more than 250,000 Cubans had served in Africa on a military or civilian basis (80 percent had served in Angola alone). By mid–1987, 24,000 scholarship students were in Cuba from 82 countries (up from 21,000 from 69 countries in 1980); two-thirds were from African countries. More than 15,000 young Africans were studying in Cuba, free of charge, by the end of 1986. The largest groups were from Angola, Mozambique, Ethiopia, Nicaragua, Congo, South Yemen, Guinea-Bissau, São Tomé and Principe, and the quasi-states of Namibia and the Spanish Sahara. Eighty percent attended primary and secondary schools, mostly at the Isle of Youth, where the "internationalist schools," founded in 1977, grew quickly to an enrollment of 12,000 in 1982 and nearly 18,000 in 1984. Since 1973 (when the first program began in the former Spanish colony of Equatorial Guinea) Cuban teachers have also served overseas. There were 4,500 Cuban teachers abroad in 20 countries in 1983 (up from 2 countries in 1976 and 14 in 1980), most of them in Mozambique, Ethiopia, Angola, and Nicaragua; all but 200 were in primary and secondary education. By early 1987 more than 20,000 Cuban teachers had served overseas.[102] An overseas sports program, begun in 1970, expanded greatly after 1977. In 1983, 90

Cuban sports specialists worked in 15 countries; in 1987, 48 sports specialists were working in 18 countries.[103]

In 1983, 3,044 Cuban health workers—up 13 percent from 1983 (and up from 492 in 1976)—were posted in 27 countries; they included 1,675 medical doctors, 58 dentists, 742 nurses, and 516 intermediate-level health technicians. In all, about 8 percent of Cuba's doctors and 2 percent of its nurses and health technicians were overseas. Cuba's emphasis on the use of doctors to provide health care added to its prestige, although it may have set too costly a model for other countries to emulate. In some areas of medicine, a third of Cuba's specialists had served overseas by 1984. In addition, 766 doctors and dentists from Third World countries had graduated from Cuban medical and dental schools; some 1,491 others from 79 countries were on scholarship in Cuba in 1984. About 7 percent of University of Havana medical and dental school graduates in 1987 were foreign scholarship students. Cuba founded a medical school in South Yemen in 1976, and is partially staffing medical schools in Angola, Ethiopia, and Nicaragua.[104]

Cuban health personnel first arrived in 1963 in Algeria, where the overseas health program began. Later in the 1960s the program was extended to Guinea, Mali, Tanzania, the Congo, and Vietnam; it boomed in the 1970s. In 1978, Cuba supplied more than 70 percent of all the physicians in Cape Verde, Angola, Equatorial Guinea, and São Tomé and Principe, and a majority of those in South Yemen and Guinea-Bissau. But countries that paid for health services in convertible currency, such as Iraq and Libya, accounted for half of all Cuban health personnel overseas that year.[105] As late as 1983 2 of every 3 doctors in São Tomé and Principe were Cubans. In 1984 the 23 Cuban medical doctors and dentists in Guyana, and a comparable number of Guyanese doctors and dentists trained in Cuba, made up half of the professional medical force of Guyana's health ministry.[106]

Cuba's overseas construction worker program began in 1970 in Peru in the aftermath of a major earthquake. Beginning in 1979 many Cuban construction projects have been carried out under profit-making contracts. By 1981 Cuba's state-owned multinational construction firm, UNECA, had 7,000 construction workers in 10 countries. It earned 70 million pesos in the first half of 1981, a threefold increase over the same period in 1980, and was among Cuba's best foreign exchange earners. In 1982 the 8,000 overseas construction workers represented 3 percent of all Cuban construction workers. From 1981 through 1985, 33,000 Cuban construction workers were posted in 20 countries overseas, and Cuba earned 430 million pesos from the projects on which they worked.[107]

Founded in 1977, UNECA distinguishes between countries that receive projects as donations (such as Laos, Vietnam, and Grenada) and those that ordinarily pay in convertible currency, such as Iraq, Libya, Algeria, and, at times, Angola (until mid-1984) and Nicaragua (until 1985). UNECA is paid extra for finishing projects ahead of schedule. It undersells private multinational firms. The most important Cuban contract has been with Libya, which employed 2,500 Cuban construction workers in 1983 (down from 3,000 in 1982). From 1979 through 1983 Cubans in Libya built schools for $7.3 million, 1,042 housing units for $47 million, two highways in the desert for $53 million, and other projects for a total of $115 million. Libya even canceled some projects with private firms and awarded them to Cuba.[108]

The following list summarizes the scope and location of Cuba's main overseas civilian programs, not including trade in goods, in the late 1980s.[109]

In Africa

Algeria. Begun in 1963. Fishing, health, agriculture, light industry, higher education, research and development, sports, construction.

Angola. Construction (in 1987, down to 1,700 Cubans), education, sports, health, fishing, forestry, sugar industry, trade organization, poultry farming, labor organization, party organization.[110]

Benin. Begun in 1977. Health, education (over 100 students from Benin have studied in Cuba), sports, fishing, livestock, trade and labor organization, sugar industry.[111]

Burkina Faso. Begun in 1984. In September 1986, 600 students from Burkina Faso arrived at the Isle of Youth.[112]

Burundi. Health; after 1983, also agriculture, education, sugar industry.[113]

Cape Verde. Health, education, transportation, culture, trade organization.

Congo. Livestock, dairy industry, poultry farming, education (900 students from the Congo were in Cuba on scholarships in 1983), sports (begun in 1984), agriculture, construction, health.[114]

Equatorial Guinea. Health, education (begun in 1973); later, also agriculture, forestry, communications, and military advice (these programs were curtailed in the late 1970s and resumed after the overthrow of President Macías in 1979).[115]

Ethiopia. Begun in 1977. Health, education, construction, veterinary medicine, aviculture, agriculture, labor organization, planning organization, sugar industry.[116]

Ghana. Begun in early 1960s, stopped in 1966, resumed in 1982. Education (secondary and higher education scholarships in Cuba), sports.[117]

Guinea. Begun in 1961. Health, agriculture, sports (stopped by end 1986),[118] education, fishing, leadership training, construction (including building two airports).

Guinea-Bissau. Communications, construction, education, sports, health.[119]

Libya. Health (begun in 1977; 213 Cuban medical personnel in 1983, down from 650 in 1978), construction.[120]

Malagasy Republic. Sugar industry, agriculture, sports (ended by early 1987),[121] education.

Mali. Health, sports.[122]

Mozambique. Begun in 1976. By 1981, hundreds of Cubans were in 7 of its 10 provinces. Agriculture, food industry, forestry, health, construction, education (including 4,300 scholarships to Cuba), sports, fishing, transportation, communications, sugar industry, chemicals.[123]

Nigeria. Sugar industry, sports.[124]

São Tomé and Principe. Health, education, fishing, livestock, communications, planning, trade organization, transportation, agriculture, construction, sports.[125]

Seychelles. Begun in 1978. Health, agriculture, education.[126]

Tanzania. Education, sports, construction, health.[127]

Uganda. Begun in 1981. Health, education.[128]

Zaire. Sugar industry.[129]

Zambia. Begun in June 1986. Unspecified.[130]

Zimbabwe. Begun in March 1986. Education, health.[131]

In Asia and the Middle East

Afghanistan. Education (begun in April 1978).[132]

Iraq. Construction (roads, 1,500 housing units), agriculture, sugar industry, fishing, sports, health (begun in 1977; 372 Cuban medical personnel in 1986, down from 506 in 1983).[133]

Kampuchea. Health (Cuba supplies 4 percent of its stock of medical doctors); communications.[134]

Kuwait. Sports (probably commercial contract).[135]

Laos. Construction (78 Cuban workers), agriculture and livestock, health.[136]

Sri Lanka. Health, education.[137]

South Yemen. Begun in 1972. Transportation, agriculture, fishing, light industry, steel, health, education (590 secondary school students from South Yemen on Isle of Youth in 1982), poultry farming, livestock, mining, sports, construction.[138]

Syria. Education, health (in 1973 during war with Israel).[139]

Vietnam. Begun in 1968. Health, agriculture, construction, fishing, sugar industry, education, sports,[140] research and development.

In Latin America

Bolivia. Begun in 1987. Donation of 3 intensive care units.[141]

Dominican Republic. In 1987, Cuba agreed to donate materials and labor to build a technical school worth $2.8 million.[142]

Guyana. Begun in 1974 with a fishing agreement (since expired); in late 1980s sugar industry, forestry, agriculture, health, light and food industries, mining, transportation, trade and labor organization.

Nicaragua. Education (over 2,000 Cuban teachers in Nicaragua and 1,200 Nicaraguans on scholarships in Cuba), sports, health (over 250 Cuban medical personnel in Nicaragua), fishing, construction.[143]

Panama. Agriculture, sports, education.[144]

Peru. Sports.[145]

This list shows the variety of countries and activities in Cuba's overseas aid program and emphasizes the importance of Cuban activity in education, sports, fishing, construction, and health. All but construction had been successful sectors in Cuba, and were important elements in its move into other countries by the 1970s. The number of programs (especially in health, education, and sports) and the number of countries in which Cuba operates have grown, despite renewed U.S. efforts in the 1980s to curtail Cuban influence. The largest single increase occurred in the mid-1970s, as Cuba became one of the closest allies of all the successor states to the Portuguese empire. Cuba at times has charged commercial rates (though lower than prevailing world market rates) for its construction, health, and other services, but in general its services have been donated. The Angolan and Grenadan programs illustrate both contract and grant approaches common to Cuba's overseas agreements.[146] About 15,000 Cuban civilians were posted overseas in the early 1980s (Cuban estimates ranged from 11,000 to 25,000). By the end of 1985 about 50,000 Cuban civilian and military personnel were working in 30 countries: about 35,000 of these were military. More countries were added to the list in 1986 and 1987.[147]

The most controversial Cuban overseas program, of course, is military. The first overseas deployment of the Cuban armed forces took place in 1963 when Cuba assisted Algeria in the war against Morocco, sacrificing its own good trade relations with Morocco in the process, at a time when Cuba badly needed foreign exchange. Cuba sent 300 to 400 tank troops and some 40 tanks, which engaged in combat.[148] In 1965 Cuba also sent troops to Brazzaville (Congo) to train regular, militia, and guerrilla forces that were fighting for the independence of Portugal's African colonies. Cuban troops also helped Guinea's Sekou Touré in maintaining internal security and in repelling foreign aggression.[149] Cuba has acknowledged that it has provided military aid to South Yemen, Guinea-Bissau and, since 1979, to Nicaragua.[150] Independent observers have reported that Cuban military training has occurred in Mozambique and Benin, and Cuba has confirmed that military doctors were engaged in the personal service of Mozambique's President Samora Machel at the time of his death in October 1986.[151] As described earlier, the largest Cuban deployments were to Angola in 1975 and to Ethiopia in 1977, and Cuban troops and workers died fighting in Grenada in 1983.

In 1980 Cuba's customary overseas armed forces amounted to about 35,000 (higher than the number the United States posted in Vietnam, relative to its population, at the peak of that war), even though victory was already assured in the Ogaden, the Angola-Zaire crises over Shaba were past, and no South African incursion against Angola would occur for another year.[152] By early 1982, 120,000 Cuban troops had served overseas.[153] From 1981 through 1985, 100,000 Cuban troops completed overseas tours of duty.[154] Cuba's Interior Ministry also posted personnel abroad as part of most Cuban overseas programs.[155] By 1988, Cuban overseas military deployments were above the 1980 level, although concentrated in Angola. In addition, many Cuban civilians were reservists, so that Cuba's effective combat capability overseas is much greater than is indicated by the number of military personnel.[156]

Cuba and Nicaragua

Cuba supported the Nicaraguan revolutionary movement until the Somoza family dynasty was overthrown in July 1979. That same month, the first Cuban medical personnel and emergency material aid arrived.[157] The first 1,200 Cuban teachers arrived in November 1979.[158] The speed of Cuba's response impressed Nicaragua's new Sandinista government. Cuba's quick involvement in Nicaragua was facilitated by the prevailing international environment. Most governments, including the U.S. government, had come to support Somoza's departure from power, wished the new Nicaraguan government well, and provided it with assistance.

By 1984, 5,000 young Nicaraguans were studying in Cuba, 1,500 of them to become teachers.[159] In 1983 Castro said that there were about 4,000 Cubans in Nicaragua, of whom half were teachers and about 500 were health workers. There were also several hundred construction workers, many building Nicaragua's first coast-to-coast highway, and a smaller group in agriculture. Castro also said there were only 200 military advisers— about a tenth of what the U.S. government had alleged. (A Cuban defector, Brigade General Rafael del Pino, reported that there were 300 to 400 Cuban military advisers in Nicaragua in 1987.)[160] Cuba's educational assistance to Nicaragua was its largest such commitment in the world, probably because language was no obstacle. Many Cuban teachers worked on Nicaragua's literacy campaign, which was patterned on Cuba's. Cuba's aid in the area of health rivaled in size the Angolan program; in 1982 Cuba supplied about a third of all health personnel in Nicaragua.[161] Cuba estimated that its educational aid to Nicaragua from 1979 to 1984 was worth about $20 million; the 5,000 Cuban teachers who had, by then, served in Nicaragua had worked with 250,000 students (or almost 10 percent of Nicaragua's 2.6 million people).[162]

Using Nicaraguan sources, Theodore Schwab and Harold Sims estimate that Cuban nonmilitary aid to Nicaragua was worth $286 million from 1979 through 1982.[163] In 1985 the U.S. government estimated that between 7,500 and 9,000 Cubans were in Nicaragua, of whom 3,000 were in the military and on internal security missions. U.S. and other diplomatic sources in Nicaragua also indicated that, by 1986, Cuban pilots were flying Soviet helicopters for the Sandinista armed forces.[164]

In 1979–80 Castro praised U.S. aid to Nicaragua and counseled the Sandinistas to "go slow," "be realistic," and "not be extremists."[165] As war clouds gathered over Central America in late 1980, Cuba contributed to the heightened conflict, notably by supporting revolutionaries in El Salvador. By 1982 Cuba was endorsing a negotiated settlement to Central America's conflicts as the surest means to consolidate Nicaragua's Sandinista regime, which faced U.S.-backed efforts to overthrow it. Cuba has pledged that it will withdraw its advisers from Nicaragua if there is regional agreement.

Having learned from the events in Grenada in 1983, Castro decided "to choose the [civilian] cooperation personnel who had the physical conditions to resist any invasion there, in other words, to join the Nicaraguans and take on the kind of struggle that might be waged there." In short, Cuba's combat capability in Nicaragua is much greater than is suggested by the number of military personnel alone. In 1986 Castro also said that Cuba would increase its support for the Nicaraguan government to match increased U.S. support for those who sought to overthrow it (commonly known as the "contras"). But, as in Grenada, he also said that Cuba would not send military reinforcements if U.S. troops invaded Nicaragua.[166]

As in the Angolan case, Cuban technical and economic aid to Nicaragua has taken the form of a gift as well as of a business transaction. One large project, the construction of a sugar mill in Nicaragua (begun in 1982) reflected Cuba's comparative advantage in such endeavors based on its own sugar industry. About 400 Cubans worked on the project regularly, and another 700 for brief periods. It was financed by a $50 million line of credit from Cuba to Nicaragua, repayable in 12 years at 6 percent interest (the cost of comparable Soviet projects in Nicaragua were repayable in 12 years but bore only 3 percent interest).[167] The funds were to pay for the equipment, materials, and labor sent from Cuba. In January 1985 the "Victoria de Julio" sugar mill went into operation, despite a worldwide sugar surplus and, consequently, in spite of prevailing world market prices well below the costs of production. Cuba thereupon canceled Nicaragua's debt for the project, which amounted to a total of $73.8 million. This policy was consistent with the shift of Cuban projects in Angola from commercial transactions to donations. Both Angola and Nicaragua were then facing serious military situations.[168]

Cuba's commitment to, and impact on, Sandinista Nicaragua has been more significant than the Soviet Union's, partly as a result of Cuba's support for, and Soviet aloofness from, the insurrection that overthrew Somoza. As early as 1979 Nicaraguan Interior Minister Tomás Borge admitted, "I will not deny that the Cuban revolution has exerted a certain very positive influence [in Nicaragua] . . . The influence of the USSR is rather more remote."[169]

In mid-1984 Borge described Nicaragua's relations with Cuba as "excellent" and those with the USSR as "good." He preferred Cuban over Soviet military advisers "for practical reasons;" the Cubans, Borge said, "speak our language and are more keen on our way of life." The Cubans know Soviet equipment, Borge continued, and "if we need technical advice about Soviet weapons, then the Cubans can play that part." Borge also perceived that the presence of Soviets in Nicaragua might be thought too provocative by other countries: in deciding to rely on Cuban, rather than Soviet, military advisers, the Sandinistas thus sought to "not . . . give our enemies a reason" to attack Nicaragua's government.[170] In fact, Soviet relations with Nicaragua during 1979–80 were limited, and the sharply increased Soviet commitment to Nicaragua dates from 1981.[171] The nature and sequence of events suggests that, as in Grenada, Cuba's leaders drew the Soviets into a deeper commitment to Nicaragua than the Soviets might have undertaken on their own.

The Coordination of Cuban and Soviet Aid Programs

The most comprehensive U.S. government evidence on the distribution of Cuban and Soviet bloc personnel in aid programs worldwide since the mid-1970s is summarized in Table 6.1. In fact, U.S. government information on Cuba's presence overseas is often incomplete and tends to underestimate its extent.[172] Nonetheless, these numbers are generally consistent with other evidence. No matter how it was measured, no statistically significant correlation arose between the distributions of Cuban and Soviet-bloc personnel in 1977 as Cuba began to expand the scope of its international programs. There was, however, a trend over time toward a closer relationship between

Table 6.1 Correlations between distributions of Cuban and Soviet bloc economic and military personnel in Third World countries

Year	All countries Economic	All countries Military	Countries where Cubans are present Economic	Countries where Cubans are present Military
1977				
Correlation	− 0.059	0.020	− 0.101	0.112
Number of countries	35	17	9	9
Statistical significance	Not significant	Not significant	Not significant	Not significant
1978				
Correlation	0.035	0.342	− 0.063	0.491
Number of countries	42	18	14	11
Statistical significance	Not significant	0.082	Not significant	0.063
1979				
Correlation	0.202	0.114	0.075	0.676
Number of countries	42	16	15	8
Statistical significance	0.100	Not significant	Not significant	0.033
1981				
Correlation	0.593	0.272	0.444	0.771
Number of countries	42	15	11	7
Statistical significance	0.000	Not significant	0.086	0.021
1984				
Correlation	0.368	—	0.314	—
Number of countries	39	—	20	—
Statistical significance	0.011	—	0.089	—

Sources: U.S. Central Intelligence agency, National Foreign Assessment Center, *Communist Activities in Non-Communist Less Developed Countries* (Washington, D.C.): for 1977, pub. ER78-10478U, tables 2, 6; for 1978, pub. ER79-10412U, tables 3, 7; for 1979, pub. ER80-10318U, tables A-3, A-7. U.S. Department of State, *Soviet and East European Aid to the Third World, 1981* (Washington, D.C., 1983), pub. 9435, tables 7, 11; U.S. Department of State, *Warsaw Pact Economic Aid to Non-Communist LDCs, 1984* (Washington, D.C., 1986), pub. 9345, table 15.

Note: These are Pearson product-moment correlations. Statistical significance assessed by means of one-tailed t-tests; significance threshold set at $p = 0.10$. Identical numbers give a correlation of 1.0; inverse relationships give a correlation close to − 1.0; calculation includes only countries for which source gives specific number of overseas personnel.

the distributions of Cuban and Soviet bloc personnel overseas. Focusing on countries where both Cuba and Soviet bloc countries were donors of military assistance, the correlations between Cuban and Soviet bloc activity became increasingly significant from 1977 to 1981—that is, in the aftermath of Cuban-Soviet military collaboration in the Horn of Africa. Except for Jamaica and Nicaragua in 1979, moreover, Cuba sent civilian technicians only to countries that also received Soviet or Eastern European technicians. And it sent military personnel only to countries where Soviet military personnel were also present (except in Guyana, Grenada and, briefly, Nicaragua; Cuban military advisers arrived in Nicaragua in 1979, before Soviet military advisers were sent).[173] Even so, the correlations between the distribution of Soviet bloc and Cuban personnel are far from perfect. In short, Cuban and Soviet bloc policies are mutually supportive, though they focus on each government's own interests.

These results support the argument that there is a mixture of hegemony and autonomy in the Cuban-Soviet relationship. The lack of more significant positive correlations in the distribution of Cuban and Soviet bloc military and economic personnel in Third World countries indicates that each government emphasizes its own interests. That concept is at the heart of autonomy. At the same time, the increasingly close association between the distributions of Cuban and Soviet bloc military personnel underscores the continuity of hegemony.

Setbacks for Cuba Abroad
One theme in my earlier analysis of Cuban aid to Angola, Grenada, and Ethiopia was the limits of Cuba's influence. That is a wider problem. Earlier discussions noted persistent Cuban-Libyan rivalry for international revolutionary leadership, and Castro's personal failure to persuade Somali President Siad Barre to compromise with Ethiopia in 1977 in order to avoid war. Cuba was also unhappy about, and powerless to prevent, the March 16, 1984, Nkomati Accord between Mozambique and South Africa, whereby Mozambique stopped supporting the African National Congress (ANC) and its fight against South Africa and arrested or deported ANC cadres. Nonetheless, Cuba continued its aid program to Mozambique, and their relations subsequently improved again, thanks in part to South Africa's violation of its side of the bargain with Mozambique.[174]

Cuba has often been unsuccessful in protecting its friends in government from being overthrown by coups, or in preventing former friends from adopting policies of which Cuba disapproves. Cuba was close to Algeria's Ahmed Ben-Bella, for instance, and in 1963 sent troops to help his government in a war against Morocco. In 1965, Castro denounced the coup by Houari Boumedienne that overthrew Ben-Bella. By 1967, however, Cuban-Algerian relations had improved again.[175] In late 1977, South Yemen's President, Salem Robaya Ali, was awarded Cuba's "Playa Girón" National Order Medal and hailed by Castro as a "hero." In June 1978, however, Cuba stood back while Ali was overthrown by Soviet-backed forces. Cuba eventually assisted in the consolidation of the new government in South Yemen; their good relations resumed.[176] Nonetheless, neither Cuba nor the Soviet Union could prevent the murderous shootout and civil war among the factions within the South Yemeni regime in 1986.[177] Beginning in 1973, Cuba supported President Nguema Macías of Equatorial Guinea, notwithstanding the atrocities committed by his regime, and disapproved of his overthrow in August 1979 (Cuba did curtail its aid to Macías in the late 1970s, but did not stop it). Relations quickly improved after 1979.[178] In Guinea in 1984, a coup swept away the remaining leaders of the late Sekou Touré's regime to whom Cuba had been close; Cuba expressed its disapproval of the new regime's policies. In Burkina Fasso in 1987, Cuba's ally Thomas Sankara was overthrown and killed. In each case, Cuba continued to honor its treaty obligations.[179]

Complex, too, were Cuba's relations with Guyana. Diplomatic relations were established in 1972. Cuba sought to maintain good relations with government and opposition parties because both had revolutionary credentials. Despite the Cuban-Guyanese cooperation that developed during the 1970s, relations were set back in 1980, when Walter Rodney, the head of a small left-wing opposition party, was assassinated and the Cuban press published reports implicating Guyana's government. Nevertheless, Cuba continued its cooperation with Guyana. Relations improved again when Guyana's relations with Venezuela and the United States deteriorated in the early 1980s.[180]

With regard to the Congo, in the mid-1960s President Alphonse Massemba-Debat welcomed the Cuban military to train his forces. In June 1966, Captain Marien Ngouabi's troops mutinied; they demanded the repatriation of the Cubans. The Cuban military entered combat to protect government officials until Massemba-Debat prevailed. In August 1968, Massemba-Debat was overthrown. By 1975, Cuba's relations with his successor, President Ngouabi, were so good that Brazzaville became a key stopover point for Cuban troops en route to Angola; yet Cuba could not prevent Ngouabi's assassination in 1977. Though Cuban-Congolese relations deteriorated in 1977–1979, they improved again thereafter.[181]

These examples outline the limits of Cuban influence over other governments. They also indicate that Cuba has dealt with various types of rulers and that it usually establishes good relations with the new government soon after its ally is overthrown. Its commitment, as Castro said after Bishop's overthrow in Grenada, is not to individuals but to a longer-range conception of Cuba's interests. These setbacks for Cuban policy, moreover, have stemmed from its very success. Cuba often has been so enmeshed in the affairs of countries the world over that its achievements have brought burdens.

More dramatically, Cubans have been expelled from Ghana in 1966 (in the wake of the coup that overthrew Kwame Nkrumah), from Chile in 1973 (after the overthrow of Salvador Allende), from Somalia in 1977 (as Cuba sided with Ethiopia in the war), from Kampuchea in 1978 (by Pol Pot's government), from Jamaica in 1981 (within a year of Prime Minister Edward Seaga's election), from Grenada in 1983 (by the U.S. and English-Caribbean invasion), and from Suriname in 1983 (out of fear of U.S. intentions just after the U.S. intervention in Grenada).[182] In Chile, Jamaica, and Grenada, Cuba's role was a contentious issue between incumbent and opposition and proved a liability in the long run for Cuba's local allies. In Grenada, Cuba's presence was a key reason for the U.S. and English-Caribbean intervention. In Grenada, Jamaica, and Somalia the Cuban aid program was large enough to be materially significant. In these seven cases, Cuba was powerless to prevent events it opposed; it lost influence and, in the Horn of Africa and Grenada, the lives of its people.

Cuba portrays itself as an example of successful socialism in the Third World. It has led the Soviets in Grenada, Nicaragua, and Angola, and it has played the role of broker between the Soviets and these and other Third World allies. But Cuba has also worked in partnership with, and has supported, Soviet policies—most clearly in Ethiopia. Characteristically, Cuba has been quicker to make international commitments than the USSR. Its policies have occasionally failed, even when Cuba's key interests were at stake. Military force could not always be translated into readily useful political power in specific contexts. Cuba has made mistakes at times out of ignorance of foreign situations. But after some setbacks Cuban leaders have been patient enough to wait through difficult periods until relations with other governments often, though not always, have improved again.

Cuba's policy of supporting other revolutionary states has been generally successful, although there have been serious costs and some setbacks. Its foreign policy reflects its ideological and strategic conceptions within the context of its Soviet alliance. The circumstances of the international system have been decisive in determining the relative success or failure of Cuba's activities abroad. The nature of each international situation has also affected the timing and results of Cuban involvement; it has been most successful in southern and eastern Africa and least so in the Caribbean. Cuba has built on its innovations at home to propel its policy abroad, especially in the military arena but also in some civilian spheres. In addition to gaining influence in the world and with the Soviets, some Cuban activities have promoted commerce in goods and services. Domestic and international factors, therefore, jointly explain the projection of Cuban power overseas.

Cuba's Relations with Capitalist Countries

7

The most serious challenge to the revolutionary government's survival was the attempt by the U.S. government to overthrow it. The United States launched a major effort in the early 1960s, with the eventual support of most Latin American governments, to isolate, punish, and, it hoped, topple the Cuban government. The Cuban government survived, though at great cost to Cuban society, economy, and politics. At home, its leaders built a tough authoritarian regime and a centralized economy; they acted on their own ideas on organizing national affairs, but were also justified in part by the need to face the enemy abroad. Internationally, Cuba fought the United States wherever it could, helping revolutionary movements and states and building an alliance with the Soviet Union. But Cuba also fought the United States by means of trade and conventional political relations with Western Europe, Canada, and Japan. In the process, Cuba participated in the world sugar market and incurred debts to the governments and banks of market-economy countries.

The international system is not uniform or centralized, and the actions of governments in different spheres are somewhat independent of each other.[1] Political adversaries may engage in trade, for example, while close trading partners may not see eye to eye in politics. In the non-Communist world, the United States has exercised a loose hegemony, neither requiring nor imposing fealty to all its preferences upon its allies. The structure of world capitalism permits a range of business opportunities to many private firms. Within the context of the independence of U.S. allies (and, even more, that of nonaligned countries or U.S. adversaries) from much of U.S. policy and the decentralization of world capitalism, Cuba found room to maneuver after 1959. In general, Cuba systematically gave priority to political over economic interests—a choice that explains the deterioration in Cuban relations with Western European countries and Canada in the late 1970s. But when both political and economic interests coincided, Cuban relations with market-economy countries were mutually beneficial. The structure of the international political economy, including the differences in interests among the advanced capitalist countries, and domestic and international measures adopted by the Cuban government, permitted the survival of revolutionary rule in Cuba.

Cuba could not have entirely separated itself from the world market, even if it wished to do so. Susan Eckstein has argued cogently that world capitalism continues to constrain Cuba because it must still engage in market transactions with many countries, even with its partners in the Council for Mutual Economic Assistance (CMEA). There is one world economy, and it is capitalist.[2] The CMEA, for example, sets its prices in relation to average international market prices, with adjustments for time lags, CMEA scarcities, and politics.[3] Thus Cuba has remained shackled to the world market price system, even though some of its leaders—especially Fidel Castro—have detested the arrangement; it is compelled to trade within that system.

Moreover, most Cuban trade with the CMEA countries is in "transferable rubles," a unit of accounting for goods and services that are bartered. The transferable ruble cannot be converted freely into other internationally traded currencies and is not traded outside the CMEA. This restricts Cuba's flexibility to obtain goods and services not readily available from CMEA countries, or not available at the quality Cuba had come to expect before the revolution. It is also politically confining. For these reasons, and also to obtain recent Western high technology, Cuba trades with non-CMEA countries, above all with the industrialized market-economy countries. This trade is carried out in freely convertible currency such as Swiss francs or Japanese yen. Some Cuban-CMEA trade (including some petroleum and sugar transactions with the USSR) is also carried out in convertible currency.

If Cuba could not escape the structure of the world economy, its leaders argued, it might as well use that economy. Mistakes have been made, especially with regard to the world sugar market in the early 1960s. But, in general, Cuban economic diplomacy has been effective as it has sought to join, rather than avoid, the world market; the exception was the early 1980s, when Cuba disengaged from the non-Communist world market and deepened its dependence on the USSR and other CMEA countries. This policy created new problems and was partly reversed in December 1984. In the second half of the 1980s Cuba has sought to resume its links with the world market economy, though limited in its capacity to trade by its own domestic economic problems. For the most part, Cuban trade has been strongly responsive to the market, and Cuba has manipulated effectively the politics and economics of market-economy countries.

Markets and Politics in Cuban Foreign Policy

The 1960s

Western Europe, Canada, and Japan never went along with the U.S. and Latin American isolation of Cuba. Instead, they contributed through trade to the survival of revolutionary rule in Cuba. Despite dominance in its relations with other industrialized market-economy countries, the United States has been unable to coerce compliance on a wide array of economic issues. As a result, the international system is less hierarchical and more polycentric in political-economic areas than in political-military areas. The industrialized market-economy countries had economic interests of their own in Cuba: moreover, their continued relations with Cuba became, for some, a symbol of their independence from parts of U.S. policy.

In 1961, as the United States tightened its trade embargo and supported an invasion of Cuba, Cuban exports to the United Kingdom, Japan, and West Germany increased from their 1960 level; Cuban exports to Canada fell. That same year Cuban imports from Canada and Japan rose, though imports from West Germany and the United Kingdom fell.[4] The following list presents the percentage distribution of the value of Cuban trade with non-Communist countries *other than the United States* in the first years of revolutionary rule.[5]

	Percentage of Cuban exports to non-Communist countries	*Percentage of Cuban imports from non-Communist countries*
1960	23.0	32.8
1961	21.9	26.3
1962	17.2	17.1
1963	32.6	14.8
1964	40.8	32.5
1965	21.8	24.0
1967	18.8	20.9

Cuban trade with the non-Communist world (excluding the United States) fell from 1960 to 1962, as the U.S. government hoped it would. The world price of sugar nearly tripled from 1962 to 1963, however, and the value of Cuban exports to the non-Communist world rose again in 1963 and 1964. Cuban imports from non-Communist countries increased sharply in 1964. The world price of sugar fell again late in 1964, and subsequent Cuban trade with non-Communists declined in value.

The initial decline in Cuban trade with non-Communists after 1960 reflected many other countries' accommodation of U.S. policy, the decisions adopted by the Latin American countries to break with Cuba, and policies adopted by France and Spain for their own reasons. The cutback in Cuban imports reflected the Cuban economy's collapse and its inability to buy imports from 1961 to 1963. The recovery of Cuba's non-Communist trade in 1963 and 1964 shows a powerful market response from both Cuba and its non-Communist trade partners. Their trade boomed. Thus economic trends, on balance, explain much of the variation in Cuban trade with non-Communist countries.

Nonetheless, politics shaped the market. Cuba's relations with France, Spain, the United Kingdom, and Switzerland in the 1960s illustrate aspects of its economic diplomacy. In part because of Cuba's strong support for Algeria's war of independence against France, Cuban exports to France fell from 1.4 percent of the total value of Cuban exports in 1960 to 0.3 percent in 1962; imports from France fell from 2.0 percent of the Cuban total to 0.2 percent over the same period. Cuba's political and ideological goals outweighed its trade interests. After Algeria's independence, this obstacle to good Franco-Cuban relations was removed. Moreover, General Charles de Gaulle's government sought to demonstrate its independence from the United States, while Cuba wanted both trade in high-quality products and more independence from the USSR in the wake of the 1962 missile crisis. According to Castro, "We always saw with sympathy DeGaulle's independent spirit."[6] In 1964, Cuba signed a contract with the French firm Berliot to buy three hundred heavy trucks and tractors worth ten million dollars; this purchase was financed by a three-year trade credit. By 1967 France was buying 2.1 percent of Cuban exports and supplying 4.1 percent of Cuban imports.[7]

Trade with Spain throughout the 1960s also reflected political events. On January 20, 1960, speaking on nationwide television, Castro denounced a conspiracy to overthrow his government. He described the conspirators as the U.S. and Spanish ambassadors in Cuba, landowners, war criminals, and thieves. The outraged Spanish ambassador, Juan Pablo de Lojendio, went to the studio where Castro was speaking to protest. A brawl ensued on camera, and the next day Cuba demanded Lojendio's removal.[8] In 1961 the Cuban government's struggle with the Roman Catholic church reached a climax. In September the government arrested 131 priests (18 percent of the total in Cuba), 86 of whom were Spaniards, and deported them to Spain.[9] Also in 1961 the Spanish government refused to import tobacco from Cuba until the Cuban government paid what was owed to the former owners of tobacco firms that had been expropriated in Cuba. Cuban exports to Spain fell from 1.2 percent in 1960 to 0.8 percent in 1961; Cuban imports from Spain fell from 2.1 to 0.8.[10] By 1963 Spain's official airline, Iberia, had suspended all flights to Cuba for fear that the U.S. government would prevent it from flying to the United States.[11]

Spain's relations with Cuba, its last colony in the Americas, were complex. Neither government broke off diplomatic relations. The Spanish government did not reward Ambassador Lojendio, and it soon came to see the religious conflict as a dispute between the Cuban government and the Roman Catholic church, not as a dispute between Cuba and Spain. Although Spain's trade with Cuba declined in part because Spain retaliated against Cuba, Spain never formally supported the U.S. trade embargo.[12]

Spain and Cuba made a deal to settle their differences. The Spanish government wanted to discourage Cuban support for opposition to General Francisco Franco's dictatorship. Cuba, for its part, did not wish to turn the resident Spanish population against the regime. In 1970, 74,026 Spanish citizens were permanent residents of Cuba, accounting for 58 percent of all foreigners permanently residing there.[13] Castro also recognized "Spain's resistance to the pressure that the United States put on it to break commercial relations with Cuba." He was conscious that ordinary Cubans, who consumed products imported from Spain, would be hurt by a trade break. And, he said, in the face of U.S. efforts to isolate Cuba, "it was a matter of sheer necessity for our country" to develop its relations with Spain.[14]

In November 1963 Spain and Cuba signed a three-year trade treaty—the first formal breach of the U.S.-initiated embargo by a Western European government. Spain agreed to pay Cuba $0.1142 per pound of sugar in 1963, well above prevailing world prices. It further agreed to pay $0.0983 per pound in 1964 and 1965. (The Soviet price had been set at $0.0611 per pound in June 1963 and remained at that level for the rest of the decade.) Cuba began to buy Spanish trucks and merchant and fishing ships, giving Spain an outlet for its manufactured exports (Spain was often uncompetitive in such exports in the international market). Iberia resumed flights to Cuba.[15] Cuba formulated the rule of the precedence of state-to-state relations (see Chapter 5) and applied it to Franco's Spain, pledging that it would not interfere in Spain's internal affairs. Franco and Castro began a relationship that proved to be beneficial for both.

Spain became Cuba's largest non-Communist trading partner (ranking fourth or fifth overall in its purchases of Cuban exports) and its first- or second-ranking non-Communist supplier of imports for the remainder of the 1960s.[16] In 1964, after Cuban exile groups killed three crewmen while attacking a Spanish merchant ship trading with Cuba, Spain's information minister, Manuel Fraga, publicly criticized U.S. policy toward Cuba. Because Fraga had always spoken for Spain's conservatives, this event highlighted the Franco regime's internal consensus about its relations with Cuba. In 1965 the trade treaty was renegotiated. Spain agreed to buy Cuban sugar for five years at $0.0671 per pound, three times the prevailing world price and still above the Soviet price. In 1966 Spain raised, but did not press, a concern for thirty-three Spanish citizens who were political prisoners in Cuba.[17] In sum, in these most difficult years for Cuba, its relations with Franco's Spain were excellent. No wonder Cuba observed official mourning when Franco died in 1975. A decade later Castro told the Spanish press of his personal appreciation for Franco's decision to oppose the United States: "'Do not touch Cuba' was his clear command."[18]

By contrast, Cuba's relations with the United Kingdom were tortuous. During the revolution, the British sold twelve war planes to the Batista government after the United States cut off its arms sales in March 1958.[19] In retaliation Castro decreed, on October 19, 1958, that all British property would be subject to expropriation after revolutionary victory.[20] Surprisingly, two weeks after victory Castro visited the British ambassador to Cuba and assured the British government of his desire for good relations. Nonetheless, the Cuban workers of a partly British oil refining company operating in Havana, Royal Dutch Shell, went on strike. On February 6, 1959, Castro affirmed that Shell property would not be expropriated "because that would be a bad tactic at this time." He approved Shell's offer to remove its top management, to raise salaries by 50 to 100 percent, and to donate $250,000 to the new government for housing and agrarian projects. He asked the workers to end the strike, the government to rescind his wartime decree, and the Cuban public to call off a solidarity boycott against British products.[21] The British released five war planes, bought by Batista but not yet delivered, in May 1959. When in the fall Cuba sought to buy more war planes from the British, the British refused, in part because the United States objected.[22]

Nonmilitary U.K.-Cuban trade continued, however. British purchases of Cuban exports rose yearly from 1960 through 1963; Cuban imports from Britain during the same period fell principally because Cuba lacked hard currency.[23] Cuba's trade breakthrough with the United Kingdom occurred in January 1964, when Leyland Motors, backed by the British government, agreed to sell Cuba four hundred buses worth $11.2 million, plus $1 million in spare parts; this purchase was financed by a five-year trade credit.[24] Together with Cuba's new contracts with Spain and France, this agreement broke the U.S. global trade embargo. Henceforth, Cuban trade with Western European countries would rise or fall depending mostly on Cuba's ability to pay, not on U.S.-imposed political constraints.

The next turning point in Cuba's economic diplomacy resulted largely from Swiss actions. In 1964, to ensure that relations with Western Europe and Canada would remain unimpaired, Castro announced Cuba's willingness to discuss compensation for expropriated property. Initial discussions with the United Kingdom did not succeed.[25] Switzerland followed through on Cuba's offer to seek compensation for Nestle and other Swiss properties that had been expropriated in Cuba. The discussions were slow and difficult because Cuba was looking for a "model" to apply in other cases. On March 2, 1967, Cuba agreed to pay Nestle 18.04 million Swiss francs for its three food plants over eight years. Compensation payments began immediately and continued on schedule. In return, Switzerland agreed to buy 40,000 tons of sugar per year for eight years at prevailing world prices. The Swiss government calculated that about one-third the value of its sugar purchases would be used by Cuba to pay for Nestle's compensation.[26]

This was a creative solution to a thorny problem. The Swiss drove a hard bargain; their firm was compensated and they bought sugar (unlike Spain or the Soviet Union) at prices no higher than world market prices. But Cuba set a precedent for future compensation cases; it ensured a modest but steady market for its sugar in Switzerland; and it demonstrated its pragmatism at a time when relations with the USSR and with Latin American countries had deteriorated. As Cuba's most radical period in domestic and foreign policy began, its agreement to compensate the Swiss created new opportunities for flexibility.

France followed the Swiss example and signed a compensation agreement with Cuba on March 16, 1967. Cuba agreed to pay 10.86 million French francs for expropriated French property over five years. Unlike Switzerland, France already had substantial trade with Cuba (see Table 7.1); thus no additional trade agreement was made.[27] Canada also began negotiations with Cuba over compensation for expropriations, but no agreement would be reached until 1980. Nonetheless, the discussions in the 1960s on this issue paved the way for improved Cuban relations with Canada.[28] Canadian banks had not been formally expropriated in 1960; they reached their own compensation agreement with Cuba and stopped operations there. These banks continued to serve as Cuba's international bankers. In the early 1960s, apart from the socialist countries, Cuba maintained convertible currency accounts only in the Royal Bank of Canada and in the Bank of Nova Scotia.[29]

Cuba's compensation agreements with Switzerland and France were possible because the claims of each country were modest and because none had subscribed to U.S. policies against Cuba. Spain, whose claims were much larger, could not reach a compensation agreement with Cuba until 1986. Spain first raised the question of compensation in 1965; a broad framework for discussions, but no settlement, was reached in 1967. Spain raised the subject again in 1975, but not until 1978 did Cuba even agree to a detailed discussion of issues preventing a settlement.[30] Unsurprisingly, no progress was made on compensating U.S. firms.

By the end of the 1960s, as Cuba's relations with the Soviet Union, China, the United States, and most of Latin America deteriorated and as Cuba increased its support for revolution in other countries, relations with Western Europe, Canada, and Japan, though not warm, were generally correct; though not close, they were mutually beneficial; and though not fundamental for either partner, they undermined the U.S. embargo's efficacy. Cuba's trade relations with capitalist countries had broken its commercial and political isolation. Cuba had not managed well what it should have handled best—its relations with Communist countries and its support for revolutionary movements—but it made very good use of economic and political opportunities in the capitalist world. At the moment of its greatest international revolutionary militancy, Cuba paradoxically showed a pragmatic streak in its relations with the non-Communist world.

The 1970s and 1980s

Market factors as well as political conditions during the first half of the 1970s were much more favorable for Cuban international relations than in the 1960s. However, both deteriorated during the second half of the 1970s in response to worsened international economic conditions and to the unanticipated costs of Cuban political decisions.

During the early 1970s Cuba achieved political and economic breakthroughs in its relations with industrialized market-economy countries, thanks both to its greater political moderation in some areas of policy and to the rise in the world price of sugar. Cuba was perceived as more moderate because of the bargains it made with increasing frequency after 1969 with Latin American governments; Cuba turned away from supporting revolution in those countries in exchange for diplomatic relations and pledges not to support hostile actions against Cuba.

The average world market price of sugar increased fifteenfold from 1968 to 1974; the Soviet price for Cuban sugar only tripled over the same period. The average world price exceeded the Soviet price for Cuban sugar in both 1972 and 1974. In 1971 the USSR bought 32 percent of Cuba's sugar ex-

Table 7.1   Cuban trade with selected capitalist countries, 1958–1986

	1958	1965	1970	1975	1977
Percent of total Cuban exports going to:					
Spain	2.1	4.9	3.9	7.7	3.9
Sweden	0.7	0.6	0.9	0.6	0.3
Switzerland	0.9	0.4	0.2	0.2	0.6
France	1.1	1.5	1.3	0.6	0.8
West Germany	1.0	0.1	0.3	0.2	0.3
United Kingdom	5.0	1.9	1.7	0.4	0.6
Canada	2.2	0.7	0.9	2.2	1.4
Japan	6.4	3.1	10.3	7.5	1.5
Percent of total Cuban imports coming from:					
Spain	1.7	5.4	2.8	4.9	4.5
Sweden	0.5	0.2	0.5	1.5	1.0
Switzerland	0.4	0.2	1.0	0.8	0.6
France	0.9	2.2	4.6	3.4	2.0
West Germany	3.1	0.6	2.6	4.5	1.9
United Kingdom	2.8	5.8	4.5	4.1	1.4
Canada	2.3	1.8	2.1	3.2	1.6
Japan	0.6	0.5	2.6	11.6	8.4
Cuba's balance of trade with (millions of pesos):					
Spain	2.6	− 12.9	3.9	74.1	− 41.9
Sweden	1.0	1.8	2.6	− 27.3	− 26.4
Switzerland	3.1	0.7	− 11.6	− 18.7	− 4.7
France	0.9	− 8.9	− 46.6	− 88.0	− 47.6
West Germany	− 16.8	− 4.6	− 30.8	− 135.5	− 56.7
United Kingdom	15.0	− 37.6	− 41.5	− 115.1	− 31.7
Canada	− 2.1	− 10.3	− 19.1	− 34.0	− 14.4
Japan	42.2	17.1	74.7	− 138.5	− 248.4

ports by value; Japan bought 15 percent. In 1972, however, the Soviets bought only 26 percent of Cuban sugar exports by value, while the Japanese bought 23 percent. The non-Communist world's share of Cuban exports rose to an all-time high of 47.3 percent in 1972 and remained high at 43.3 percent in 1974. The non-Communist world's share of Cuban imports reached 39.5 percent in 1974 and peaked at 51.4 percent in 1975.[31] Cuba thus proved remarkably responsive to the market. It sold wherever it could get the highest price and, after accumulating reserves, it bought wherever it

1978	1979	1980	1981	1982	1983	1984	1985	1986
1.7	2.3	1.2	1.5	1.8	1.7	1.2	1.7	—
0.1	0.2	0.1	0.4	0.1	0.1	0.1	0.1	0.1
0.8	0.3	1.8	0.6	1.1	0.6	0.7	1.2	1.0
0.7	0.7	0.6	1.1	0.9	1.1	0.6	1.1	0.9
0.5	0.8	0.4	0.3	0.9	1.2	0.3	0.3	0.2
0.3	0.5	0.4	0.4	0.5	0.6	0.3	0.5	0.3
1.7	2.1	2.9	2.8	0.9	0.7	0.8	0.5	0.7
2.8	2.2	2.8	2.8	0.9	1.3	0.9	1.3	2.1
2.1	2.9	3.0	3.2	1.7	1.7	1.5	2.2	—
0.4	0.5	0.8	0.7	0.6	0.3	0.4	0.3	0.3
0.6	0.8	0.9	1.0	0.3	0.5	0.3	0.3	0.3
1.1	1.1	2.6	2.1	0.6	1.6	1.4	1.2	0.7
2.1	2.0	1.8	1.9	1.0	1.0	1.3	1.0	1.1
1.6	1.7	1.7	1.2	0.9	1.5	1.3	1.3	1.0
1.1	1.0	2.4	1.5	0.9	0.6	0.8	0.7	0.7
4.2	3.4	3.9	3.1	2.5	1.4	3.0	2.7	3.5
−14.6	−26.4	−92.7	−98.9	−7.2	−13.1	−43.3	−75.1	—
−11.5	−13.8	−33.7	−22.2	−28.7	−13.7	−29.0	−20.8	−14.1
6.3	−16.6	33.4	−26.4	38.1	2.7	17.8	46.0	30.3
−15.9	−17.0	−93.6	−59.8	11.5	−38.7	−64.3	−30.9	−6.5
−57.7	−46.8	−66.1	−85.7	−9.7	3.7	−77.1	−65.9	−73.6
−46.8	−41.8	−62.3	−46.9	−25.4	−62.0	−77.3	−77.7	−61.9
19.1	36.8	4.0	40.9	−1.1	1.9	−12.9	−26.6	−16.2
−54.9	−49.3	−70.1	−41.6	−64.8	−15.5	−167.3	−140.6	−154.0

Sources: Comité Estatal de Estadísticas, *Anuario estadístico de Cuba, 1982, 1983, 1984, 1985, 1986* (Havana).

could get the best deal. It diversified its trade relations, moving away from the Soviet Union and the CMEA, and found no significant political obstacles to this expanded trade with capitalist countries. This diversification of trade was accomplished in part by increased Cuban sugar output after 1972; at key moments, however, Cuba actually diverted sugar deliveries from Communist and toward capitalist countries. For example, from 1971 to 1972 sugar cane output fell by 12.6 percent; crude sugar exports to the USSR fell by 30.6 percent, but crude sugar exports to Japan fell by only 0.3 percent.[32]

The first half of the 1970s was atypical in its high sustained world prices for sugar and, consequently, in the high levels of Cuban trade with capitalist countries. The more normal, long-run trends in Cuban trade with selected capitalist countries are summarized in Table 7.1. In general, these countries' shares of Cuban exports and imports over time are stable, with some noteworthy variations. Trade with capitalist countries increased in 1980–81, when world sugar prices rose substantially (see Table 4.1), compared with the late 1970s, indicating yet again Cuba's responsiveness to the market. Cuba diverted sugar shipments from the USSR to sell to capitalist countries. Overall, the quantity of Cuban raw sugar exports fell by 14 percent from 1979 to 1980; the quantity shipped to the USSR fell by 29 percent, while the quantity shipped to Japan fell by only 10 percent.[33] Nevertheless, Cuba diverted less of its trade away from the CMEA countries than it had done in the earlier periods of high world market sugar prices (see also Tables 4.2 and 4.3).

Cuban trade policy changed markedly after 1981. Cuba had cut in half its imports from the industrialized capitalist countries by 1982. The eight countries listed in Table 7.1 supplied 17.1 percent of Cuban imports in 1980, but only 8.5 percent in 1982. The primary reasons for the change were financial. Cuba had increased its imports from these countries in 1980–81 because it had earned more convertible currency from sugar sales; as the world price of sugar fell, Cuba—which had an already high and rising negative trade balance—had to cut back sharply on imports. The deepening of Cuba's dependence on trade with the CMEA stemmed in part, then, from Cuba's inability to export enough to pay for the imports it needed from the industrialized West; therefore, it had to turn to the CMEA.

Cuba has had great difficulty in managing abundance; it is more effective at managing scarcities and shortages. In 1963–64, the first high world sugar prices led to an import buying binge that increased Cuba's overall trade deficit from 12.3 million pesos in 1961 to over 300 million pesos per year in 1963 and 1964. Foreign Trade Minister Alberto Mora was dismissed in the summer of 1964 and import purchases were sharply restricted; by 1965 the overall trade deficit fell to 175 million pesos.[34] A comparison between 1970 and 1975, years of low and high world sugar prices, respectively, shows the same pattern. Cuba's trade deficit worsened in 1975 in relation to every country in Table 7.1 except Spain. Cuba reduced its trade deficit with the industrialized capitalist countries only by 1978, when world sugar prices were at their lowest point in the second half of the 1970s. The same pattern can be seen in 1980–81, when world sugar prices were high compared with either 1978 or 1982. In 1980 Marcelo Fernández, Cuba's foreign trade minister, was also dismissed.

A related though slightly different problem arose in 1984. From 1983 to 1984, after a period of sluggish growth, the Cuban economy grew officially by 7.4 percent (in terms of global social product, GSP, at constant prices). Imports from market-economy countries increased 41 percent from 1983 to 1984, and Cuba's trade deficit with these countries jumped from 45.8 million pesos in 1983 to 579.6 million pesos in 1984. An emergency revision of the government's 1985 economic plan was adopted in December 1984, imposing new austerity measures and reorganizing the economy to generate exports.[35] In June 1985 Humberto Pérez, president of the Central Planning Board and the architect of Cuba's economic policies for nearly a decade, lost his job.

Cuba has faced a U.S. trade embargo, economic sanctions from most Latin American countries, and mismanagement of and inefficiencies in its economy. Its leaders have learned best how to manage with less. The infrequent periods of high world market prices for sugar erode the restraint of government leaders and agencies. A Spartan society, disciplined in the face of adversity, behaves like a child in a candy store in the rare moments of abundance. Cuba's trade deficit is worse when sugar prices are higher because its discipline in import purchases breaks down. Thus the U.S. government's ongoing embargo on trade with Cuba may have an effect that is the opposite of what the U.S. government intends. What the Cuban government manages best is U.S. economic hostility; what it manages least well are episodes of prosperity and active engagement in the world market. It is the specter of wealth, not of scarcity, that haunts the Cuban revolution.

This pattern can be seen in specific cases. Cuban trade with Japan, for example, has reponded almost exclusively to market forces. (By Japan's count, in 1973 the Japanese-Cuban community consisted of only 694 people, including Cuban citizens of Japanese origin and Japanese citizens who were Cuban residents.)[36] Japan never adhered to the U.S. trade embargo on Cuba. In 1981 Cuba accounted for about 0.14 percent of Japan's worldwide trade.[37] In general, the significance of trade with Japan for Cuba has declined since the mid-1970s, as Cuba has deepened its relations with the CMEA and as Japan has relied on other sugar suppliers. Japan's retreat from trade with Cuba stemmed largely from a Cuban miscalculation in 1975. Japan was ready to sign a multiyear trade agreement, guaranteeing a minimum price of $0.17 per pound for one million tons of sugar. This amounted to about half of Cuban exports to the world market. When Cuba held out for a minimum price of $0.19, Japan found other suppliers.[38]

In the view of Vice President Carlos Rafael Rodríguez, Cuban trade with Japan in the 1980s was also hurt by U.S. policies, although he reported that "we have excellent relations with Japan despite its government which always agrees with the United States."[39] On the whole, however, market factors explain most of the reduction in Cuba's trade with Japan in the 1980s: Japan has less reason to buy from Cuba, and Cuba has less foreign exchange to buy from Japan.

Spain's relations with Cuba responded to market forces in the 1970s more than in the 1960s. Spain had typically paid a price for Cuban sugar that was well above the world price and often higher than the price paid by the USSR. The Soviet price for Cuban sugar was 134 pesos per ton in 1965; the Spanish price was 140 pesos; the Soviet price was 482 pesos in 1975, while the Spanish price was 569.[40] In December 1974, with the world price over $0.60 per pound, Spain agreed to pay Cuba $0.30 per pound in 1975 and $0.23 per pound in 1976 and 1977. The world price in 1975 turned out to be $0.20, and it declined, oscillating between $0.12 and $0.08 in 1976 and 1977. Then, Spain increased domestic sugar production and cut back its purchases from Cuba. Though Spain agreed to pay $0.21 per pound in 1978 (about triple the prevailing world price), its share of Cuban exports fell to less than a quarter of the 1975 level.[41] The long-term effect of the premium prices that Spain paid for Cuban sugar was to stimulate Spain to cut sharply its purchases of Cuban sugar.

In the cases of Japan and Spain, Cuba's efforts to obtain sugar prices well above world market levels backfired. Japan refused to sign a trade agreement with Cuba because it would be too expensive. Spain did sign, but it later found ways to ensure that it would never again pay such high prices for Cuban sugar. Cuba's greed thus cost it its two most important non-Communist sugar markets.

Although Cuba's relations with the industrialized capitalist countries responded largely to market conditions, politics continued to influence these relations. Cuba's political relations with France deteriorated after de Gaulle's presidency.[42] In the early 1970s Cuban exports to and imports from France were well below the annual averages of the previous decade.[43] Just as Franco-Cuban relations seemed ready to improve in 1975, the French Interior Ministry expelled three Cuban diplomats because of their contacts with the international terrorist Carlos, who had killed two French police officers days before. Though Cuba denied that its agents had participated in any of Carlos's acts of violence and asserted that it opposed terrorist methods, Franco-Cuban relations were set back.[44] (Cuban officials probably did have contacts with Carlos in order to be informed about his plans—more evidence of Cuba's relations with untrustworthy movements.)

Relations deteriorated further when France supplied airplanes in March 1977 to transport Moroccan troops that were sent to Zaire's Shaba province to help President Mobutu repel the invasion of former Shaba gendarmes based in Angola. Relations continued to deteriorate when French paratroopers were sent to Shaba in May 1978 to repel a second invasion from forces based in Angola. Although Cuban troops were involved in neither invasion, the French appeared to expect a military confrontation with Cuba. Vice President Rodríguez charged that France had "assumed the most aggressive role in Africa" of all the "neocolonial powers."[45] Franco-Cuban trade—especially Cuban imports from France—fell in the late 1970s.

Trade recovered somewhat, as did political relations, after François Mitterrand's election as President in 1981. French firms built paper and cardboard factories and thermoelectric plants in Cuba. But part of the U.S. trade embargo—the U.S. ban on buying French products that included nickel imported from Cuba—continued to hurt Franco-Cuban trade in the 1980s. France had to cut back its Cuban nickel imports as a result.[46] Also in the 1980s Cuba welcomed French opposition to U.S. policy toward El Salvador and Nicaragua. Still, Cuban officials worried about the reduction in French economic aid to Nicaragua (begun in 1983) and the increased French criticism of Sandinista policies. In 1986 Franco-Cuban political relations deteriorated somewhat when Ricardo Bofill, a dissident Marxist scholar active in a human rights group in Cuba, found asylum for five months in the French embassy in Havana; Cuba subsequently expelled Agence France Presse and Reuters correspondents in Havana who were working on stories on the human rights group.[47]

Cuban relations with Canada show a similar trend. Trade increased during the first half of the 1970s in response to market conditions, but Canada was also motivated by politics. In 1974 the Canadian government guaranteed the Montreal Locomotive Works–Worthington Ltd.'s agreement to sell twenty-five locomotives to Cuba even though the U.S. firm Studebaker Worthington owned 52 percent of the company. Under U.S. law, the firm could thus not sell to Cuba.[48] In 1975 Canada granted Cuba $100 million (Canadian) in trade credits that could be used within a year and were repayable in ten years. Canada also donated $3 million (Canadian) for technical assistance in health.[49] Subsidized Canadian loans to Cuba in 1975 amounted to an additional $9.8 million (Canadian).[50] In January 1976 Canada's Prime Minister, Pierre Trudeau, became the first head of a NATO government to visit Cuba. Both countries explored possible Canadian investments to develop Cuba's nickel resources; had this project gone forward, it might have provided Cuba with an alternative to the slow-moving CMEA investments in Cuban nickel.[51]

Difficulties were also apparent in Cuban-Canadian relations, however. In

January 1977 Canada expelled five Cuban diplomats engaged in intelligence work, accusing them of recruiting undercover agents to go to southern Africa. Cuba admitted that part of the accusation was true, saying that its relations with "third parties" were designed to prevent anti-Cuban Angolans from operating against Cubans and the Luanda government.[52] In 1977, Cuban-Canadian trade fell to half the 1975 level, and trade remained generally lower in subsequent years than in the early 1970s. Nonetheless, Cuba's relations with Canada remained good in some areas. In May 1977 Canada agreed to allow Cuba's fleet to fish within Canada's 200-mile maritime zone—a right Canada denied to U.S. fishing fleets. In 1980 Cuba at last agreed to pay $850,000 (Canadian) over a three-year period to compensate Canadians for expropriations at the beginning of revolutionary rule (in 1978 Canadian Shell, the main owner in 1960 of Royal Dutch Shell of Cuba, had transferred its shares of Shell of Cuba to a Netherlands-based company, thereby removing an economic obstacle to the settlement of other Canadian claims).[53]

Cuba's political relations with Spain had improved somewhat in the early 1980s as Spain's new Socialist government, headed by Felipe González, sought to prevent U.S. military intervention in Nicaragua. Relations were then set back in December 1985 after four Cuban embassy employees attempted to kidnap, on a Madrid street, a Cuban vice minister (who admitted accepting nearly $500,000 in illegal commissions) who was trying to defect in Spain; passersby stopped the kidnapping, and Spain expelled the four Cubans.[54] To improve relations González visited Cuba in November 1986, obtaining at last Cuba's agreement to pay about $41.6 million to Spaniards in compensation for all property seized in the early years of revolutionary rule; $15 million would be paid in cash, and the remainder in merchandise, over a fifteen-year period. (Spanish owners were not pleased; they had valued their property in 1959 at about $3 billion.)[55]

After the visit, however, several events underscored the complexities of Cuban-Spanish relations. At Spain's request Cuba freed Eloy Gutiérrez Menoyo, a Spanish citizen who had served twenty-one years in prison having been convicted of trying to overthrow the Cuban government. In December 1986 the Spanish Parliament excluded Cuba from participating in the Fourth Conference of Iberoamerican Democratic Parliaments, held in Spain (the Cuban National Assembly was a member of the Latin American Parliament since 1985).[56] Such political issues were likely to continue to keep democratic Spain occasionally at odds with Marxist-Leninist Cuba. Nevertheless, four months later the Spanish government awarded Cuba a $50 million credit to finance Cuban purchases of Spanish products. From

1982 to 1985 Spain was Cuba's principal trade partner in Western Europe and the one Western European country most likely to buy a wide array of products from Cuba.[57] Such economic interests were likely to sustain Cuban-Spanish relations through momentary crises.

Cuba's ties to illegal and unconventional international operations hurt its efforts to improve its relations with France, Canada, and Spain. Although Cuba often blames the United States or other adversaries for its international setbacks, in these cases Cuba bore most of the blame. Cuba's overseas military activities also hurt its relations with the industrialized West.

Sweden is a case in point. Sweden did not have embassy-rank diplomatic representation in Cuba until the 1960s. Although Cuban-Swedish trade fell in the early 1960s in response to the Cuban economy's weakness, Sweden never joined the U.S. trade embargo, and Cuban imports from Sweden became significant in the early 1970s. After 1970 Sweden included Cuba in its foreign aid program, increasing its aid to Cuba every year from 1970 to 1975, when it reached over 12 million pesos. Upon the overthrow of Chilean President Salvador Allende in 1973, Cuba asked Sweden to represent its interests in Chile. In July 1975, the Cuban press reported that "Sweden is the western nation that has been the friendliest to Cuba."[58] In response to Cuba's dispatch of troops to Angola only weeks later, however, Sweden cut its aid to Cuba for 1976 from $13.8 to $9.2 million.[59] Cuban-Swedish trade declined in the late 1970s. All the Scandinavian countries adopted the view that Cuba's overseas programs meant that it did not need their aid; they reduced their grants to Cuba while retaining trade credits.[60] Nonetheless, the Scandinavian countries, Sweden in particular, continued some grants.[61] They also opposed U.S. policy toward Nicaragua in the 1980s—a position that Cuba applauded.

Western European countries reacted even more negatively to Cuba's second overseas military expedition—to Ethiopia in 1977–78. For example, the Dutch government in the mid-1970s signed an agreement to provide technical aid to Cuba in the form of donations or loans on easy credit terms to clean up Havana harbor, to install pollution-reduction equipment, to buy medical equipment, and to develop the Cuban baby food industry. Dutch low-interest credits to Cuba from 1975 to 1978 were worth a cumulative total of $18.4 million.[62] In 1978, however, coinciding with the Cuban involvement in Ethiopia, the Netherlands decided not to renew its grant programs to Cuba, though it continued small subsidized credit programs.[63]

Cuban trade relations with the United Kingdom deteriorated after Cuba's intervention in Angola and remained at a lower level than during the 1960s for the next decade. After Cuba's entry into the Horn of Africa, in early

1978 British Foreign Secretary David Owen criticized Cuba so sharply that the Cuban government criticized him personally and publicly in the press.[64] Nonetheless, displaying the same pragmatism first evident in the late 1960s, in October 1978 Cuba agreed to compensate thirty-nine British citizens whose property had been seized in the early years of revolutionary rule—a total sum of 350,000 pesos. British citizens who were not U.S. residents were paid immediately; with regard to those residing in the United States, Cuba agreed only to hold the amount due in a "suspense account" from which payment would be made only if such a person became a resident of a country other than the United States. The claims of several British companies (and of the still partly British Shell of Cuba) were not settled, however, nor are these claims being actively pursued by the firms.[65] Although this settlement removed an irritant in British-Cuban relations, bilateral relations remained impaired compared to the period before Cuba's entry into wars in Africa. Cuba's subsequent relations with the United Kingdom are no better and no worse under Margaret Thatcher's government than under the preceding Labor government,[66] but they are considerably worse than under Labor and Tory governments before 1975. The cost to Cuba of its overseas activities, therefore, includes worsened relations with several industrial democracies. The political climate deteriorated, and trade and economic aid declined.

A final case in point is West Germany. Of all Western Europe, the Federal Republic has had the most politicized relations with Cuba for reasons that have little to do with U.S. policy. Cuba signed its first long-term commercial agreement with East Germany in December 1960; other agreements soon followed, and East Germany extended credits to Cuba for economic development. But Cuba delayed establishing formal diplomatic relations with East Germany until 1963 in order not to hurt its relations with West Germany. Following its standard policies, West Germany cut off diplomatic relations with Cuba after Cuba established formal ties with East Germany, although trade—conducted mostly by German subsidiaries in Spain—continued at a reduced level.[67] West German purchases from Cuba during the first half of the 1970s, when sugar prices were high, did not increase, though Cuban purchases of German goods did grow.[68] When West Germany established relations with East Germany and with other Eastern European countries, it changed its policy toward Cuba as well. Diplomatic relations were reestablished in 1975.

In late 1982 the Christian Democrats returned to power in the Federal Republic and reactivated a dormant issue: Because of its relations with East Germany, Cuba did not recognize West Berlin as part of the Federal Republic. West Germany has relations with all Warsaw Pact countries, regardless of their views on Berlin, but Cuba is not a member of the Warsaw Pact and is, therefore, not exempt from West Germany's insistence that all other countries recognize Berlin as West German or suffer poor relations with the Federal Republic. (West Germany takes literally Cuba's standing as a member of the Nonaligned Movement.) In the late 1980s the issue remained unresolved, weakening Cuban relations with West Germany.[69] Relations also deteriorated as a result of the change in West German policy toward Central America under the Christian Democrats. Their government edged closer to the U.S. government's positions, cut aid to Nicaragua, and increased it to El Salvador. Nonetheless, trade and tourism relations continued with Cuba, though at a low level, through the 1980s.[70]

In general, then, Cuba had surprisingly successful relations with the industrialized capitalist countries, other than the United States, in the 1960s—a development that helped break Cuba's political and commercial isolation. As Cuba became more politically moderate (by bargaining with Latin American governments), and as the price of sugar rose in the early 1970s, Cuba's relations with the industrialized capitalist countries improved further. They worsened after 1975, however, even though the U.S. embargo had weakened considerably. The reasons varied: Cuba's greed with regard to sugar prices in its relations with Japan and Spain, Cuba's ties with illegal political movements in the cases of France and Canada, and Cuba's overseas wars and foreign aid programs. The results were uniform: cooler political relations and loss of aid from and trade with the industrialized West in the late 1970s and, after a respite in 1980–81, again in the first half of the 1980s. Cuba's deepened dependence on CMEA countries, in short, did not stem only from their preferential treatment of Cuba or Cuba's fears of retaliation by U.S. allies. It was also the direct or indirect consequence of Cuban policies. Cuba lost an opportunity for excellent relations with Western Europe and Japan in the mid-1970s; that opportunity has not yet been regained.

Nonetheless, Cuban relations with industrialized market-economy countries (other than the United States) were on the whole fairly good in the 1980s. There were no major political disputes, although most European governments were critical of some of Cuba's African policies. Several disputes—such as the status of Berlin—seemed subject to eventual resolution. Cuba welcomed the steps taken by most West European governments in the 1980s to restrain U.S. actions against the Nicaraguan government. There were no serious political obstacles to greater Cuban trade with these countries—a major part of Cuba's economic strategy for the second half of the

1980s. In fact, during Cuba's big push to increase its exports in 1985, exports to market-economy countries increased twice as fast as exports to CMEA countries. And when Cuban exports fell in 1986, exports to market-economy countries fell only half as fast as exports to CMEA countries.[71] The main problem was the condition of the sugar market, hurt by European Economic Community (EEC) policies, and the lack of other products Cuba could export to earn hard currency and pay for debts.

The International Sugar Market

Cuba misjudged its interests in the world sugar market in the early 1960s, but the lessons it learned made it more effective in later years. The central questions for Cuba remained the same over time: How should it maintain its access to sugar importers in the non-Communist world? How could it keep the price of sugar in the world market high enough to make that trade profitable and to provide a high base line for calculating the price of sugar sold to Communist countries? The link between the world price of sugar and that paid by Communist countries was the unbreakable bond between the subsidized sugar trade with Communist countries and the world market. Cuba could not escape what it perceived as the curse of capitalism: prices that responded to supply and demand.

Sugar can be obtained from cane and from beets, and can be produced, therefore, in tropical and temperate climates. Thus sugar is one of the most widely produced agricultural commodities in the world. In the long run most countries that can produce sugar have done so. The ratio of world net exports to production fell from about a third in the early 1950s to a quarter in the late 1960s as more countries became self-sufficient in sugar production. About 60 percent of world sugar exports are traded through preferential agreements, such as those that the United States, the EEC, and the CMEA have had with their suppliers. The remainder—the so-called world market—has encompassed a steadily smaller share of the world sugar output since the early 1950s. Price trends in this residual market are strongly shaped by the output of a handful of large producer-exporters, including Cuba.[72]

In 1958, 65 percent of Cuban sugar exports by value went to the United States, amounting to 38 percent of U.S. consumption. The United States paid Cuba about twice the prevailing world market price in the 1950s.[73] Before as well as after the revolution, then, the Cuban sugar economy has depended on substantial external subsidies; these subsidies have been higher since the mid-1970s than before 1959.

Cuban sugar trade with the Soviet Union and Eastern Europe has been complex. The sugar production of the Soviet bloc doubled from the early 1950s to the late 1960s, but consumption more than doubled. Bulgaria and East Germany became net importers of sugar in the 1960s; Czech, Hungarian, and East German sugar production fell during the 1960s. The USSR, Poland, and Rumania increased their production during that decade, however; Poland remained an exporter of sugar and Rumania became one.[74] When the United States cut off its sugar imports from Cuba in 1960, CMEA countries did not need much Cuban sugar. Since that time they have increased their sugar consumption and have reached trade agreements on sugar that have benefited Cuba since the mid-1970s. In the early 1960s, however, they bought Cuban sugar and resold much of it in the world market, thereby contributing to market destabilization.

Before the Cuban revolution the world market was governed by the International Sugar Agreement, signed in 1953 by most exporting and importing countries and renewed in 1955 and 1958; the agreement set minimum and maximum prices.[75] Its main instrument was the allocation of quotas to exporting countries. In 1953 the Cuban quota was 43.2 percent of the world market by quantity. Its quota rose somewhat by 1958, but its market share fell to 37.2 percent because of the growth of world output.[76] Exports to the U.S. market were excluded from the agreement, but exports to Communist countries were included. If the world price fell below the minimum set by the agreement, quotas would be cut; if it rose above the maximum, quotas would be increased. The treaty served the interests both of exporters and of importers by maintaining the stability of price and supply. Because the agreement had worked well in the 1950s, the Castro government ratified the 1958 extension in July 1959.

In July 1960 Cuba was forced to violate the agreement by the U.S. government's decision to stop importing sugar from Cuba. To survive, Cuba sharply increased its exports to Communist countries. In September 1961 the international sugar conference met in Geneva. At the time, the world price of sugar was at an eighteen-year low, well below the standard set by the International Sugar Agreement. A key issue was the change in Cuba's trade patterns. A deal was offered to Cuba. The world quotas of the countries that had taken Cuba's place as a supplier of sugar in the U.S. market would be cut by one-third of their new exports to the United States. Cuba's world quota would rise to 5.65 million tons, equal to its 1958 world quota (2.415 million tons) plus its "predicted" U.S. quota in 1961 (3.235 million tons—115,000 tons higher than Cuba's U.S. sugar quota in 1960). This proposal allowed for only a slight increase of Cuban sugar production between 1958 and 1961.

Raúl Cepero Bonilla, Cuba's chief delegate, rejected this proposal. Cuba wanted a world quota of 6.8 million tons, which would take into account its much higher sugar production in 1961. (This higher production, of course, had helped to lower the world market price.) Cepero argued that Cuba's sales to Communist countries represented a net expansion of world demand and not simply a diversion of trade; he estimated the net growth in demand at 4 million tons. The original proposal would require Cuba either to cut back its expanded trade with the CMEA or to lose its traditional customers. Cepero admitted that Cuba had to sell more sugar to derive the same income because of the loss of U.S. preferential prices. However, the bargaining committee at the Geneva conference calculated, with Cuba's assent, that in 1960 the Communist countries had reexported to the world market 800,000 of the 2,271,000 tons of sugar they had bought from Cuba. (In fact, the actual net increase in world demand in 1960 was only about 1 million tons.) At the conference, Cuba got a second offer, raising its world quota to 6.15 million tons, which Cuba also rejected.[77]

This was a strategic error on Cuba's part. Cuba failed to recognize that its large 1961 harvest was an aberration and that its trade in sugar with non-Communist countries was already declining. Even in 1961 Cuban sugar exports were only 5.87 million tons, barely above the first proposed compromise; the second proposal would have allowed Cuban exports to grow. While Cuba estimated its sugar exports to Communist countries accurately for 1961, it had predicted 1.9 million tons of exports to non-Communist countries; in fact, it exported only 900,000 tons. Its total sugar exports fell to only 3.52 million tons in 1963.[78] In the 1960s, when world demand for sugar increased in fact only slightly, Cuba's sugar exports were simply diverted from one area of the market to another. Cuba's actions wrecked the international agreement (which ceased to function), damaged the structure of the world sugar market, and hurt itself because prices became unstable and generally lower.

When Cuban sugar production rose again in the late 1960s the modest growth in world demand and the lack of an international agreement brought world prices to lows unprecedented in decades. The Communist countries, especially the USSR, helped to keep world sugar prices low because they reexported about 56 percent of the sugar they imported from Cuba (about 1.874 million tons) between 1966 and 1970. In the short run, however, Communist reexports helped Cuba. These countries paid Cuba higher than world market prices; they relieved Cuba of the burden of finding buyers as prices fell; and they kept Cuba's direct exports to the world market within the boundaries of past export patterns, strengthening its position for the negotiations of a new sugar pricing agreement in the future.[79]

In October 1968 most sugar importing and sugar exporting countries signed a new International Sugar Agreement. Cuba was allocated a world quota of 2.15 million tons. The problem of reexports by Communist countries was addressed by imposing ceilings on Soviet sugar exports and on Cuban exports to other Eastern European countries.[80] The agreement cut world production and contributed to the recovery of the world sugar price in 1969. World prices then continued to rise (owing to production shortfalls) and, as a result, the agreement's procedures to regulate supply and demand broke down. Cuba abided by the terms of the agreement, cutting its net exports to the world market as required in 1969 and increasing them as required in 1970 and 1971. Its own production fell in the early 1970s, contributing to the continued sugar price rise. The United States did not sign the agreement because it objected to Cuba's participation; the EEC also did not sign because it did not accept restrictions on exports.[81] Cuba's reversal of its 1961 stand and its adherence to the agreement of 1968, at the moment of its greatest international revolutionary militancy, was noteworthy because Cuba signed even though it objected to several of the agreement's provisions.[82] As in the compensation agreements with the Swiss and the French, Cuba again showed its pragmatism.

A new international sugar conference met in 1973 as prices rose rapidly. Cuba proposed that the world sugar price be allowed to fluctuate between $0.06 and $0.09 per pound, compared with the 1968 agreement's range between 3.25 and 5.25 cents. Importer countries had proposed a price between 4.5 and 7.0 cents per pound. The extreme Cuban proposal allowed Brazil and Australia to play more moderate roles, proposing a price between 5.4 and 7.9 cents, but to no avail. No agreement was reached, and prices continued to rise.[83] During the 1973 conference Cuba collaborated with other Latin American countries, thus helping to improve its political relations with them. In November 1974, as sugar prices peaked, the Latin American and Caribbean sugar exporters—Cuba included—met for the first time and agreed to act in concert.[84]

In response to these high prices, world sugar output increased and prices fell again. In 1977, with world sugar prices below 8 cents per pound, another international sugar conference convened in Geneva and reached a new agreement. It was a triumph for Cuba, whose preferential trade with the CMEA was exempted from the agreement while most other preferential sugar trade agreements (the U.S., British, and Portuguese) had expired. Cuba still received the largest world export quota, even though Australia and Brazil had been exporting more sugar to the world market than Cuba in the years preceding the agreement. Marcelo Fernández, Cuba's foreign trade minister, compromised on various points but not on Cuba's decision to expand its sugar production and exports. At this conference Cuba again worked closely with other Latin American sugar exporters.[85] As Vice President Rodríguez put it, "Although temporary political differences sometimes separate us"—the Latin Americans had imposed collective economic sanctions on Cuba for a decade—"common economic interest . . . draws us close and moves us toward unity."[86]

The 1977 agreement was a failure in practice, however. The world sugar price was below the agreed-upon minimum of 11 cents per pound for all but twelve months of the seven-year agreement, despite the cuts in export quotas and other efforts to bolster prices. In response to bad harvests, the price skyrocketed in 1980, despite the suspension of the export quota limitations and other efforts to limit price increases. And prices fell just as drastically after 1981, despite the reimposition of quotas and of other measures.

The agreement was sabotaged by the EEC, the world's only major sugar producer that refused to sign it. The EEC's Common Agricultural Policy heavily subsidized high-cost sugar producers and their exports. Although the EEC was a net deficit area in sugar production in 1975, it became the world's second largest net exporter of sugar by 1981 and the largest by 1984, with a quarter of world market exports—almost twice Cuba's. EEC exports by quantity were larger than the entire reduction in exports undertaken by all other producers to bolster prices when these fell in 1981. The EEC reduced the volume of its exports, but not its market share, from 1982 to 1984.[87]

The United States, though a signatory, also undermined the agreement in response to pressures from domestic sugar producers. The U.S. Agriculture and Food Act of 1981 reinstated protection for domestic sugar producers, which had been discontinued in 1974. U.S. domestic sugar prices were propped up through tariffs and fees on imported sugar. In 1982, as world prices continued to fall, President Reagan reimposed restrictive import quotas on sugar, thereby diverting to the residual world market sugar that had been imported to the U.S. market; as a result, the world market price of sugar fell further.[88]

Cuba, too, contributed to the decline in world sugar prices by increasing the volume of its exports to the world market 19 percent from 1983 to 1984.[89] Cuba contributed to world overproduction by building sugar mills in Angola, Nicaragua, and Nigeria, and by giving technical assistance and other services to the sugar industries in these and in eight other countries. In 1987 Cuba agreed to build sugar mills in Vietnam and in Zaire.[90] Although it was rational in the short run for Cuba to export its services in an industry in which it has much experience, Cuban support for world sugar overproduction is not beneficial in the long run.

The 1977 agreement expired in December 1984; negotiations for a new agreement were unsuccessful. The world price of sugar fell to 4 cents a pound in 1985 though it rose from 6 to about 12 cents from 1986 to 1988. Cuba's market position weakened as exports from the EEC, Australia, and Brazil surged. Australia wanted a new agreement that included all internationally traded sugar, including Cuba's trade with the CMEA, while the EEC wanted its exports to be accepted. Cuba wanted an agreement that would keep prices from dropping and ensure its continued access to capitalist markets; it offered to include its sales to non-CMEA Communist countries (China and Yugoslavia) under the agreement and to cut its basic quota of 2.5 million tons to 2.35 million tons. But it refused to include its trade with the CMEA and to accept a proposed quota of 2.2 million tons. The only bright spot in the negotiations was the political situation of Cuba's continued collaboration with other Latin American sugar exporters.[91]

The logic of the market, of the U.S. domestic sugar industry, of Western Europe's autonomous politics—which had served Cuba so well before 1975—and of Cuba's own need to increase exports brought down the world sugar price in the mid-1980s. This decline foreshadowed drops in the price the CMEA might pay for Cuban sugar later in the 1980s. In 1984, at a time when Cuba had adopted a strategy to export more to countries that would pay in convertible currency, the price of its key export tumbled. The recovery of the world sugar price in 1986–88 was too modest to allow for sustained economic growth.

Alternatives to Sugar Dependence

Generations of Cubans have looked unsuccessfully for alternatives to dependence on sugar. Sugar exports have accounted for about 75 to 85 percent of the value of Cuban exports for the bulk of its history. In 1958 that proportion was 82 percent; in 1986 it was 80 percent (excluding reexports of Soviet crude oil). Cuba's traditional exports are sugar and its derivatives, tobacco and tobacco products, and raw and semiprocessed minerals. Nontraditional exports accounted for 9.8 percent of the value of exports in 1958 and for 18.3 percent in 1985. In 1985, however, 8.8 percent of Cuban exports were crude oil reexports (worth 527 million pesos), which were really a Soviet incentive to Cuban energy conservation. The crude oil reexports were crucial financially for Cuba—they were worth three times

Cuba's earnings in convertible currency from sugar exports to the world market in 1985—but were not part of its export profile. Thus true nontraditional exports (fish and other seafood, citrus, and other products, excluding crude oil) amounted to 9.5 percent of the value of Cuban exports (excluding crude oil) in 1985 and 10.4 percent in 1986. Exports earning convertible currency of all products other than sugar and crude oil were 84 percent of the 1983 figure in 1984, 116 percent in 1985, and 95 percent in 1986.[92]

Cuba's prospects for diversifying its exports may now be better than these numbers suggest, however. The preeminence of sugar and nickel in Cuba's export profile after 1975 has resulted from massive price subsidies from the USSR and other CMEA countries. Not all Cuban exports have been subsidized to the same extent; in fact, the real rate of growth of nonsugar exports has been higher than that of sugar exports.[93] Cuba has had some success stories in exporting nontraditional products and in increasing their share of exports. For example, the Cuban catch of fish and other seafood products, most of which are exported at unsubsidized prices in convertible currency, increased tenfold from 1958 to 1978. The output of citrus fruits and citrus exports also rose substantially; most Cuban citrus exports went to CMEA countries and were sold at subsidized prices.[94]

Nevertheless, in almost all cases, the products being exported in 1986 were already exported in 1958. In fact, Cuban exports of a great many traditional and nontraditional products fell from the 1950s to the 1960s, then increased again in the 1970s. To be sure, the increases since the 1970s have at times been substantial. For example, only 401 tons of cement (worth 6,000 pesos) were exported in 1958 as compared with over 200,000 tons (worth over 4 million pesos annually) from 1980 to 1984 (though falling drastically in 1985 and in 1986). Steel exports were worth only 11,000 pesos in 1958 but surpassed the multimillion mark in the early 1980s. Nonetheless, the 1958 level for exports of chemical products was surpassed only in 1981, and that for medicines only in 1983; exports of rope and string have yet to reach the 1958 level.[95]

In the 1980s Cuba began to export small quantities of many nontraditional products, though almost exclusively to non-CMEA countries.[96] By 1984, for example, Cuba exported over sixty different articles of sports equipment (especially for boxing) to twenty countries. By 1985 it exported about a million books a year to Latin American countries, plus several million textbooks to Angola and Nicaragua. By 1986 it exported two million tropical plants to European countries.[97] However, Cuba's diversification of trade has often been stymied by domestic problems. For instance, in 1984 the Cuban government estimated that about $500,000 worth of lobsters for potential exports had been stolen.[98] A major plant in Jagüey Grande exporting citrus fruit shipped its products through Cienfuegos harbor, where shipment delays, along with the poor quality of the product, caused the loss of export sales.[99] Despite Cuba's investments in modern tobacco technology, the quality of its cigars for export has fallen, according to the Cuban government, because of disorganization, inefficiency, poor training, poor quality control, statistical falsification, and labor absenteeism.[100]

Other problems have stemmed from Cuba's limited marketing experience. After years of wondering why some exports did not sell well, in the 1980s the government tried market research. When it found that Cuban candy was too sweet for international tastes, a new candy was developed for export. Cuban liqueurs were also too sweet and remain so, but new bottles were designed for duty-free exports. Cuban fresh tomatoes and avocados are too delicate for successful export to Europe; Cuba will have to invest in new methods of processing them for export. Cuban oranges are too sweet for Western European tastes; they also have dark spots, even when their quality is excellent, and they are more difficult to peel than Israeli or Moroccan oranges that sell well in Western Europe. The lemons that sell best in Western Europe are yellow; Cuba's lemons are green. Cuba will, therefore, have to invest in processing frozen citrus concentrates in order to export citrus products to Western Europe. Some Cuban products have sold well in some markets but not in others. Cuban mango juice is too sweet for Western European markets, for instance, but sells well in Saudi Arabia. The quality of Cuban double-boilers is too low for European markets, but they sell well at low prices in less developed countries. In the same way, Cuba has targeted less developed countries for the export of its manufactured products; in 1985 and 1986, all of Cuba's exports to Cape Verde were manufactured products.[101]

In addition to U.S. government pressures (discussed in the next chapter) and the Cuban-West German political problems described earlier, there have been political obstacles to the development of Cuba's exports. Tobacco industries in many countries are heavily protected, making it difficult for Cuba to export tobacco. It is also difficult to export Cuban rum to the EEC because of EEC measures to protect the rum industries of Martinique and Guadeloupe, which are French departments. Rum exports have been complicated by a legacy of Cuba's own revolution: Before 1959, the Bacardi rum firm had registered its trademark worldwide; the Cuban government could not continue to use it after it expropriated the firm. Cuba's Havana Club rum lacks Bacardi's brand name loyalty and exposure even though it is made in Bacardi's old plants.[102]

In general, then, Cuba found serious internal obstacles to increasing its exports. The lack of product diversification and the low quality of Cuban products by international standards held back exports.[103] All was not bleak, however. With better investments and improved efficiency, by the mid-1980s Cuba had shown that it could diversify its exports beyond sugar, selling small quantities of many products worldwide, and even selling some manufactured products in less developed countries. Even so, only a tenth of Cuban exports were nontraditional products. Dependence on sugar exports, whether at depressed world market prices or politically managed CMEA and Soviet prices, was still the path to the economic future.

Cuba has also sought other alternatives to dependence on sugar. It earns foreign exchange by selling services, the main area of which is construction. The value of its construction projects in Libya in the early 1980s exceeded both the value of all seafood exports and the value of all citrus exports in 1982. Moreover, Cuba's increased cement exports in the 1980s were promoted by its construction service contracts, which in turn were often tied to the purchase of Cuban cement.[104] Cuba's construction contracts were not limited by ideology; it sought profits, not revolution. In 1984, for example, Cuba began a commercial construction relationship with the Sheikdom of Kuwait.[105] Nonetheless, Cuba's political decision in the mid-1980s to shift contracts in Angola and Nicaragua from a commercial to a grant basis curtailed this source of income.

Organizational innovations helped to promote Cuba's international transactions. The Cuban government created firms that were registered as private companies, even though it owned them and they were run by Cuban officials. One is Contex S.A., which is Cuba's largest manufacturer of men's, women's, and children's wear, and jewelry for export. It is a subsidiary of Cimex, ostensibly a Panamanian holding company run by Cuban officials; Cimex promotes Cuban trade with market-economy countries.[106] To facilitate trade, the National Bank of Cuba has operated a bank in London registered under British law since the late 1960s. And in 1984 it authorized the creation of a private bank, of which the Cuban government is the sole shareholder, the Banco Financiero Internacional, to operate in international markets.[107]

Financial transactions have, indeed, earned foreign exchange. In 1984 and early 1985 Cuba could not meet its sugar delivery obligations to the Soviet Union. As a result, it bought 201 million pesos' worth of sugar at the current low world prices in convertible currency and resold the sugar to the Soviets at the agreed-upon subsidized price in transferable rubles (a total of 1,529 million pesos). In July 1985 Cuba again bought half a million tons of sugar in convertible currency (at some of the lowest prices ever in the world market) and resold it to the USSR at the subsidized price.[108]

In February 1982 Cuba also authorized new direct foreign investments in the form of joint ventures.[109] Tourist facilities in Cuba have since been developed jointly with Argentine and Spanish firms. These have been primarily "turn-key" operations—the facility is turned over to Cuba once it has been built—rather than ongoing, direct investments by foreign companies. By early 1985, despite talk of other prospects, only one foreign firm had registered a direct investment project in Cuba: a Spanish firm recycling metal products.[110]

Since the late 1970s Cuba has promoted tourism as a source of convertible currency. The agency managing Cuba's tourist facilities, Havanatur, is another Cuban firm registered privately in Panama though wholly owned by the Cuban government. One group of clients has been Cuban Americans who, beginning in late 1978, were allowed to return from the United States for short visits. After 102,381 Cuban Americans returned during 1979, creating internal security problems that served as background to the exodus of 125,000 Cubans from Mariel harbor to the United States in 1980, the number of returning Cuban Americans had stabilized at about 10,000 per year by 1983–84. These tourists paid Cuba $1,200 per week for hotel accommodations even if they stayed with their relatives. Cuba cut off such tourism in May 1985, in retaliation for the U.S. government's Radio Martí broadcasts to Cuba, but allowed tourists to visit again beginning in June 1986. The total number of tourists to Cuba (mostly from Canada, West Germany, the USSR, Spain, Mexico, and the returning Cuban Americans) exceeded 267,000 in 1986; the resulting income to Cuba was 107.6 million pesos (98 million in convertible currency). But the proportion of tourists who return to Cuba for a second visit is among the lowest in the Caribbean; visitors to Cuba complain of problems with Cuban Airlines, the airport, the hotels, and the restaurants. The prospects for developing more income from tourism depend on improving the quality of tourist services.[111]

Although all of these measures have provided Cuba, to some degree, with alternatives to dependence on sugar, that overwhelming dependence is still the central fact of Cuba's international transactions.

Cuba's Convertible Currency Debt

In August 1982 the Cuban National Bank, on behalf of the government, requested the rescheduling of its debt in convertible currency to governments and multinational banks from market-economy countries. Cuba had accumulated a large debt as a result of its persistent trade deficits in convertible currency (see Table 7.1). This situation was consistent with the experience of most Latin American and many other Third World countries, though in the late 1970s and early 1980s Cuba's management of its debt in convertible currency was prudent in comparison to others.

Because of the Cuban economy's weakness and U.S. policies that limited its access to the international financial system, Cuba incurred only a modest debt in convertible currency in the 1960s. In 1969 Cuba's convertible currency debt was 291 million pesos. As Cuba's engagement in the world economy increased with the rise in sugar prices, its appetite for imports grew. Its annual trade deficits with market-economy countries ranged between 559 and 713 million pesos from 1975 to 1977. Although the amount declined, Cuba had deficits in its convertible currency balance of payments current account through 1980. To finance these deficits, Cuba borrowed in the international capital markets. The need to borrow reflected a problem, but the ability to borrow reflected an international recognition of Cuba's improved economic performance in the 1970s. The National Bank reported a surplus in Cuba's convertible currency current account for 1981; subsequently published data on the balance of trade indicate that the situation may have been worse. Moreover, the National Bank's own data show that Cuba had a high debt service ratio—that is, payments on the convertible currency debt as a percentage of exports earning convertible currency—of over 46 percent from 1980 to 1982. This ratio weakened its bargaining position on the debt.[112]

In 1982 the National Bank argued that Cuba's debt crisis was not its fault, that it had been caused by factors beyond Cuba's control: the subsidized overproduction and export of sugar by the EEC; the intense ideological hostility of the Reagan administration, which led to the elimination of most U.S. tourism to Cuba in April 1982; and the worldwide increase in interest rates after 1978, which hurt all borrowing countries. The high interest rates stemmed mainly from U.S. actions and policies. In this instance, Cuba suffered from U.S. policies that were not targeted against it. Compared with the damage from high interest rates, the partial reimposition of the U.S. ban on travel to Cuba was minor.

The National Bank of Cuba listed other factors that hurt Cuba's ability to service its debt but, though the bank did not say so, Cuba bore some responsibility for these problems. One factor was the drop in the world price of sugar after 1980, as a result of overproduction; Cuba had contributed to this decline by increasing its raw sugar exports 25 percent from 1980 to 1982.[113] Another was Japan's increased sugar production and its increase in sugar imports from Australia; Cuba induced that change by its price hawkishness in the mid-1970s. The same happened with the Spanish market, which came to be supplied from Spain's own production. A third factor was

Cuba's lack of access to the financial markets in 1981–82, caused in part by the trends in the sugar market, by Cuba's high deficits in convertible currency trade and balance of payments in previous years, and by the poor credibility of its price statistics for 1980–1982.

There were also factors that the National Bank of Cuba did not mention, such as the deterioration of Cuba's terms of trade with the USSR as a result of the cut in Soviet sugar prices from 1980 to 1981 and the sustained rise in prices paid by Cuba for imports from the USSR (to be sure, Cuba's terms of trade had deteriorated even more with market-economy countries that did not subsidize their trade with Cuba). The Soviet and Eastern European economies also slowed down in the early 1980s, hurting Cuba. Moreover, fearful over the possibility of debt defaults, the international private banks in early 1982 began to cut back on loans to all Latin American countries regardless of each country's performance.

To its credit, the Cuban National Bank had foreseen aspects of the looming debt crisis and, under the circumstances, acted prudently in the late 1970s and early 1980s, though it could not stave off the 1982 debt crisis. One warning signal was the trend in Cuba's debt maturity structure—the time available to repay loans—which was shortened twice before the 1982 economic crisis. Political and economic trends were so closely connected in the issue of Cuba's debt repayment that it is difficult to disentangle them; my analysis assumes a lag of several months to a year between external events and their impact on Cuba's debt structure. For example, before 1972 Cuba received no credits repayable in more than eight years; its economy had performed badly, world sugar prices were low, and Cuba was a political pariah. In the first half of the 1970s, however, world sugar prices rose, Cuba's economy improved, and Cuba improved its relations with other governments. Between 1973 and 1975, 25 to 45 percent of the credits Cuba received were repayable in over eight years. In 1975–76, there was a world recession, sugar prices fell, and Cuba intervened in Angola. In 1976 and 1977 only 10 percent of the loans Cuba received were repayable in over eight years. The world and the Cuban economy recovered, and Cuban relations improved, even with the United States in 1977. The proportion of loans Cuba received that were repayable in over eight years rose to 26 percent in 1978, then fell again to less than 15 percent beginning in 1979 in response to Cuba's intervention in the Horn of Africa in 1978 and the renewed 1979 world recession.[114]

Therefore, expecting debt problems, the Cuban National Bank reduced Cuba's external nominal debt in convertible currency from 3,267 million pesos in 1979 to 3,227 million pesos in 1980, then to 3,170 million pesos in 1981. Though only a drop of 3 percent from 1979 to 1981, that compares favorably to other Latin American countries whose external nominal debt increased, on the average, 32 percent from 1979 to 1981.[115]

Nonetheless, the underlying economic forces overrode the gains from prudent management and Cuba had to ask for a rescheduling of its debts. On June 30, 1982, the National Bank of Cuba stated that it believed it owed about 2,914 million pesos in convertible currency, of which 1,616 million was owed to private banks, 1,252 million to other governments, and the remainder to multilateral institutions (such as United Nations agencies) and to suppliers. In fact, the bank later discovered that the actual numbers were lower. In 1982 Cuba owed 2,669 million pesos in convertible currency, of which only 1,327 was owed to the private banks, 1,276 to other governments, with the remainder to multilateral institutions and suppliers.[116] The National Bank of Cuba was correct all along on two key points: Cuba's debt situation was not worse than that of the rest of Latin America, and Cuba could meet its obligations if it received terms that were also no worse than those for the rest of Latin America.

Agreements on debt repayment were made between Cuba and the private banks and between Cuba and creditor governments. The negotiations were not easy. Cuba signed a first agreement with most creditor governments in Paris in March 1983. Although Cuba came out well compared with other Latin American countries and their settlements, it did not do well by its own standards. Cuba had asked the creditor governments to reschedule debts falling due during the next forty months; instead, the debts rescheduled were due over the next fifteen months. Cuba asked to be allowed to repay the rescheduled debt over ten years; the agreement allowed eight and a quarter years. Cuba also asked for a forty-month grace period (when no repayment of principal was required) and got it. Cuba signed a second, more favorable agreement with creditor governments in Paris in July 1984; it was allowed a five-year grace period and a total repayment time of nine years. Another agreement was reached with creditor governments in July 1985. Cuba's negotiations with the private banks took even longer; a first agreement was reached only in December 1983, the second in December 1984, and the third in 1985. There were two reasons for the delay. One was that Cuba negotiated slowly in order to establish acceptable precedents. The other was the position of the United States and West Germany. The West German government did not sign the Paris agreements in either 1983 or 1984—a refusal consistent with worsened Cuban-German political relations after 1982. The U.S. government had made no loans to Cuba and prohibited U.S.-based banks from doing so, but its policies still affected the negotiations. Just before the December 1983 deal was closed, one of Cuba's creditors, London's Trade Development Bank, was bought by the American Express Company, which, by U.S. law, could not help bail Cuba out. The matter was settled when American Express sold its share of Cuba's debt to a non-U.S. bank.[117]

The agreements negotiated in the years 1983–1985 were reasonable. Comparative data are available on the rescheduling of debts coming due in 1982–83, owed by twelve Latin American countries to private international banks. These countries paid a premium over the prevailing international standard for interest rates, the London Inter-Bank Offering Rate (known as LIBOR), to refinance their debts. The median premium was 2.25 percent—which was also paid by Cuba. The median repayment time for the countries' rescheduled loans was between seven and eight years; for Cuba, it was eight. The median grace period granted to the Latin American countries was three years, as it was for Cuba. The median commission paid to the banks by the Latin American countries was 1.25 percent—also paid by Cuba. Data are also available on the rescheduling of debts coming due in 1983–84, owed by six Latin American countries to the banks. In these, the median premium paid over LIBOR was 1.75 percent; Cuba paid 1.88 percent. The median repayment time for the Latin American countries, and for Cuba, was nine years, with five years' grace. The median commission was between 0.75 and 0.88 percent; Cuba paid 0.88 percent. Although given terms slightly worse than the median for the Latin American countries, Cuba—like most of those countries—received more favorable terms from the banks in the second round of negotiations than in the first. The pattern was the same in the rescheduling of debts coming due in 1984–85, owed by twelve Latin American countries to the banks. The median premium paid over LIBOR was 1.39 percent; Cuba paid 1.5 percent. The median commission was 0.025; Cuba paid 0.38 percent. The median repayment time was twelve years; for Cuba it was ten. Cuba's terms continued to improve in relation to its own in previous agreements but Cuba fell further behind the Latin American median—even though the amounts it rescheduled were smaller each time than the times before.[118]

Nevertheless, Cuba's convertible currency debt rose every year after 1982. It reached 3,559 million pesos in 1985—a 33 percent increase over 1982. The debt rose because the balance of payments current account in convertible currency showed a deficit every year after 1983 and because, during the grace period, Cuba did not have to repay the principal it had rescheduled. The amount of interest to be paid also rose 11 percent from 1984 to 1985. The composition of the debt also changed. Whereas Cuba's debt to other governments rose 31 percent, its debt to private banks fell 13 percent from 1982 to 1985. Governments, not banks, were willing to bail Cuba out, confirming its own government's belief in the greater reliability of politics over markets. Because of the drop in the international oil price, Cuba expected that its crude oil reexports would earn $300 million less in 1986 than it had first anticipated. In 1986 the National Bank projected a large deficit in the balance of payments current account in convertible currency.[119]

In July 1986, Cuba's National Bank unilaterally suspended all interest and principal payments on the debt falling due in 1986 until it could reach a new agreement with its creditors. The Cuban economy was already in a recession. As the government sought simultaneously, for ideological reasons, to reduce the role of monetary incentives to workers, productivity began to fall.[120]

Cuba received a short-term credit from the banks to cover interest payments due to the banks through June 1987. Debts falling due in 1986 were rescheduled by the creditor governments (but not by the banks) for repayment over ten years. By the end of 1986 Cuba's convertible currency debt had climbed to 3,870 million pesos; Japan had become Cuba's main creditor (holding 800 million pesos). In 1987 Cuba's global social product fell 3.2 percent; the current account deficit in convertible currency was 750 million pesos in 1987. Negotiations continued to reschedule Cuba's debts falling due in subsequent years, but Cuba's bargaining position had been weakened by three factors: its poor economic performance in 1986 and 1987, the increase in the size of its convertible currency debt (it reached 5,657 million pesos at the end of 1987), and rising creditor distrust of Cuba that stemmed from Cuba's unilateral suspension of payments in mid-1986.[121]

In general, Cuba's debt to market-economy countries parallels that of other Latin American countries. Cuba got into trouble for reasons not unlike theirs: Trade deficits and balance of payments deficits in convertible currency, financed through borrowing, were exacerbated by the rise in interest rates and the drop in commodity prices. Cuba's debt problem was less severe than that of other Latin American countries because its convertible currency debt was small by world standards and its management in the late 1970s and early 1980s had been more prudent. Cuba's bargaining position was made worse by several factors, however. First, too much of its economy was shrouded in the statistical secrecy of its relations with the Soviet bloc; second, there was reason to doubt the accuracy of some optimistic Cuban economic statistics in 1980–1982; third, Cuba's performance in exporting products to earn convertible currency was poor, and world sugar prices fell in the first half of the 1980s; fourth, Cuba refused to cut back on its non-income producing personnel overseas as part of its austerity program; and, fifth, the U.S. government was quite hostile. Despite these problems Cuba came out well, on balance, in its financial negotiations in 1982–1985. The results are a tribute to Cuba's financial diplomacy and to the pragmatism of the private banks and most creditor governments. Since mid-1986, however, Cuba has had much greater difficulty in paying its debts and in obtaining credits to import goods; as a result, in 1987–1988 the Cuban government adopted a very severe economic austerity policy.[122]

In response to their own economic interests and to their wish to show political independence from the United States, several industrialized market-economy countries retained commercial ties to Cuba that were essential for the revolution's survival. As a result of these ties Cuba gained political and economic breathing space in its U.S. and Soviet relations and also gained access to new technology and to products that either do not exist or exist only at lower quality in CMEA countries.[123]

At the outset of revolutionary rule Cuba did not fully understand the importance of the world market. It nearly broke with Spain and sabotaged the 1961 international sugar conference. But Cuban relations with Spain soon became a model of reciprocal nonideological pragmatism. In 1967–68, Cuba's mixture of revolutionary militancy and market pragmatism was on full display. As Cuba increased its support for revolution in Latin America and confronted the U.S., Soviet, and Chinese governments over many issues, it also agreed to compensate Swiss and French firms for property it had expropriated years earlier; moreover, it reversed its policy toward the world sugar market, signing the International Sugar Agreement of 1968 in spite of the constraints it imposed on Cuban exports.

Cuban relations with market-economy countries prospered during the first half of the 1970s. Trade grew; Cuba became credit-worthy enough to get into debt in the international capital markets; its leadership of the world sugar market was recognized even by the U.S. government. Cuba was remarkably responsive to the market, even diverting sugar exports from the Soviet Union to obtain higher world sugar prices at key moments.

The political environment that had allowed economic relations to flourish was soured, however, by Cuba's decision to intervene in Angola in 1975 and on Ethiopia's side in the war against Somalia in late 1977. Other problems with particular countries arose as well, from Cuban hawkishness on sugar prices for Japan and Spain to political problems with France, Canada, Spain, and the Federal Republic of Germany. Cuba emphasized its relations with CMEA countries in the early 1980s, thus further curtailing trade with market-economy countries; such trade was promoted again only after 1984, though the success of this new policy was limited by Cuba's own domestic economic problems.

In the early 1980s the Cuban economy was hurt most not by anti-Cuban policies of the U.S. government but by general market trends: the world-wide rise of interest rates and the subsidized sugar policies of the United States and the EEC. Cuba then faced its own convertible currency debt crisis. It had to submit its economy to the indirect supervision of market-economy governments and banks and adopt more orthodox economic policies. Its December 1984 economic plan resembled an agreement negotiated with the International Monetary Fund, calling for austerity measures in consumption, budget discipline, improved efficiency, and export promotion. This policy was one result of the engagement of socialist Cuba in the world market economy. Ironically, Cuba has pledged to honor all its own debts even as it has counseled Latin American countries to do otherwise.

Market-economy countries have always conducted their relations with Cuba in a political environment. Relations therefore flourished in the early to mid-1970s, when Cuba behaved most conventionally; they were impaired at other times, when Cuba emphasized its role as a world-class revolutionary power. But the polycentric structure of the international system always permitted such relations, for they were economically and politically beneficial for all. Cuba gained from its trade relations with capitalist countries, especially when it was most vulnerable in the early 1960s and most prosperous in the early to mid-1970s. But as it projected its military power overseas, became more militant once again, and tightened military and political ties with the USSR after 1975, its pursuit of world power over gains from trade curtailed the benefits of its relations with capitalist countries.

Cuba's Diplomacy in the Americas and the Third World

8

Cuba's foreign policy has been designed to ensure protection against the United States and to gain influence through a vast network of diplomacy. Beyond its relations with Communist and capitalist states, and with revolutionary movements and states, Cuba has managed and improved its relations with many governments in Africa and Asia and, since 1969, in Latin America and the Caribbean.

Cuba's attention to Africa and Asia was first intended to make up for its increasing isolation in the Americas; this strategy was modestly successful in the 1960s. But Cuba's diplomacy succeeded best in Asia, Latin America, and especially Africa, in the 1970s. In that decade, Cuban diplomacy in relation to the Third World brought it leadership in the Nonaligned Movement, despite Cuba's close association with the Soviet Union. Consistent with Cuba's central foreign policy goal of reshaping world politics and economics, membership in the Nonaligned Movement has been viewed by the Cuban government as a means to acquire political leverage. Along with its relations with revolutionary states and its willingness to deploy troops, Cuba's leadership in the Nonaligned Movement propelled it onto the world stage as an actor others ignored only at their peril.

In the early to mid-1970s the increase of Cuban political influence worldwide did not impede improvements in U.S.-Cuban relations. Only in the late 1970s, after the spread of Cuban military power overseas, did relations falter. Cuba faced severe challenges as the 1970s ended, resulting from Cuba's wars in Africa. Others were self-inflicted wounds, especially in 1979–80, when Cuban foreign policy seemed to have lost its bearings. Some of the setbacks stemmed from Cuba's tight alliance with the USSR—notably its unwillingness to criticize Soviet intervention in Afghanistan. When Cuba's duties to the Nonaligned Movement and its duties to its Soviet ally have conflicted, the latter have taken precedence. Only a few of Cuba's difficulties could be attributed to U.S. policy.

The balance of success and failure in foreign policy during more than thirty years of Castro's government reflected both Cuba's ambitions to act as a major power and its limited resources as a small, vulnerable, and relatively underdeveloped country. As with most powers, its successes and failures were due in part to the structure and trends of the international system. A window of opportunity opened for Cuba in the first half of the 1970s, when the U.S. engagement in Vietnam was increasingly unpopular within the United States and elsewhere. During this period, Cuba found common ground with other governments. The Vietnam War, conflicts in the Middle East, and U.S. emphasis on improving its Soviet relations diverted U.S. attention and resources away from most of the Third World. As one consequence, the United States was less apt to view third countries' relations with Cuba as a test of their relations with itself. These shifts made it easier for Cuba to improve its foreign relations everywhere, especially in Latin America. The 1973 oil crisis increased the political autonomy of oil-producing countries, with whom Cuba improved relations. Finally, the last burst of decolonization in Africa after the 1974 Portuguese revolution brought to power several revolutionary movements that had been helped by Cuba. No single event advanced Cuban influence more than its intervention in Angola in 1975–76: the goals of independence, liberation, and the struggle against racism all came together to justify, in the eyes of many, Cuba's military activities there.

The setbacks experienced by Cuban foreign policy had even more mixed sources than its successes. Some were typical of a world power's problems: arrogance toward less powerful neighbors, interference in the internal affairs of other countries, and increasing concern of others about the open-ended Cuban military engagement in Africa. Some setbacks, on the contrary, stemmed from the fact that Cuba was not a major power; it had to be loyal to the USSR on the issue of Afghanistan, for instance, even at the cost of influence in the Nonaligned Movement. And its inability to meet the needs of its own people led to domestic turbulence in 1979–80 that hurt its relations with Latin America and the United States.

Cuba and the Nonaligned Movement

After World War II decolonization created newly independent states in Asia, and later in Africa and the Caribbean, thereby transforming the international system. Many new states sought to detach their foreign policy from the Cold War. Unlike the old-style neutrality (still exemplified by Switzerland), the nonalignment of new states in what came to be called the "Third World" was more activist. These states helped colonies become independent, at times supporting armed struggle when the colonial power resisted, as did France in Algeria and Portugal in all its colonies. The first steps toward what would become the Nonaligned Movement were taken in Africa and Asia with the 1945 foundation of the Arab League, and later the Colombo conference of government heads from newly independent Asian states. In April 1955 an Afro-Asian conference, including aligned and non-aligned governments, met at Bandung. After 1959 Cuba looked to these continuing developments as a new source of power to project its influence worldwide and to help it ward off the United States.

In 1959, Cuba's ambassador to the United Nations, Manuel Bisbé (a respected moderate in Cuban politics), still often sided with the United States. Cuba voted to include the question of China's intervention in Tibet on the General Assembly's agenda, for example—supporting U.S. condemnation of the Chinese action. Bisbé called a Soviet disarmament plan "utopian" because it did not provide adequate inspection procedures. But that same year, Cuban foreign policy slowly began to alter. Cuba abstained on the question of seating the representative of the People's Republic of China (whereas the United States had voted against and the USSR for it); Bisbé condemned Latin American dictatorships, several of which were U.S. allies; and he voted for Poland (not for U.S.-backed Turkey) as a member of the United Nations Security Council. Outside the United Nations, the same policy shift was apparent. Cuba's ambassador to the Organization of American States (OAS), Raúl Roa, condemned de Gaulle's Algerian policy and denounced a past (1954) U.S. intervention in Guatemala.[1] By 1960 Cuba had moved away from the U.S. position on most international issues: It voted to seat the delegate from the People's Republic of China, to accept a Soviet disarmament proposal, to condemn the formation of United Nations Peacekeeping Forces for the Congo, and to support the Congo's Patrice Lumumba.[2]

In 1961 Yugoslavia, which wanted to create a group of states separate from both major global power blocs, called the founding meeting of the Nonaligned Movement in Belgrade. Several Latin American governments were invited to the conference but only Cuba sent a full delegation, led by President Osvaldo Dorticós, hoping for support beyond the Americas as it fought against the United States and most Latin American governments. Although Cuba was already allied with the Soviet Union, Dorticós stressed its right to membership in the movement: Cuba was not a formal member of any military pact, he said, and it joined other founding members in supporting decolonization, development, and opposition to racism. The Belgrade conference supported Cuba's contention that the U.S. naval base at

Guantánamo violated Cuba's sovereignty and territorial integrity, and it backed Cuba's right to choose its own political and social system. The conference also set a precedent by accepting as a full member a "national liberation movement," Algeria's Provisional Government, as if it were an independent state.[3]

The next conference of the Nonaligned Movement was held in Cairo in October 1964. The members asked the United States to return the Guantánamo base to Cuba and to lift its trade embargo on Cuba. They also called on all participants "to offer every type" of support to "the freedom fighters in territories under Portuguese colonialism."[4] Dorticós, who once again led the Cuban delegation, was pleased that "it was made clear at the conference that non-alignment is not the same as neutrality but that it only means not participating in some military bloc; that is good to make clear, because Cuba is aligned perfectly."[5] The movement's third conference, held at Lusaka in September 1970, issued a more general declaration that made no specific reference to Cuba.[6]

Cuban diplomacy benefited from support from Nonaligned Movement countries. For example, Latin American governments had excluded Cuba from their United Nations caucus since 1964. Because of the importance of the caucus system in United Nations politics, Cuba had thus become a pariah. In 1969, when two places allotted to Latin America became vacant on the U.N. Development Program's Council, the Latin American caucus nominated Mexico and Argentina. Cuba ran as an independent with Nonaligned Movement support in the General Assembly election; Cuba and Mexico won. It was the first reversal of the Latin American blacklisting of Cuba in the United Nations.[7] Similarly, at the insistence of the Latin American governments, Cuba had been excluded from the so-called Group of 77—the caucus for less developed countries—within the U.N. Conference for Trade and Development (UNCTAD) since its founding in 1964. Cuba was not invited to the Group's 1967 ministerial meeting in Algiers. At the second UNCTAD conference in New Delhi, Cuba was excluded from the Group of 77's task forces and from participation in the nomination process. Finally in 1971—at Peru's initiative with backing from the nonaligned countries—the group admitted Cuba.[8]

In the early 1970s Cuba continued to strengthen its relations with the Nonaligned Movement, though its closeness to the USSR presented some difficulties within the movement. In 1972 and again in 1973 Castro visited several African countries. These trips proved to be turning points for Cuba's African policies because Castro refocused his government's attention on Africa and, generally, on the Third World. Castro also led the Cuban delegation to the fourth Nonaligned Movement summit conference, held in Algiers in September 1973. He thus upgraded the significance of the Nonaligned Movement for Cuban policy and shrewdly exploited the ongoing changes in the international system to increase Cuban influence.

At the conference, Castro defended the USSR and his government's alignment with it. Many heads of government were angry at Castro for claiming to be both a nonaligned country and a Soviet ally. Two days later, to improve Cuba's standing in the movement, Castro announced that Cuba was breaking off diplomatic relations with Israel, thereby departing from Cuba's own "policy of not being the one to break relations so as not to contribute to the imperialist tactic of isolation."[9] Cuba's policy toward Israel had differed from the USSR's since the 1967 Arab-Israeli war, when the Soviets broke with Israel. The reversal of Cuban policy in 1973 is best explained as a response to pressure from Arab governments within the Nonaligned Movement. Cuba could not remain in good standing with the movement while maintaining relations with Israel and defending the Soviet Union. Its shift was thus consistent with Soviet policy but probably not caused by it.

Castro's ploy worked. The final declaration of the Algiers conference was a success for Cuba. The declaration called on members "to provide active material support to the armed struggle of liberation movements in Africa," as Cuba had been doing. It repeated the demand that the Guantánamo base be returned to Cuba and, for the first time, went on to adopt many Cuban-sponsored resolutions about Latin America: It backed Puerto Rico's independence, called for the return of the Canal Zone to Panama and for the removal of U.S. bases in Panama and Puerto Rico, included Latin American countries among those struggling for liberation against imperialism, backed nationalist economic policies, and called for solidarity with the leftist policies of the governments of Peru and Salvador Allende's Chile.[10]

Cuba's success at Algiers was reflected in several United Nations events. In 1973 the General Assembly approved a Cuban resolution calling for Puerto Rican independence—an issue Cuba had raised unsuccessfully every year since 1965—by a vote of 104 to 5; only the United Kingdom, France, Portugal, and South Africa joined the United States in voting against the measure.[11] In 1974 Cuba was elected to the Special Committee on Decolonization: in January 1975 it was welcomed back by the Latin American caucus. That spring Cuba was elected a member of the Economic and Social Council.[12]

Cuba's relations with the Third World continued to grow. From 1959 to 1969 Cuba signed 34 bilateral agreements with governments in Africa,

Asia, and the Middle East. During the same period Cuba established diplomatic relations with 9 African countries. From 1970 through 1976 it signed 102 bilateral agreements with African, Asian, and Middle Eastern governments. In 1976 alone, agreements with these countries made up 23.4 percent of Cuba's total bilateral agreements. Propelled by Castro's trips to Africa and Cuba's 1975 entry into the Angolan War and 1977 entry into the Horn of Africa War, Cuba established diplomatic relations with 28 additional African countries between 1970 and 1977, and with 8 more between 1978 and 1983, when Cuba had diplomatic relations with a total of 42 African countries. The widening range of Cuban bilateral transactions with Asian, Middle Eastern, and especially African countries enabled Cuba to break out of the diplomatic isolation the United States had sought to impose on it.[13]

When Vice President Carlos Rafael Rodríguez led the Cuban delegation to the movement's fifth conference, held in Colombo in August 1976, the United States had recently been defeated in Indochina, Latin American governments were acting more independently from the United States, and Cuba was at a point where it could savor its own international triumphs. The conference rewarded Cuba for its military intervention in Angola and for its support for other liberation movements in the former Portuguese colonies. It elected Cuba the movement's chairing nation, scheduling its sixth conference for Havana in September 1979. The conference's declaration reiterated earlier condemnations of U.S. policies toward Cuba and went further by asking the United States to pay Cuba reparations for damages. More militant than statements of earlier conferences in support of Cuba-backed liberation movements and against U.S. policies, the declaration asserted, "Latin America is one of the world's regions that has suffered most intensely from colonialist aggression and U.S. imperialism." The declaration also asked the United Kingdom to grant independence to Belize and to return the Malvinas (Falkland) islands to Argentina.[14] In short, Cuba used the movement to gain support in the 1960s and to spread its influence in the 1970s.

Coming Home to America

The great breakthrough in Cuban foreign policy occurred in the first half of the 1970s. Cuba's improved relations with Western Europe, Canada, and Japan, and its greater effectiveness in the United Nations, depended in part on Cuba's improved relations with Latin American countries and the United States. Three factors contributed to the breakthrough. First, U.S. policy changed. Although the United States remained hostile to Cuba, much of the attention of the U.S. foreign policy apparatus turned to the Vietnam War, the Middle East, and improved Soviet relations. The U.S. commitment to detente with Communist countries also softened its views about relations with Cuba. Second, Cuba's overall situation in Latin America changed. Cuba's declining militancy in the hemisphere helped to improve U.S.-Cuban relations, while the decline in U.S. attention to Latin America and Cuba made it easier for Latin American governments to reexamine their own relations with Cuba. Moreover, the ascension to power in several Latin American countries of governments committed to foreign policy innovation created "diplomatic space" for Cuban initiatives. Third (as discussed in Chapter 5), Cuba changed its foreign policy, becoming more willing to bargain with governments and to play down, or forgo, its support for revolutionary movements.

In 1969 Cuba's bargaining with Chilean President Eduardo Frei's Christian Democratic government led to the reestablishment of trade; its bargaining with Venezuelan President Rafael Caldera's Christian Democratic government and with Peruvian President Juan Velasco's reformist military government led to improved political relations. By reestablishing trade with Cuba, Chile was the first country to breach the collective inter-American sanctions imposed five years earlier (Mexico had never adhered to them). In July 1969 Castro praised the Peruvian military government's "patriotic" measures, which had, in his view, "an objective revolutionary character." On June 13, 1971, Peru reestablished trade with Cuba.[15]

In September 1970 Salvador Allende, leading a Socialist-Communist coalition, was elected Chile's President; soon thereafter Chile reestablished full diplomatic relations with Cuba. In November 1971 Castro began a month-long visit to Chile, his first to a Latin American country since 1959.[16] During this visit, Castro articulated his new policy: "We subordinate whatever other difference or whatever other problem exists [between Cuba and another government] to the fundamental one: defiance of the dictates of the United States." In practice, Castro said, "one operational test of an independent foreign policy is establishing relations with Cuba." He stated his willingness to reestablish diplomatic relations with Peru and Ecuador.[17] Conventional diplomacy, rather than support for revolution, Castro now believed, would serve the same historic goal: defiance of the United States.

In May 1972 Peru moved that the OAS permit members to establish relations with Cuba. Seven members voted in favor of the proposal, three abstained, and thirteen voted against. In June Peru reestablished full diplomatic relations with Cuba. In December 1972 Barbados, Guyana, Jamaica, and Trinidad and Tobago did so as well; Jamaica had retained consular relations all along.[18] Though Cuba had been fairly inactive in the English-speaking Caribbean, in 1973 it began an activist policy toward its smaller neighbors.[19]

Argentina's return to civilian rule in mid-1973 led it to reestablish relations with Cuba; on June 4 the two governments signed a trade agreement, and the value of Cuban imports from Argentina skyrocketed to 105.5 million pesos in 1975. Panama reestablished relations with Cuba in August 1974; Venezuela followed suit in December. Both had been trading with Cuba since 1973. Colombia reestablished full relations with Cuba in March 1975. Cuba also strengthened its relations with Mexico, which had never severed diplomatic or trade relations with Cuba; Cuban imports from Mexico doubled between 1972 and 1975. To reassure its new friends that they had nothing to fear from the Cuban armed forces, Cuba invited military observers from all Latin American and Caribbean countries it had relations with to observe the Cuban Central Army's maneuvers in December 1973.[20]

Setbacks also occurred. On September 11, 1973, for example, Chile's armed forces overthrew President Allende; the new government broke off all relations with Cuba. Cuban support for Allende had been one factor that had polarized Chilean politics and frightened the armed forces, which claimed that Cuban weapons were being smuggled into Chile. Some Cuban weapons probably did enter Chile, but the nature of Cuba's involvement there remains unclear.[21]

The United States and Cuba in the 1970s
U.S.-Cuban relations, hostile since 1959, remained poor at the beginning of the 1970s. In 1970–72, the U.S. government arrested Cuban fishermen on charges of violating U.S. waters on three separate occasions; blocked the participation of Cuban technicians in the Fourteenth Congress of the International Association of Sugarcane Technicians, held in Baton Rouge; and seized Cuban films intended for screening at a New York film festival. For its part, Cuba in 1971 terminated a bilateral migration agreement signed in 1965, which had brought a quarter-million Cubans to the United States in orderly fashion.[22]

But there were some signs of improved relations. In 1971 Castro signaled his government's willingness to sign an anti-hijacking agreement, thus resuming negotiations begun, without success, in October 1969. In 1968 a rash of air piracy had begun in the Caribbean, with many flights diverted to Cuba. At that time Cuba's policy was to safeguard the crew, passengers, and airplanes, and allow the flight to continue. However, the Cuban government generally disapproved of hijacking because it had lost 264 planes and boats, which had not been returned, through hijacking to the United States between 1960 and 1970. As a result hijackers to Cuba were typically arrested, although some were given political asylum. In the early 1970s Cuba signed several anti-hijacking treaties, even with countries it had no other relations with, such as Venezuela.[23] In March 1973 the United States and Cuba signed an agreement to prevent air and sea piracy.[24]

In November 1974 William D. Rogers, U.S. assistant secretary of state for inter-American affairs, began secret negotiations with the Cuban government. On March 1, 1975, Secretary of State Henry Kissinger said that there was "no virtue in perpetual antagonism with Cuba." Cuba responded by extraditing the hijacker of a U.S. plane and returning a $2 million ransom seized in another hijacking.[25] At the same time, other countries, notably Canada and Argentina, pressured the United States to allow firms under their jurisdiction to trade with Cuba, even if they were subsidiaries of U.S.-based multinational firms—something that was then illegal under U.S. law.

On July 29, 1975, with U.S. support, the collective inter-American sanctions on Cuba were lifted. Only Chile, Paraguay, and Uruguay were opposed; Brazil and Nicaragua abstained. To rid itself of pressure from its own allies, the U.S. government modified its embargo policies toward Cuba on August 21. It stopped denying aid to countries that allowed their ships or aircraft to carry goods to or from Cuba, and permitted the docking in the United States of ships of third countries engaged in such traffic. The U.S. government agreed to grant licenses permitting trade in foreign-made goods between Cuba and U.S. subsidiaries based abroad. It also agreed to authorize, "on a case by case basis," exports to Cuba by U.S. subsidiaries in third countries that included an "insubstantial proportion of U.S. origin materials," defined as "20 percent or less of the value of the product to be exported from the third country."[26]

On September 23 Rogers announced, "We are prepared to improve our relations with Cuba." But Cuba's intervention in the Angolan Civil War halted the secret talks in November 1975 and ended the improvement in U.S.-Cuban relations. At the last negotiating session, although Rogers objected to Cuba's Angola operation, he proposed that the talks continue; the Cubans declined, probably because they did not expect fruitful results after their decision to intervene in Angola.[27]

In 1977 the Carter administration moved again to improve U.S.-Cuban relations. In April the governments agreed to delimit maritime boundaries where their claims overlapped; they agreed also to grant each other reciprocal fishing rights. In June they agreed to establish diplomatic "interests sections" in each other's capitals. The U.S. lifted the ban on tourist travel to Cuba and granted tourist visas to some Cubans. It also permitted the resumption of charter flights between the two countries. Cuba agreed to a U.S. request to permit the repatriation of U.S. citizens who were long-term Cuban residents and their families. Eventually, Cuba released all U.S. citizens in its prisons.[28]

Cuba's decision to send troops to help Ethiopia defeat the Somali invasion in late 1977 soured U.S.-Cuban relations again. The U.S. government opposed Somalia's invasion of Ethiopia, but it also opposed the Soviet and Cuban defense of Ethiopia. When the Shaba exiles invaded Zaire for a second time in May 1978, Carter blamed Cuba, with some—though not much—justification; the U.S. government ignored Cuba's offer to join the United States in defusing the Zaire situation.[29] Relations deteriorated further when the United States learned in November 1978 that MiG-23F combat aircraft had arrived in Cuba. In August 1979 the United States discovered the presence of Soviet military personnel organized as a "brigade" in Cuba—remnants of the Soviet forces that arrived in Cuba in 1962. This event contributed to the failure of the U.S. Congress to ratify the U.S.-Soviet Strategic Arms Limitation Treaty (SALT II).

Decisive though Cuban participation in the Ethiopian-Somali war proved to be for U.S.-Cuban relations, its importance was less evident at the time. The Carter administration had warned Cuba in November 1977 not to send troops to Ethiopia, and it reacted strongly to Cuba's ultimate intervention.[30] Nonetheless, in mid-January 1978, at the peak of Cuba's troop deployment to Ethiopia, the U.S. Coast Guard and Cuba's Border Guard Troops held talks in Havana to improve communications, to cooperate on search-and-rescue operations in international waters, and to curb drug traffic and terrorism. They established teletype links, and Cuba lifted a seventeen-year ban on the use of Cuban water and air space by the U.S. Coast Guard. The Coast Guard and the Border Guard Troops held further talks in Washington in May 1979. Cuba continued to repatriate U.S. citizens and their families who wanted to leave Cuba in 1978–79. In late 1978 Castro released most Cuban political prisoners (about 3,600 were released within the year); approximately 1,000 emigrated to the United States with their families. He also announced that Cuban-Americans could return to visit their families. This decision was in part a response to the U.S. government's human rights interests, in part an attempt to generate tourist revenue, and in part a humanitarian gesture.[31]

Cuban officials interviewed in March 1985 stressed that U.S.-Cuban negotiations continued during and after Cuba's entry into the Ethiopia-Somali war, and that the intervention was a serious but not an overriding issue on the U.S. agenda in discussions with Cuba. They argued that it was only after subsequent events soured the relationship late in the Carter administration that this war emerged, retrospectively, as the turning point.[32] According to this interpretation, improved U.S.-Cuban relations in certain areas were possible without affecting the overseas posting of Cuban troops.

In fact, the two governments still collaborated after the Ethiopian-Somali war, though most new initiatives came from Cuba. But for each improvement on a matter of moderate importance, there was a setback on a matter of major importance. For the U.S. government, security concerns were paramount. Cuba's unwillingness to meet those concerns killed the "normalization" of relations.[33] That the two governments accomplished much in those years shows that both can benefit from negotiations; nonetheless, even when some limited agreements are reached, issues of greater concern for both governments remain unresolved and may undermine the few areas of agreement.

Cuba's decision to give priority to leading the international revolutionary movement—especially its pursuit of greater influence in Africa—and to its alliance with the USSR, at the expense of improving U.S. relations, clarified its policies. The prospects for U.S. trade or for other modest gains from better U.S.-Cuban relations paled in comparison with these goals.

Cuba's decisions were brilliant in many ways. Its leaders correctly concluded that the United States would back neither South Africa in Angola nor irredentist Somalia on the warpath. They also correctly concluded that the United States would not back leftist regimes in Angola or Ethiopia, leaving the field clear for Cuba and its allies to win on the ground and to gain international influence by backing causes popular with African governments. Cuba was thus able to oppose the South African regime in one war and to protect the sanctity of established borders in the other. Cuba also judged that, in the immediate aftermath of the Vietnam War, the United States would not enter another distant war. By its activities in Africa, Cuba demonstrated its political and military worth to the Soviet Union; the Cuban government might not manage its economy well, but it could secure political and military victory. The Soviets and the East Europeans rewarded Cuba with massive economic subsidies beginning in 1976 (see Chapter 4).

Cuba may have overreached its limits, however. Its deployment of troops to Africa twice in a thirty-month period alarmed the United States. Although U.S.-Cuban relations did not worsen immediately, progress toward normalization halted. Cuba's growing overseas influence was also portrayed in the United States as a failure of the Carter administration, energizing its opposition and increasing antagonism to detente. Cuba's African policy and the tightening of Soviet-Cuban relations that helped to kill SALT II did not elect Ronald Reagan President by themselves, but—along with Castro's April 1980 decision to send criminals from Cuban jails through Mariel harbor to the United States (see below)—they helped to defeat Jimmy Carter in 1980, the President who had tried hardest to alter U.S. policy toward Cuba.

Unsuccessful Cuban Foreign Policy in the Americas
In the second half of the 1970s Cuban relations with Latin America and the Caribbean at first continued to improve. Within days of the lifting of collective inter-American sanctions in 1975, Cuba was admitted as a founder of the Latin American Economic System—an organization to promote economic collaboration among Latin American governments. From 1975 to 1976 the value of Cuban exports to Peru and Venezuela grew, as did its imports from Mexico, Argentina, and Colombia. To demonstrate its willingness to abide by agreements, Cuba continued to trade with the repressive military government that came to power in Argentina early in 1976: Cuba still imported goods valued at 115 million pesos from Argentina in 1977.[34] Costa Rica established full diplomatic relations with Cuba in February 1977; Ecuador, St. Lucia, and Suriname did so in 1979.

Yet trends were already under way that eventually led to a major deterioration in Cuba's relations with its neighbors. The first setback for Cuba was unexpected. On October 6, 1976, a bomb exploded in a Cuban Airlines civilian plane flying over Barbados; all aboard were killed. Castro alleged that Venezuelan territory was used to plot the crime, but he said he was confident that Venezuela would prosecute those responsible. He blamed the CIA for sponsoring terrorist attacks on Cuba, although he did not provide proof, and he canceled the U.S. hijacking agreement, although, in practice, Cuba has continued to honor it.[35] In the end, the event hurt Cuban-Venezuelan relations. When in 1980 the military prosecutor in a Venezuelan court dropped all charges against those accused of bombing the Cuban plane, Cuba recalled its embassy personnel from Caracas. Cuban-Venezuelan relations also suffered in 1979–80, when the Venezuelan embassy in Havana granted political asylum to several Cubans, and when the Venezuelan government sided with the United States against Cuba in the continuing competition for influence in Central America.[36]

Cuban-Peruvian relations, meanwhile, deteriorated after the shift to the right within the Peruvian military government in 1975, although trade continued. Peru and Cuba also clashed over the activities of the Cuban fishing fleet in Peruvian waters; the Peruvian Navy sank two Cuban fishing boats, and Peru canceled its fishing agreement with Cuba. In 1980 a serious incident arose at the Peruvian embassy in Havana, one that eventually affected Cuban relations not only with Peru but with other Latin American countries and the United States as well. Some Cubans broke into the embassy seeking political asylum, which was granted. Castro, furious, removed the Cuban guards at the embassy. After the mass media announced the removal, thousands of people entered the embassy grounds seeking to leave Cuba. After tense negotiations, some Cubans left for Peru and Costa Rica. Each departure embarrassed the Cuban government and damaged its image in Latin America because the emigrés were received as heroes abroad (especially by Costa Rican President Rodrigo Carazo, whom the Cuban press denounced). Then Castro decided not to allow any more Cubans to go to other Latin American countries. Instead, he invited Cuban Americans to come by boat from the United States to Mariel harbor to pick up their relatives from the Peruvian embassy and from other parts of Cuba.[37]

On his own, Castro thus defied U.S. immigration laws; at his encouragement, more than 125,000 Cubans (often known as "Marielitos") entered the United States in a period of weeks. Castro later admitted that his government invited common criminals to leave prison for the United States; but those guilty of "crimes of blood" were not asked to emigrate, he insisted, although he acknowledged, "there are some who have gone by mistake."[38] Cuban officials required each boat that came looking for relatives to pick up some criminals. U.S. scholars estimate that one-third of the Marielitos had been in jail in Cuba, and that just under half of these had committed common crimes; Cuban scholars estimate that 45 percent of the Marielitos had been in jail in Cuba, and almost all of these had committed common crimes. The Cuban government also encouraged the departure of homosexuals, at times using intense harassment against them.[39] In staging the exodus of common criminals, the Cuban government committed an act of aggression against the people of the United States, not just its government.

In the short run, the Cuban government outwitted its enemies. Many criminals emigrated, tarnishing the image of Cuban exiles; and the U.S. government, which had at first welcomed the new migration, panicked and sought to stop it. But in the long run, in Western Europe and Latin America, the Cuban policy created the image of its government as one that unleashed common criminals on another society in order to cover up and divert attention from its problems at home.

Difficulties continued in Cuba's relations with other Latin American governments in 1980. Problems of asylum also arose at Ecuador's embassy in Havana. When the Cuban police stormed that embassy. to capture those seeking asylum, Ecuador protested sharply.[40] With regard to Colombia, Cuba decided to support Colombia's revolutionary M-19, a step that led Colombia to break off diplomatic relations with Cuba in March 1981. In a short time Cuban relations worsened with Venezuela, Peru, Ecuador, Colombia, and Costa Rica. Despite Cuban willingness to continue, the Argentine government curtailed trade; Cuban imports from Argentina reached a low of 13 million pesos annually in 1979 and 1980.[41] Relations with these six countries had produced Cuba's diplomatic breakthrough a decade earlier. By the early 1980s Cuba's Latin American policy again lay in ruins.

These setbacks were masked somewhat by the 1979 revolutionary victories in Grenada and Nicaragua. Even those victories, however, had negative repercussions. Other Latin American governments began to worry that Cuba was again supporting those who sought to overthrow them. The revolution in Grenada planted the fear of Cuban intervention for the first time in the English Caribbean, with which Cuba had developed good relations in the 1970s.

Cuban-Jamaican relations, for example, had improved markedly by 1975. Before Cuba's entry into the Angolan War in 1975, more Cubans were posted in Jamaica than in any other country; thereafter, Jamaica ranked second to Angola in Cuban overseas presence.[42] U.S.-Jamaican relations, meanwhile, had worsened in 1974, when U.S. aid to Jamaica stopped. Cuba helped Jamaica during several natural disasters and also agreed to build several construction projects. Prime Minister Michael Manley's government increasingly collaborated with Cuba on foreign policy. Through 1981 Cuba claims to have donated 3 junior high schools and a sports training facility; built 14 housing units, 6 small dams, and 5 plants to build components for prefabricated buildings; and donated 50 tractors with spare parts and 26,000 cartons of condensed milk. Cuban health personnel in Jamaica recorded roughly a million patient visits, and Cuban personnel trained about a thousand Jamaicans in various fields. Cuba became so involved in Jamaican internal affairs that its presence became an issue in the 1980 national elections. In October 1981, a year after Manley's People's National Party lost to Edward Seaga's Jamaican Labor Party, the Seaga government broke off diplomatic relations with Cuba.[43]

Relations with the Bahamas also worsened. On May 10, 1980, the Cuban Air Force, in full daylight, attacked a large, clearly marked Bahamian Coast Guard vessel, the HMBS *Flamingo,* which had stopped two Cuban fishing boats in Bahamian waters. The *Flamingo* was sunk and four of its crew were killed. The next day, the Cuban Air Force impeded Bahamian efforts to rescue the survivors. Instead of apologizing immediately for its mistake, Cuba accused the Bahamian boat of serving unspecified U.S. interests and claimed the right to take the same actions in the future. Disputes over fishing rights had been common, but this response was unprecedented; in earlier cases, Cuba had yielded to the Bahamas. Later in the same month Cuba apologized, but only after the Bahamas and several English-Caribbean countries threatened to take the case to the United Nations Security Council. Cuba compensated the government of the Bahamas and the families of the four dead seamen.[44]

The Grenadan revolution and U.S. discovery of the Soviet military presence in Cuba in 1979, and the Bahamian incident in 1980, focused the attention of the Carter administration on the Caribbean. U.S. economic aid to Caribbean English-speaking countries rose markedly; the budget proposal for fiscal year 1981 was the first to request military aid for them. The combination of U.S. aid and fears about Cuban actions led Barbados, Trinidad and Tobago, and St. Vincent and the Grenadines to keep their distance from Cuba. Elections in Dominica and St. Lucia brought to power governments less friendly to Cuba. Even Guyana, which had developed good relations with Cuba in the 1970s, was poised for a break in 1980 (see Chapter 6). By the end of 1980 Cuban diplomacy in the English Caribbean, like its relations with Latin America, was in a shambles.

The failure of Cuban foreign policy in the Americas between 1979 and 1981 was second only to its collapse in the early 1960s. In contrast to the first instance, the United States played only a modest role in the later period, mostly in the English-Caribbean. Cuba's problems were primarily of its own creation: notably, the attack on the Bahamian boat, excessive involvement in Jamaica's internal affairs, support for guerrillas seeking to overthrow the Colombian government, and mishandling of bilateral relations with Venezuela, Peru, Ecuador, Costa Rica, and Guyana in 1980. In brief, the setbacks for Cuban foreign policy are best explained by a combination of arrogance and ineptitude on Cuba's part, with modest assistance from U.S. policy and bad luck.

Leading the Nonaligned Movement

Economic Relations

While Cuba's relations with governments in the Western hemisphere began to deteriorate in the late 1970s, its relations with the members of the Nonaligned Movement remained good. Cuba provided substantial military, economic, and technical assistance to twenty-eight members of the movement, at the time of the 1979 Havana Summit.

Trade with these countries was important for Cuba. Less developed countries were the main market for Cuba's increasing exports of refined sugar; Libya, Iraq, and Algeria, were the main customers for Cuban sales of services. Including Angola and Ethiopia, less developed countries were also a good market for Cuba's new manufactured exports. The value of Cuban exports to African countries in 1980–81 exceeded the value of Cuban exports to the European Economic Community. By the early 1980s the value of Cuban exports to Algeria, Egypt, Iraq, Syria, and India had become as high as the value of exports to many individual Western European countries.[45]

Cuba's sugar trade with several Nonaligned Movement members for which data are available became especially valuable in the early 1980s because these countries paid prices higher than prevailing real world market prices (see Table 8.1 and Appendix B). Until 1977, when Cuba was chosen to lead the movement, Cuba typically sold sugar to Angola, Iraq, Algeria,

Table 8.1 Ratios of sugar prices paid to Cuba by selected less developed countries, 1965–1986

Year	Angola	Iraq	Algeria	Morocco	Egypt	Vietnam
1965	—	0.61	0.67	0.87	0.60	0.72
1970	—	0.72	1.01	0.87	0.94	0.75
1975	—	0.53	0.74	0.68	0.75	0.26
1977	0.58	0.51	0.55	0.54	0.54	0.02
1978	0.82	0.98	1.01	—	1.03	1.10
1979	0.95	0.93	0.96	—	0.83	1.03
1980	1.22	1.04	1.06	—	0.96	0.26
1981	1.99	1.05	1.26	—	1.37	0.73
1982	1.55	1.30	1.17	—	1.21	1.47
1983	1.82	1.15	1.65	—	1.48	1.73
1984	1.19	1.30	1.43	—	1.46	2.32
1985	1.79	1.44	1.24	—	1.25	3.25
1986	1.19	1.17	1.08	—	1.26	1.49

Sources: Comité Estatal de Estadísticas, *Anuario estadístico de Cuba, 1982, 1983, 1984, 1985, 1986* (Havana).

Note: Ratios are calculated as the price paid by each country divided by the "real world market price" (see Appendix B). A ratio below 1.00 means the country paid less than the real world market price; a ratio above 1.00, that it paid more.

Morocco, Egypt, and Vietnam at prices below those paid by major market-economy customers. After 1977 Cuba generally increased sugar prices for the five of those countries that continued to trade with it (Vietnam was an exception in 1980–81). Morocco cut off its trade with Cuba in 1978 to protest Cuban support for the Polisario revolutionary movement. Since the 1979 Havana Summit, Angola, Iraq, Algeria, and Egypt have paid higher prices for Cuban sugar than did Japan, Spain, or Canada. Indeed, Angola paid a premium of 80 percent or higher over the real world market price in 1983 and 1985. Cuba may have underpriced its sugar to these countries before 1977 as a means to gain political influence, while it may have raised relative prices in the early 1980s to offset the reduction in the Soviet price for Cuban sugar in 1981 and the general downward trend in world sugar prices. In spite of these factors, some oddities are difficult to explain. Why has war-ravaged Angola paid generally more than war-ravaged Iraq since 1979? Why has Angola paid generally more than Algeria, a country not at war? And why, in 1979–80, did Egypt—which had poor political relations with Cuba—get better sugar prices from Cuba than did Angola, Iraq, and Algeria, whose political relations with Cuba were much better? Whatever the explanations, the fact remains that certain nonaligned countries were politically and economically important to Cuba.

The Havana Summit

Cuba's approach to the Nonaligned Movement was primarily political, not economic.[46] It worked hard to prepare for the movement's sixth summit conference in Havana in September 1979. Contrary to some expectations, Cuba's leadership of the meeting was not out of line with the movement's traditions. The final documents were primarily critical of the United States and its allies rather than the USSR and its allies, but the same had been true of previous declarations. Though longer and more detailed, the final documents were not markedly more "leftist" than those of earlier summits, nor did they make significant departures even with regard to Latin America.[47]

Three main disputes erupted at the summit.[48] One was over which of two competing Kampuchean delegations should be seated. In early 1979 Vietnam had invaded Kampuchea, overthrown Pol Pot's government, and installed one led by Heng Samrin, which Cuba backed. Among the countries that the Cuban press identified as having taken a stand on the Kampuchean question, 23 favored the Pol Pot government, 15 backed Heng Samrin's, and 6 favored leaving the seat vacant. Overt support for Heng Samrin's government was limited to Cuba and its close allies. Among recipients of Cuban assistance, only North Korea favored Pol Pot. However, only 12 of the 28 delegations that received Cuban aid took a clear stand in favor of Heng Samrin's government, suggesting the limits of Cuban influence. Cuba backed off and used its role as conference leader to shape a "consensus"; it proposed that Kampuchea's seat be left vacant, thus adopting a minority position that was, nonetheless, approved as the least objectionable alternative to the contending parties.

The second controversy centered on the formerly Spanish western Sahara, which Morocco had annexed. There was resistance in the Sahara to that action, and civil war had broken out. Cuba had backed the Polisario revolutionary movement; at the Havana conference, 29 participants sided openly with Polisario, and only 6 with Morocco. The final declaration endorsed the Sahara's independence and asked Morocco to withdraw its forces.

In the third controversy—over Egypt's continued membership in the Nonaligned Movement—the conference condemned the Camp David Accords and the March 1979 treaty signed between Egypt and Israel. Some Arab members, with Cuba's support, proposed Egypt's expulsion from the movement. A moderate view prevailed, however; the question of Egypt's continued membership was referred to a committee for study, where it was quietly shelved.

Cuba's main objective in hosting the summit was to emerge as the Third World's recognized leader. At first that goal seemed within reach. Soon after the meeting, Castro spoke at the United Nations General Assembly, as he said, on behalf of the Nonaligned Movement. His eloquent, hard-hitting speech emphasized North-South rather than East-West themes. But political disaster soon struck when the Soviet Union invaded Afghanistan in late 1979. Cuba voted with the USSR against the General Assembly's condemnation of the invasion, even though Cuba did not specifically endorse the invasion and its officials' public statements suggested unhappiness with the Soviet action.[49] A majority of movement members voted to condemn the Soviet invasion. Among the 25 recipients of Cuban aid that were also United Nations members, 7 voted with Cuba and the Soviets, 12 abstained, and 6 condemned the invasion.[50] This vote shows not only the limits of Cuban influence in the Nonaligned Movement but also the compatibility of its views with a few core Third World allies.

As leader of the movement, in the fall of 1979 Cuba sought election to the U.N. Security Council. Its opponent was Colombia. Cuba led in the 154 separate votes in the General Assembly, once coming within 4 votes of the two-thirds majority needed for election. After the Soviet invasion of

Afghanistan, however, support for Cuba plummeted, and movement members defected. Cuba withdrew its candidacy in favor of Mexico.[51]

Cuba's term as movement chairing nation turned out to be less decisive than it had hoped. Soviet hegemony over Cuban policy was exposed at an inopportune time, and Cuba's 1980 foreign policy debacle in the Americas put it at odds with most Latin American and Caribbean members or observers of the movement. When Cuba's term ended at the seventh movement summit in New Delhi in March 1983, Castro chose to talk about economics, not politics—that is, not about what the movement really represented and what mattered most for Cuba.[52]

Salvaging Cuban Foreign Policy in the 1980s

The Americas

In the first half of the 1980s Cuba worked to mend its international relations within the Americas. Relations with Guyana began to improve in 1981, when the Reagan administration vetoed an Inter-American Development Bank loan to Guyana because of its government's socialist policies. As a result, Guyana turned to Cuba for support.[53] Also in 1981, Cuba resumed cultural, sports, and educational exchanges with Venezuela, and Venezuela began again to export small quantities of petroleum to Cuba. When three airplanes flying over Venezuela were hijacked to Cuba, Cuba swiftly returned the crews, passengers, and planes, announcing that it would try the hijackers; Cuba and Venezuela also renewed their hijacking agreement. In June 1984 eleven Cubans, who had been in Venezuela's embassy in Havana for years, voluntarily returned to their homes; Cuba promised not to prosecute them. In September 1984 Cuba and Venezuela jointly presented a plan for Puerto Rico's self-determination to the United Nations Decolonization Committee.[54] In the late 1980s, however, Cuba still objected to Venezuela's support for the government of El Salvador and regretted Venezuela's growing hostility toward the government of Nicaragua.

In April 1982, Cuba strongly supported the Argentine military government during its war with the United Kingdom over the British islands in the south Atlantic. Cuba condemned British military actions, and offered to send Argentina military aid. (The United States sided with the United Kingdom.) Castro, then still head of the Nonaligned Movement, helped Argentina garner support from member countries at a meeting in Havana.[55] Cuban-Argentine relations continued to improve after the return of civilian rule in Argentina; in June 1984 Argentina granted Cuba an annual trade credit of $200 million for each of three years, at 7.5 percent interest. In early 1986 Cuba awarded a contract for $120 million dollars to Argentine firms to build eight hotels on Cuba's Varadero beach. In October 1986 Argentina's President, Raúl Alfonsín, visited Cuba; shortly thereafter, the two governments signed an agreement to promote cooperation in the development of nuclear energy.[56]

Castro developed good, though informal, relations with Colombia's Conservative party President, Belisario Betancur, in power from 1982 to 1986. Although formal relations were not reestablished, Cuba praised Colombia's criticism of U.S. economic policy, its membership in the Contadora Group, which was seeking a negotiated solution to the wars in Central America, and its relief efforts in Nicaragua. In 1983 Colombia and Spain helped to evacuate Cubans captured by U.S. armed forces in Grenada, and the Cuba-Colombia agreement on hijacking was renewed in 1984.[57]

Relations also improved with Ecuador and Peru. Cuba donated medicines to Ecuador after several disastrous floods in 1983, and the two governments upgraded their diplomatic relations in 1984. In 1985 Ecuador's conservative President, León Febres Cordero, visited Cuba. In mid-1985 Castro greeted Peru's new, young, and popular President, Alan García, with some jealous hostility. By year's end, however, Cuba went out of its way to court the new government. The Peruvian Prime Minister visited Cuba twice within a year to sign economic, scientific, and technical cooperation agreements. To make amends for Cuba's past behavior in fishing rights disputes, Cuba sent to the Pacific two trawlers whose catch would be donated to Peru for six months.[58]

In addition to rebuilding relations that had deteriorated, Cuba made some net gains. From modest beginnings in 1980, Cuba developed trade, cultural, and sports relations with Brazil; Brazilian-made soap operas became a hit on Cuban national television. Castro referred to General João Figueiredo, President of Brazil, as "correct and dignified." In June 1986, more than a year after the return of civilian rule, Brazil reestablished diplomatic relations with Cuba.[59] Moreover, the return of civilian rule in Bolivia and in Uruguay led to the reestablishment of Cuban diplomatic relations with Bolivia in January 1983 and with Uruguay in December 1985; some trade with both resumed as well. In 1985 representatives of the Cuban National Assembly were admitted to the Latin American Parliament and, in December, Cuba was elected president of the Council of the Latin American Economic System. In 1987 Cuba strengthened its informal relations with the Dominican Republic.[60]

Cuban relations with Panama and Mexico had weathered the crisis in relations with Latin America. As mentioned in Chapter 7, Cuba used Panamanian registration for government-controlled firms trading with market-economy countries. In his February 1986 address to the third congress of the Cuban Communist party, President Castro praised Panama's military leaders—the only Latin American armed forces that he praised.[61]

Cuba's relations with Mexico remained cordial into the 1980s. In the past, Mexico had supplied fuel products to Cuba in emergencies and Cuba had sold sugar to Mexico even when its own production was short. In the early 1980s trade improved further. As Mexico's sugar industry sputtered, Cuban sugar exports to Mexico boomed. The value of Cuban exports to Mexico had ranged between one and two million pesos annually from 1975 to 1979; that figure jumped to 185.6 million pesos in 1980. From 1980 to 1986 Cuba sent exports worth 326 million pesos to Mexico. By 1984 the two governments had signed sixteen agreements covering exchanges in technology, industry, culture, petroleum, tourism, and other areas; a new agreement, worth 400 million pesos to both countries, was signed in 1984 to promote collaboration in the steel, machinery, and sugar industries. Cuba and Mexico enjoyed greater reciprocity in fishing rights than did either country with the United States.

Political relations were even more important than trade, and Mexico's increased purchases of Cuban products in 1980 had a political dimension. Mexican President José López Portillo announced a state visit to Cuba in the midst of Cuba's difficulties at the Peruvian embassy and at Mariel harbor. Mexico also supported Nicaragua's Sandinista government and opposed U.S. policy in El Salvador. Under President Miguel de la Madrid, however, Mexico's position on Central America diverged from Cuba's and moved closer to that of the United States; Mexico improved its relations with El Salvador and curtailed aid to Nicaragua. Nonetheless, Mexico was closer to Cuba on Central American issues than any Latin American government other than Nicaragua. More generally, as de la Madrid delicately put it, "a positive sign of the political maturity of Commander Castro is his respect for different economic and social processes from which he also demands respect." This was a restatement of Cuba's rule of the precedence of state-to-state relations, especially with Mexico, which had defied U.S. policy toward Cuba. Cuba would not support revolutionary movements to overthrow such a government.[62]

Since 1982 Cuba has supported negotiations to end the war in El Salvador and wider regional agreements to enable Nicaragua to live in peace with its neighbors; Cuba backed the mediation by the Contadora Group (made up of Colombia, Panama, Venezuela, and Mexico), under the assumption that a regional settlement would strengthen Nicaragua's government. More-over, given the then-weakened military position of the Salvadoran guerril-las, a negotiated solution to that internal war would give revolutionaries more power than they could win on the battlefield. Indeed, Castro's only public criticism of the Contadora Group was that it had neglected to pro-mote a negotiated settlement in El Salvador.[63] Cuba's support for negotia-tions enhanced its relations with most Latin American governments, which opposed both direct U.S. military intervention in the region and indirect efforts (by the United States or Cuba) to overthrow existing regimes. Thus statesmanship and revolutionary goals coincided in Cuban policy toward Central America in the mid- to late-1980s.

Despite its successes in Latin America, Cuban relations with most En-glish-Caribbean governments continued to deteriorate. Jamaica, Barbados, Dominica, St. Vincent and the Grenadines, St. Lucia, and Antigua joined the United States in the Grenada invasion in 1983. But Cuba did improve its relations with Guyana and Trinidad and Tobago, which did not support the invasion.[64] In addition, Suriname, which had developed close ties to Cuba in the preceding two years, became frightened by the U.S. interven-tion in Grenada. To avoid provoking the United States, the Suriname gov-ernment asked Cuban advisers to leave and ordered that the Cuban embassy staff be cut to two people. Cuba withdrew all its personnel and suspended, without actually breaking off, relations.[65]

Cuba's generally improved relations with Latin American governments after 1981 did not reach the degree of cordiality that prevailed in the mid-1970s. Symbolic of Cuba's pragmatism, but also of its recognition of the limits of its influence in Latin America, was Vice President Rodríguez's statement at the Latin American Economic Conference held in Quito in January 1984: "This is an economic conference. We will exclude, there-fore, political comments as a contribution to our necessary unity."[66] Cuba's relations with much of the English-Caribbean and Suriname did not re-cover. The main reason for Cuba's difficulties in the Caribbean was the unprecedented assertion of U.S. power in a region where the United States had always deferred to European powers. The explanation for the outcome in Latin America was Cuba's patience and skill in working to overcome the legacy of its problems of 1979–1981.[67] The United States could not prevent the improvement of Cuban relations with Latin America. Even conservative presidents in Colombia, Ecuador, and Brazil had reasons for better relations with Cuba. In March 1987, of the eight Latin American members of the United Nations Human Rights Commission, only Costa Rica voted with the United States to place on the commission's agenda a discussion of violations of human rights in Cuba. The events of the first half of the 1980s showed both the inefficacy and the capability of both Cuban and U.S. foreign policy in different parts of the hemisphere. Cuba's was not a bad record for a small country, but not as good as it had been a decade earlier.[68]

The Third World
After the damage done by its support for the Soviet invasion of Afghanistan, Cuba had to work hard to reestablish its credibility among Nonaligned Movement countries. In some senses, it made a full recovery. In the fall of 1983 Cuba was elected vice president of the U.N. Council for Social, Humanitarian, and Cultural Affairs; later in the fall it was elected to the Governing Board of the International Atomic Energy Agency. In the fall of 1984, with the support of the Latin American caucus, Cuba was elected Vice President for the Thirty-ninth Session of the U.N. General Assembly.[69]

Not all went well in other respects. Three revolutionary movements with close ties to Cuba had damaging internal divisions in 1983. First, open warfare broke out in Lebanon among factions of the Palestine Liberation Organization (PLO), which Cuba had supported strongly (Cuba welcomed the reunification of the PLO in 1987). Second, a rivalry within El Salvador's Popular Forces of Liberation (FPL)—one of the two strongest Salvadoran guerrilla forces—led to the murder and suicide of its two top commanders (Ana María and Marcial, pseudonym for Cayetano Carpio), to a deepened split within the FPL, and to the secession from the Farabundo Martí National Liberation Front, the umbrella revolutionary military organization, of Marcial's faction—a rift that weakened the unity of Salvadoran revolutionaries. Third, Grenada's New Jewel Movement split, beginning the sequence of events that ended in the invasion by the United States and six English-Caribbean countries. As a result of these events, Cuba emphasized the need for unity among revolutionary forces even more strongly in the mid-1980s.[70] Although the U.S. government took advantage of some of these events, the divisions themselves cannot be explained by U.S. policy.

In southern Africa in the early 1980s, the U.S. government worked hard to induce a settlement between South Africa and its neighbors, hoping to force Cuban troops to leave Angola and to halt the efforts of Angola, Mozambique, and South Africa to overthrow one another's governments.[71] The success of this policy in 1984 led to frictions between Cuba and Angola, and Cuba and Mozambique. In February 1984 Angola and South Africa agreed at Lusaka on procedures for the South African withdrawal from Angola and for Angolan restraint in support of SWAPO guerrillas in Namibia. Cuba was apparently surprised by this agreement. After some intense high-level consultation, Cuban-Angolan policy coordination improved by late 1984. Continued South African support for Jonas Savimbi's UNITA guerrillas against the Angolan government, and the U.S. decision in 1985 to send funds and military supplies to UNITA, subsequently strengthened Cuban-Angolan relations.

A bigger setback for Cuban policy was the Nkomati Accord signed in March 1984 by Mozambique and South Africa. This agreement ended Mozambique's support for the African National Congress, which was fighting against the South African government, in exchange for South Africa's pledge to end its support for the rebels seeking to overthrow Mozambique's government. Displeased with Mozambique's actions, Cuba nevertheless continued to work with that country. In November 1984 the two countries' ruling parties renewed their collaboration agreement; Mozambican students remained in schools in Cuba. Relations have continued to improve because South Africa has not honored its side of the bargain with Mozambique. In this case, Cuba showed diplomatic maturity even in adversity.[72]

We can make three generalizations about Cuban foreign policy in the Third World in the 1980s. First, the fact that Cuba's engagement is global means that at any moment it is likely to encounter a mixture of successes and setbacks, which need not be directly related to each other. Second, successful U.S. policy contributed to the setbacks Cuba encountered in southern Africa but not elsewhere. In general, the specific twists and turns of Cuban foreign policy in the mid- and late-1980s cannot be explained either by changes in the structure of the international system or by U.S. actions. Instead, the specific details of each situation hold the key to explanation. Third, evolution in the conduct of Cuban foreign policy has enabled the Cuban government to manage a complex international situation with diplomatic dexterity and maturity well beyond that of its earlier ventures.

The United States and Cuba in the 1980s

"The issue is our effort to promote democracy and economic well-being in the face of Cuban and Nicaraguan aggression, aided and abetted by the Soviet Union," President Ronald Reagan told his nation in May 1984 in explaining his government's policies toward Central America. Cuba, he continued, was involved in a "bold attempt," with the USSR and Nicaragua, "to install communism by force throughout the hemisphere." Moreover, he said, "El Salvador's yearning for democracy has been thwarted by Cuban-trained and armed guerrillas." Thus he summarized his view of Cuba and its foreign policy.[73]

According to the Cuban government, as Castro told the Cuban Communist party congress in December 1980, "a bitter ideological struggle has been waged by our imperialist enemy and the Cuban revolution—a struggle that has been and will continue to be fought not only in the realm of revolutionary and political ideas but also in the sphere of our people's patriotic national feelings." In his opinion, the future was bright because "our people's communist and internationalist consciousness has undoubtedly been increased in recent years."[74]

The U.S. and Cuban governments simply do not share the same ideas of freedom, justice, democracy, equality, order, the role and nature of violence, prosperity, and the nature of the good society. There are, and there should be, profound and lasting differences between the values and the interests of the two sides. Thus reconciliation is probably impossible, though that need not mean that they must wage war on each other. In fact, since the mid-1960s, when a "live-and-let-live" mutual security agreement was reached regarding the U.S. naval base at Guantánamo,[75] and when the United States focused its attention on Vietnam, direct U.S.-Cuban clashes had been rare—until the events of October 1983 in Grenada. On specific issues, of course, U.S.-Cuban disputes continued.

The United States has long objected to Cuba's military relations with the Soviet Union, to Cuba's deployment of troops and other military personnel overseas, and to its support for revolutionary movements. The main geographic areas of U.S. concern over Cuban activities are Central America and southern Africa. The United States also has substantial outstanding claims against Cuba for property seized in 1959–60.[76] It objects to Cuba's insistence on Puerto Rico's independence, to Cuba's use of emigration as a weapon against the United States, to the authoritarian nature of Cuba's political regime, and to the Cuban government's violations of human rights and its imprisonment of political opponents.[77]

Cuba objects to U.S. economic sanctions, to efforts to undermine or overthrow the Cuban government, and to the continued U.S. occupation and use of the Guantánamo naval base. (The treaties governing U.S. use of Guantánamo set no end date; the United States can occupy the base area until both governments agree otherwise.)[78] Cuba also objects to U.S. efforts to impede Cuban relations with third countries, especially the USSR, and to U.S. policies toward Angola and Nicaragua. Cuba believes the United States owes it reparations for damages stemming from U.S. policies. A host of other, smaller issues also troubles their relations.[79]

For most of the 1980s neither government tried very hard to address the issues of most importance to the other. The U.S. government was reluctant to rely on negotiations for fear of a recurrence of the 1975–1978 events, when, notwithstanding active U.S.-Cuban negotiations, Cuba sent troops to Angola and to Ethiopia. As an assistant secretary of state for inter-American affairs, Thomas Enders, has stated, the United States tried that approach and it failed: "Not only did it not induce Cuba to moderate its behavior, arguably it resulted in, or at least was followed by, even bolder, more aggressive action by Castro."[80] Cuba, for its part, has insisted that its relations with third parties—whether the USSR, Angola, or Nicaragua—are not the business of the U.S. government.

The sanctions imposed by the U.S. government against Cuba in the early 1960s have remained in place, except as modified in 1975 and 1977. Few economic transactions have occurred between the two countries; thus the United States has few tools to punish Cuba further; most feasible punishments have already been imposed. Nonetheless, in the 1980s the U.S. government continued its attempts to punish Cuba economically. Cuba's access to international capital markets was marginally impeded because U.S. banks could not participate in normal lending consortia and debt reschedulings; of course, Cuba got itself into debt, but probably at terms that were more onerous than if U.S. policy had been different. Merchant shippers, similarly, charged a premium above normal world prices for carrying cargo to and from Cuba as insurance against U.S. retaliation.

The United States also opposed loans to Cuba by multilateral institutions. The only organizations to which both countries belong where the issue has arisen are part of the United Nations system. Cuba has received funds from the Food and Agriculture Organization, the U.N. Development Program, the International Atomic Energy Agency, UNESCO, and UNICEF—but probably in smaller amounts than if the United States were not opposed; in return, Cuba has made donations of goods and services to these and other organizations in the system.[81] Even after the changes in the U.S. embargo against Cuba in 1975, exports to Cuba by subsidiaries of U.S. multinational firms based in third countries continue to be prohibited when more than 20 percent of the product's contents are of U.S. origin, and imports of products with Cuban content are also still prohibited. In practice, this rule has applied mostly to steel and other industrial imports from Western Europe and Japan that include Cuban nickel.[82]

The Reagan administration reversed some but not all of the 1975–1978 relaxations of U.S. policy. The governments' respective "interests sections" still operate, but the 1977 fishing agreement was allowed to lapse in 1982. Under Reagan, the U.S. government enforced existing legislation more vigorously. To stop some U.S. subsidiaries in third countries from trading with

Cuba, twelve U.S. firms were fined in 1981 for exceeding the limits of U.S. law, and eighteen firms in the United States, Panama, and Jamaica were designated as Cuban "fronts" intended to break the U.S. embargo; it became illegal for U.S. firms to trade with the eighteen firms. In 1982 the U.S. government accused the Cuban government of participating in the drug trade (see Chapter 5); Cuba responded by abrogating its 1978 agreement with the U.S. Coast Guard. Also in 1982 the U.S. government reimposed a partial ban on travel by U.S. citizens to Cuba (it prohibits tourism but allows visits by Cuban Americans to see their relatives or visits for scholarly, journalistic, and diplomatic purposes). Enforcement of the ban on imports of products made with Cuban nickel in Western Europe and Japan was also tightened in 1983–84.[83] The U.S. government has also sought to intimidate Cuba through warlike language and through the increased scope and frequency of U.S. military exercises near Cuba; Cuba has had to divert scarce resources to its defense. And yet, after surviving the effects of U.S. policies for so many years, the harm done to Cuba by the Reagan administration did not change Cuba's fundamental policies.[84]

As in times past, during the 1980s bilateral relations on technical matters continued routinely. The United States and Cuba exchanged weather information,[85] and cooperated on civil aviation, and on postal, telegraph, and telephone services. Cuba behaved responsibly in hijacking cases even without a bilateral agreement.[86] Routine exemptions to the U.S. embargo permitted the financial transactions needed for these relations.[87] Small, joint scholarly projects also continued.

There were two high-level contacts between the two governments between 1981 and 1988: a meeting in Mexico City between Secretary of State Alexander Haig and Vice President Carlos Rafael Rodríguez in November 1981, and another in Havana between Ambassador-at-Large Vernon Walters and Castro four months later. These meetings led nowhere.[88] The two countries came nearest to agreement on several issues in late 1984, when, facing strained relations with the Soviet Union, Cuba sought to improve its relations with the United States. At that time, Angola and Cuba came close to accepting key U.S. proposals linking Namibia's independence to a Cuban troop withdrawal from Angola. Cuba also expressed its appreciation of the U.S. government's stricter enforcement of its own antiterrorist laws, which included arresting and convicting those who had attacked Cuban diplomats in the United States.[89] In December 1984 Cuba agreed to permit the repatriation of 2,746 Cubans who had come to the United States in 1980 and were excluded under U.S. laws; both governments also agreed to regularize their migration relations. Henceforth the U.S. government was to treat emigrating Cubans as immigrants, not as refugees from Communism. The Reagan administration argued in U.S. federal court that those about to be repatriated to Cuba need not fear that the Cuban government would not protect their human rights.[90] This process stopped in May 1985, when the U.S. government's Radio Martí began broadcasting to Cuba, and Cuba suspended the migration agreement in retaliation. Soviet-Cuban relations improved about the same time, and the war in Angola intensified.

In late 1987, once more at a moment of difficulty in Soviet-Cuban relations, Cuba took several initiatives to establish a possible new framework for its relations with the United States. U.S.-Angolan-Cuban negotiations over southern Africa intensified again (see Chapter 6), thanks in part to Cuba's agreement to negotiate a schedule for the withdrawal of all of its troops from Angola. In November 1987, Cuba reinstated the migration agreement, tacitly accepting Radio Martí. The general improvement in U.S.-Soviet relations, and the improvement in Cuban-Soviet relations, permitted further steps in 1988. Early in the year Cuba allowed a delegation of private U.S. citizens to inspect its prisons and to interview political prisoners. Also in early 1988 Cuba allowed the chief of the U.S. Interests Section in Havana to tour the nuclear plant under construction near the city of Cienfuegos. The U.S. government reciprocated by taking steps to attempt to induce South Africa to withdraw its troops from Angola, by responding responsibly to Cuba's change of policy with regard to the migration agreement, and by beginning to explore other areas for possible agreement.

For Cuba the major long-standing issue has been its wish to be treated as a sovereign country on a par with the United States. For the United States, that recognition might not cost much objectively, but it would be difficult politically. Having weathered the administrations of seven U.S. presidents, the Cuban government is in no hurry to compromise on matters it deems significant. In response to Reagan administration policies, Cuba built up its armed forces with Soviet assistance and did not discontinue actions the U.S. government found objectionable. In Cuba's view, the United States should recognize that it has lost this "war" of thirty years and should accept Cuba's rightful place among nations. Acceptance is unlikely, regardless of the party in power in Washington. Overall, the prospects for good relations between the United States and Cuba are poor.

For the United States, the issues were first defined in 1808 by Thomas Jefferson's Cabinet, which agreed that U.S. agents should tell "influential persons in Cuba" that the United States would be "extremely unwilling to see you pass under the dominion or ascendancy" of any of the major world powers. However, the U.S. government would not commit itself to support

Cuba in the event its leaders were to adopt an independent policy. The Jefferson Cabinet's orders said only that, "should you choose to declare independence, we cannot now commit ourselves by saying we would make common cause with you but must reserve ourselves to act according to the then existing circumstances, but in our proceedings we shall be influenced by friendship to you, by a firm belief that our interests are intimately connected, and by the strongest repugnance to see you under subordination" of any of the world's other leading powers.[91] The United States remains just as unhappy about Soviet "ascendancy" in Cuba today as it was about Spanish domination in 1808, but it has been unwilling to adopt policies that might induce Cuban leaders to act more independently of the USSR. Although U.S.-Cuban interests remain "intimately connected," in 1988, unlike 1808, the U.S. government cannot credibly claim that it professes friendship for the Cuban government. The key issues have not changed much, nor have relations between the governments become more cordial nearly two centuries later.

How Cuban Foreign Policy Is Made

9

Cuban foreign policy results from the coordinated actions of many agencies, groups, and individuals; it is not just the extension of one person's thoughts, inclinations, and actions, although Fidel Castro has certainly stamped it with his ideas. Castro designed the framework for Cuban foreign policy. He makes the boldest and riskiest decisions and, at times, oversees implementation in minute detail. Cuban foreign policy would not be what it is without Castro, but it would also not be what it is if only Castro were responsible for it. Both personal and organizational factors combine in foreign policy decisions. Having examined the content and effects of Cuban foreign policy in previous chapters, let us turn to how foreign policy is made and what individuals and organizations have been involved in making it.

Fidel Castro as a Decision Maker

Castro combines strategic and tactical abilities rarely surpassed among world leaders. His approach to decision making is shaped by several fundamental ideas that he has held since his youth. The first is his belief that the long-range interests of Cuba and the United States are incompatible. This concept, which goes well beyond Marxism-Leninism, stems from Castro's sense of his own and Cuba's identity. It was exhibited, for example, in a letter of June 5, 1958, to his long-time associate Celia Sánchez, in which Castro swore that "the Americans will pay very dearly for what they are doing." After victory in the revolutionary war, he added, "a much longer and bigger war will begin for me: the war that I will make against them."[1] The same idea has appeared in his public statements. For example, he told the second congress of the Cuban Communist party in December 1980: Across the centuries, "the United States has been the sworn enemy of our nation . . . Imperialism has never stopped attacking our Cuban national spirit, putting it to the test."[2] The corollary of this concept for Castro is that all Cubans should combat the United States; revolutionaries ought to be in the vanguard of that historic struggle.

A second fundamental idea is that it is not only possible to recognize the march of history but also desirable to speed its progress. This approach to history made Marxism intriguing to Castro, and this approach to revolutionary leadership made Leninism essential. Castro stated in the Second Declaration of Havana in 1962: "In America and in the world, it is known that the revolution will be victorious." But, he continued, "it is improper revolutionary behavior to sit at one's doorstep waiting for the corpse of imperialism to pass by." Therefore, "it is the duty of every revolutionary to make the revolution."[3]

A third key idea is that revolution in only one country is not possible, at least not for long. Castro believes that international activism must be an inherent component of a revolutionary's thought and action, not just an option or a tactic. Without such activism, revolutionaries—if they succeeded in gaining power—would be snuffed out by their enemies. Castro believes that the United States has designed and governs a world system that affects each and every country. To struggle against it in Cuba, it is necessary to struggle against it everywhere. According to this view, the United States is not just a static presence. Its politics is inherently expansionist—it is the spirit of capitalism to grow—and U.S. culture shapes thoughts, images, and values throughout the world. "Imperialism," in Castro's view, must be understood as a world system, not just as one aspect of U.S.-Cuban relations. He sees his struggle against imperialism as the struggle of a citizen of the world against a world system of domination.

These three ideas led Castro to participate as a young man in attempts to overthrow the governments of the Dominican Republic and Colombia. More recently, they have helped him understand the defeat of the Grenadan revolution. They continue to be at the heart of the support for international revolution, an essential element of Cuba's foreign policy.

Castro has other, more particular beliefs about himself that also shape his approach to foreign policy. Most important, he believes that he has a historic mission, as was clear in his first major statement to the people of Cuba, made during his trial for attacking the Moncada army barracks on July 26, 1953: "Condemn me; it does not matter to me. History will absolve me." At another crisis in his political life—after Cuba's failure to achieve the ten-million-ton sugar harvest targeted for 1970 and the resulting dislocation of the Cuban economy—Castro reiterated this theme: "If we have an atom of value, that atom of value will be through our service to an idea, a cause, linked to the people."[4] He told an interviewer in 1985, "Let me state, in all frankness, that I have never harbored personal doubts or lack of confidence . . . if you see your actions as objectively correct, then not having doubts is good."[5]

Castro maintains that individuals, himself above all, can overcome obstacles through sacrifice and hard work. The more apparently unreachable the political goal, the more worthy it is of pursuit. Willful political action and tactical boldness work in the long run, even if there are temporary setbacks. This belief led him to attack the Moncada barracks against apparently impossible odds in 1953; to launch a crazy expedition against the Batista regime in 1956; once in power, to defy the United States; and, first in the late 1960s and again in the late 1980s, to attempt to transform the Cuban people into ideological beings committed to revolutionary ideals and unsoiled by the dirty motivation of money. "Don Quixote's madness and the madness of revolutionaries are similar," Castro told an interviewer; "the spirit is similar . . . that spirit of the knight-errant, of righting wrongs everywhere, of fighting against giants."[6]

Castro believes that no subject is beyond his intellectual grasp, from battlefield tactics to the genetics of cattle breeding.[7] No detail is unworthy of his attention. His interference in the most minute economic decisions at all levels of government is a major explanation for the disorganization, wild experimentation, and eventual collapse of the Cuban economy in the late 1960s. Castro's style of leadership has caused great problems for managing Cuban public policy. But it is also an important part of his public appeal and charm—a head of state knowledgeable about chromosomes, worried about the fate of a little village in a remote region, and involved in the intricacies of sugar mill operations.

Castro may cultivate the public image of a leader who resists the formation of a cult of personality, but one has subtly developed nevertheless. His beard, a symbol of past struggles, is a physical reminder of his historic role. Tall by Cuban standards, Castro uses his physique in conversation to make points, to create intimacy, to generate warmth and at the same time awe. A world-class orator, able to express ideas thoughtfully and at great length, he can address sophisticated audiences on esoteric subjects and can speak simply, with affection and humor, to little children. A man of extraordinary energy, a renowned night owl, he projects an image of omniscience and hides the reality of his near omnipotence in Cuban politics. Wise but not overbearing is the image he has chosen; the reality is that he is flawed, ruthless, and enormously powerful.[8]

Castro's approach to decision making explains many aspects of Cuban foreign policy, particularly tension with the United States and support for revolution overseas. It provides a rationale for Cuba's persistence even in the face of setbacks, for its patient expectation that revolutionaries will prevail in the end, and for the bold actions it has taken to bring about revolution.

Castro performs best when he can orchestrate or anticipate a crisis that helps him advance toward his strategic goals. In late 1959 and early 1960, for example, he provoked conflict with the U.S. government, to the latter's bewilderment, that helped pave the way for the break with the United States and alliance with the Soviet Union. Similarly, Castro expected the Bay of Pigs invasion in April 1961 and responded to it effectively.[9]

Castro's capacity for strategic crisis management was also displayed in 1977. He began again to improve U.S.-Cuban relations—an improvement that had been interrupted because of Cuba's intervention in Angola—even though Cuban troops remained in Angola. Late that year, Cuba intervened in the Ethiopian-Somalia war after Castro had failed in his intensive mediation efforts. Cuba also reactivated its support for Central American revolutionaries in late 1977.[10] Each crisis had its own roots and particularities. All had global consequences, and Castro did make "strategic decisions" to deal with these effects.[11] Castro had no master plan, but he made masterful decisions.

In handling crises that involve unforeseen elements, however, Castro has been less successful. In 1962, after the deployment of Soviet strategic weapons in Cuba, Castro was not surprised by the ensuing crisis with the United States. But he was shocked and furious when the Soviets yielded to U.S. demands that the missiles be removed. His behavior during that crisis was seriously flawed. Because Castro was ready for nuclear war, he impeded the settlement that avoided it. He envisaged leading the Cuban people to collective suicide. Although years later he said that he was wrong in 1962—that he had not fully appreciated that the settlement would help consolidate his regime—Castro has never repudiated two views he held at the time: that the Soviets should have consulted with him before acting and that the statement "never surrender to the United States" remains a valid principle in times of crisis. Castro's performance was calmer and more effective in subsequent crises with the United States that did not include such surprises.

The principle that Cuba should never surrender to the United States has a rational basis. It is intended to persuade the United States that the cost of war will be very high. It is logical that the leader of a weak state make such statements to show that he cannot be intimidated and that he will resist military blackmail. Visible and wide-ranging preparations for war have to be undertaken to convince the United States that the whole Cuban people will resist; Cuba's willingness and capacity to fight in Angola and Ethiopia have further deterred the United States from attacking Cuba.[12] However, the "never surrender" principle is not rational in the extreme form in which Castro applies it, because in a crisis it can prevent a settlement or lead to casualties that no longer serve the purpose of deterring or terminating war.

Castro handled effectively the Soviet-Cuban crisis of 1967–68, a conflict that had built up gradually as a result of Cuba's own decisions. One reason for the different outcome is that the emotions the United States stirs in Castro are not evoked by the USSR. The crisis was also not a military one; no bloodshed or national suicide was at issue. Largely for these reasons, Castro gave in to the Soviet position.

Castro also handled well the decisions to intervene in Angola and Ethiopia. In each case, the crisis evolved during a period of months, Cuba prepared for it, and U.S. behavior was highly restrained. Gabriel García Márquez has discussed Castro's crisis management in the early stages of the Angolan War in 1975. "Fidel Castro kept up on even the smallest war details," according to García Márquez. He saw off all the ships; he spoke with the troops; he personally drove the commanders of the special forces unit to the airport for the first flight to Angola. García Márquez wrote:

> Castro remained in the General Staff command room for up to 14 hours at a stretch, sometimes without eating or sleeping . . . He followed the battle operations with colored pins on detailed maps as big as the walls and was in constant communication with the MPLA high command on the battlefield . . . There was not a point on the map of Angola he could not identify or a jot in the terrain he did not know by heart. His concentration on the war was so intense and meticulous that he could cite any figure about Angola as if it were Cuba, and he spoke of its cities, its customs and its people as if he had lived there all his life.[13]

During Cuba's difficult year of 1980, its government's crisis management was poor, with Castro himself responsible. The year began badly for him with the death of his long-time personal secretary and confidante, Celia Sánchez. Cuba was in economic and political turmoil. Although Castro had known about the situation for months, he responded to specific events with anger, not analysis. He was furious that the Peruvian and Venezuelan embassies had become havens for Cubans seeking asylum. His decision to remove the guards from the Peruvian embassy, thus allowing unlimited numbers of Cubans to enter the building, was impulsive ("we lost our patience"); it was intended to burden the Peruvians with such unexpected guests in their embassy—"no matter what the price."[14] That thousands of Cubans should decide to emigrate at a moment's notice was a shock to Castro. What had been a minor police problem became a major domestic and international crisis through Castro's personal misjudgment. His subsequent handling of other aspects of the crisis was also flawed. Castro did not foresee how tarnished his regime's image was until the first emigrants to Costa Rica and Peru were received there as heroes.[15]

Castro's reaction to the October 1983 invasion of Grenada most resembles his reaction to the 1962 missile crisis. Castro was not surprised by the invasion itself; indeed, he had analyzed possible Cuban responses to an invasion in his communications with the Grenadan government. But he was surprised by the behavior of his military officers in Grenada. His instructions had been: "Do not surrender under any circumstances." Colonel Pedro Tortoló, the commander of the Cuban forces in Grenada, had wired back: "Commander in Chief, we will carry out your instructions and we will not surrender. Fatherland or Death. We shall overcome." Cuba's ambassador to Grenada added that the Cubans in Grenada had pledged "that they will fight to the last man and the last bullet." In fact, Castro's orders were disobeyed. Though the ambassador wired at 11:00 A.M. on October 26 that "the combatants at our last position did not surrender and died for the fatherland," only 24 of 784 Cubans died in Grenada.[16] Whereas the Cuban government has continued to praise the Cuban construction workers' resistance as military reservists in Grenada (in Cuba they became a special construction brigade called "Grenada's Heroes"), the military officers who commanded them were demoted for conduct unbecoming an officer.[17]

Castro plainly expected the Cubans in Grenada to fight to the last man. If they did not, he feared, the United States would think Cuba weak.[18] There was a rational basis for this fear. However, the Cuban reservists' performance in combat sufficed to impress the United States with the courage and combat readiness of ordinary Cuban civilians. They fought so well that, at first, U.S. commanding officers overestimated their number. Despite eventual surrender, their performance proved that the costs of a direct U.S. attack on Cuba would be prohibitively high. If Cuban reservists fought so loyally and courageously far from home, surely the U.S. government would respect even more Cuba's regular armed forces defending the homeland. Once again, as in 1962, Castro carried a rational position to an irrational extreme and stripped the surviving Cuban officers of their rank and their honor. In short, surprise rattles Castro. And in the context of a crisis with the United States, surprise can lead him to irrational behavior.

The Foreign Policy Leadership Team

In governing Cuba, Castro has relied on a small circle of associates since the revolutionary war; the same pattern is found in the making of Cuban foreign policy. Of the eleven members of the party's founding Political Bureau and Secretariat (the leading policy-making and implementation units within the Communist party) in 1965, only one (Dorticós) had died and only one other (Chomón) had been demoted twenty years later. All of the vice presidents of the Council of State in 1985 had been members of the party's National Directorate—the first formalized party leadership body— in 1962 and of the Political Bureau since 1965. Of the fourteen members of the Political Bureau in 1985, nine had been members of either the Political Bureau or the Secretariat since 1965; four others had been ministers of government as early as 1959–60; only one, Jorge Risquet, had been added to the top leadership as recently as the late 1960s. Fidel Castro's designated successor, and Cuba's second most powerful person, is his brother Raúl, armed forces minister, first vice president of the Councils of State and Government, and second party secretary. As these examples indicate, Castro has delegated power to his long-time trusted associates, and only to them.

For the first time since 1960, major changes were made at the top of the regime in anticipation of the 1986 Third Party Congress. Ramiro Valdés, minister of the interior, and Guillermo García, vice president for transportation and communication, were relieved of their government posts and of membership in the party's Political Bureau. Sergio del Valle, minister of health (and former interior minister) and the ailing Blas Roca (who died in 1987) also left the Political Bureau and their government posts. Antonio Pérez Herrero was dismissed as party secretary for ideology; a rising star in Cuban politics, he had also been an alternate member of the Political Bureau in charge of the party's propaganda and the mass media. Humberto Pérez was also dismissed as president of the Central Planning Board. These high-level changes led to many more at lower levels. Those who remained in power in government and party posts were still long-time personal comrades of Fidel Castro.

Personal Responsibility in Foreign Policy
Although, as we shall see, many agencies and officials are responsible for implementing foreign policy, a handful of leaders have retained authority over the most important decisions. At times, the top leaders themselves implement the most delicate foreign policies. For example, in the 1960s— during the long tenure of Foreign Minister Raúl Roa—Prime Minister Fidel

Castro, Armed Forces Minister Raúl Castro, and President Osvaldo Dorticós carried out the key foreign policy missions. In the spring of 1959, for instance, Fidel Castro went to the United States to gain time to consolidate his rule; in September 1960, he went to the United Nations to meet Nikita Khrushchev; and in 1963 and 1964 he went to the Soviet Union to renegotiate the terms of relations. Raúl Castro went to Moscow in July 1960 to sign the military alliance with the USSR and in the summer of 1962 to discuss the deployment of Soviet strategic weapons in Cuba. He returned to Moscow for Communist party conferences in 1965 and 1966. Dorticós represented Cuba at the first two Nonaligned Movement conferences. In June 1960 he toured Latin America, and in 1962 he represented Cuba at Punta del Este when Cuba was suspended from the Organization of American States. Dorticós accompanied Raúl Castro to Moscow for the 1966 conference of Communist parties. Roa did not even go on any of these crucial trips to Moscow. Clearly it was felt that only top leaders could be entrusted to negotiate the regime's survival.

In the 1970s Fidel Castro personally supervised the expansion of Cuba's ties with African countries. He spent two months traveling in Africa, the USSR, and Eastern Europe in 1972. He attended the Nonaligned Movement conference in Algiers in 1973. Over the years he has spent several months in Africa. One of his most significant, albeit unsuccessful, efforts was his personal shuttle diplomacy during five weeks in 1977, an attempt to avoid war between Ethiopia and Somalia. Castro's chairmanship of the Nonaligned Movement also demanded considerable personal attention. He has hosted leaders from many Eastern European and African countries on their visits to Havana, as well as some from Western Europe, Canada, and Latin America, and has lavished personal attention on visiting members of the U.S. Congress and others in U.S. politics, mass media, and business.

In the early 1970s Castro also worked personally to repair relations with the USSR. He went there twice in 1972: in July to join the Council for Mutual Economic Assistance (CMEA) and in December to reschedule debts and to sign other economic agreements. In January 1974 he hosted Leonid Brezhnev in Havana. He attended Brezhnev's funeral in 1982, Andropov's in 1984, and the Soviet Communist party congresses in 1976, 1981, and 1986. To help overcome Cuban-Soviet tensions in 1984–85, Castro visited the USSR twice in 1986, spending several weeks developing a relationship with Mikhail Gorbachev. In 1987 Castro returned for the seventieth anniversary of the Russian Revolution, again to patch up difficulties with the Soviets.

General Raúl Castro has also continued to share in the conduct of military and political relations with the Soviet Union. After 1970 Dorticós became gradually more detached from foreign affairs; his place was taken by Carlos Rafael Rodríguez, who manages economic relations with the USSR and other CMEA countries as well as playing an important role in relations with Western Europe, Latin America, the United States, and the Nonaligned Movement. When the elderly Raúl Roa was replaced as foreign minister by Isidoro Malmierca in December 1976, the minister's role did not change. Malmierca has spent much time traveling on protocol missions, not making the most sensitive decisions nor carrying out the most important foreign policy missions.

Highly centralized foreign policy management imparts coherence and allows greater speed of response; it creates channels to handle problems that go beyond formal government relations. However, Cuba's reliance on highly personalized decision making and implementation in foreign policy has had its costs. It has made U.S.-Cuban relations more difficult, for example; the U.S. government has insisted that Cuba use regular channels, through the two countries' diplomatic Interests Sections. The personal emphasis has also at times impaired Cuban relations with some Latin American governments whose presidents have been reluctant, for their own reasons, to be seen hobnobbing with Fidel Castro. The same factor helped defeat U.S. Senator Frank Church in the 1980 elections, when Church's opponent, Stephen Symms, made an issue of Church's personal relations with Castro.

The personal element in foreign policy helps explain both Cuba's difficult relations with the USSR in the 1960s and their improvement in the 1970s. Castro's personal outrage at Khrushchev's decision, without consulting Castro, to remove strategic missiles from Cuba in the fall of 1962 seriously impaired Cuban-Soviet relations. Vice President Rodríguez called attention in 1982 to the personal factor as one of the many causes of worsened relations with the USSR in the late 1960s. Cuban and Soviet Political Bureau members, he said, "had taken fifteen years to establish close" personal relations.[19] He also dated the improvement in Cuban-Soviet relations from Brezhnev's visit to Cuba in 1974—evidence that the personal touch could also benefit Cuba in foreign relations.

As in most countries, when leaders take personal responsibility for foreign policy, they are judged on the quality of their performance by the results of the policy they promote. For instance, Foreign Trade Ministers Alberto Mora and Marcelo Fernández lost their jobs in 1964 and 1980, respectively, because top leaders judged that they had mismanaged foreign trade. Military commanders are also often judged by how their actions affect Cuba's relations with other countries. Colonel Pedro Tortoló, for example, lost his rank after his command of Cuban forces in Grenada was deemed unbecoming an officer. In May 1980 the Air Force mistakenly attacked a Bahamian Coast Guard boat and sank it; in December 1980 Francisco Cabrera, the Air Force commander, was the only division general not included as a full Central Committee member at the Second Party Congress. (He was also replaced as Air Force chief.)

Good performance in overseas military engagements has also been rewarded. Division General Abelardo Colomé, founder of the Twenty-sixth of July Movement, was publicly commended by the Cuban government for his fulfillment of "several internationalist missions," above all his "brilliant leadership" of the Cuban troops in Angola in 1975–76. Colomé was promoted ahead of other, more senior division generals to a post in the party's Political Bureau in 1986. Division General Arnaldo Ochoa, who joined the rebellion as a teenager in early 1958 and fought alongside Castro, has also been publicly honored by the Cuban government for his work on "several internationalist missions under adverse and difficult circumstances . . . [which] included his brilliant performance as leader of the Cuban troops in Ethiopia" in 1977–78.[20] He was promoted to division general and armed forces deputy minister over more senior officers.

Vice President Rodríguez was a minister without portfolio in the late 1960s, having lost his earlier, higher rank. His prudent and careful work in improving Cuban-Soviet relations paid off for Cuba (and for him) in the early 1970s. Rodríguez helped to convince the USSR to invest additional resources in Cuba after the economic mismanagement and political disarray of the 1960s. His appointment as deputy prime minister (later vice president of government) in 1972 and his membership on the party's Political Bureau since 1975 are a tribute to his effectiveness in foreign policy.

During Deputy Foreign Minister Ricardo Alarcón's long tour of service as United Nations ambassador, Cuba gradually overcame its position as a pariah state in the United Nations. Alarcón's effective work with African and Asian countries contributed to Cuba's emergence as a leader of the Nonaligned Movement. He was Cuba's foremost contact with the U.S. government when no formal diplomatic links existed, and has remained Cuba's most important diplomat in U.S. relations, contributing to agreements reached during the Carter administration. Alarcón also negotiated Cuba's only agreement with the Reagan administration (that on migration, signed in December 1984). He was promoted to deputy foreign minister and appointed as one of the youngest party Central Committee alternates in December 1980.

The cases of General Cabrera, party Secretary Antonio Pérez Herrero, and Vice President Rodríguez indicate that the Cuban government gives some people a second chance. General Cabrera remained division general until his retirement in 1983, when he was appointed ambassador to Ethiopia. He was replaced by Pérez Herrero in 1986. Vice President Rodríguez's political fortunes recovered in the early 1970s. This pattern exists at lower ranks as well. José Pérez Novoa, Cuba's ambassador to Ethiopia, intervened in Ethiopia's internal affairs in 1978 and was expelled by Ethiopia. Pérez Novoa became ambassador to India in 1981.

A second chance is possible because Cuban leaders believe in learning from experience, as is evident in the career of Fidel Castro, who had become one of the world's most experienced statesmen in international affairs by the late 1980s. General Vernon Walters has given his impressions of Castro, whom he met first in 1959, when Walters translated for Vice President Richard Nixon during Castro's visit to the United States and again in Havana in 1982, when Walters visited as U.S. special ambassador: "I must say the Castro I saw in 1982 was a very different Castro from the one I'd seen twenty-five years before . . . Much more sure of himself, much more relaxed, and extraordinarily courteous."[21] Castro has learned to deal more successfully with the United States and with the Soviet Union, recovering from the 1967–68 debacle and limiting the conflicts of 1984–85 and 1987. He has learned as well the importance of the international understandings that developed in the aftermath of the 1962 missile crisis and has changed Cuban policy to prop up those understandings.

There has also been a change in the government's analytical capacity, which had been generally poor until the late 1970s. For example, Raúl Valdés Vivó, the Communist party's secretary for international relations, published a book on Ethiopia in 1977 which suggests that his own knowledge about Ethiopia was limited.[22] A former high Ethiopian official confirms that Cubans were "naive" about domestic politics in his country on the eve of their intervention. Moreover, Cuba was surprised at how difficult it was to bring Ethiopia and Somalia to a peace table, and at the complexity of the Ethiopian government's internal processes. This naiveté has begun to change. In the late 1970s serious analysis of other countries and of international relations received more emphasis at the universities. The Center for Western European Studies was also founded. In the early 1980s new Centers for African and Middle Eastern Studies, for American Studies, and for Studies of the World Economy, among others—several of them formally subordinate to the party's Central Committee staff—began to produce good scholarship. They provide advice and help to improve the training of Cuba's foreign policy establishment.[23]

Learning is also in evidence in the practice of Cuban foreign policy. In 1973, at the Nonaligned Movement summit in Algiers, Castro and Mohammar Khadaffy engaged in a shouting match over the USSR's global role and Cuba's links to the Soviets and the movement. Cuba, behaving prudently, has gradually and greatly improved its relations with Libya since then. Cuba's recovery of its diplomatic standing in parts of Latin America and in Guyana in the early 1980s was a tribute to its diplomatic efficacy and maturity. Cuba responded with anger and opposition to South Africa's accords with Angola at Lusaka and with Mozambique at Nkomati but honored its agreements with both, improving relations with Angola quickly and with Mozambique somewhat slower. In early 1984 a military coup in Guinea overthrew the government that had replaced President Sekou Touré within a week after his death and adopted policies to dismantle Touré's legacy. Cuba had worked closely with Touré and disapproved of the new measures, but it honored its agreements with Guinea. Even more striking, despite Castro's contempt for capitalism, Cuban troops have successfully guarded Gulf Oil's installations in Angola since 1975. These Cuban foreign policy accomplishments resulted not only from Castro's learning to be an effective leader in international affairs, but also from the growing skill of his foreign policy team.

Factions and Coalitions in Foreign Policy Making

This foreign policy team had to be constructed in the early years of revolutionary rule. Scholars have often speculated about factions in the Cuban leadership and about the policy disputes that they may reflect. What minimal evidence can be found does suggest that leaders have built coalitions in support of a broad framework for Cuban foreign policy, and especially to foster leadership cohesion at times of risky endeavors or new departures in foreign policy. One example is the decision to commit Cuban personnel to Ernesto (Che) Guevara's expedition to Bolivia in the late 1960s. Although no general consensus existed among Cuban leaders in the mid-1960s about the wisdom of supporting revolution in other countries, a majority coalesced in support of the Guevara expedition—the makeup of which (many members of the Cuban leadership or those with close ties to the leadership) served to build this coalition.

The expedition included many Cubans.[24] For example, Juan Vitalio Acuña and Antonio Sánchez Díaz were commandants (then the highest military rank in Cuba) and members of the Communist party's Central Committee from 1965 until their deaths in Bolivia. Acuña had joined Fidel Castro's guerrillas in 1957 and remained close to him for the next decade; he had also served for a time as Guevara's deputy and, near the end of 1958, under Political Bureau member Commandant Guillermo García. Gustavo Machín had worked with the leader of the university students' Revolutionary Directorate (Faure Chomón, a Political Bureau member in 1965) in the failed effort to assassinate Batista and had fought with directorate troops along with Guevara's Twenty-sixth of July Movement troops in late 1958. After 1959 Machín was Guevara's deputy minister of industries; he also served as chief of the general staff of the Matanzas Army Corps. Israel Reyes had fought under Raúl Castro and later under Commandant Abelardo Colomé. In 1959 Reyes worked for Deputy Interior Minister Manuel Piñeiro, a Central Committee member since 1965, and eventually became a bodyguard for Raúl Castro. Octavio de la Concepción Pedraja had served during the guerrilla war with the military medical corps led by Jose Ramón Machado, a government minister in the mid-1960s. René Martínez Tamayo served in military security after 1959 and eventually joined the Interior Ministry. Alberto Fernández Montes de Oca had come from Mexico with Pedro Miret (government minister in the mid-1960s) to join the guerrillas; he served in 1958 under Guevara and, after 1959, as a manager of enterprises for Guevara's Ministry of Industries. Orlando Pantoja Tamayo had fought under Guevara and Fidel Castro in the 1950s. After 1959, he worked for the Interior Ministry, becoming first chief of the ministry's Border Guard Troops. In short, the key members of Guevara's expedition were drawn from the close associates of major Cuban leaders and from the most important government organizations. The Interior Ministry had a leading role in promoting the expedition. The only leadership group missing from the coalition supporting the Guevara expedition was the prerevolutionary Communist party.

Many prerevolutionary Communist party members aligned themselves with the USSR and the Moscow-oriented Latin American Communist parties to oppose the view that the armed struggle was the only way to revolutionary power. Thus they opposed Guevara's efforts to promote a revolution in Bolivia. As Cuba's conflict with the Soviets deepened, so too did the conflict between this faction and the majority of the leadership, which squelched this "microfaction" in January 1968. Former members of the prerevolutionary Communist party then split. Carlos Rafael Rodríguez and Blas Roca sided with Fidel and Raúl Castro; the other group of old Communists, who sided with Aníbal Escalante, were defeated, and many were imprisoned. The 1968 crisis was the last time until 1985 that any Cuban official was demoted for reasons publicly linked to foreign policy. The coalition that emerged from the events of 1968 was strengthened in the 1970s: Roca and Rodríguez joined the Political Bureau in 1975, Cuban relations with the USSR and with Soviet-oriented Communist parties in Latin America were greatly improved, and the new consensus supported the initiatives in Angola, Ethiopia, and Central America.

Then a new crisis developed in the Cuban leadership near the end of 1984, when Castro sought to improve Cuba's relations with the United States, Western Europe, and Latin America. He wanted to lessen the serious tensions with the United States and to create a more favorable environment for Cuba's new exports to market-economy countries; one tangible result was that a migration agreement was signed with the United States. Antonio Pérez Herrero, the party's secretary for ideology, objected to Castro's abrupt switch in December 1984 from profound hostility toward the U.S. government to rapprochement. He objected as well to Castro's invitation to several U.S. Roman Catholic bishops to discuss affairs of state with him, and to the implication that discussions with Cuba's bishops would follow. Castro called an extraordinary meeting of the party's Central Committee, which praised his recent foreign policy stands and asserted that "only these positions" have "ideological validity," and which removed Pérez Herrero from his post in the Secretariat and as Political Bureau alternate (though he remained a member of the Central Committee). The officials directly in charge of party propaganda and the state's radio and television monopoly were also replaced because they were part of Pérez Herrero's team.[25]

Although Castro shapes Cuban foreign policy, he has had to build and maintain a consensus within the regime's leadership. Since the disputes of the 1960s, the leadership has agreed on the basic outlines of foreign policy. Nonetheless, the 1985 dismissal of a key party leader over a foreign policy dispute suggests that there is opposition to Castro's breaking out of the framework of consensus, or doing so too quickly—a consensus that has rested on hostile relations with the United States. Coalitions are required to manage the domestic politics of Cuba's foreign policy, to support the foreign policy leadership team, and to make the foreign policy apparatus work effectively.

Cuba's Foreign Policy Apparatus

State and Party Policy-Making Organizations
In Cuba, unlike most other Communist states, the Constitution, approved in 1976, requires that the same person be head of state and of government.[26] That person, Fidel Castro, is also the first secretary of the Communist party and the commander-in-chief of the armed forces. Before 1976 the Fundamental Law of 1959 provided that different people serve as head of state

and head of government. From 1959 until December 1976 Osvaldo Dorticós was President; Fidel Castro was Prime Minister. As President, Dorticós
(a Political Bureau member until his suicide in 1983) participated actively
in foreign policy making.

The Constitution gives the National Assembly the right to set the general
framework for foreign policy, to declare war, and to approve peace treaties.
In fact, the National Assembly is in session only about five days a year.
Since its first meeting in December 1976, it has yet to have a substantive
discussion of foreign policy, military, or security affairs. The National Assembly elects a Council of State, many of whose thirty-one members also
belong to the party's Political Bureau and Secretariat, which meets more
frequently. The Constitution assigns to the Council of State the power to
appoint and receive ambassadors, to ratify treaties, and to assume the assembly's powers of making war and peace whenever the assembly is not in
session—most of the time. The irrelevance of the National Assembly to
foreign policy is clear. Even the council's powers are mostly formal, however; foreign policy debates and decisions occur elsewhere.

The key institution making foreign policy is the party's Political Bureau.
Half the size of the Council of State, the Political Bureau includes only the
most important leaders. It was the Political Bureau, not the council or the
assembly, that decided to send Cuban troops to fight in Ethiopia in late
1977, for example.[27] Similarly, the foreign policy debate of 1984–85 occurred within the party, not the state, organizations, and Pérez Herrero's
dismissal resulted from a Political Bureau recommendation to the Central
Committee.[28]

The Central Committee, the party's deliberative body, has at times played
an important role as a sounding board for lower-level leaders. It has had a
role in decisions on every major foreign policy issue with actual or potential
domestic repercussions. The Central Committee was founded in 1965, but
before the First Party Congress in 1975, it met rarely. Meetings were held
in May 1967, however, when Venezuela captured Cubans working to overthrow the Venezuelan government; in October 1967, when Guevara's expedition to Bolivia failed and he and two members of the Central Committee were killed; and in January 1968, in the midst of the domestic and
international crisis involving the "microfaction" and the Soviet Union.
After 1975 the Central Committee has met regularly (about twice a year)
and in emergency sessions, such as the one on the Pérez Herrero dismissal.

The Central Committee's staff for international relations is split into two
departments, one for the Americas and the other, the General Department
for International Relations, for the rest of the world. The General Depart-

ment oversees all party personnel policies in international affairs (even personnel assignments in the Western Hemisphere) and supervises the international activities of the mass organizations—those for labor, youth, and women.[29] The Americas Department has been headed by Manuel Piñeiro, formerly deputy minister of the interior, since 1974. The General Department was headed by Raúl Valdés Vivó until his demotion in 1979, and then by Jesús Montané until 1986. Both Piñeiro and Montané have been Central Committee members since 1965. According to Foreign Relations Deputy Minister Ricardo Alarcón, also a Central Committee alternate, "the party directs everything but it does not do everything."[30] In other words, the party sets general foreign policy, which is then carried out by government agencies. Much high-level coordination between party and government organizations is thus necessary.

Cuban foreign policy making remains one of the most centralized areas within a highly centralized regime. Centralization results in part from the necessity for an embattled regime to concentrate authority in order to act effectively in international affairs. It also reflects above all Fidel Castro's overwhelming power and preferences. Although key foreign policy decisions are highly centralized, implementation of policy falls to many agencies and officials. In Cuba, as elsewhere, agencies and individuals make many decisions about how to carry out the government's broad policies.

The Ministries of Foreign Relations and Foreign Trade

In 1959 Cuba's Foreign Relations Ministry was ill equipped to serve a revolutionary government; it had focused on managing relations with the United States and with international organizations. Not until September 1959 did it even have a Department of Latin American Affairs. At that time, the government also revoked the tenure of all foreign service personnel so that anyone considered disloyal to the regime could be dismissed.[31] In fact, the frequent dismissal or defection of Cuban ambassadors and other diplomats was a serious problem between 1959 and 1961. In October 1961 a further reorganization created Departments for Western European Affairs, Socialist Countries, and Afro-Asian Affairs within the Foreign Relations Ministry. All diplomats posted overseas were required to return to Cuba for a month every year to "familiarize themselves with the progress of the revolution." Ministry personnel also had to contribute "productive" labor; during weekends and after work they operated a dairy enterprise.[32]

In July 1963, at the conclusion of the first plenary congress of the ministry's personnel, Foreign Minister Raúl Roa chided all personnel because "this is a Ministry of Foreign Relations and, in the voluminous and meaty report which has been read, there is no evaluation of Cuba's foreign policy during the year."[33] Indeed, the bulk of the staff's time was spent ensuring participation in productive work, attendance at political meetings, reduction of labor absenteeism, and the loyalty of diplomats.[34] President Dorticós added, "There have been traitors in this Ministry."[35] Distrusted by the leadership, demoralized by its treatment, and plagued by personnel turnover, the Foreign Relations Ministry at first played only a modest role in the conduct of Cuban foreign policy.

In July 1960 the new Bank of Foreign Trade was given a monopoly over all international trade; it was replaced in February 1963 by the new Foreign Trade Ministry, headed by Alberto Mora. The new ministry's state enterprises carried out international trade.[36] In August 1964 the Foreign Trade Ministry's binge of import buying in convertible currencies forced Cuba to break trade contracts, and Mora was replaced as minister by Marcelo Fernández.

Both the Foreign Trade Ministry and the Foreign Relations Ministry came under attack in March 1966. The government purged them of what it called "anti-social elements," at once dismissing about fifty officials. Castro denounced the Western European embassies in Havana as sources of corruption of Cuban diplomats and foreign trade officials, and criticized the personnel of the two ministries for "soft living" and for their susceptibility to "subtle forms of bribery."[37] Foreign Trade Minister Fernández announced measures to make his ministry "more revolutionary and to purify it"; he forbade all personnel to accept gifts when posted overseas. On March 18 the Cabinet barred Cuban officials from all foreign embassies in Havana in order to avoid "dancing, drinking, and dirty jokes." In June both deputy foreign trade ministers were dismissed.[38] Neither ministry could protect its personnel from the ensuing wave of social radicalism that swept the country in the late 1960s.

Despite these problems, the Foreign Relations Ministry managed the twists and turns of Cuban diplomacy and brought Cuba from diplomatic relations with 42 countries in 1958 to relations with 57 in June 1960 (22 countries established relations with Cuba between 1959 and 1961, but 20 broke them from 1959 to 1964).[39] The Foreign Trade Ministry managed the reorientation of Cuban trade from West to East. By 1963 both ministries had achieved breakthroughs in relations with Western Europe and, gradually, with the Nonaligned Movement. Not until the 1970s, however, would their professionalism and accomplishment be recognized. Cuba had diplomatic relations with 81 governments in 1975 and with 121 in 1986, thanks to its expansion of ties with African and Asian countries and to its reestablishment of relations with many Latin American and Caribbean countries.[40]

The training of Cuban diplomats improved by the mid-1980s. At the end of 1974 the Foreign Service Institute graduated the first students from a full four-year course; a decade later, over forty people per year were graduating.[41] A similar trend occurred in the Foreign Trade Ministry. In 1986, 21 percent of this ministry's staff was made up of university graduates; another 19 percent were studying part time at the university.[42]

A measure of the Foreign Relations Ministry's strength is its share of ambassadorial appointments by the mid-1980s; ambassadors are appointed by the Council of State and report to the Foreign Relations Ministry. I have selected two periods for analysis to assess whether the criteria for appointment were sensitive to changes in Cuban domestic politics. The first period, from February 1984 to February 1985, was mostly uneventful in terms of personnel changes in domestic politics; the appointments of twenty-nine ambassadors were announced in the Cuban press during these months. The second period, from February 1986 to February 1987, followed upon the Third Party Congress in February 1986 and coincided with many personnel changes in domestic politics; the appointments of nineteen ambassadors were announced during these months.

Two-thirds of the forty-eight ambassadors appointed in both periods had worked for the Foreign Relations Ministry before, either as ambassadors or as staff—a proportion that suggests a highly professional corps of ambassadors (there were no significant differences between the two periods in the likelihood of appointment from the Foreign Relations Ministry). The remaining sixteen ambassadors came from twelve different government and party agencies. No more than two came from any one organization besides the Foreign Relations Ministry. However, there was a difference between the two periods. In the first, seven of the nine nondiplomats had worked on international issues before their appointment; in the second period, only two of the seven nondiplomats had done so. Some of those appointed ambassador during the second period seem to have been demoted from their positions in domestic politics; one was Antonio Pérez Herrero, demoted as party secretary for ideology in February 1985 and appointed ambassador to Ethiopia in March 1986.

Two-thirds of the forty-eight ambassadors appointed in both periods were moved from a staff job in Cuba to an overseas post; this ensured the principle established in 1961 that diplomats overseas be familiar with "the progress of the revolution" (there were no significant differences between the two periods in the likelihood of such rotation). Nine others went from one embassy to another (another seven were simply named ambassador to another country concurrent with their existing appointment; the background of one was not reported).

Among twenty-one appointees in both periods whose prior work had been in the area of foreign policy (excluding the seven who had been named ambassador to a new country while retaining an appointment in another country), the government sought not only to build up expertise on particular regions but also to create generalists by assigning some people to posts outside their previous area of expertise. Ten of the twenty-one were appointed to a post within the geographic region of their expertise, while eleven were sent to regions on which they had not worked. But the patterns were not the same in both periods; twice as many ambassadors in the second period were appointed to countries within the region of their expertise as were appointed to regions on which they had not worked. This change seems unrelated to domestic politics, however; the government probably sought to foster both kinds of diplomatic expertise in the long run. Thus, the impact of domestic politics on ambassadorial appointments is quite modest; the professional diplomatic expertise of Cuba's ambassadors is considerable.

In addition to the influence it gained as a result of greater professionalism, the political clout of the foreign relations establishment increased also because of its closer links to the party. There was no Communist party cell in the Foreign Relations Ministry until April 1967.[43] The foreign relations establishment—the Foreign Trade and Foreign Relations Ministries and the State Committee for Economic Collaboration (CECE)—accounted for only 3 percent of the full members of the party's Central Committee from 1965 to 1975 but for not less than 6 percent since then. More important, since the 1970s Cuba has centralized power overseas in one official, the ambassador, who represents the interests of both state and party. There is no formal party mission overseas, although there are party cells in each embassy. By the mid-1980s almost all Cuban ambassadors were also Communist party members, whereas in the past, some ambassadors had represented the party even though they were not party members.[44] The ambassador's powers affect other agencies. For example, a Ministry of Culture official might be named a cultural attaché; that person might, then, leave the Ministry of Culture and join the Foreign Relations Ministry so that there would be no doubt about the ambassador's complete authority. (The Foreign Trade Ministry is a partial exception: it has separate offices abroad but they must also respond to the ambassador.)[45]

The Foreign Trade Ministry's history is somewhat different. It, too, lacked a party cell when it was "purified" in 1966, and in January 1980 Foreign Trade Minister Marcelo Fernández lost his job over his management of Cuban trade. But at the fifteenth congress of the Cuban Confederation of Labor, in 1984, ministry personnel received awards for their good work. Vice President Rodríguez noted the high percentage of ministry personnel in the party, observing that the majority of the younger staff belonged to the Communist Youth Union.[46] The Foreign Trade Ministry had a staff of 4,083 people in early 1984 (up from 3,500 in late 1981), organized in specialized agencies and in state enterprises for international trade. They conducted Cuban trade with over one hundred countries.[47] Many Cuban enterprises, not directly under the Foreign Trade Ministry, also imported or exported a part of their production with the ministry's help.[48] The complexity of Cuba's international economic transactions, however, required further government reorganization, which reduced the Foreign Trade Ministry's preeminence in that field, especially with regard to trade with other Communist countries. Since 1976 the Foreign Trade Ministry has dealt mainly with foreign private firms and with Cuban and foreign state firms engaged in international trade; it also signed international agreements outside the CMEA area.

International Technical and Economic Organizations
Cuban-Soviet economic coordination began to improve in 1969. In 1970 the Cuban-Soviet Joint Commission for Economic, Scientific, and Technical Collaboration was founded, with Carlos Rafael Rodríguez heading the Cuban side.[49] Cuba has created similar joint commissions with other Eastern European countries and elsewhere. In November 1976 the CECE was created, with authority over all the joint commissions. The CECE negotiates economic agreements with other governments and international organizations, often coordinating technical relations between agencies not engaged in trade. The CECE also negotiates purchases of complete "turn-key" plants; it supervises Cuba's agreements to supply nonmilitary services overseas and Cuba's receipt of such services; the CECE works with most civilian state agencies that provide or receive such services. It managed the booms in Cuban trade with CMEA countries and in Cuba's deployment of civilian personnel overseas.[50]

When Cuba joined the CMEA in July 1972, its "complicated procedures and complex structure" were an "enigma" to Cubans responsible for CMEA relations.[51] Thus Cuba had to learn to deal with the CMEA as a system of multilateral institutions. This explains in part the great delay in Cuba's receipt of benefits from CMEA membership. In November 1976 Cuba created the Permanent Secretariat for CMEA Affairs, headed by Vice President Rodríguez, to represent Cuban interests before CMEA institutions.[52]

Before 1972 Cuba belonged only to three CMEA multilateral institutions;

it had joined seven others by 1975, another five by 1980, and one more by 1982. Of the twenty-seven CMEA multilateral institutions in which Cuba was eligible for membership in 1983 (those not limited to European members), it belonged to only sixteen. Thus Cuba was only partially integrated into the CMEA at the end of its first decade of membership. Although it had joined all the CMEA institutions specializing in scientific and technical matters, it had joined only 45 percent of those engaged directly in economic activities.[53] Similarly, Cuba belonged to only 40 percent of the CMEA's long-term development programs in the early 1980s.[54] Cuba's gains from CMEA membership remained limited in part because of organizational problems, for which it and the CMEA were responsible. Nonetheless, the gains eventually materialized, thanks to the learning that did occur and the effective work of Vice President Rodríguez and Cuba's CMEA staff.

Cuba's growing exposure to the CMEA system has brought it into contact with a variety of foreign economic policy-making approaches in Eastern Europe. Cuban academics and government technocrats are learning that the USSR does not provide the only model of socialist organization. More decentralized approaches can work, including Hungary's bolder market-socialist approaches.[55] Indeed, the Soviet system may be second best. For example, Jorge Valdés Miranda found that the East German approach to trade with market-economy countries is superior to the USSR's. When East Germany buys in market-economy countries, it requires the foreign seller to buy East German products of comparable worth in order to maintain bilateral trade equilibrium. The East German government is well organized to implement this policy; the Cubans and the Soviets were not.[56]

Cultural Organizations

Beyond political and economic relations with governments, several Cuban agencies promote other aspects of international relations. Casa de las Américas was founded in April 1959 to promote Cuba's cultural relations with Latin America and with intellectuals in many other countries. After collective inter-American sanctions were imposed in 1964, Casa prevented the full severance of Cuba's ties with Latin America by bringing many intellectuals from Latin America to Cuba, operating as a high-quality publisher since 1960, and giving out awards every year for the best Latin American literature. During its first decade, Casa honored only literature in Spanish. In 1973 prizes were added for literature in Portuguese; in 1976 prizes were extended to the English-speaking Caribbean, and in 1978, to the French-speaking Caribbean.[57]

Casa de las Américas also sought to maintain a relatively open intellectual climate—one loyal to the revolution but open to various forms of artistic expression. Among intellectuals who were not "pro-imperialist," it looked for quality before dogma, funding and publishing or exhibiting their work. It pointedly did not limit itself to "socialist realism."[58] But the government's increasingly narrow definition of loyalty and of acceptable behavior gradually brought it into conflict with many, though not all, of Cuba's best intellectuals. Censorship and self-censorship tightened. Many intellectuals emigrated; some, Heberto Padilla most spectacularly, were arrested and forced to confess their errors. The 1971 "Padilla affair" brought protests from many of the same world-renowned Latin American and Western European intellectuals who had earlier supported the Cuban revolution. In response Castro called them "intellectual rats." These events brought about a historic break between Cuba and many of those intellectuals, staining—deservedly—the Cuban government's reputation as a champion of intellectual freedom.[59]

Prensa Latina, Cuba's official international wire service, was founded in June 1959. By the end of 1960 it had to close its office in Washington and in fifteen Latin American countries because of the deterioration of Cuba's official relations with these countries; in Latin America it operated only in Mexico, Chile, and Uruguay. But it later grew impressively. By the mid-1980s it had thirty-seven correspondents permanently stationed overseas. It dispatched 7,800 news items per day in Spanish, English, French, and Portuguese (but not in Russian). It was linked to the Intersputnik and the Intelsat satellite systems, the first run by the Soviets and the second by market-economy countries. It published two magazines (one in Spanish and Russian and the other in Spanish, English, and Portuguese). It diffused worldwide the Cuban government's news about itself and its views of world affairs.[60]

The Cuban Institute for Friendship with Peoples was created in October 1960 to invite and host foreign visitors, arranging for translation, lodging, tours, and transportation. It supervises international events and conferences, works with foreign residents in Cuba, and promotes organizations of friendship with Cuba in other countries (over ninety in 1975). It is the lead agency for contacts with individuals and private associations abroad.[61]

In short, the Cuban government defended itself from isolation in the 1960s and projected its influence in the 1970s and 1980s by circumventing hostile governments to reach out to intellectuals and the public in other countries. The organizations engaged in such cultural relations were part of the supporting cast for Cuba's worldwide policies. Their success was closely tied to Cuba's general international fortunes and, in the area of culture, to trends within Cuba.

Organizations Supporting Revolution

Not much is known about Cuba's system of support for revolutions just after 1959, since many arrangements were ad hoc and the government was badly organized. In the mid-1960s new organizations were created to support such movements. The Tricontinental Conference, held in Havana in January 1966, led to the foundation of the Organization for Solidarity with the Peoples of Africa, Asia, and Latin America (OSPAAL), with headquarters in Havana. In the early 1980s its work focused primarily on Latin American countries. It has always had Cubans as secretaries-general and in other key positions.[62] OSPAAL was Cuba's first stable "front organization" to support revolution. Its first twelve-member secretariat included representatives of the governments of Syria, the United Arab Republic, Guinea, and North Korea, as well as revolutionary movements from Venezuela, the Dominican Republic, Pakistan, the Congo (Leopoldville), the liberation movements of the Portuguese Colonies, the Vietcong, and more moderate movements in Puerto Rico and Chile.[63]

At the 1966 Tricontinental Conference, the twenty-seven Latin American delegations also founded the Organization for Latin American Solidarity (OLAS), which gave priority attention to the Dominican Republic, Venezuela, Colombia, Guatemala, and Peru. The OLAS had an intense though short life. Its only continental conference was held in the summer of 1967 at the peak of Cuba's commitment to support for Latin American insurgencies. Havana was chosen as the organization's headquarters and a Cuban official as its secretary-general. Following Guevara's death and the defeat of most guerrilla forces in Latin American countries in the late 1960s, OLAS was absorbed by OSPAAL.[64]

From its foundation, OSPAAL published two journals and many pamphlets; it held workshops and seminars. It became especially active in Africa. As Edouard Marcel Sumbu of the National Council for the Liberation of the Congo said: "In Africa, all the movements that fight colonialism receive aid" from OSPAAL. "Our delegation has proofs demonstrating that the Organization is up to its task of aiding these movements for liberation from colonialism."[65] Paulo Jorge, a member of the Popular Movement for the Liberation of Angola (MPLA), head of the Conference of National Organizations of the Portuguese Colonies, and later Angola's foreign minister, gave examples of OSPAAL's work: publicity for revolutionary movements, work to promote unity and mobilize world public opinion, and appeals for "concrete and effective solidarity."[66] OSPAAL was also directly involved in military support for revolution. OSPAAL stated in mid-1968 that its watchword was "arms, money, and equipment for the liberation struggle of Latin America." And it founded a school in late 1966 to train cadres for revolutionary movements.[67]

A third "front organization" was the Continental Organization of Latin American Students (OCLAE). Congresses of Latin American students had met in the past; the Cuban government called the fourth such conference for August 1966 in Havana, at which the organization was founded. Havana became the permanent headquarters of the OCLAE, and the Cuban university students' federation became OCLAE's head organization. In the early 1980s OCLAE was officially committed to the use of "all means, legal and clandestine," to support revolution, focusing on Nicaragua and El Salvador, where support included "gathering and sending material and financial aid."[68]

The Cuban Communist party supervises OSPAAL and OCLAE. It also has direct relations with revolutionary movements. Its Central Committee's General Department staff is in charge of support for SWAPO, Polisario, and the PLO, which are treated as quasi-states; its Americas Department does the same for revolutionary movements in Central America.[69]

The Interior Ministry

The Interior Ministry is in charge of maintaining internal order and security. It also has extensive involvement in foreign policy. It gathers intelligence and counterintelligence information in Cuba and abroad; it cooperates with the domestic security agencies of Cuba's allies; it deploys elite troops to foreign countries for special missions; it performs covert operations abroad; and it guards Cuba's frontiers. "There is practically no glorious page of [Cuba's] internationalist history in which Interior Ministry fighters are not present," Castro noted in 1976.[70]

In early November 1975, 650 of the Interior Ministry's Special Troops were deployed to Angola in the vanguard of Cuba's combat forces.[71] Independent of the armed forces, the elite Special Troops have been employed in several overseas missions. The Interior Ministry also advises and cooperates with domestic security forces in other countries, including Nicaragua. It receives support from and works closely with its Soviet counterpart.[72] At least as late as the 1968 crisis, the Interior Ministry was also a source of Cuban independence from the Soviets. Ministry staff undertook the surveillance of Soviet personnel in Cuba who had been close to the "microfaction," for example. At the peak of that crisis, the chief of the ministry's Soviet advisers sought the arrest of Deputy Interior Ministry Manuel Piñeiro for having kept the investigation secret.[73]

The Interior Ministry also commands the Border Guard Troops, which protect Cuba's coastline and are the first line of defense against invasion. The Border Guard enforces Cuban maritime jurisdiction up to twelve miles; it cooperated with the U.S. Coast Guard on search and rescue missions during the period 1978–1982. Jointly with the Border Brigade of the armed forces, the Border Guard surrounds the U.S. naval base at Guantánamo.[74]

Another function of the Interior Ministry is to operate against the regime's enemies abroad. As discussed in Chapter 7, the ministry's covert overseas activities have at times hurt Cuban relations with other governments. In France its agents were in touch with terrorist groups, in Canada they recruited undercover agents, and in Spain they even sought to kidnap a high Cuban official seeking to defect. The ministry has planted double agents in the United States, within the Cuban American community— among them, Carlos Rivero Collado, son of Batista's last Prime Minister and President-elect in late 1958.[75]

The Interior Ministry played a key role in staffing Guevara's expedition to Bolivia in the 1960s. To signal that support for revolutionary movements overseas remains central to its mission, in 1984 the ministry established a new award to honor Eliseo Reyes, a staff member who died with Guevara in Bolivia.[76] The ministry works with the Central Committee's Departments of the Americas and General International Relations to support revolutionary movements. A personal link facilitates this relationship: Central Committee member Manuel Piñeiro served as deputy interior minister in charge of these operations until he became head of the Americas Department.

The Interior Ministry has also been politically powerful. By 1976 it had the highest percentage of party and Communist Youth Union membership of any large Cuban agency, including the armed forces.[77] In the mid-1980s, however, the ministry's political clout fell. Interior Minister Ramiro Valdés was fired curtly in December 1985. His successor, Division General José Abrantes, a Central Committee member since 1965, was not asked to join the Political Bureau when Valdés was dropped from it in February 1986. For the first time since the Political Bureau's foundation, the interior minister is not a member. Interior Ministry representation among Central Committee full and alternate members fell from thirteen to eight; nine of the thirteen ministry representatives on the 1980 Central Committee were dropped in 1986—a far greater purge than that endured by the armed forces or the civilian Central Committee members. The ministry was blamed for failing to stop a domestic crime wave, for corruption and abuses of power, and for failing to detect early on the disintegration of Grenada's ruling New Jewel Movement.[78]

The Armed Forces

The armed forces have been decisive in Cuba's interventions in the Angolan and Ethiopian wars and have also supplied military advisers and trainers in Angola, Ethiopia, and other countries. Although the first Cuban troops were deployed in 1963 to support Algeria in its war against Morocco, the Cuban armed forces have gone overseas in a major way only since the early 1970s. The armed forces claim a large proportion of national resources, though it is difficult to say exactly how much. One measure is the military and domestic security expenditures in the national budget, figures that are available consistently only since 1978 (see Table 9.1).

Budgeted military expenditures doubled from 1974 to 1978 as a result of Cuba's entry into African wars. They remained high but stable in the late 1970s. Beginning in 1981 (when military disbursements were 10.5 percent higher than budgeted figures), they, as well as actual military disbursements, rose rapidly, to nearly double again by 1984 in response to worsened U.S.-Cuban relations. Though the 1985 budget, prepared in 1984, projected a further increase of military expenditures, the improvement in U.S.-Cuban relations during the first half of 1985 saved Cuba 135.2 million pesos in military disbursements in 1985. Military expenditures stabilized in the mid-1980s.

The Soviet Union has supplied weapons to Cuba free of charge since 1962; thus weapons purchases do not appear in Cuba's budget (which covers mainly personnel costs). According to the Cuban government, Soviet weapons deliveries nearly doubled Cuba's arsenal in 1981–82, when the weapons the USSR had agreed to deliver in 1981–1985 were delivered on an expedited basis.[79] The U.S. government estimated that Soviet weapons deliveries to Cuba jumped from an average of 30,000 metric tons per year in 1976–1980 to an average of 61,400 metric tons per year in 1981–1984.[80] In the early 1980s Cuba began to develop and manufacture various types of light weapons. By late 1984 Castro said that Cuba had tripled its stock of weapons from all sources during the first half of the 1980s.[81]

Other important military expenditures do not appear in the budget. The Territorial Troop Militia, first organized in 1980, is funded by "voluntary" contributions from mass organizations, state enterprises, and individuals. The Cuban Labor Confederation alone contributes about 20 million pesos per year.[82] Some incentives for officers and draftees to reenlist, and to vol-

Table 9.1   Military budget, 1972–1988

Year	Budgeted military expenditures (million pesos, current prices)	Budgeted military expenditures as a percentage of the national budget	Actual military disbursements (million pesos, current prices)	Actual military disbursements as a percentage of national budget disbursements
1972	365.0	—	—	—
1974	400.0	—	—	—
1978	784.0	8.6	—	—
1979	840.9	8.9	—	—
1980	810.9	8.5	—	—
1981	842.1	7.5	930.7	8.6
1982	923.8	9.4	—	—
1983	1,115.5	10.8	1,133.1	9.9
1984	1,403.5	12.5	1,385.7	11.7
1985	1,470.9	13.0	1,335.7	10.6
1986	1,307.1	10.9	1,331.7	11.2
1987	1,302.6	11.1	—	—
1988	—	18.0	—	—

Sources: Granma Weekly Review, August 6, 1972, p. 4; January 1, 1978, p. 3; January 29, 1979, p. 3; January 6, 1980, p. 3; January 11, 1981, p. 4; January 10, 1982, p. 5; January 12, 1986, p. 12. *Granma,* December 29, 1982, p. 4; January 3, 1985, p. 5; December 29, 1986, p. 3; December 31, 1987, p. 3. Banco Nacional de Cuba, *Economic Report,* August 1982, p. 53; February 1985, p. 18; March 1986, p. 14; May 1987, p. 18. Frank Mankiewicz and Kirby Jones, *With Fidel* (Chicago: Playboy Press, 1975), pp. 118–119.

unteer for overseas service, result in nonfinancial costs for civilians; for example, at least since 1980, veterans have been given preference in employment, housing allocations and, since 1981, in admissions to some university schools.[83]

Cuba relies on a standing regular force that is relatively small considering its responsibilities for war overseas and the defense of the homeland. All males are subject to the military draft; women may volunteer to join the armed forces. Labor force studies—the best independent source of information on the size of the Cuban armed forces—and other information suggest that the regular armed forces shrank from over 350,000 troops in the mid-1960s (when there was a serious domestic insurgency and when troops also worked in production) to below 225,000 during the first half of the 1970s (when the domestic insurgency had been defeated, overseas missions had not yet been undertaken, and troops were less often used in production). The size of the regular armed forces remained unchanged during the period of the "great wars" in Angola and Ethiopia (1975–1978) but increased thereafter to about 319,000 troops in 1980.[84]

The regular armed forces were kept small thanks to the existence of military reserves. All men under fifty and all women under forty have a military reserve classification, based on age, skill, and prior military experience, which determines the length of time every year they can be required to spend in military training, including participation in major war games along with the regular forces. The shortest period is twelve days a year; the longest, three months. A three-month period disrupts the reservists' lives as well as the work centers that employ them. Reservists accounted for 70 percent of the Cuban troops in Angola in 1975–76, and for about half of those in Ethiopia in 1977–78.[85] Of the 784 Cubans in Grenada in October 1983, only 8.3 percent were regular military personnel.[86] Since 1980 the size of the reserves has expanded, thanks to the addition of the Territorial Troop Militia, whose main task is to protect civilian installations and to free the regular armed forces and the ready reserves for combat. The militia and the reserves reached 1.5 million in early 1985.[87]

The Cuban armed forces started from a low professional base. Its leaders were not good at logistics in 1960. Commander of the Revolution Guillermo García hid some of the first Soviet tanks so well that, according to General Raúl Castro, "later no one knew where they were hidden."[88] Educational levels were also quite low. In April 1959, for example, the first school for 1,518 Rebel Army officers and troops opened. Of these, 500 were illiterate and another 543 had completed only the second grade; only 256 had as much as a sixth-grade education.[89]

On the eve of Cuba's entry into the Angolan War in 1975, most officers who commanded troops were high school graduates. Military engineers and Air Force officers were required to be university graduates; artillery officers and naval officers had about a junior college education.[90] The experience of combat and the need to handle the more complex equipment scheduled to arrive in the early 1980s has led the armed forces to raise educational standards again. Since 1982 all new officers have had the equivalent of a university education.[91] To improve the quality of draftees, policies changed in 1979 to draft first male skilled workers and male high school graduates before they entered the University; this reversed the previous policy of deferments for educational or productive reasons.[92] By the end of 1982 the minimum educational requirement for noncommissioned officers was completion of the ninth grade.[93]

The Armed Forces are politically powerful. Officers on active duty (drawn from the armed forces and the Interior Ministry) accounted for 32 percent of the full members of the Communist party's Central Committee at the 1975 First Party Congress, for 24 percent at the 1980 Second Party Congress (their number actually grew because the Central Committee expanded), and for 18 percent at the 1986 Third Party Congress. The brunt of the 1986 reduction was borne by the Interior Ministry and the Navy. Whereas in 1986 the Interior Ministry lost its slot on the party's Political Bureau, an Army division general joined the Political Bureau for the first time, and another one joined the Secretariat. The armed forces also have impressive powers to draft young men, mobilize reservists, and command the resources necessary for war. The armed forces are Cuba's premier institution, its essential instrument of defense, and its most effective means to project its power overseas.

Social and Political Factors in Cuba's International Activities

The overseas spread of the Cuban revolution has involved hundreds of thousands of Cubans. Many have volunteered to go abroad; others have agreed to do so in response to job incentives; yet others have gone in fear of penalties to themselves or their families if they refused. For many Cubans, especially those in the armed forces, service overseas is a routine part of their career. Not everyone who volunteers can go abroad, however; in every case, the Cuban government selects those who do.

Some information is available about Cubans who have served abroad. For example, of the 24 Cubans who died in combat in Grenada in October 1983, 8 were members of the Communist party, another was a candidate for membership, and 4 were members of the Communist Youth Union. Nine were nonwhites. The median time they had been in Grenada was ten months. Their places of birth indicate that they were drawn from all over Cuba, but that the eastern provinces were underrepresented.[94] That one-third of the dead were Communist party members is noteworthy because only about one-sixth of the Cuban labor force belongs to the party.[95] That Cubans in Grenada were more likely than Cubans in general to be Communist party members suggests either that Communists are more likely to volunteer to serve in other countries or that the Cuban government relies on committed militants in overseas missions.

To assess the significance of race in the deployment of workers to Grenada, I compared the proportion of nonwhites in Cuba's population with that of Cubans killed in Grenada.[96] Among the Cubans dead in Grenada, nonwhites were overrepresented by 25 percent. Nonwhites may have been more likely than whites to volunteer to work in a black country as well as to be selected by the Cuban government for such purposes.[97] This evidence indicates that Cuba's overseas personnel are not drawn from a random cross-section of the population.

Cuba also published some information on 679 other Cubans who survived in Grenada. Most were male construction workers. Before going to Grenada, 70 percent lived in metropolitan Havana or in neighboring Matanzas province (which together accounted only for 25.6 percent of Cuba's population in the 1981 census).[98] This suggests that Cuba sends entire "brigades" of construction workers, regardless of their attitudes toward service abroad, rather than creating new units of volunteers from various regions.

The ages of Cuban personnel in Grenada imply a further consideration in determining who goes abroad. The list below presents the ratio of the percentage of Cuban personnel in each age group in Grenada to that age group's percentage of the Cuban labor force in the 1981 census (students, housewives, and others not in the labor force are thus excluded). A ratio below 1.00 indicates that there were fewer Cubans in Grenada in a particular age group than one would expect from their share of Cuba's labor force; a ratio above 1.00 indicates that the age group was overrepresented.[99]

Age group	Ratio
19	0.14
20–24	0.64
25–29	1.31
30–34	1.44
35–39	1.40
40–44	1.15
45–49	1.06
50–54	0.88
55–59	0.54
60–64	0.41

Those workers under 25 and over 49 were underrepresented among Cubans in Grenada. The most overrepresented groups were in their thirties— and were therefore aged 6 to 15 when the revolution came to power. Maurice Zeitlin has suggested that age group differences may influence revolutionary commitment: the most revolutionary population groups are those who experienced the revolution at a crucial formative period. In the 1980s, the middle-aged were more committed to the regime than either younger or older workers.[100] In short, political loyalty, gender, age, and race shaped the group of workers who volunteered and were selected to go to Grenada.

The same factors influence the makeup of Cuban personnel in Nicaragua and Angola. Of 201 Cuban medical interns in Nicaragua in 1983, 92 percent were members of the Communist Youth Union, thereby suggesting the Cuban government's use of political loyalty as a criterion to choose volunteers to send abroad; 60 percent of the 201 were men and 33 percent were nonwhite.[101] There are few Nicaraguan blacks; the racial distribution of Cubans in Nicaragua simply matches Cuba's. The high proportion of men may reflect the Cuban government's 1981 decision to manipulate medical school admissions quotas to give preference to men; the government claims that other countries accept men more readily and that posting men overseas presents fewer social problems at home and abroad.[102] The bias in favor of men is also evident among Cuban teachers in Nicaragua; 50 percent of 554 Cuban teachers sent to Nicaragua in November 1979 were men as compared with only 38 percent of those in the "teaching and research staff" category in the 1981 census—a 32 percent overrepresentation of men.[103]

In Angola, politically loyal men who are disproportionately nonwhite predominate. Most Cubans in Angola are male soldiers. In 1979, there were 394 Cuban primary school teachers in Angola, of whom 72 percent were members of the Communist Youth Union and 21 percent were party members or candidates for party membership.[104] In April 1984, 14 Cuban construction workers—all men—were killed in Angola. Only one was aged 24 or less; most were middle-aged. Twelve of the 14 came from just two Cuban provinces—further evidence that existing construction worker brigades are sent instead of new brigades of volunteers from various regions. Nonwhites were overrepresented by 70 percent, compared to their share of the population of the two provinces (Sancti Spíritus and Ciego de Avila) from which most of those who were killed came.[105]

In general, then, Cubans abroad are committed to their government. Disproportionately drawn from the Communist Youth Union and party, they are likely to come from the age group for which the revolution was the most intense formative experience. Cuban nonwhites are overrepresented in majority-black countries. The overrepresentation of men among nonmilitary personnel stems in part from discriminatory policies of the Cuban government.

Another question regarding Cubans abroad is whether they can talk with foreigners. Surprisingly, language training is not emphasized in Cuban schools. Castro told the 1986 Third Party Congress that even university students' knowledge of foreign languages was "poor."[106] As Cuba became more involved overseas, fewer adults studied a foreign language. Nationwide adult enrollment in language courses dropped every year after 1975–

76, for a cumulative decline of 37 percent by 1980–81 (when enrollment in language courses for adults was between 22,000 and 24,000 students). In the Nicaro region, where thousands of Soviets were at work on Cuba's nickel production facilities, the Russian language was not taught, nor was Spanish taught to the Soviets.[107]

Cubans' lack of language training has had several effects. One was the enthusiasm for service in Nicaragua. If Cubans had to go abroad to demonstrate their revolutionary credentials, it was easier not to have to learn another language. Second, English was more apt to be used when another language would have been more appropriate; for example, students from South Yemen in Cuba were taught in English, not in Arabic.[108] Third, Cubans erroneously seem to believe that the Spanish and Portuguese languages are so close that Cubans need not learn Portuguese.[109]

Interpersonal relations between Cubans and foreigners are limited also by government policies. For example, most foreign secondary and primary school students who study in Cuba are taught in the Isle of Youth, south of the main island, in schools for their own people. Only 0.5 percent of the Republic of Cuba's population lives on that island. Therefore, the foreign students have little contact with most Cubans. Although many of these students are black, they are not taught in one of Cuba's three majority-black provinces; two-thirds of the Isle of Youth's Cuban population is white.[110]

Few foreigners have emigrated to Cuba.[111] While foreigners rarely wish to come to a poor, struggling country, Cuban policy also discourages immigration. Cuba attempts to dissuade those who come to study in Cuba from marrying and remaining, insisting that students return to their home country and not contribute to a "brain drain" there.[112] Immigration is also discouraged because of the housing shortage and the belief that foreigners might not adapt well to life in Cuba. The problem seems especially serious for male Cubans returning from East Germany with foreign spouses.[113]

The red tape involved in bringing a loved one to Cuba can be staggering. For example, Cuban journalist Pedro de la Cruz, who served in Cuba's medical corps in Angola in 1976, rescued and adopted a twelve-year-old boy, Zacarías Dunge Kito, but he could not bring the boy to Cuba. After taking the case all the way to the Cuban Communist party's Central Committee and to Castro personally, de la Cruz was allowed to bring his son to Cuba; the government even arranged for Cruz to be assigned in Angola so that Kito could keep in touch with his home country.[114]

In addition, Cubans' limited social interactions with citizens of other countries have objective, practical deterrents: Even if Cubans want to maintain friendships with foreigners, it is difficult to do so because mail, telephone, and airline service are poor. In 1979 it took months for mail to get from Cuba to countries where Cubans were posted; in 1983 it still took a week for a letter to get from Havana to Managua.[115] In 1984 Cuban Airlines reported an improvement in its service: only 31 percent of its international flights had had problems![116]

The low level of interpersonal communication with other countries stems in part from lack of interest. Before the Angolan War in 1975, Marifeli Pérez-Stable interviewed fifty-seven Cuban workers in fifteen "model" state enterprises identified by the government. Thirty of the workers were labor union leaders; of the twenty-seven rank-and-file workers, seventeen were picked by the government. In short, this "sample" greatly overrepresented supporters of the regime. Pérez-Stable coded the answers for interest in international affairs, counting any reference to international issues or Cuba's standing in the world. Only 35 percent of these most revolutionary of workers referred to international issues. As expected, the middle-aged were more likely to do so.[117] Ordinary Cubans were presumably even less likely to be interested in international affairs.

Surveys taken between 1977 and 1983 also show little interest in Cuban radio news programs, especially among people under age thirty—in part because programs are of poor quality. The government thus cut the air time of radio news programs from 25 percent in 1980 to 16 percent in 1982 to increase the time for entertainment programs. This policy persisted until 1985 when, possibly in response to the beginning of broadcasts by the U.S. government's Radio Martí, the air time of Cuban radio news programs rose again to 20 percent of total programming.[118]

Some Cuban officials believe that foreign ideas and values may be subversive of Cuban society. Armed Forces Minister Raúl Castro has played a leading role in combatting "ideological diversionism." Education Minister Belarmino Castilla warned in 1971 against the introduction of "alien" ideas. In 1972, the First National Congress on Education and Culture endorsed the need to "combat the possible infiltration of imperialist cinema and television through the system of satellites" and tightened the rules for permissible relations with foreign intellectuals.[119] In 1977 party Secretary for Ideology Antonio Pérez Herrero warned that because the U.S. policy of destroying the regime by force had failed, "the ideological struggle [has taken on] more importance as a factor in our country's foreign relations and as an element of the greatest importance in defending our socialist society."[120] The effort to prevent ideological diversionism has curtailed Cuba's cosmopolitanism.

This government obsession has led to repression. In 1980, some intellectuals were arrested and accused of "nordomania," which the government defined as excessive love for things from the north. They had to leave universities and other cultural institutions for months of manual labor to "learn from the proletariat" and to "deepen their revolutionary consciousness."[121]

Between 1959 and 1982 about a million people—a tenth of the population—emigrated from Cuba.[122] Most settled in southern Florida. Thus many Cubans have relatives or friends abroad. In late 1978, the Cuban government authorized visits by returning Cuban Americans; 102,381 visited in 1979. In 1980 the government limited the number of visits to about 10,000 per year because the visits exposed Cubans to "alien" political and consumerist ideas. In 1986 the Cuban government further cut the number of visits to about 2,000 per year. These cutbacks have limited the most intense personal international contacts of the Cuban people.

To their credit some Cuban officials are aware of the costs of parochialism. Political Bureau member and Minister of Culture Armando Hart has called for awareness of the "bourgeois cultural heritage," arguing that "the critical study of the West's art and culture, of its forms and techniques, can help to enrich and develop our own culture and permit the better implementation of our unyielding policy of [revolutionary] principles."[123]

Cuban society is simply not internationalist. Cubans are not likely to learn other languages, and they have little serious interest in learning about the world beyond Cuba's borders. Their government discourages the formation of deep interpersonal relations with foreigners. It combats seductive ideas from other ideologies, from other cultures that nurtured Cuba's society before the revolution, and from Cuban Americans. Cuban involvement overseas has, therefore, grown not from the internationalization of Cuban society but from the internationalization of the regime's policies.

The conduct of Cuban foreign policy has outgrown the agencies in charge of diplomacy and trade. Gradually, most Cuban organizations have become engaged in international affairs because the regime has connected many of its domestic policies, and even individual career incentives, to overseas service. For example, in 1975 Castro told the First Party Congress that Pedro Rodríguez Peralta, who had fought with the revolutionaries in Guinea-Bissau against the Portuguese Army, which captured and imprisoned him for several years, was joining the party's Central Committee because of his prior service abroad.[124] Whereas 8 percent of the delegates to the First Party Congress had served in other countries, that proportion has exceeded 30 percent at the 1980 and the 1986 Party congresses. Those who served abroad were thus rewarded with representation at major party events.[125]

International service is recorded on a citizen's labor and military records (thus its absence can be detected) and is taken into account in job evaluations. Admission to university requires the demonstration of "political" merit. Although this requirement had been in effect since the early 1960s, procedures for evaluating political merit were formalized after 1977. Castro has also indicated that better jobs will be given to university graduates whose political behavior is superior. Service overseas helps to demonstrate political merits.[126]

Cuban overseas personnel are given direct material incentives. In addition to their Cuban salaries, they receive a stipend from the host government as well as in-kind services from the Cuban and the host governments. The majority are able to save most of their salary for use after they return or to improve their families' standard of living.[127]

Despite such incentives, some Cubans go overseas for more subjective reasons. Like their leaders, many believe that international service is right and that people the world over should help each other. These sentiments may propel members of the minority of Cubans who are internationalists. Such feelings, of course, are neither uniquely Cuban nor uniquely Marxist. Some may also go overseas to see the world and to search for adventure.

At times the government's international priorities have clear costs in terms of domestic welfare. As Castro said in late 1978, "in Cuba . . . there is a need to build schools, but we are, nevertheless, building schools in Jamaica and Tanzania . . . We still have a shortage of hospitals, but we are, nevertheless, building a hospital in Vietnam . . . still short of roads . . . [but we are] building roads and highways in Guinea and Vietnam."[128]

The government claims that Cubans overseas volunteer for their service. Considering the powerful factors that may motivate volunteers, the claim is credible—though the extent to which personal decisions to go abroad are genuinely voluntary varies greatly from case to case, and though the government always retains the final say as to who goes abroad. Many government organizations—involving the armed forces and internal security personnel, construction workers, school teachers, medical doctors and nurses, and sports coaches—work overseas; indeed, it is a rare government agency that has not changed its internal procedures to induce its personnel to serve abroad. The regime's domestic policies have propelled both government organizations and political activists to contribute to the overseas spread of the Cuban revolution.

Appendixes

Notes

Index

Appendix A:
Interviews Conducted
in Cuba and Elsewhere

My research for this book included three trips to Havana: two weeks in March 1985, and one week each in June 1986 and April 1988. The purpose of the first was to conduct interviews; the second, to discuss a preliminary draft of the manuscript with some Cuban academics; and the third, to update my data. The trips were funded by a Ford Foundation research grant.

On each occasion, I was invited by Cuba's Center for American Studies (CEA), a research institution formally subordinate to the Communist party's Central Committee. I am impressed with CEA's seriousness of purpose and commitment to its own research and publications work. In 1985 and in 1988 I had told the CEA in advance about my research interests and about the types of people I sought to interview. The CEA arranged for interviews, selecting the persons I would meet. It also selected those who would read my manuscript and discuss it with me in June 1986. The center's judgment was excellent each time. Although I would have liked to interview and discuss the manuscript with more people, had time permitted it, there is no doubt that the CEA's selections advanced my research. I am very grateful to the CEA staff, especially the director, Luis Suárez, and the head of the Department on the United States, Rafael Hernández, for their friendship and professionalism. Moreover, I was free in these, as in my earlier trips to Cuba in January 1979 and August 1980, to move about and to meet others on my own.

During the visits in 1985 and in 1986, the CEA invited me to speak on U.S.-Cuban relations at its headquarters and to meet informally with its researchers to discuss their work. In addition, the University of Havana's Department for Research on the United States (DISEU) invited me to speak on studies of Cuba conducted in the United States; I also met informally with many of the DISEU's researchers. In 1988 I spoke again on U.S.-Cuban relations, and on U.S. politics and society, at the University's renamed Center for U.S. Studies and at the Foreign Ministry's Foreign Service Institute. I am grateful to these institutions for hosting me. Although each department chose the audience for each lecture (rather than allowing my lectures to be open to the public), my talks made it easier for me to meet other researchers and officials, formally and informally.

In March 1985 I conducted interviews with government and party officials and with Cuban scholars. The shortest interview lasted an hour and fifty minutes; the longest lasted four hours. The median time was about two-and-a-half hours. A CEA staff member accompanied me when I met with a government or party official; I was usually on my own when I met with academics in interviews arranged by the CEA and was not accompanied by a CEA staff member in meetings I arranged. In all formal interviews, I asked for and was given permission to take notes. I had decided in advance not to carry a tape recorder.

No academic insisted on anonymity. Government and party officials generally made no mention of the issue, but at times they wanted to be certain that the interview was for a book, not for a newspaper article. I took this preference as a request for confidentiality with regard to the content of their remarks. No one asked that his or her name not be mentioned in the book. Some social situations also turned into interviews. Because of the initial setting, I had not taken paper and pen nor had I asked in advance for the right to take notes. After such meetings, I reconstructed and recorded the discussion from memory as accurately as possible.

In most instances, I have not specified whether the person interviewed was an official or a scholar, or the manner in which the interview developed. Instead, the book's text and notes explicitly identify the person interviewed only when it seemed to me that the person would not be compromised if so identified. When I was in doubt on this point, or when I felt the person might be compromised, I did not identify the interviewee; the book's notes simply refer to an interview with an anonymous person in that case. This is standard scholarly procedure for researchers working in any country; it extends the protection of confidentiality beyond what was explicitly requested. In my judgment, this self-imposed constraint is regrettable but prudent.

The procedure is troubling because it infringes on a standard of scholarship, namely, replicability; that is, another scholar should be able, in principle, to retrace my steps to assess my results. Nothing prevents someone else from seeking to arrange the same interviews, of course; that is one reason for providing below the list of people I interviewed. In practice, however, I am conscious that my opportunity was extraordinary. I had never had such an opportunity before, and I know that few have had it under any circumstances. The vagaries of U.S.-Cuban travel restrictions complicate matters further. It is especially troubling that scholars whose work has been more critical of the Cuban government than mine would find it particularly difficult to retrace my steps.

Consequently, I have intentionally made less use of interviews in this book than I otherwise might have. Whenever a published Cuban source supports a fact, I have used that source rather than an interview. In some instances, both published sources and interviews are cited to warn the reader that the text is supported only in part by the published record. I have relied on interviews as the sole source of information only when there is no alternative. One indirect result of these decisions is that interviews, especially when cited anonymously, are more likely to be relied on in discussions partly or wholly unfavorable to the Cuban government, since it is easier to find published Cuban statements favorable to the official position. It is not my intention to use interviews only with a critical purpose; in fact, interviews also helped to inform my thinking on matters in which the Cuban government appears in a favorable light. The pattern of the use of interviews in this book, then, is a function only of the availability of other sources. Of course, the inferences and conclusions are my own, and at times they are clearly at odds with the opinions and preferences of particular people I interviewed.

I interviewed, formally or informally, the following Cubans in Havana in March 1985.

Ricardo Alarcón, deputy minister for foreign relations; alternate member, Communist party Central Committee

Miguel Alfonso, faculty, Foreign Service Institute, Ministry of Foreign Relations

José Antonio Arbesú, deputy chief, Americas Department, Communist party Central Committee staff

Jesús Arboleya, member, North America Directorate, Ministry of Foreign Relations

Osvaldo Cárdenas, staff, Center for Studies on Western Europe; formerly ambassador to Suriname and director for the Caribbean on the staff of the Americas Department of the Communist party Central Committee

Alfonso Casanova, faculty, Center for Research on International Economics

Arnaldo Coro, faculty, Foreign Service Institute, Ministry of Foreign Relations

Armando Entralgo, director, Center for Studies on Africa and the Middle East

Jesús Escandel, secretary for international relations; member, Executive Committee, Cuban Confederation of Labor

Julio Fernández de Cossío, official, National Bank of Cuba

Santiago Frayle, staff researcher, Center for Studies on Western Europe

Domingo García, director, Center for Studies on Western Europe

Alfredo García Almeyda, chief, North American section, Americas Department, Communist party Central Committee staff

Isidro Gómez, adviser to the president of the Cuban Institute for Friendship with Peoples

Daniel Hernández, faculty, Center for Research on International Economics

Jesús Hernández, staff researcher, Center for American Studies; formerly with the National Bank of Cuba

Rafael Hernández, head of the Department for Research on the United States, Center for American Studies

Francisco López Segrera, academic dean, Foreign Service Institute, Ministry of Foreign Relations

Fernando Martínez, staff, Center for American Studies; formerly editor of *Pensamiento crítico*

Osvaldo Martínez, director, Center for Research on the World Economy

Carlos Martínez de Salsamendi, adviser to Council of State Vice President Carlos Rafael Rodríguez

Marta Núñez, faculty, Center for Research on International Economics, University of Havana

Oscar Pino Santos, adviser to the Council of State; founder of the Center for American Studies and of the Center for Research on the World Economy

Hugo Pons, director, *Economía y desarrollo* (journal); acting director, Department for Research on the United States, University of Havana

José Luis Rodríguez, deputy director, Center for Research on the World Economy

Luis Suárez, director, Center for American Studies; formerly Americas Department, Communist party Central Committee staff

Eloy Valdés, deputy chief, General Department for International Relations, Communist party Central Committee staff

Juan Valdés Paz, head of the Department for Research on Central America, Center for American Studies

Antonio Villaverde, general secretary, Chamber of Commerce of Cuba

Ismael Zuaznábar, faculty, Center for Research on International Economics

In June 1986 the following persons read early drafts of the chapters and appendixes in this book (listed by current chapter and appendix): Chapter 1, Francisco López Segrera; Chapter 2, Rafael Hernández; Chapter 3, Juan Valdés Paz; Chapter 4, José Luis Rodríguez; Chapter 5, Fernando Martínez; Chapter 6, Osvaldo Cárdenas; Chapter 7, José Luis Rodríguez; Chapters 8 and 9, and Appendix A, Miguel Alfonso; Appendix B, José Luis Rodríguez.

Altogether, these discussions of the manuscript took about twenty hours. The commentators were thoroughly and consistently professional; their readings were careful, detailed, and thoughtful and often spurred me to make changes in response. At times the discussions were spirited and vigorous, but never offensive; on some issues we simply agreed to disagree. For example, there was generally strong objection to my characterization of Soviet-Cuban relations as hegemonic, to my discussion of Soviet subsidies to Cuba, and to what was viewed as my insufficient allocation of blame to the U.S. government for the pattern of U.S.-Cuban relations; moreover, the readers held a much more benign interpretation of Cuban foreign policy than I. All of the readers, I am convinced, would still take strong exception to my discussion of these and many other issues in the chapters that they read. By contrast, there was no objection to my description and analysis of many other crucial issues, and I was able to conclude that the book, on the whole, presents Cuban foreign policy fairly and accurately.

In April 1988 I met with Vice President Carlos Rafael Rodríguez and again with Ricardo Alarcón and José Antonio Arbesú, as well as with many of the same researchers I had met during previous visits.

On these and other trips I have also discussed Cuban affairs with each chief of the U.S. Interests Section in Havana since its establishment in 1977.

Since the mid-1970s, at Harvard and on various trips I have also discussed Cuban affairs with each person who has served as the U.S. State Department's Coordinator for Cuban Affairs and with officials knowledgeable about Cuba from the U.S. Departments of Defense, Treasury, Commerce, Agriculture, and Justice; with officials of the Immigration and Naturalization Service, the National Security Council, the Central Intelligence Agency; and with officers of the U.S. Army, Navy, Air Force, Marines, and Coast Guard. Similarly, I have conducted interviews on Cuban issues and affairs with high government officials from Mexico, Guatemala, El Salvador, Honduras, Nicaragua, Costa Rica, Panama, Colombia, Venezuela, Peru, Argentina, Brazil, Haiti, Jamaica, the People's Republic of China, the Soviet Union, Ethiopia, Spain, the United Kingdom, Sweden, the Federal Republic of Germany, and Canada.

Appendix B:
Technical Notes on Soviet-Cuban Economic Relations

Soviet Sugar Prices and Subsidies

The Soviet contract price for sugar and the price actually paid by the Soviets at times differ somewhat. I have used for all calculations only the prices actually paid by the Soviets.

The difference between Soviet and world market prices for sugar is the conventional measure of Soviet sugar subsidies to Cuba. However, very little of the world's sugar is actually traded in what is called the "world market" (an international spot market). Less than a third of world sugar production is traded internationally, and more than half of what is traded is sold outside the world market through preferential agreements (such as Cuba's agreements with the USSR and some other Eastern European countries, and the U.S. and European Economic Community sugar market arrangements) or medium-term contracts. This is true even for Cuban sales of sugar to many market-economy countries. Therefore, a more realistic measure of the sugar subsidy is needed.

I have calculated the "real" Soviet sugar subsidy as the difference between the Soviet price and the price Cuba might have received from key market-economy partners and on the international spot market, to which it could have sold its sugar if the Soviets had not bought it.[1] Canada, Japan, and Spain have been the three most important non-Communist purchasers of Cuban sugar over time; Japan and Canada have also been two of the top five sugar buyers in the world market for years.[2] In addition, Cuban sugar statistics show a category called "other countries," which includes smaller and often nonrecurring sales to minor clients and to those on the international spot market. The purchases by Canada, Japan, Spain, and "others" were weighted and added to create a basis for calculating the real world market price. The difference between the Soviet price and this weighted market-economy price is the real weighted Soviet subsidy for Cuban sugar shown in Table 4.2.

This real world market price is also the basis for the calculations that generated the statistics in Tables 4.3 and 8.1 and for references to sugar subsidies in the text. However, the sugar subsidies for the 1960s reported in Chapter 3 were calculated conventionally as the difference between the Soviet price and the average daily price on the international spot market. Cuba has not published enough data to permit the real world market price to be calculated for the 1960s.

The year 1975 exemplifies differences in the measures of the Soviet sugar subsidy. As Table 4.1 shows, the Soviet price in 1975 was higher than the world market price: a conventional calculation would therefore result in a net Soviet subsidy. In fact, however, Japanese and Spanish prices for Cuban sugar in 1975 were 613 and 569 pesos per ton, respectively—higher than the Soviet price of 482 pesos per ton (only the Canadian price quickly followed the overall market price downslide to 330 pesos per ton). Therefore, Cuba in effect gave the USSR a subsidy in the form of lower sugar prices worth 261 million pesos in 1975 (Table 4.2); Soviet sugar purchasers did better for their consumers than did Spanish and Japanese capitalists.

It is difficult to relate Cuba's subsidies from other countries to Cuba's gross domestic production because Cuba uses different prices for its domestic and international accounts. Consequently, the last two rows of Table 4.2 merely illustrate the relative financial importance of two Soviet subsidies (of a great many) to Cuba. Negative numbers in these rows indicate a Cuban "subsidy" to the USSR. This situation occurred when Cuba had bilateral trade surpluses with the Soviet Union, as it did in 1975–1978. The global social product (GSP) is Cuba's widest measure of aggregate production.

Other Soviet subsidies—such as the free weapons transfers or oil subsidies in the form of preferentially lower prices for Cuba—are crucial but, because Cuba has no significant alternative supplier, it is difficult to calculate how much they are really worth, though it is clear that the Cuban government could not have survived without them.

Cuban Terms of Trade with the USSR

"Terms of trade," a measure of the amount of imports a country can buy with its exports, is imperfect. While it measures price shifts for primary products fairly well, it does not capture well the effect of technological improvements in the manufacture of existing products or the introduction of new products; it is even less effective in measuring trade in services. These general problems are compounded in Cuba's case because its government does not publish information about all of Cuba's imports, nor does it publish sufficiently discrete trade data for product categories to allow accurate calculations of unit prices. Moreover, Cuban data on trade with CMEA countries combine transactions in transferable rubles and in convertible currencies, which have different economic effects. Furthermore, Cuban-Soviet trade is primarily barter trade; political factors often affect the negotiated prices for products. Therefore, all references to Cuba's terms of trade, in this book or in any other publication, ought to be taken at best as rough estimates.

The effort to calculate the terms of trade needs to be made, however, because the Cuban government has made this measure its primary indicator of its economic relations with the USSR. To reduce some of the many uncertainties, terms of trade have been calculated only for Cuban trade with the Soviets. But it is most likely that Cuba's terms of trade with market-economy countries have deteriorated much more than with the Soviets. Table 4.2 also shows terms of trade calculated only for Cuban sugar and Soviet petroleum. The prices for these products are relatively easy to measure, and Cuba has emphasized them in its trade with the Soviets.

Cuba's overall net barter terms of trade with the USSR have been computed as follows. Export and import products traded between Cuba and the Soviet Union for which evidence was found were converted to their equivalents in 1975 prices; these were then totaled to indicate Cuban imports from, and exports to, the USSR in 1975 prices. The value of the imports and exports for each year, multiplied by 100, was divided by the value of imports and exports in 1975 constant prices, resulting in indexes for Cuban import and export prices in its trade with the USSR. The overall Soviet-Cuban net barter terms of trade resulted from dividing the index for Cuban exports in constant prices, multiplied by 100, by the index for Cuban imports, also in constant prices. The same procedure, though simplified, was also used to calculate Cuba's net barter terms of trade in sugar and oil with the Soviets.

Table 4.2 includes most Cuban exports to the Soviet Union (the lowest percentage of the total was 87 for 1983 and 1984). The coverage of imports from the Soviet Union was above 92 percent until 1977 and between 60 and 70 percent from 1978 through 1986. All export data have been updated through 1986. Because Cuba has not published the data necessary to calculate the price it paid for petroleum in 1986, data on imports and terms of trade are calculated only through 1985. Cuba's 1986 statistical yearbook was used to update final figures for 1985 and earlier years.[3]

Currency Exchange Rates

Since 1961 the peso has not been freely exchanged in international markets. Until the end of 1971 the Cuban government set the dollar-peso exchange rate at 1.00; since then, it has set the peso's relationship to other currencies on a controlled floating basis.

In 1971 the Cuban central bank's peso bought 1.09 dollars. The peso officially appreciated with regard to the dollar for most years through 1980, when one peso bought 1.41 dollars. On the black market and in unlicensed international transactions, the peso also appreciated against the dollar from 1972 (when one peso bought 0.10 dollars on average) to 1976 (when one peso bought 0.112 dollars on average), but it depreciated thereafter (the peso bought 0.07 dollars on average in 1979). The official peso began to depreciate with regard to the dollar in 1981, when it bought 1.18 dollars, continuing to 1985, when it bought 1.09 dollars. In 1986 the official peso appreciated; it bought 1.21 dollars.[4]

Because the unofficial peso is traded in a very limited market, it is not a good guide to the peso's "real" value. Because the official peso is set artificially higher than market values in order to capture more foreign exchange earnings from tourism, it, too, is not a good guide to the peso's real value. Because calculations on either exchange rate make little sense, they have not been made in this book.

U.S. government estimates of Soviet subsidies to Cuba generally use the official peso exchange rate, thereby overestimating their dollar value. For example, the U.S. Central Intelligence Agency estimated Soviet sugar subsidies for 1979 at $2,287 million dollars. The CIA estimated total trade subsidies as $2,667 million and total Soviet financing for Cuba's trade deficit with the Soviets as $440 million dollars for that year, the highest combined sum for the 1970s. Were the CIA to use the unofficial peso rate, the dollar value of Soviet subsidies would fall dramatically.[5]

Notes

Introduction

1. Interview on a Havana street curb, January 1979.

2. For my analysis of internal Cuban affairs, see *Cuba: Order and Revolution* (Cambridge, Mass.: Harvard University Press, 1978), and "Revolutionary Politics: The New Demands for Orderliness," in *Cuba: Internal and International Affairs,* ed. Jorge I. Domínguez (Beverly Hills: Sage Publications, 1982).

3. This formulation differs from that in my earlier "Cuban Foreign Policy," *Foreign Affairs* 57, no. 1 (Fall 1978): 83–108.

1. The Formative Years

1. Russell Fitzgibbon, *Cuba and the United States, 1900–1935* (Menasha, Wis.: Banta, 1935).

2. For a discussion of regimes, see the special issue of *International Organization* 36, no. 2 (Spring 1982).

3. For comparison, Jorge I. Domínguez, *Cuba: Order and Revolution* (Cambridge, Mass.: Harvard University Press, 1978), chaps. 2 and 3.

4. Fernando Henrique Cardoso and Enzo Faletto, *Dependency and Development in Latin America,* trans. Marjory Mattingly Urquidi (Berkeley: University of California Press, 1979).

5. Robert F. Smith, *The United States and Cuba: Business and Diplomacy, 1917–1960* (New Haven: College and University Press, 1960), pp. 157–164.

6. Domínguez, *Cuba: Order and Revolution,* pp. 67–68, 114–119, 142.

7. Cuban Economic Research Project, *A Study on Cuba* (Coral Gables: University of Miami Press, 1965), pp. 287–288, 399, 403, 607, 614, 616, 618.

8. Jaime Suchlicki, *University Students and Revolution in Cuba, 1920–1968* (Coral Gables: University of Miami Press, 1969), pp. 47–54.

9. Carlos Franqui, *Diary of the Cuban Revolution* (New York: Viking, 1980), pp. 9–19.

10. Herbert Matthews, *Revolution in Cuba* (New York: Charles Scribner's Sons, 1975), p. 84.

11. *Treaties and Other International Acts Series, 1951* (Washington, D.C.: U.S. Government Printing Office), no. 4692; hereafter cited as *TIAS, 1951.*

12. *New York Times,* February 5, 1958, p. 1; February 14, 1958, p. 1; February 19, 1958, p. 14; March 28, 1958, p. 9.

13. Earl E. T. Smith, *The Fourth Floor* (New York: Random House, 1962), p. 97.

14. U.S. Department of State, *American Foreign Policy: Current Documents, 1958* (Washington, D.C.: U.S. Government Printing Office), document 74; hereafter cited as *Current Documents,* by year.

15. Smith, *The Fourth Floor,* p. 99.

16. *TIAS, 1951,* no. 4092.

17. *Current Documents, 1958,* document 81; Smith, *The Fourth Floor,* p. 137; *New York Times,* June 28, 1958, p. 1; June 29, 1958, p. 1; Franqui, *Diary,* pp. 325–326, 356–358; Hugh Thomas, *Cuba: The Pursuit of Freedom* (New York: Harper and Row, 1971), pp. 1000–1001.

18. Dwight D. Eisenhower, *Waging Peace* (Garden City, N.Y.: Doubleday, 1965), p. 520; Smith, *The Fourth Floor,* p. 111; U.S. Department of State, *Bulletin* 39, no. 999 (August 18, 1958): 282.

19. Franqui, *Diary,* pp. 429–430; *New York Times,* October 22, 1958, p. 1; October 24, 1958, p. 1; October 27, 1958, p. 1.

20. Smith, *The Fourth Floor,* p. 166.

21. John Dorschner and Roberto Fabricio, *The Winds of December* (New York: Coward, McCann and Geoghegan, 1980), pp. 152–154, 157–161.

22. Smith, *The Fourth Floor,* p. 170.

23. Domínguez, *Cuba: Order and Revolution,* chap. 4.

24. Franqui, *Diary,* p. 290.

25. Royal Institute of International Affairs, *Documents on International Affairs, 1959* (London: Oxford University Press, 1963), pt. 4, statements of January 21, 1959, and May 15, 1959.

26. Text in Franqui, *Diary,* p. 421.

27. George J. Boughton, "Soviet-Cuban Relations, 1956–1960," *Journal of Inter-American Studies and World Affairs* 16, no. 4 (November 1974): 437–443.

28. Andrés Suárez, *Cuba: Castroism and Communism, 1959–1966* (Cambridge, Mass.: MIT Press, 1967, chap. 1.

29. Stanley Hoffmann, *Gulliver's Troubles, or The Setting of American Foreign Policy* (New York: McGraw-Hill, 1968), chap. 2.

30. *Revolución,* January 3, 1959, p. 1.

31. On internal events, see Domínguez, *Cuba: Order and Revolution,* and Thomas, *Cuba: The Pursuit of Freedom.*

32. *Revolución,* January 29, 1959, p. 6.

33. Ibid., March 6, 1959, p. 1.

34. Fidel Castro, *El pensamiento de Fidel Castro* (Bogota: Ediciones Paz y Socialismo, 1963), p. 69; *New York Times,* March 5, 1959, p. 6.

35. Philip W. Bonsal, *Cuba, Castro, and the United States* (Pittsburgh: University of Pittsburgh Press, 1971), pp. 47, 53.

36. Fidel Castro, *Discursos para la historia* (Havana: Impresa Emilio Gall, 1959), pp. 30, 34–35; *Revolución*, January 13, 1959, p. 2.

37. *Current Documents, 1959*, document 75.

38. Castro, *Discursos para la historia*, pp. 125–126.

39. *Revolución*, March 21, 1959, p. 2.

40. *New York Times*, March 4, 1959, p. 1; March 28, 1959, p. 5; Dwight D. Eisenhower, *Waging Peace, 1956–1961* (Garden City, N.Y.: Doubleday, 1965), p. 523.

41. Bonsal, *Cuba, Castro, and the United States*, p. 63.

42. "Castro's Challenge," *Frontline*, Public Broadcasting System, WGBH-TV production, first aired April 10, 1985.

43. *Revolución*, April 3, 1959, p. 1.

44. "Castro's Challenge," *Frontline;* see also *Revolución*, April 17, 1959, p. 15.

45. Pazos, interview, 1984, "Central America Project," WGBH-TV Educational Foundation. See also *Revolución*, April 30, 1959, p. 1. For U.S. government confirmation, *New York Times*, April 15, 1964, p. 8.

46. *Revolución*, April 10, 1959, p. 2.

47. Ibid., July 9, 1959, p. 1.

48. Domínguez, *Cuba: Order and Revolution*, chap. 11.

49. *Current Documents, 1959*, document 86; Bonsal, *Cuba, Castro, and the United States*, pp. 70–73.

50. *Revolución*, June 15, 1959, p. 1.

51. *New York Times*, October 23, 1959, p. 1.

52. Fidel Castro, *Speech to the People of Cuba, October 26, 1959* (Havana: Cooperativa Obrera de Publicidad, 1959), p. 30.

53. *Revolución*, October 22, 1959, p. 16; October 23. 1959, pp. 8, 16.

54. Alexandr Alexeev, "Cuba después del triunfo de la revolución: Primera parte," *América Latina*, no. 10 (October 1984): 56–67; quotation from p. 61. *Revolución* did not report his presence until December 15, 1959.

55. Ibid., pp. 63–64, 66–67.

56. Years later, this was confirmed by Fidel Castro and Carlos Rafael Rodríguez; see Rodríguez, "25 años de la victoria de Playa Girón y de la declaración del carácter socialista de la Revolución Cubana," *Cuba socialista*, no. 2 (1986): 23.

57. Alexeev, "Cuba después del triunfo de la revolución: Primera parte," pp. 57, 64, 65; Boughton, "Soviet-Cuban Relations, 1956–1960," pp. 443–444, 454.

58. Castro, *Discursos para la historia*, pp. 133–135; *Revolución*, March 21, 1959, p. 2; August 13, 1959, p. 1; October 1, 1959, p. 1.

59. Alexeev, "Cuba después del triunfo de la revolución: Primera parte," pp. 57–58, 67; Edward Gonzalez, "Castro's Revolution, Cuban Communist Appeals,

and the Soviet Response," *World Politics* 21, no. 1 (October 1968): 39–68.

60. "Castro's Challenge," *Frontline.*

61. *Revolución,* February 18, 1960, p. 13; Alexandr Alexeev, "Cuba después del triunfo de la revolución: Segunda parte," *América latina,* no. 11 (November 1984): 59.

62. Alexeev, "Cuba después del triunfo de la revolución: Primera parte," pp. 58, 65; ibid., "Segunda parte," pp. 58–59: Ivan Shkadov, Pavel Zhilin, Thelma Bornot Pubillones, and Victor Volski, *Valentía y fraternidad: El internacionalismo y la amistad combativa entre las fuerzas armadas de Cuba y la URSS* (Havana: Editorial de Ciencias Sociales, 1983), pp. 101–102, 173, 180, 234; Andrés García Suárez, "Los tanques soviéticos que combatieron en Playa Girón," *Bohemia* 78, no. 20 (May 16, 1986): 11.

63. *Revolución,* June 7, 1960, p. 1; June 8, 1960, p. 1; June 11, 1960, p. 1; June 17, 1960, p. 1.

64. Arkady Shevchenko, *Breaking with Moscow* (New York: Knopf, 1985), p. 105.

65. *Revolución,* February 20, 1959, p. 1.

66. Ibid., August 7, 1959, p. 18; October 21, 1959, p. 19.

67. Ibid., November 14, 1959, p. 18.

68. Ibid., December 18, 1959, p. 1.

69. *Current Documents, 1960,* document 67.

70. *Revolución,* January 28, 1960, p. 1.

71. Amoedo's testimony in *New Leader,* April 27, 1964, pp. 10–12.

72. Eisenhower, *Waging Peace,* p. 525.

73. *Current Documents, 1960,* document 71.

74. *Revolución,* March 2, 1960, p. 1.

75. Fidel Castro, *Sabotage of La Coubre* (Havana: Office of the Prime Minister, 1960).

76. Eisenhower, *Waging Peace,* p. 533.

77. *Revolución,* June 8, 1960, p. 2

78. Ibid., June 20, 1960, p. 19.

79. Ibid., July 11, 1960, p. 20.

80. Maurice Zeitlin and Robert Scheer, *Cuba: Tragedy in Our Hemisphere* (New York: 1961).

81. Bonsal, *Cuba, Castro, and the United States,* pp. 149–150.

82. *Revolución,* July 6, 1960, p. 6.

83. Ibid., July 11, 1960, p. 4.

84. Ibid., July 21, 1960, p. 1.

85. Ibid., October 14, 1960, p. 1; October 17, 1960, p. 1.

86. Ibid., December 20, 1960, p. 10; January 1, 1961, p. 1; U.S. Department of State, *Bulletin* 44, no. 1126 (January 23, 1961).

87. "Twenty-five Years of Aggression," *Tricontinental,* no. 88 (April 1983): 33.

88. Senate Select Committee to Study Governmental Operations with respect to

Intelligence Activities, "Alleged Assassination Plots Involving Foreign Leaders," *An Interim Report,* 94th Cong., 1st sess. (Washington, D.C.: U.S. Government Printing Office, 1975), pp. 73, 74–82, 255.

89. *Revolución,* March 8, 1961, p. 4; March 14, 1961, p. 1.

90. See its leader's anguish on camera: Manuel Ray's testimony in "Castro's Challenge," *Frontline.*

91. Lloyd S. Etheredge, *Can Governments Learn? American Foreign Policy and Central American Revolutions* (New York: Pergamon Press, 1985); Peter Wyden, *Bay of Pigs: The Untold Story* (New York: Simon and Schuster, 1979); Lucien S. Vandenbroucke, "The Decision to Land at the Bay of Pigs," *Political Science Quarterly* 99, no. 3 (Fall 1984): 471–491.

92. *Current Documents, 1961* document 96.

93. J. Lloyd Mecham, *The United States and Inter-American Security, 1889–1960* (Austin: University of Texas Press, 1961), chaps. 13 and 14.

94. Castro, *Discursos para la historia,* p. 129.

95. *Revolución* July 30, 1959, p. 2; July 31, 1959, p. 18; August 7, 1959, p. 19; August 10, 1959, p. 1.

96. Ibid., February 5, 1960, p. 14; March 29, 1960, p. 6; Joseph Gold, *The Cuban Insurance Cases and the Articles of the Fund* (Washington, D.C.: International Monetary Fund, 1966), pp. 2–3, 47.

97. House Committee on Foreign Affairs, "Inter-American Relations," *Hearings,* 93d Cong., 1st sess. (Washington, D.C.: U.S. Government Printing Office, 1973), pp. 202–203.

98. *Revolución,* September 3, 1960, p. 1.

99. House Committee on Foreign Affairs, "Inter-American Relations," p. 203.

100. Ibid., pp. 227–232.

101. *Current Documents, 1962,* document 59.

102. *New York Times,* October 24, 1962, p. 23; October 25, 1962, p. 1; October 26, 1962, p. 16; October 27, 1962, p. 9; October 28, 1962, pp. 1, 26; October 31, 1962, pp. 1, 18; December 2, 1962, p. 30.

103. U.S. Department of State, *Bulletin* 48, no. 1252 (June 24, 1963).

104. House Committee on Foreign Affairs, "Inter-American Relations," pp. 537–538, 571–573, 638–664.

105. Ibid., p. 235.

106. *Obra revolucionaria,* no. 18 (1964): 30.

107. Rolando Bonachea and Nelson P. Valdés, eds., *Revolutionary Struggle, 1947–1958: The Selected Works of Fidel Castro* (Cambridge, Mass.: MIT Press, 1972), pp. 164–221.

108. Ibid., pp. 346, 354–355, 366, 388.

109. See "Castro's Challenge," *Frontline.*

110. Quoted in Alexeev, "Cuba después del triunfo de la revolución: Primera parte," p. 63.

111. Lee Lockwood, *Castro's Cuba, Cuba's Fidel* (New York: Vintage Books, 1969), pp. 155, 163.

112. Susana Tesoro, "Setenta años de una vida plena," *Bohemia* 75, no. 20 (May 20, 1983): 56.

113. Lockwood, *Castro's Cuba, Cuba's Fidel,* p. 163.

114. *Daily Worker* (New York), August 5 and 10, 1953, quoted in Thomas, *Cuba: The Pursuit of Freedom,* p. 842.

115. Lockwood, *Castro's Cuba, Cuba's Fidel,* pp. 162–163.

116. Franqui, *Diary,* p. 269.

117. Fidel Castro, *El pensamiento de Fidel Castro* (Havana, 1962); *Revolución,* December 2, 1961.

118. *Revolución,* December 22, 1961.

119. Ibid., January 18, 1962.

120. Lockwood, *Castro's Cuba, Cuba's Fidel,* pp. 160–162.

121. Ibid., pp. 162, 165. See also *Fidel y la religión: Conversaciones con Frei Betto* (Havana: Oficina de Publicaciones del Consejo de Estado, 1965), pp. 158–168.

122. On regime support, Domínguez, *Cuba: Order and Revolution,* chaps. 5 and 6.

2. The Security Regime

1. *Revolución,* April 17, 1961; May 2, 1961.

2. Robert Jervis, "Security Regimes," *International Organization* 36, no. 2 (Spring 1982): 357–378; Joseph S. Nye, Jr., "Nuclear Learning and U.S.-Soviet Security Regimes," *International Organization* 41, no. 3 (Summer 1987): 371–402.

3. *Revolución,* July 27, 1962, p. 1.

4. For 1961–62 U.S.-Cuban trade, see Cuban Economic Research Project, *A Study on Cuba* (Coral Gables: University of Miami Press, 1965), pp. 708, 712.

5. Senate Select Committee to Study Governmental Operations with respect to Intelligence Activities, "Alleged Assassination Plots Involving Foreign Leaders," *An Interim Report,* 94th Cong., 1st sess. (Washington, D.C.: U.S. Government Printing Office, 1975), pp. 83–85.

6. *Revolución,* July 27, 1962, p. 1; April 20, 1963, p. 6; *New York Times,* April 16, 1963, p. 1; April 19, 1963, p. 14.

7. Jorge I. Domínguez, *Cuba: Order and Revolution* (Cambridge, Mass.: Harvard University Press, 1978), chaps. 5 and 6.

8. Roger Hilsman, *To Move a Nation* (New York: Delta Books, 1967), p. 170.

9. Anatoly Gromyko, "The Caribbean Crisis," *Soviet Law and Government* 11, no. 1 (Summer 1972): 9.

10. *Revolución,* July 3, 1962, pp. 1–2; July 7, 1962, p. 1; July 14, 1962, p. 1; April 20, 1963, p. 6.

11. Ibid., August 18, 1962, p. 1.

12. Ibid., September 3, 1962, p. 1.

13. Quoted in David Larson, ed., *The Cuban Crisis of 1962* (Boston: Houghton Mifflin, 1963), p. 3.

14. Fen O. Hampson, "The Divided Decision-Maker: American Domestic Politics and the Cuban Crises," *International Security* 9, no. 3 (Winter 1984–85): 134–149.

15. Quoted in Theodore C. Sorensen, *Kennedy* (New York: Harper and Row, 1965), p. 670.

16. Raymond L. Garthoff, "The Meaning of the Missiles," *Washington Quarterly,* Autumn 1982, pp. 81–82.

17. *Verde olivo* 25, no. 2 (January 12, 1984): 36; T. N. Dupuy and Wendell Blanchard, *The Almanac of World Military Power,* 2d ed. (Dunn Loring, Va.: T. N. Dupuy Associates, 1972), p. 24.

18. In *Cuba: Order and Revolution,* I gave the inaccurate impression (p. 349) that these planes arrived only as late as 1965.

19. Graham Allison, *The Essence of Decision: Explaining the Cuban Missile Crisis* (Boston: Little, Brown, 1971), pp. 103–105; Raymond Garthoff, "American Reaction to Soviet Aircraft in Cuba, 1962 and 1978," *Political Science Quarterly* 95, no. 3 (Fall 1980): 428; *Granma Weekly Review,* October 9, 1983, p. 12.

20. Hilsman, *To Move a Nation,* p. 193.

21. *Revolución,* October 24, 1962, p. 7.

22. Hilsman, *To Move a Nation,* p. 224.

23. U.S. Department of State, *Bulletin* 47, no. 1220 (November 12, 1962): 743.

24. Text in Larson, ed., *The Cuban Crisis of 1962,* p. 3.

25. *Revolución,* September 3, 1962, p. 1.

26. Herbert Matthews, *Revolution in Cuba* (New York: Charles Scribner's Sons, 1975), pp. 209–210.

27. Hugh Thomas, *Cuba: The Pursuit of Freedom* (New York: Harper and Row, 1971), pp. 1387–93.

28. Carlos Franqui, *Family Portrait with Fidel* (New York: Random House, 1984), pp. 183–187; Arkady N. Shevchenko, *Breaking with Moscow* (New York: Knopf, 1985), pp. 110, 116–117.

29. Tad Szulc, "Friendship Is Possible But . . . ," *Parade Magazine,* April 1, 1984, pp. 5–6; "The MacNeil/Lehrer Newshour," Public Broadcasting System, February 15, 1985.

30. Gromyko, "The Caribbean Crisis," p. 20; Lieut. Col. José Rodda Romero, "La crisis de Octubre por dentro," *Verde olivo* 23, no. 43 (October 28, 1982): 40.

31. On Soviet motivations, see Jacques Levesque, *L'URSS et la revolution cubaine* (Montreal: Presses de l'université de Montréal, 1976), pp. 58–65; Allison, *Essence of Decision,* pp. 230–244. Garthoff, "The Meaning of the Missiles," pp. 76–82, assesses whether the missile deployment posed a military threat to the United States.

32. Franqui, *Family Portrait with Fidel*, p. 187.

33. *Revolución*, November 2, 1962, p. 5.

34. Lee Lockwood, *Castro's Cuba, Cuba's Fidel* (New York: Vintage Books, 1969), pp. 224–225.

35. Matthews, *Revolution in Cuba*, p. 213, based on many interviews with Cuban leaders about the crisis.

36. Pedro Prada, "Guardianés de los cielos," *Verde olivo* 25, no. 24 (June 14, 1984): 30–33.

37. Jorge Luis Blanco, "Donde ella me necesite," *Verde olivo* 24, no. 19 (May 12, 1983): 31, 33.

38. Quoted in Frank Mankiewicz and Kirby Jones, *With Fidel* (Chicago: Playboy Press, 1975), p. 171.

39. Franqui, *Family Portrait with Fidel*, p. 193.

40. Szulc, "Friendship Is Possible, But . . . ," p. 6.

41. *Revolución*, July 3, 1964, p. 1.

42. Ibid., January 22, 1965, p. 4.

43. U.S. Department of State, *Bulletin* 47, no. 1220 (November 12, 1962): 742.

44. Hilsman, *To Move a Nation*, p. 220.

45. U.S. Department of State, *American Foreign Policy: Current Documents, 1962* (Washington, D.C.: U.S. Government Printing Office), document 104; hereafter cited as *Current Documents, 1962;* see also document 105, and *Revolución*, November 20, 1962, p. 1.

46. See also book sponsored by the Cuban and Soviet Armed Forces: Ivan Shkadov, Pavel Zhilin, Thelma Bornot Pubillones, and Victor Volski, *Valentía y fraternidad: El internacionalismo y la amistad combativa entre las Fuerzas Armadas de Cuba y la URSS* (Havana: Editorial de Ciencias Sociales, 1983), p. 161.

47. Allison, *Essence of Decision*, pp. 224–225; Hilsman, *To Move a Nation*, pp. 220–221.

48. Franqui, *Family Portrait with Fidel*, p. 194.

49. Lockwood, *Castro's Cuba, Cuba's Fidel*, pp. 223, 225.

50. Szulc, "Friendship Is Possible, But . . . ," p. 6.

51. "The MacNeil/Lehrer Newshour," Public Broadcasting System, February 15, 1985.

52. Garthoff claims that the Cuban Army surrounded the four Soviet missile base areas for several days. "American Reaction to Soviet Aircraft in Cuba, 1962 and 1978," pp. 430, 433. I have no independent evidence of this.

53. *Revolución*, October 29, 1962, p. 2.

54. Testimony of Soviet officer in charge. Major General Igor Statsenco, "Sobre algunos aspectos político-militares de la crisis del Caribe," *América latina*, no. 3 (1978): 149.

55. *Revolución*, November 2, 1962, p. 5.

56. Garthoff, "American Reaction to Soviet Aircraft in Cuba, 1962 and 1978," p. 433.

57. *Revolución,* November 8, 1962, p. 1.

58. Garthoff, "American Reaction to Soviet Aircraft in Cuba, 1962 and 1978," p. 433.

59. *New York Times,* November 9, 1962, p. 1.

60. *Revolución,* November 13, 1962, p. 5.

61. *Current Documents, 1962,* document 105; *Revolución,* November 20, 1962, p. 1.

62. *Current Documents, 1962,* document 111.

63. U.N. Security Council, document S/5228 (1963), pp. 1–4.

64. Gloria Duffy, "Crisis Mangling and the Cuban Brigade," *International Security* 8, no. 1 (Summer 1983): 69–71; Dupuy and Blanchard, *The Almanac of World Military Power,* p. 24.

65. *Granma Weekly Review,* October 7, 1979, p. 4. Dupuy and Blanchard give the figure 3,000 for the number of Soviet military personnel in Cuba in 1969; see *The Almanac of World Military Power,* p. 24.

66. Lockwood, *Castro's Cuba, Cuba's Fidel,* p. 226.

67. McGeorge Bundy, "The Brigade Is My Fault," *New York Times,* October 23, 1979, p. 23.

68. Hilsman, *To Move a Nation,* p. 225; Garthoff, "American Reaction to Soviet Aircraft in Cuba, 1962 and 1978," p. 438; Duffy, "Crisis Mangling and the Cuban Brigade," p. 71; Cyrus Vance, *Hard Choices* (New York: Simon and Schuster, 1983), p. 359.

69. U.S. Department of State, *Bulletin* 47, no. 1224 (1962): 874–875.

70. "The Lessons of the Cuban Missile Crisis," *Time,* September 27, 1982, p. 86.

71. *Current Documents, 1962,* document 111.

72. U.N. Security Council, document S/5228 (1963), pp. 1–4.

73. *Reagan on Cuba,* publication no. 18 (Washington, D.C.: Cuban-American National Foundation, 1986), p. 50.

74. *Report of the National Bipartisan Commission on Central America* (Washington, D.C.: U.S. Government Printing Office, 1984).

75. Senate Select Committee, "Alleged Assassination Plots," p. 173; see also pp. 170–173.

76. Ibid., pp. 173–174; for Fidel Castro's views, see Mankiewicz and Jones, *With Fidel,* pp. 160–169.

77. Senate Select Committee, "Alleged Assassination Plots," p. 174. See also Henry Hurt, *Reasonable Doubt: An Investigation into the Assassination of John F. Kennedy* (New York: Holt, Rinehart and Winston, 1985), chap. 11.

78. Senate Select Committee, "Alleged Assassination Plots," pp. 148–180.

79. Ibid., pp. 89–90, 176.

80. Ibid., p. 178; *Granma,* March 1, 1966, p. 1; March 5, 1966, p. 5; March 9, 1966, pp. 5, 7, 8; March 10, 1966, p. 6; March 11, 1966, p. 3.

81. Senate Select Committee, "Alleged Assassination Plots," pp. 177–180.

82. Henry Kissinger, *White House Years* (Boston: Little, Brown, 1979), pp. 632–633.

83. Ibid., p. 634.

84. Raymond L. Garthoff, "Handling the Cienfuegos Crisis," *International Security* 8, no. 1 (Summer 1983): pp. 50–52.

85. Kissinger, *White House Years,* p. 638.

86. Ibid., pp. 649–650.

87. Testimony by U.S. Defense Intelligence Agency analysts, in House Committee on Foreign Affairs, Subcommittee on Inter-American Affairs, "Soviet Naval Activities in Cuba," *Hearings,* 91st Cong., 2d sess. (Washington, D.C.: U.S. Government Printing Office, 1971), pp. 1–26.

88. *New York Times,* August 21, 1981.

89. House Committee on Foreign Affairs, Subcommittee on Inter-American Affairs. "Soviet Activities in Cuba," *Hearings,* pts. 4 and 5, 93d Cong. (Washington, D.C.: U.S. Government Printing Office, 1974), pp. 25–40.

90. See also Wayne S. Smith, *The Closest of Enemies* (New York: Norton, 1987), p. 83.

91. House Committee on International Relations, Subcommittee on Inter-American Affairs, "Impact of Cuban-Soviet Ties in the Western Hemisphere," *Hearings,* 95th Cong., 2nd sess. (Washington, D.C.: U.S. Government Printing Office, 1978), p. 9.

92. *Granma,* September 21, 1976, p. 1.

93. Ibid., May 8, 1984, p. 3.

94. Cited in Rodda, "La crisis de octubre por dentro," p. 43.

95. Garthoff, "American Reaction to Soviet Aircraft in Cuba, 1962 and 1978," pp. 427–439.

96. *Verde olivo* 20, no. 1 (January 7, 1979): 54.

97. Ibid., 20, no. 7 (February 18, 1979): 37.

98. Vance, *Hard Choices,* p. 133.

99. Duffy, "Crisis Mangling and the Cuban Brigade," pp. 67–87; Hampson, "The Divided Decision-Maker," pp. 156–165.

100. *Granma Weekly Review,* October 7, 1979, p. 2.

101. U.S. Department of State, Bureau of Public Affairs, "President Carter: Soviet Troops in Cuba," *Current Policy,* no. 92 (October 1, 1979): 2; U.S. Department of State, Bureau of Public Affairs, "Background on the Question of Soviet Troops in Cuba," *Current Policy,* no. 93 (October 1, 1979): 3; U.S. Department of State, Bureau of Public Affairs, "Secretary of State Vance, Press Conference: Soviet Troops in Cuba," *Current Policy,* no. 95 (September 5, 1979): 1; Vance, *Hard Choices,* p. 363.

102. *Granma Weekly Review,* October 7, 1979, p. 3.

103. Ibid., p. 2.

104. Alexander M. Haig, Jr., *Caveat: Realism, Reagan, and Foreign Policy* (New York: Macmillan, 1984), pp. 98, 128–129.

105. *Reagan on Cuba,* p. 21.

106. For other views about security regimes, see Jervis, "Security Regimes," pp. 360–362, 371–378; and Nye, "Nuclear Learning," pp. 391–400.

107. U.S. Chief of Naval Operations, Admiral James D. Watkins, "The Maritime Strategy," in *The Maritime Strategy* (U.S. Naval Institute, 1986), pp. 6–7, 11; David Ronfeldt, *Geopolitics, Security, and U.S. Strategy in the Caribbean Basin* (Santa Monica, Calif.: Rand Corporation, 1983): Richard Halloran, "Reagan as Military Commander," *New York Times Magazine,* January 15, 1984; Tony Velocci, "The Cuban Threat," *National Defense,* July-August 1984, 35–41.

108. The Cuban Air Force described its 1961–1978 buildup in *Granma Weekly Review,* October 9, 1983, p. 12. Evidence of MiG-23s is presented in *Verde olivo* 24, no. 13 (March 31, 1983): 4–5, and of submarine flying the Cuban flag in *Verde olivo* 23, no. 49 (December 9, 1982): 8–9.

109. *Granma,* February 4, 1985, p. 2.

110. *Granma Weekly Review,* August 3, 1986, p. 2; August 31, 1986, p. 9; *Los Angeles Times,* September 26, 1986, p. 20.

111. Interviews in Havana, April 1988.

112. Interviews of Castro are in the *Boston Globe,* February 3, 1985 (which reprinted the *Washington Post* interview), p. 22, and Madrid's *El País,* January 21, 1985, p. 6; see also *Granma,* December 9, 1986, p. 1.

113. Interview with informed U.S. government official, March 1985. See also *Granma,* December 10, 1986, p. 1.

114. *Granma,* February 4, 1985, p. 2.

3. Cuba's Challenge to the Soviet Union in the 1960s

1. For comparison of U.S. and Soviet hegemonies within Cuba, see Jorge I. Domínguez, *Cuba: Order and Revolution* (Cambridge, Mass.: Harvard University Press, 1978), chaps. 2–5.

2. Computed from Comité Estatal de Estadísticas, *Anuario estadístico de Cuba, 1983* (Havana), pp. 289, 296, 300.

3. María Teresa Valdés, "La evolución de la producción azucarera en Cuba y su papel en las relaciones económicas externas, 1959–1983," *Revista CIEM: Temas de economía mundial* no. 10 (1984): 136.

4. Maurice Halperin, *The Rise and Decline of Fidel Castro* (Berkeley: University of California Press, 1972), chaps. 20–23.

5. Valdés, "La evolución de la producción azucarera," p. 136.

6. *Obra revolucionaria,* no. 15 (1963): 32; Fidel Castro, *El viaje de Fidel Castro a la Unión Soviética* (Montevideo: Ediciones Pueblos Unidos, 1963), p. 49; Cuban Economic Research Project, *Cuba: Agriculture and Planning* (Coral Gables: University of Miami Press, 1965), p. 142.

7. Dirección Central de Estadística, *Compendio estadístico de Cuba, 1966* (Havana: Junta Central de Planificación), p. 19.

8. Edward Boorstein, *The Economic Transformation of Cuba* (New York: Monthly Review Press, 1968), chap. 6.

9. *Revolución*, January 23, 1964, p. 1.

10. Ibid., January 25, 1964, p. 4.

11. Anatoly Bekarevich, *Cuba* (Moscow: Nauka, 1970), p. 213; Leon Goure and Julian Weinkle, "Soviet-Cuban Relations: The Growing Integration," in *Castro, Cuba, and Revolution*, ed. Jaime Suchlicki (Coral Gables: University of Miami Press, 1972), p. 170.

12. Domínguez, *Cuba: Order and Revolution*, p. 151.

13. Eric Baklanoff, "International Economic Relations," in *Revolutionary Change in Cuba*, ed. Carmelo Mesa-Lago (Pittsburgh: University of Pittsburgh Press, 1971), p. 268.

14. Yuri Gavrikov, "América Latina y los países del CAME: Algunos problemas de la colaboración," *Panorama latinoamericano* (Novosti), no. 150 (July 1, 1972): 5–6; Yuri Gavrikov, "URSS-Cuba: Colaboración y solidaridad," ibid., no. 163 (February 15, 1973); 3–5; Boris Gorbachev, "Cuba: Algunas cuestiones de su integración económica con los países del socialismo," ibid., no. 171 (August 1, 1973): 3; Boris Gvozdariov, "URSS-Cuba: Unidad de criterios y posiciones," ibid., no. 184 (April 1, 1974): 6; O. Darusenkov, "Cuba Builds Socialism," *International Affairs*, no. 11 (November 1975): 21; "Science and Education in Cuba," *International Affairs*, no. 1 (January 1976): 154.

15. Domínguez, *Cuba: Order and Revolution*, p. 150.

16. *Che Guevara Speaks*, ed. George Lavan (New York: Merit Publishers, 1967), pp. 108–109; also published in *Revolución*, February 26, 1965, p. 1.

17. Economist Intelligence Unit, *Quarterly Economic Review: Cuba, Dominican Republic, Haiti, Puerto Rico*, no. 50 (1965).

18. Technical discussion in Edward A. Hewett, *Foreign Trade Prices in the Council for Mutual Economic Assistance* (London: Cambridge University Press, 1974), pp. 43–45, 58, 178–179.

19. Goure and Weinkle, "Soviet-Cuban Relations," pp. 166, 170; these authors did not identify their source. See also *Cuban Economic News* 2, no. 11 (May 1966): 7; Economist Intelligence Unit, *Quarterly Economic Review: Cuba, Dominican Republic, Haiti, Puerto Rico*, no. 1 (1966): 6.

20. Domínguez, *Cuba: Order and Revolution*, pp. 156–157.

21. *Obra revolucionaria*, no. 20 (1963): 25.

22. *Revolución*, October 8, 1963, p. 1.

23. Andrés Suárez, *Cuba: Castroism and Communism, 1959–1966* (Cambridge, Mass.: MIT Press, 1967), pp. 201–209.

24. Jacques Levesque, *L'URSS et la revolution cubaine* (Montreal: Presses de l'université de Montréal, 1976), pp. 136–166.

25. Fidel Castro, *Division in the Face of the Enemy Was Never a Revolutionary or Intelligent Strategy* (Havana, 1965), p. 7.

26. In fact, China sold Cuba 145,900 tons of rice in 1966.

27. *Granma*, January 3, 1966, p. 4.

28. *Política internacional* 4, no. 13 (1966): 213–226; "Discurso de Fidel Castro el 13 de marzo," *Cuba socialista* 6, no. 56 (May 1966): 3–16.

29. Cuban Economic Research Project, *A Study on Cuba* (Coral Gables: University of Miami Press, 1965), p. 537.

30. Dirección Central de Estadística, *Boletín estadístico de Cuba, 1964* (Havana: Junta Central de Planificación, 1966), p. 80; Dirección Central de Estadística, *Anuario estadístico de Cuba, 1970* (Havana: Junta Central de Planificación, 1972), p. 96.

31. Computed from Comité Estatal de Estadísticas, *Anuario, 1983,* pp. 289, 291, 296, 298, 300, 302.

32. *Granma Weekly Review,* July 31, 1966, p. 11.

33. *Granma,* May 15, 1966, pp. 2–3.

34. Ibid., November 13, 1966, p. 5.

35. *Granma Weekly Review,* March 19, 1967, supplement, p. 8.

36. Ibid., July 30, 1967, p. 9.

37. Ibid., p. 5.

38. Fidel Castro, *Obras escogidas, 1962–1968,* vol. 2 (Madrid: Editorial Fundamentos, 1976), pp. 161–162.

39. *New York Times,* November 7, 1967, p. 10.

40. For a general discussion, see D. Bruce Jackson, *Castro, the Kremlin, and Communism in Latin America* (Baltimore: Johns Hopkins University Press, 1969).

41. United Nations, *Statistical Bulletin* 3 (1966): 38; *Granma Weekly Review,* January 7, 1968, pp. 2–3; Dirección Central de Estadística, *Anuario estadístico de Cuba, 1974* (Havana: Junta Central de Planificación, 1974), p. 128.

42. *Granma,* January 3, 1968, pp. 2–3, 6. Thirteen years later, Castro had developed political amnesia: "During over twenty years . . . never did any equipment stop working in our country for lack of Soviet oil . . . Never has the Soviet Union cast the slightest shadow over [our] independence." *Verde olivo* 22, no. 18 (May 3, 1981): 33.

43. *Granma,* February 12, 1968, p. 4; February 13, 1968, p. 4.

44. *Current Digest of the Soviet Press* 19, no. 50 (December 15, 1967): 15–16.

45. *Granma,* January 6, 1968, p. 9.

46. Ibid., January 13, 1968, p. 3.

47. Ibid., January 28, 1968, pp. 1–2.

48. Ibid., January 29, 1968, pp. 2–3; January 30, 1968, p. 2; February 1, 1968, p. 2.

49. Ibid., January 30, 1968, p. 2.

50. Ibid., p. 3; February 1, 1968, p. 2.

51. Ibid., January 28, 1968, p. 1; February 29, 1968, p. 4.

52. Ibid., January 28, 1968, p. 1.

53. Ibid., p. 1.

54. Henry Kissinger, *White House Years* (Boston: Little, Brown, 1979), p. 638.

55. *Granma,* February 12, 1968, p. 1.

56. Alexis Codina and Joaquín Fernández Núñez, "Apuntes en el XX aniversario del inicio de la formación de economistas," *Economía y desarrollo,* no. 71 (November-December 1982): 23.

57. *Granma Weekly Review,* March 24, 1968, p. 7.

58. Fidel Castro, *Obras escogidas, 1962–1968,* II, 182, 224.

59. Ibid., pp. 199, 203, 207, 220, 221, 223, 224.

60. *Granma Weekly Review,* January 4, 1976, p. 10.

61. Ibid., January 25, 1976, p. 10.

4. The Reestablishment of Soviet Hegemony

1. See also Cole Blasier, *The Giant's Rival* (Pittsburgh: University of Pittsburgh Press, 1983), chap. 5; Eduard Sheinin, "Vínculos internacionales de la economía cubana," *América latina,* no. 1 (1979): 100–112; Svetlana Penkina, "Cuba y la división socialista internacional del trabajo," *América latina,* no. 4 (1979): 18–34; W. Raymond Duncan, *The Soviet Union and Cuba* (New York: Praeger, 1985); and José Luis Rodríguez, "Las relaciones económicas Cuba-URSS, 1960–1985," *Revista del CIEM: Temas de economía mundial,* no. 17 (1986): 7–33.

2. Fidel Castro, *Obras escogidas, 1953–1962,* vol. 1 (Madrid: Editorial Fundamentos, 1976), p. 47; *Granma,* January 4, 1985, special supplement, p. 4.

3. Henry Kissinger, *White House Years* (Boston: Little, Brown, 1979), p. 638.

4. *Granma Weekly Review,* October 7, 1979.

5. Ibid., January 4, 1976, p. 7.

6. Dmitry F. Ustinov, "Nacidos del Gran Octubre," *Verde olivo* 20, no. 8 (February 25, 1979): 47.

7. *Verde olivo* 20, no. 1 (January 7, 1979): 12, 13.

8. *Granma Weekly Review,* June 27, 1982, p. 2; *Granma,* December 13, 1982, p. 2.

9. *Granma Weekly Review,* June 27, 1982, p. 2; *Granma,* January 4, 1985, special supplement, p. 6; *Granma,* February 4, 1985, p. 2.

10. *Granma,* December 13, 1982, p. 2; June 13, 1984, p. 1; Fidel Castro, "Main Report: Third Congress of the Communist Party of Cuba" (mimeo, Havana, 1986), p. 51.

11. U.S. Department of Defense, *Soviet Military Power* (Washington, D.C. U.S. Government Printing Office, 1985), pp. 115, 119–120.

12. *Granma,* April 22, 1975, p. 4.

13. *Granma Weekly Review,* September 19, 1971, pp. 3, 7.

14. Ibid., July 23, 1972, p. 10.

15. For changes beginning in 1969, see testimony of Cuban Interior Ministry defector, in Senate, Committee on the Judiciary, Subcommittee to Investigate the Administration of the Internal Security Act and Other Internal Security Laws, "Communist Threat to the United States through the Caribbean: Testimony of Or-

lando Castro Hidalgo," *Hearings,* 91st Cong., 1st sess. (Washington, D.C.: U.S. Government Printing Office, 1969), pp. 1424–26.

16. *Granma Weekly Review,* January 14, 1973, p. 2; Boris Asonov, "La colaboración económica U.R.S.S.-Cuba a partir del triunfo de la revolución," *Economía y desarrollo,* no. 20 (November-December 1973): 155–157. See also Theodore H. Moran, "The International Political Economy of Cuban Nickel Development," in *Cuba in the World,* ed. Cole Blasier and Carmelo Mesa-Lago (Pittsburgh: University of Pittsburgh Press, 1979).

17. María Teresa Valdés, "La evolución de la producción azucarera en Cuba y su papel en las relaciones económicas externas," *Revista del CIEM: Temas de economía mundial,* no. 10 (1984): 136.

18. Computed from Comité Estatal de Estadísticas, *Anuario estadístico de Cuba, 1978* (Havana), pp. 165, 167.

19. Documents captured by the U.S. armed forces in Grenada (now available in the U.S. National Archives): Embassy of Grenada in the USSR, "Relations with the CPSU," no date (probably late 1982), p. 4.

20. José Luis Rodríguez García, "La economía cubana entre 1976 y 1980: Resultados y perspectivas," *Economía y desarrollo,* no. 66 (January-February 1982): 121.

21. Ibid. On CMEA price policy, see "CMEA and Raw Materials Prices," *World Marxist Review* 18, no. 5 (May 1975): 139; interview with Hugo Pons, editor, *Economía y desarrollo,* March 17, 1985.

22. Interviews with Hugo Pons, Havana, March 17, 1985, and José Luis Rodríguez Garcia, deputy director of the Centro de Investigaciones de la Economía Mundial (CIEM), Havana, March 22, 1985; Rodríguez, "La economía cubana," p. 121. The Cuban armed forces expected the same: *Verde olivo* 19, no. 5 (January 29, 1978): 12.

23. Elsa Blaquier and Luis López, "¿Qué nos trajo este quinquenio?" *Verde olivo,* 21, no. 51 (December 21, 1980): 34.

24. See also Comité Estatal de Estadísticas, *Estadísticas quinquenales de Cuba, 1965–1980* (Havana, 1982), p. 61.

25. *Granma Weekly Review,* November 9, 1980, special supplement, p. 2; José Luis Rodríguez, "Un enfoque burgués del sector externo de la economía cubana," *Cuba socialista,* no. 14 (March-April 1985): 99.

26. Interview with José Luis Rodríguez Garcia, March 22, 1985.

27. Quoted in Julio Díaz Vázquez, "Cuba: Industrialización e integración económica socialista," *Economía y desarrollo,* no. 79 (March–April 1984): 67.

28. *Granma,* January 4, 1985, special supplement, p. 5.

29. Banco Nacional de Cuba, *Economic Report,* August 1982, p. 15; and interviews in Cuba, March 1985.

30. A case can be made for interest-bearing loans if they are forgiven in the future. They are more likely to motivate structural readjustments to improve economic efficiency and to reduce distortions created by price subsidies. Private communication from Jorge Pérez-López, September 19, 1985.

31. *Granma Weekly Review,* December 9, 1984, special supplement, p. 14.

32. Banco Nacional de Cuba, *Economic Report,* February 1985, p. 3; *Granma Weekly Review,* March 29, 1987, p. 11; interviews in Cuba, March 1985 and June 1986.

33. Julio A. Díaz Vázquez, "Cuba: Integración económica socialista y especialización de la producción," *Economía y desarrollo,* no. 63 (July-August 1981): 152.

34. *Granma,* August 1, 1983, p. 3.'

35. Sergei Tsukasov, "The Loveliest Blossom of the Revolution," *World Marxist Review* 27, no. 2 (February 1984): 61.

36. Interviews with Hugo Pons, who is also an energy market specialist, March 17, 1985, and with Julio Fernández Cossío, of Cuba's Central Bank, Havana, March 26, 1985; *Granma Weekly Review,* December 9, 1984, special supplement, p. 13.

37. Banco Nacional de Cuba, *Economic Report,* March 1986, p. 23.

38. For the consensus on overall trends in Cuban economic performance and the disagreements on estimates of specific growth rates, see Carmelo Mesa-Lago, *The Economy of Socialist Cuba: A Two-Decade Appraisal* (Albuquerque: University of New Mexico Press, 1981); Claes Brundenius, *Revolutionary Cuba: The Challenge of Economic Growth with Equity* (Boulder, Colo.: Westview Press, 1984); José Luis Rodríguez García, *Dos ensayos sobre la economía cubana* (Havana: Editorial de Ciencias Sociales, 1984); Andrew Zimbalist, ed., *Cuban Political Economy* (Boulder, Colo.: Westview Press, 1988), chaps. 1–5; Jorge Pérez-López, "Real Economic Growth in Cuba, 1965–1982," *The Journal of Developing Areas* 20 (January 1986): 151–172; Wharton Econometric Forecasting Associates, *Construction of Cuban Economic Activity and Trade Indexes* 1 (November 1983).

39. Castro, "Main Report: Third Congress," p. 4.

40. Ibid., pp. 28–33, 35–36. See also Jorge Pérez-López, "Cuban Economy in the 1980s," *Problems of Communism* 35, no. 5 (September-October 1986): 16–34.

41. *Granma Weekly Review,* January 10, 1982, p. 4.

42. Computed from Comité Estatal de Estadísticas, *Anuario estadístico de Cuba, 1986* (Havana), p. 100.

43. *Granma,* December 14, 1981, pp. 2–3; interviews in Havana, June 1986.

44. See also Cole Blasier, "COMECON in Cuban Development," in *Cuba in the World,* ed. Blasier and Mesa-Lago.

45. Jorge I. Domínguez, *Cuba: Order and Revolution* (Cambridge, Mass.: Harvard University Press, 1978), pp. 151–152.

46. N. V. Faddeev, "La comunidad de países socialistas," *Verde olivo* 20, no. 12 (March 25, 1979): 39.

47. Stanislaw Raczkowski, "The Influence of International Movements of Prices and Inflation on the Economies of the Socialist Countries," *Eastern European Economics* 24, no. 4 (Summer 1986): 3–28.

48. José Peraza Chapeau, *El CAME y la integración económica socialista* (Havana: Editorial de Ciencias Sociales, 1984), pp. 68–70.

49. Julio A. Díaz Vázquez, *Cuba y el CAME* (Havana: Editorial de Ciencias Sociales, 1985), pp. 70–88; interviews in Havana, June 1986.

50. Díaz Vázquez, *Cuba y el CAME,* pp. 71–72; *Granma,* August 1, 1983, p. 3; interviews in Havana, March 1985.

51. *Granma Weekly Review,* October 28, 1984, p. 3.

52. Ibid; ibid., June 24, 1984, p. 2; Juan Ibáñez, "Cuba en la división internacional socialista del trabajo," *Verde olivo* 24, no. 19 (May 12, 1983): 37–38; Marcelo Fernández Font, *Cuba y la economía azucarera mundial,* Estudios e Investigaciones, no. 5 (Havana: Instituto Superior de Relaciones Internacionales "Raúl Roa García," 1986), p. 196.

53. Ibáñez, "Cuba en la división internacional socialista," p. 38.

54. *Granma Weekly Review,* October 28, 1984, p. 3.

55. Ibid.

56. Ibid., October 28, 1984, p. 3; figure computed from *Anuario, 1985,* pp. 398–399.

57. Mercedes Ramos, "Moa," *Bohemia* 76, no. 39 (September 28, 1984): 77.

58. Elsy Fors, "Cuba: Doce años en el CAME," *Bohemia* 76, no. 26 (June 29, 1984): 71.

59. Castro, "Main Report: Third Congress," pp. 28, 48; Banco Nacional de Cuba, *Economic Report,* March 1986, p. 9; *Granma,* October 11, 1986, p. 2.

60. *Granma Weekly Review,* October 28, 1984, p. 3; *Granma,* November 5, 1986, p. 5; Bob Ubell, "Cuba's Great Leap," *Cubatimes* 4, no. 6 (September-October 1984): 16; interview with Vice President Carlos Rafael Rodríguez, Havana, April 1988.

61. Roxana Brizuela Prado, "Las relaciones América Latina-países miembros del CAME," *Economía y desarrollo,* no. 67 (March-April 1982): 60.

62. Anatoly Olshany and Julio A. Díaz Vázquez, "Las relaciones económicas entre los países del CAME y la América Latina," *Economía y desarrollo,* no. 57 (May-June 1980): 171, 179.

63. Oneida Alvarez Figueroa, "Papel del sistema socialista en el establecimiento de un nuevo tipo de relaciones internacionales," *Economía y desarrollo,* no. 66 (January-February 1982): 18.

64. Díaz Vázquez, *Cuba y el CAME,* pp. 39–70.

65. "Cuba-RDA XX aniversario," *Bohemia* 75, no. 2 (January 14, 1983): 71.

66. *Granma,* December 16, 1982, p. 3; February 24, 1984, p. 3; *Granma Weekly Review,* February 8, 1987, p. 5.

67. *Granma,* August 20, 1982, pp. 1, 3; December 16, 1982, p. 3; Serafín Marrero, "Cuba-RDA: Dos decenios de colaboración," *Bohemia* 76, no. 20 (May 18, 1984): 35.

68. *Granma Weekly Review,* December 4, 1983, p. 2; interviews in Cuba, 1985.

69. *Granma,* August 20, 1982, p. 3; interviews in Cuba, 1985.

70. Interview with Jesús Escandel, secretary for international relations, CTC, Havana, March 23, 1985.

71. N. Leonov, "U.S.S.R.-Cuba: Fraternal Cooperation in Action," *International Affairs*, no. 11 (1984): 26; Andrei Chernoschok, "Estudian en Moscú," *Bohemia* 75, no. 18 (May 6, 1983): 62; Comité Estatal de Estadísticas, *Anuario estadístico de Cuba, 1983* (Havana), p. 403; *Anuario, 1986*, p. 528.

72. *Granma*, November 6, 1984, p. 5.

73. Ibid., December 15, 1984, p. 3.

74. Frank Agüero, "La educación: Obra de todos," *Verde olivo* 24, no. 52 (December 29, 1983): 57.

75. Díaz Vázquez, "Cuba: Integración económica socialista," pp. 137, 138–139.

76. Ibid., pp. 138–139; interviews in Cuba.

77. Claes Brundenius, *Revolutionary Cuba*, pp. 61–68, 75–77; Mesa-Lago, *The Economy of Socialist Cuba*, chap. 5; 1986 figure computed from *Anuario, 1986*, pp. 427–431.

78. William LeoGrande, "Cuban Dependency: A Comparison of Pre-Revolutionary and Post-Revolutionary International Economic Relations," *Cuban Studies* 9, no. 2 (July 1979): 1–28; Ramón Pérez Cabrera, "La sustitución de importaciones en Cuba: Realidad y perspectivas," *Cuba socialista*, no. 20 (March-April 1986): 69–86.

79. *Granma*, January 4, 1985, special supplement, p. 4; Castro, "Main Report: Third Congress," p. 13.

80. LeoGrande, "Cuban Dependency," p. 25.

81. Fernando Henrique Cardoso, "Associated Dependent Development: Theoretical and Practical Implications," in *Authoritarian Brazil*, ed. Alfred Stepan (New Haven: Yale University Press, 1973).

82. LeoGrande, "Cuban Dependency," p. 26.

83. Carmelo Mesa-Lago and Jorge Pérez-López, "Imbroglios on the Cuban Economy," *Comparative Economic Studies* 27, no. 1 (Spring 1985): 47–83.

84. Text in H. Michael Erisman, *Cuba's International Relations* (Boulder, Colo.: Westview Press, 1985), pp. 123–124.

85. Henry Rowen, "The Soviet Economy," in *The Soviet Union in the 1980s*, ed. Erik P. Hoffmann (New York: Academy of Political Science, 1984); interviews in Havana, June 1986.

86. Average prices increased from $0.838 in 1982 to $0.856 in 1983; Table 4.1 reflects the effects of rounding.

87. José L. Rodríguez, Edith Felipe, and Norka Clech, "La evolución de la economía de los países socialistas," in *Informe sobre la evolución de la economía mundial en 1983* (Havana: CIEM); *Boston Globe*, January 27, 1985, pp. A43, A45.

88. *Anuario, 1986*, p. 100; Banco Nacional de Cuba, *Report on the Economic and Financial Situation of Cuba during 1987–1988*, January 1988, p. 3.

89. Claes Brundenius, "Measuring Income Distribution in Pre- and Post-Revolutionary Cuba," *Cuban Studies* 9, no. 2 (July 1979): 29–44.

90. *Verde olivo* 20, no. 8 (February 25, 1979): 73.

91. *Granma*, December 29, 1984, p. 2; January 4, 1985, special supplement; interviews in Havana, March 1985.

92. Interviews with Cuban officials confirm that following the Soviet model was their intention.

93. See also Robert A. Packenham, "Capitalist Dependency and Socialist Dependency: The Case of Cuba," *Journal of Inter-American Studies and World Affairs* 28, no. 1 (Spring 1986): 59–92.

94. *Granma,* January 4, 1985, special supplement.

95. José Luis Rodríguez, "Los precios preferenciales en los marcos del CAME: Análisis preliminar," *Revista del CIEM: Temas de economía mundial,* no. 9 (1984): 23.

96. *Granma,* January 4, 1985, special supplement, p. 11.

97. Ibid., December 29, 1984.

98. *Granma Weekly Review,* November 15, 1981, p. 5.

99. *Granma,* April 12, 1984, p. 3.

100. Interviews in Havana, 1985.

101. *Granma Weekly Review,* September 16, 1973, p. 12.

102. "The MacNeil/Lehrer Newshour," Public Broadcasting System, February 15, 1985.

103. *Granma Weekly Review,* June 3, 1984, p. 3; June 17, 1984, p. 3.

104. Yoram Shapira, "Cuba and the Arab Israeli Conflict," in *Cuba in the World,* ed. Blasier and Mesa-Lago.

105. M. Petrov, "Denuclearised Zone in Latin America, *International Affairs,* no. 8 (August 1974): 49–50; M. Petrov, "The Soviet Union and the Denuclearised Zone in Latin America," *International Affairs,* no. 12 (December 1979).

106. Interviews in Cuba, June 1986.

107. *Granma Weekly Review,* November 30, 1980, special supplement, p. 2.

108. Carlos Rafael Rodríguez, "Fundamentos estratégicos de la política exterior de Cuba," *Cuba socialista,* no. 1 (2d ser.) (December 1981): 32.

109. *Granma,* October 21, 1983, p. 5; June 15, 1984, p. 8.

110. *Granma Weekly Review,* November 4, 1984, p. 2.

111. Ibid., December 9, 1984, special supplement, p. 14.

112. *Granma,* February 4, 1985, p. 2.

113. "Playboy Interview: Fidel Castro," *Playboy* 32, no. 8 (August 1985): 62; interviews in Havana, March 1985.

114. *Granma Weekly Review,* January 12, 1986, p. 4; March 9, 1986, p. 1; November 23, 1986, p. 9.

115. Fidel Castro, "En el 53 Pleno del Consejo Nacional de la CTC," *Cuba socialista,* no. 25 (January-February 1987): 159; Banco Nacional de Cuba, *Economic Report,* May 1987, p. 14.

116. María del Carmen Ariet Garcia, "Che's Role in the Foreign Policy of the Cuban Revolution," *Tricontinental,* no. 113 (May 1987): 59; see also p. 38.

117. Foreign Broadcast Information Service, *Daily Report: Soviet Union,* SOV-87-120 (June 23, 1987): BB, 2; ibid., SOV-87-107 (June 4, 1987): I, 1–4.

118. Vladislav Chirkov, "An Uphill Task," *New Times,* no. 33 (August 17, 1987): 16–17.

119. Carlos Rafael Rodríguez, "A Difficult but Steady Ascent," *New Times,* no. 41 (October 19, 1987): 16–17.

120. Pavel Bogomolov, "Tackling the Problems of Growth," *New Times,* no. 37 (September 21, 1987): 14–15.

121. Nikolai Vasetski, "Atolladeros del pseudorrevolucionarismo," *América Latina,* no. 1 (1987): 20–21; A. Nosov, "A qué lleva el desconocimiento del objeto," *América Latina,* no. 9 (1987): 58–59.

122. *Granma Weekly Review,* December 27, 1987, p. 1; February 14, 1988, p. 6; "Carlos Rafael Rodríguez en el III Congreso de la AEALC," *Bohemia* 79, no. 49 (December 4, 1987): 78; and interview with Vice President Carlos Rafael Rodríguez, Havana, April 1988.

123. *Granma Weekly Review,* January 17, 1988, p. 1.

124. *New York Times,* January 3, 1988, pp. 1, 8.

125. For a suggestive article, Bruce E. Moon, "Consensus or Compliance? Foreign Policy Change and External Dependence," *International Organization* 39, no. 2 (Spring 1985): 297–329.

5. Support for Revolutionary Movements

1. Fidel Castro, *Obras escogidas, 1953–1962,* vol. 1 (Madrid: Editorial Fundamentos, 1976), p. 131.

2. *Documentos políticos: Política internacional de la revolución cubana,* vol. 1 (Havana: Editora Política, 1966), p. 83.

3. *Granma,* November 6, 1982, p. 2.

4. *Revolución,* April 29, 1959, p. 15.

5. *New York Times,* March 18, 1959, p. 7.

6. *Revolución,* May 8, 1959, p. 1.

7. Ibid., June 16, 1959, p. 16; June 17, 1959, p. 19; June 22, 1959, p. 20; June 26, 1959, p. 21; June 27, 1959, p. 19.

8. Alberto Recarte, *Cuba: Economía y poder (1959–1980)* (Madrid: Alianza Editorial, 1980), pp. 160–189; *El país,* January 21, 1985, p. 6.

9. Interview with a high-ranking Spanish government official.

10. *El país,* January 21, 1985, p. 6.

11. *Granma Weekly Review,* May 21, 1967, p. 8. For additional Cuban government admissions that other Cubans were killed in Venezuela fighting against that government, see *Tricontinental Bulletin,* no. 17 (August 1967): 37.

12. *El país,* January 21, 1985.

13. *Revolución,* July 29, 1964, p. 4.

14. *New York Times,* July 6, 1964, p. 1; Lee Lockwood, *Castro's Cuba, Cuba's Fidel* (New York: Vintage Books, 1969), pp. 220–223.

15. Interview with Luis Suárez, director, Center for American Studies (CEA), Havana, March 28, 1985.

16. Carmelo Mesa-Lago, *Cuba in the 1970s* (Albuquerque: University of New

Mexico Press, 1974), chap. 4; Carlos Antonio Romero, "La diplomacia de proyección y el caso cubano en el contexto nacional y regional: Las relaciones entre Venezuela y Cuba," in *Fragmentos,* vol. 11 (Caracas: Centro de Estudios Latinoamericanos "Rómulo Gallegos," 1981), pp. 12–14.

17. *Granma Weekly Review,* June 15, 1969, p. 6.

18. Ibid., August 31, 1975, p. 7.

19. In the most repressive years of President Jorge Videla's regime, Cuba imported merchandise worth $165 million in 1976, $115 million in 1977, and $78 million in 1978. Comité Estatal de Estadísticas, *Anuario estadístico de Cuba, 1980* (Havana), p. 171.

20. *O Estado de São Paulo,* September 6, 1986, p. 3. See also Heraldo Muñoz and Boris Yopo, "Cuba y las democracias latinoamericanas en los ochenta," *Documento de Trabajo PROSPEL,* no. 9 (1987): 10, 23–24.

21. *Granma Weekly Review,* November 19, 1972, p. 11; Senate Committee on Foreign Relations, Subcommittee on Western Hemisphere Affairs, "U.S. Policy toward Cuba," *Hearings,* 93d Cong., 1st sess. (Washington, D.C.: U.S. Government Printing Office, 1974), pp. 1–7.

22. *Granma Weekly Review,* April 18, 1982, p. 5.

23. *Granma,* April 29, 1982, p. 2.

24. Ibid., August 3, 1983, p. 1.

25. *Granma Weekly Review,* March 29, 1981, p. 1.

26. Interviews in Havana, March 1985.

27. See Jorge I. Domínguez, ed., *Cuba: Internal and International Affairs* (Beverly Hills: Sage Publications, 1982.

28. Anatoly Olshany, "Colaboración económica y comercial de los países miembros del CAME y Colombia," *América latina,* no. 3 (1982). Soviet scholar Nikolai Vasetsky labeled the M-19 "pseudoradical," not revolutionary, in his "Atolladeros del pseudorrevolucionarismo," *América latina,* no. 1 (1987): 20–21.

29. *Granma Weekly Review,* November 9, 1986, p. 1; *Times of the Americas,* November 26, 1986, p. 2.

30. *Granma Weekly Review,* March 19, 1967, special supplement.

31. Fidel Castro, "Che: Universal Inspiration to Struggle," *Tricontinental Bulletin,* no. 8 (September-October 1968): 102–104.

32. "Editorial," *Tricontinental Bulletin,* no. 31 (October 1968): 11.

33. Carlos Fonseca Amador, "Zero Hour in Nicaragua," *Tricontinental Bimonthly,* no. 14 (September-October 1969): 33, 35, 36.

34. Arnoldo Cardona (pseudonym), "Guatemala, Dogma and Revolution," *Tricontinental Bimonthly,* no. 8 (September-October 1968): 38.

35. Roque Dalton, "El Salvador, Isthmus and Revolution," *Tricontinental Bimonthly,* no. 11 (March-April 1969): 15.

36. *Documentos políticos,* I, 97–99; interviews in Havana, June 1986.

37. *Granma Weekly Review,* October 13, 1968, p. 12; October 20, 1968, p. 12.

38. Ibid., May 3, 1970, pp. 2–5.

39. "Declaration of the Meeting of Communist Parties of Latin America and the Caribbean," *Tricontinental Bimonthly,* no. 44 (July-August 1975): 84, 92, 95, 96, 99.

40. "The National Liberation Movement in Latin America and the Caribbean," *Tricontinental Bimonthly,* no. 75 (February 1981): 94, 99.

41. *Tricontinental Bimonthly,* no. 73 (1980): p. 34.

42. *Granma Weekly Review,* June 1, 1980, p. 8.

43. Nguyen Thi Binh, "Viet Nam: Nixon's Maneuvers," *Tricontinental Bimonthly,* no. 15 (November-December 1969): 10; Ivan Shkadov, Pavel Zhilin, Thelma Bornot Pubillones, and Victor Volksi, *Valentía y fraternidad: El internacionalismo y la amistad combativa entre las Fuerzas Armadas de Cuba y la URSS* (Havana: Editorial de Ciencias Sociales, 1983), p. 250.

44. *Granma Weekly Review,* April 1, 1979, p. 2; August 24, 1980, p. 2; November 30, 1980, special supplement, p. 5.

45. *Granma,* July 5, 1982, p. 7; *Granma Weekly Review,* May 18, 1982, p. 3; July 4, 1982, p. 1; November 28, 1982, p. 3; July 22, 1984, p. 9; Juana Carrasco, "Los pueblos revolucionarios se hermanan," *Verde olivo* 23, no. 18 (May 6, 1982): 12–13; interviews in Havana, March 1985.

46. Manuel Somoza, "Western Sahara: A War That's Nearing the End," *Tricontinental Bimonthly,* nos. 69–70 (1980): 88–89; *Granma,* August 5, 1982, p. 5; November 19, 1982, p. 6; March 1, 1983, p. 7; October 3, 1984, p. 3.

47. *Verde olivo* 20, no. 37 (September 16, 1979): 34–35.

48. Point eloquently made by Armando Entralgo, director, Center for Studies on Africa and the Middle East (CEAMO), Havana, March 21, 1985.

49. John Damis, "The Role of Third Parties in the Western Sahara Conflict," *The Maghreb Review* 7, nos. 1–2 (January–April 1982): 12–13.

50. Interview with Eloy Valdés, deputy chief, General Department for International Relations, Central Committee staff, Communist party of Cuba, Havana, March 26, 1985.

51. *Granma,* October 9, 1982, p. 7; *Granma Weekly Review,* July 25, 1982, p. 8; *Verde olivo* 20, no. 37 (September 16, 1979): 34; and Sam Nujoma, "La independencia de Namibia es inevitable," *Bohemia* 75, no. 12 (March 25, 1983): 69.

52. *Granma Weekly Review,* November 25, 1979, p. 6; *Granma,* October 21, 1983, p. 2; February 23, 1987, p. 2. Juan Benemelis, a Cuban foreign service official in Africa in the 1960s, reports that the secret training of Namibians in Cuba began then (personal communication).

53. *Granma Weekly Review,* November 25, 1984, p. 10; December 2, 1984, p. 9.

54. *Granma,* October 9, 1982, p. 7; November 19, 1982, p. 8; *Verde olivo* 23, no. 22 (June 3, 1982): 11. See also Juan Abugattas, "The Perception of the Palestinian Question in Latin America," *Journal of Palestine Studies* 11, no. 3 (Spring 1982): 117–128; Damián J. Fernández, *Cuba's Foreign Policy in the Middle East*

(Boulder, Colo.: Westview Press, 1988), pp. 70–75; and Yoram Shapira, "Cuba and the Arab-Israeli Conflict," in *Cuba in the World,* ed. Cole Blasier and Carmelo Mesa-Lago (Pittsburgh: University of Pittsburgh Press, 1979).

55. *Tricontinental Bulletin,* no. 28 (July 1968): 37.

56. Yasser Arafat, "The Road of Armed Struggle," *Tricontinental Bimonthly,* no. 41 (January-February 1975): 93–99.

57. *Granma,* July 22, 1982, p. 4.

58. Interview with Armando Entralgo, Havana, March 1985; personal communication from Juan Benemelis; Carlos Martínez de Salsamendi, "El papel de Cuba en el Tercer Mundo: América Central, el Caribe y Africa," in *Cuba y Estados Unidos,* ed. Juan Gabriel Tokatlian (Buenos Aires: Grupo Editor Latinoamericano, 1984), p. 183.

59. Gabriel García Márquez, "Operation Carlota," *Tricontinental Bimonthly,* no. 53 (1977): 4–25; José M. Ortiz, "Angola: From the Trenches," *Tricontinental,* no. 96 (June 1984): 48–50; *Granma Weekly Review,* May 24, 1987, p. 2. For Castro's admission that Cuban military personnel and weapons arrived a month before Angolan independence, see *Granma,* April 20, 1976. Juan Benemelis places the arrival of Cuban military advisers for the MPLA by March 1975 (personal communication).

60. Agostinho Neto, "A Victory for Africa," *Tricontinental Bimonthly,* no. 48 (March-April 1976): 9–10; Fidel Castro, "Shattered Myths," in ibid., pp. 13–16; Ortiz, "Angola," p. 50; *Granma,* April 20, 1976; Shkadov et al., *Valentía y fraternidad,* p. 253; Martínez de Salsamendi, "El papel de Cuba en el Tercer Mundo," p. 188; Bruce D. Porter, *The USSR in Third World Conflicts* (Cambridge: Cambridge University Press, 1984), pp. 155–170.

61. "Resolution on Angola," *Tricontinental Bulletin,* nos. 7–8 (October–November 1966): 37; "Interview with Paulo Jorge from the MPLA," *Tricontinental Bimonthly,* no. 7 (July-August 1968): 154–156; Fidel Castro, "Closing Speech at the First Congress of the Communist Party of Cuba," *Tricontinental Bimonthly,* nos. 46–47 (November 1975–February 1976): 108–109; Limbania Jiménez Rodríguez, "Heroines of Angola," *Tricontinental,* no. 3 (1986): 29; *Granma Weekly Review,* February 15, 1976, p. 10; interview with informed Cuban, 1983.

62. Alfonso Iglesias García, "Algunos aspectos del pensamiento político de Agostino Neto," *Revista de Africa y Medio Oriente* 1, no. 1 (1983): 173; Fidel Castro, "Main Report: Third Congress of the Communist Party of Cuba" (mimeo, Havana, 1986), pp. 77, 104; Jorge I. Domínguez, *Cuba: Order and Revolution* (Cambridge, Mass.: Harvard University Press, 1978), pp. 224–227, 483–485; Carlos Moore, *Cuban Race Politics: The Shaping of Castro's Africa Policy,* forthcoming.

63. John Marcum, *The Angolan Revolution: Exile Politics and Guerrilla Warfare, 1962–1976* (Cambridge, Mass.: MIT Press, 1978), pp. 272–273; William LeoGrande, "Cuban-Soviet Relations and Cuban Policy in Africa," in *Cuba in Af-*

rica, ed. Carmelo Mesa-Lago and June Belkin (Pittsburgh: Center for Latin American Studies, University of Pittsburgh, 1982); and Nelson P. Valdés, "Revolutionary Solidarity in Angola," in *Cuba in the World,* ed. Blasier and Mesa-Lago. On the U.S. decision, see Nathaniel Davis, "The Angola Decision: A Personal Memoir," *Foreign Affairs* 57, no. 1 (Fall 1978): 109–124.

64. Both in "Castro's Challenge," *Frontline,* Public Broadcasting System, WGBH-TV production, first aired April 10, 1985.

65. Arkady N. Shevchenko, *Breaking with Moscow* (New York: Knopf, 1985), p. 272.

66. Amilcar Cabral, "Determined to Resist," *Tricontinental Bimonthly,* no. 8 (September-October 1968): 120, 124–125; *Granma Weekly Review,* March 21, 1982, p. 3; Castro, "Closing Speech," pp. 93–94; Fidel Castro, *Nada podrá detener la marcha de la historia* (Havana: Editora Política, 1985), pp. 147–148.

67. Two interviews, Havana, March 1985.

68. Samora Machel, "Report from the Central Committee of FRELIMO to the Third Congress," *Tricontinental Bimonthly,* no. 52 (1977): 30–31, 47; Castro, *Nada podrá detener,* p. 147.

69. Alex LaGuma, "Specifics of the Liberation Struggle in South Africa," *Tricontinental Bimonthly,* nos. 69–70 (1980): 5–6; *Granma Weekly Review,* September 19, 1982, p. 8.

70. Fermín Arraiza, "Appeal on the Colonial Case of Puerto Rico," *Tricontinental Bimonthly,* no. 43 (May-June 1975): 119; Ricardo Alarcón, "The Force of Solidarity," ibid., pp. 123–124; Osvaldo Dorticós, "Similarities of Two Historical Processes," ibid., no. 45 (September-October 1975): 117.

71. *Tricontinental Bulletin,* no. 44 (November 1969): 36; "Puerto Rico: Colony in Revolution," ibid., no. 48 (March 1970): 21.

72. For differing views, see *New York Times,* September 8, 1985, p. 38, and *Castro's Puerto Rican Obsession,* publication no. 21 (Washington, D.C.: Cuban-American National Foundation, 1987).

73. "Editorial," *Tricontinental Bimonthly,* nos. 4–5 (January–April 1968): 1–2; "On the Shores of the Red Sea," ibid., pp. 65–70; *Tricontinental Bulletin,* no. 45 (December 1969): 31.

74. *Granma Weekly Review,* July 1, 1984, p. 4.

75. Interviews in Havana, March 1985; discussion with Carlos Moore, February 15, 1985.

76. Castro, "Closing Speech," p. 108; García Márquez, "Operation Carlota," pp. 7, 9.

77. Olga Pellicer de Brody, *México y la revolución cubana* (Mexico: El Colegio de México, 1972); *Granma Weekly Review,* August 31, 1975, pp. 4, 7, 8; May 27, 1979, p. 3; July 5, 1981, p. 1; August 16, 1981, p. 1. For precedence regarding African states, see ibid., June 25, 1978, p. 2.

78. García Márquez, "Operation Carlota," pp. 9–11; interviews in Havana, March 1985. For more detail, see Moore, *Cuban Race Politics.*

79. *Granma,* August 30, 1982, p. 2; September 1, 1982, pp. 2–3; September 2, 1982, p. 2; October 12, 1982, p. 2; February 19, 1983, p. 2; Alfredo Reyes Trejo, "Su ejemplo inmortal," *Verde olivo* 23, no. 40 (October 7, 1982): 27–30; Regis Debray, *¿Revolución en la revolución?* (Havana; Casa de las Américas, 1967); *The Complete Diaries of Che Guevara,* ed. Daniel James (New York: Stein and Day, 1968).

80. "Revolution in Nicaragua," *Frontline,* Public Broadcasting System, WGBH-TV production, first aired April 11, 1985.

81. Three interviews in Havana, two in March 1985 and a third in June 1986. See also *Granma Weekly Review,* March 13, 1988, special supplement, p. 7.

82. *Bohemia* 73, no. 37 (September 11, 1981): 49; ibid., 73, no. 39 (September 25, 1981): 57.

83. Michael Taber, ed., *Fidel Castro Speeches, 1984–1985: War and Crisis in the Americas* (New York: Pathfinder Press, 1985), pp. 121, 162.

84. Norma Guevara, "El Salvador: Paper Presented at the Anti-Imperialist Scientific Conference," *Tricontinental Bimonthly,* no. 76 (March 1981): *Granma,* January 22, 1983, p. 3; Mario del Cueto, "Hay que movilizar aún más la opinión pública mundial," *Bohemia* 76, no. 18 (May 4, 1984): 75–76; *Granma Weekly Review,* February 8, 1987, p. 11; July 5, 1987, p. 1; April 10, 1988, p. 12.

85. "The International and the National in the Working Class Movement," *World Marxist Review* 24, no. 9 (September 1981): 58.

86. *Tricontinental Bulletin,* no. 31 (October 1968): 9–11; *Granma Weekly Review,* June 8, 1980, p. 14; March 7, 1982; *Granma,* August 4, 1983, p. 3; Mario Menéndez Rodríguez, "El Ejército Guerrillero de los Pobres," *Bohemia* 73, no. 42 (October 16, 1981): 76–77.

87. *Granma Weekly Review,* May 28, 1978, p. 1; June 11, 1978, p. 2.

88. Ibid., June 25, 1978, p. 2. For a convergent U.S. view, see Cyrus Vance, *Hard Choices* (New York: Simon and Schuster, 1983), p. 90.

89. House Committee on Foreign Affairs, "U.S. Response to Cuban Government Involvement in Narcotics Trafficking and Review of Worldwide Illicit Narcotics Situation," *Hearings,* 98th Cong., 2d sess. (Washington, D.C.: U.S. Government Printing Office, 1984), pp. 21, 29, 33, 39.

90. *Granma Weekly Review,* November 21, 1982, p. 5; Santiago Valdés, "Drogas en Estados Unidos: La 'Cuban Connection,'" *Verde olivo* 24, no. 20 (May 19, 1983): 15; John S. Martin, "Cuba and Drugs: The Real Dope," *Cubatimes* 4, no. 3 (March–April 1984): 1, 3–5; interview with high-ranking U.S. Coast Guard officer, August 1986.

91. Taber, ed., *Fidel Castro Speeches, 1984–85,* pp. 140–142.

92. Enrique Baloyra, *El Salvador in Transition* (Chapel Hill: University of North Carolina Press, 1982); Tommie Sue Montgomery, *Revolution in El Salvador* (Boulder, Colo.: Westview Press, 1982).

93. Edward Gonzalez, *Cuba under Castro: The Limits of Charisma* (Boston: Houghton Mifflin, 1974), pp. 133–141; Herbert S. Dinerstein, "Soviet Policy in

Latin America," *American Political Science Review* 61, no. 1 (March 1967): 80–90; and Jacques Levesque, *L'URSS et la revolution cubaine* (Montreal: Presses de l'université de Montréal, 1976), pt. 2.

94. Written personal communication from Juan Valdés Paz, Havana, June 17, 1986 (see Appendix A).

95. For convergent views among authors who otherwise disagree, see Jiri Valenta, "The U.S.S.R., Cuba, and the Crisis in Central America," *Orbis* 25, no. 3 (Fall 1981): 715–746; Robert Pastor, "Cuba and the Soviet Union: Does Cuba Act Alone?" in *The New Cuban Presence,* ed. Barry Levine (Boulder, Colo.: Westview Press, 1983); William LeoGrande, "Foreign Policy: The Limits of Success," in *Cuba,* ed. Domínguez; Edward Gonzalez, "Institutionalization, Political Elites and Foreign Policies, in *Cuba in the World,* ed. Blasier and Mesa Lago; James LeMoyne, "The Guerrilla Network," *New York Times Magazine,* April 6, 1986.

96. *Granma Weekly Review,* December 19, 1982, p. 4.

6. Support for Revolutionary States

1. Raymond Vernon, *Sovereignty at Bay: The Multinational Spread of U.S. Enterprises* (New York: Basic Books, 1971), chap. 3; Neil Hood and Stephen Young, *The Economics of Multinational Enterprise* (London: Longman, 1979), pp. 44–62; Jean François Hennart, *A Theory of Multinational Enterprise* (Ann Arbor: University of Michigan Press, 1982), pp. 131–164; Walter H. Goldberg, "Introduction," in *Governments and Multinationals: The Policy of Control vs. Autonomy,* ed. Walter H. Goldberg with Anant Negandhi (Boston: Oelgeschlager, Gunn and Hain, 1983), p. 3.

2. Jorge I. Domínguez, *Cuba: Order and Revolution* (Cambridge, Mass.: Harvard University Press, 1978), chap. 9; *Granma,* February 4, 1985, p. 2; interviews in Havana, June 1986.

3. Carlos Moore, *Cuban Race Politics: The Shaping of Castro's Africa Policy* (forthcoming); Comité Estatal de Estadísticas, Oficina Nacional del Censo, *Censo de población y viviendas, 1981: República de Cuba,* vol. 16 (Havana, 1984), p. cvii, hereafter cited as *Censo, 1981.*

4. Dirección Central de Estadística, *Anuario estadístico de Cuba, 1974* (Havana: Junta Central de Planificación), p. 23; Comité Estatal de Estadísticas, *Anuario estadístico de Cuba, 1978* (Havana), p. 33; ibid., *1985,* p. 58.

5. *Censo, 1981,* pp. cixxv, 149; Carmelo Mesa-Lago, *The Economy of Socialist Cuba* (Albuquerque: University of New Mexico Press, 1981), p. 164.

6. *Anuario, 1985,* pp. 484–487.

7. Paula J. Pettavino, "The Politics of Sport under Communism: A Comparative Study of Competitive Athletics in the Soviet Union and Cuba" (Ph.D. diss., University of Notre Dame, 1982), chap. 4.

8. Domínguez, *Cuba: Order and Revolution,* pp. 184–185; *Anuario, 1985,* p. 525.

9. Mesa-Lago, *The Economy of Socialist Cuba,* p. 70.

10. Domínguez, *Cuba: Order and Revolution,* pp. 186–188.

11. Sergio Roca, "Economic Aspects of Cuban Involvement in Africa," in *Cuba in Africa,* ed. Carmelo Mesa-Lago and June Belkin, Latin American Monograph and Document Series, no. 3 (Pittsburgh: Center for Latin American Studies, University of Pittsburgh, 1982), p. 178; Jorge Pérez-López, "Comment: Economic Costs and Benefits of African Involvement," in ibid., pp. 185a–186.

12. Edith Felipe, "Cuba y la colaboración económica con el mundo subdesarrollado," *Revista del CIEM: Temas de economía mundial,* no. 15 (1985): 87–88.

13. "Discurso pronunciado por el Comandante en Jefe Fidel Castro Ruz, Primer Secretario del CC del Partido Comunista de Cuba y Presidente de los Consejos de Estado y de Ministros, en la clausura del II período de sesiones de la Asamblea Nacional del Poder Popular. Palacio de las Convenciones," December 27, 1979, mimeo; *Granma Weekly Review,* December 12, 1976, p. 1.

14. *Anuario, 1985,* p. 57.

15. *Granma Weekly Review,* August 8, 1976, p. 3; April 16, 1978, p. 3.

16. Ibid., December 2, 1984, p. 9; *Fidel Castro Speeches 1984–85: War and Crisis in the Americas* (New York: Pathfinder Press, 1985), pp. 133–134; James Brooke, "Cuba's Strange Mission in Angola," *New York Times Magazine,* February 1, 1987; *General del Pino Speaks* (Washington, D.C.: Cuban-American National Foundation, 1987), p. 15.

17. *New York Times,* September 22, 1985, p. 20; November 23, 1985, pp. 1, 5; February 1, 1987, pp. 1, 12; Chester Crocker, "The U.S. And Angola," in U.S. Department of State, Bureau of Public Affairs, *Current Policy,* no. 796 (1986).

18. *Granma Weekly Review,* September 14, 1986, p. 9; September 21, 1986, pp. 9–10.

19. Ibid., August 9, 1987, p. 1; August 23, 1987, p. 4; November 29, 1987, p. 11; February 7, 1988, p. 8; February 14, 1988, p. 1; *New York Times,* September 22, 1987, p. 17; August 9, 1988, pp. A1, A11; *Boston Globe,* December 6, 1987, p. 11; May 4, 1988, p. 10; and interviews in Havana, April 1988.

20. *Granma Weekly Review,* June 25, 1978, p. 2; *Granma,* August 30, 1982, p. 6; September 21, 1986, p. 10; Armando López Rivera, "Sudáfrica: ¿Defensa o militarización?" *Verde olivo* 23, no. 18 (May 6, 1982): 21; Fidel Castro's closing speech to the Third Party Congress, February 1986, on television; and "Angola: Continued Occupation," *Africa,* no. 133 (September 1982): 31.

21. *Granma Weekly Review,* April 3, 1977, p. 1; September 21, 1986, p. 9.

22. Domínguez, *Cuba: Order and Revolution,* Chap. 9.

23. "Intercambio Cuba-Angola: Prometedoras perspectivas," *Bohemia* 76, no. 39 (September 28, 1984): 31.

24. Irving Kaplan, ed., *Angola: A Country Study,* Foreign Areas Studies Series, American University, 2nd ed. (Washington, D.C.: U.S. Government Printing Office, 1979), pp. xiii-xiv, 69–72, 112–115.

25. *Granma Weekly Review,* February 12, 1984, p. 12; Kaplan, ed., *Angola,* p. 114.

26. Neiva Moreira and Beatriz Bissio, *Os cubanos na África* (São Paulo: Global

Editora, 1979), p. 70; Ezzedini Mestiri, *Les cubains et l'Afrique* (Paris: Editions Karthala, 1980), pp. 168–169.

27. *Granma Weekly Review,* February 12, 1984; February 22, 1987, p. 1.

28. Marta Rosa Martínez, "Embajadores de la salud," *Verde olivo* 23, no. 3 (January 21, 1982): 18–19. Julio Díaz Vázquez cites 800 health workers in 17 provinces at about the same time; "Cuba: Colaboración económica y científico-técnica con países en vías de desarrollo de Africa, Asia, y América Latina," *Economía y desarrollo,* no. 68 (May–June 1982): 30–31.

29. *Granma Weekly Review,* April 3, 1977, p. 1.

30. Díaz Vázquez, *"Cuba: Colaboración,"* pp. 30–31; *Granma Weekly Review,* February 23, 1983, p. 9; *Granma,* April 5, 1984, p. 2.

31. Interviews in Havana, March 1985.

32. Interviews in Havana, March 1985; Carlos Martínez de Salsamendi, "El papel de Cuba en el Tercer Mundo: América Central, El Caribe, y Africa," in *Cuba y Estados Unidos,* ed. Juan Gabriel Tokatlian (Buenos Aires: Grupo Editor Latinoamericano, 1984), pp. 144–145; *Granma Weekly Review,* April 15, 1987, p. 3; Mestiri, *Les cubains et l'Afrique,* p. 176; *Fidel Castro Speeches 1984–85,* pp. 134–135; *General del Pino Speaks,* p. 13.

33. *Granma Weekly Review,* June 25, 1978, pp. 2–3; ABC News, "Issues and Answers," transcript, June 18, 1978.

34. *Granma,* February 6, 1982, p. 6.

35. Colin Legum, "Under South Africa's Shadow," *New African,* no. 198 (March 1984): 12–13; Colin Legum, "Lusaka Accord in Danger," *New African,* no. 204 (September 1984): 28–29.

36. *Granma Weekly Review,* March 25, 1984, p. 1, my emphasis.

37. Ibid., November 25, 1984, p. 10; U.S. Department of State, Bureau of Public Affairs, "U.S. Policy toward Namibia," *Current Policy,* no. 663 (February 21, 1985).

38. Interviews in Havana, March 1985.

39. William M. LeoGrande, "Cuban-Soviet Relations and Cuban Policy in Africa," in *Cuba in Africa,* ed. Mesa-Lago and Belkin, p. 47.

40. Interviews in Havana, March 1985.

41. Gabriel García Márquez, "Operation Carlota," *Tricontinental Bimonthly,* no. 53 (1977): 4–25.

42. Interview conducted on February 28, 1980. Interviewees in Havana, in March 1985, also stressed Cuba's quick and enthusiastic commitment to Mengistu's government. On Castro's mediation, see Nelson P. Valdés, "Cuba's Involvement in the Horn of Africa: The Ethiopian-Somali War and the Eritrean Conflict," in *Cuba in Africa,* ed. Mesa-Lago and Belkin.

43. Keith Somerville, "Angola: Major Defeats for UNITA," *New African,* no. 196 (January 1984): 28; *Granma Weekly Review,* February 9, 1986, p. 3; March 29, 1987, p. 3.

44. Gerald J. Bender, "Angola, the Cubans and American Anxieties," *Foreign*

Policy, no. 31 (Summer 1978): 25–26. There is no direct evidence, however, that the Cuban ambassador supported Alves; surprise was expressed by scholars and officials in Havana in 1985 and 1986 when I suggested during interviews that the Cuban response to the Alves coup attempt may have been divided.

45. U.S. Department of State, *Soviet and East European Aid to the Third World, 1981,* publication 9345 (Washington, D.C., 1983), pp. 14, 20.

46. *Granma Weekly Review,* March 26, 1978, p. 5.

47. Ibid., May 7, 1978, pp. 2, 5; ABC News, "Issues and Answers," p. 3; Fidel Castro, *The Nonaligned Countries Will Know How to Fulfill the Duty That the Present Demands of Them* (Havana: Editorial de Ciencias Sociales, 1975), p. 13.

48. Eliseo Alberto, "De Etiopía a Cuba, de corazón a corazón," *Verde olivo* 20, no. 36 (September 9, 1979): 55; *Granma Weekly Review,* September 3, 1979, pp. 6–7.

49. Interviews in Havana, March 1985.

50. *Granma Weekly Review* August 8, 1976, p. 8.

51. Interview with a former high-ranking Ethiopian official, February 28, 1980.

52. Whether Cuban troops also may have fought on the government side in Eritrea is unclear. For an argument that they did, see William E. Ratliff, *Follow the Leader in the Horn: The Soviet-Cuban Presence in East Africa,* publication no. 17 (Washington, D.C.: Cuban-American National Foundation, 1986), pp. 12–15; for an argument that they did not, Martínez de Salsamendi, "El papel de Cuba en el Tercer Mundo," p. 195.

53. Prensa Latina press dispatch, July 4, 1984, teletype; *Granma,* February 6, 1985, p. 2; "Setbacks in the Horn," *Africa,* no. 136 (December 1982): 27; Colin Legum, "Ethiopia: New Front Opens Up," *New African,* no. 196 (January 1984): 33; Victor Ndovi, "Cubans Withdrawing from Ethiopia," *New African,* no. 198 (March 1984): 32; V. Sharayev, "Milestone in Ethiopian History," *International Affairs,* no. 10 (1984): 36. The estimate of 10,000 troops derives from the Cuban-Ethiopian mail flow; *Bohemia* 74, no. 8 (February 19, 1982): 80.

54. U.S. Arms Control and Disarmament Agency, *World Military Expenditures and Arms Transfers, 1969–1978* (Washington, D.C.: U.S. Government Printing Office, 1980), pp. 38, 47, 80, 89.

55. *Granma,* December 4, 1979; *Granma Weekly Review,* October 3, 1982, p. 9; Felipe, "Cuba y la colaboración económica," p. 96.

56. *Granma Weekly Review,* October 28, 1984, p. 9.

57. Ibid., August 22, 1982, p. 12; October 24, 1982, p. 3; September 2, 1984, p. 4; *Granma,* May 16, 1984, p. 6.

58. Díaz Vázquez, "Cuba: Colaboración," p. 33.

59. Said Yusuf Abdi, "Cuba's Role in Africa: Revolutionary or Reactionary?" *Horn of Africa,* no. 1 (October-December 1978): 19, 24; International Institute for Strategic Studies, *Strategic Survey, 1978* (London: IISS, 1979), p. 97.

60. Interviews in Havana, March 1985.

61. In Havana, interviews with Carlos Martínez de Salsamendi, adviser to

Council of State Vice President Carlos Rafael Rodríguez, March 27, 1985; Eloy Valdés, deputy chief, General Department for International Relations, member, Communist party Central Committee staff, March 26, 1985; and Armando Entralgo, director, Center for Studies on Africa and the Middle East (CEAMO), March 21, 1985.

62. Interview with José Antonio Arbesú, deputy chief, Americas Department, member, Communist party Central Committee staff, Havana, March 28, 1985; Jorge Luna, *Granada: La nueva joya del Caribe* (Havana: Editorial de Ciencias Sociales, 1982), p. 87.

63. *Granma Weekly Review,* April 22, 1979, p. 1; September 23, 1979; October 7, 1979, p. 3.

64. Documents captured by the U.S. armed forces in Grenada (hereafter cited as CD): K. Fraser to E. Louison, "Material Means Recieved [*sic*] from Foreign Countries, within the period 1979–81," no date (probably October 1981), pp. 1–2. These documents are available in the U.S. National Archives.

65. Díaz Vázquez, "Cuba: Colaboración," p. 41; José Cazañas and Luis López, "El aeropuerto de Granada," *Verde olivo* 24, no. 44 (November 3, 1983): 59; *Granma Weekly Review,* June 29, 1980, p. 10; November 28, 1982, p. 7; *Granma,* March 29, 1982, pp. 4–5; December 9, 1982, p. 5; *Bohemia* 74, no. 12 (March 19, 1982): 65; Luna, *Granada,* p. 207; and interviews with U.S. government officials.

66. CD, "Protocol of the Military Collaboration between the Government of the Republic of Cuba and the People's Revolutionary Government of Grenada," and its "Annex no. 2, Protocol of the Military Collaboration about the Material Means, Services and Assuring Personnel," no date (probably late 1981).

67. CD, W. Richard Jacobs, "Grenada's Relations with the USSR" (Moscow: July 11, 1983), p. 2.

68. CD, "Agreement between the Government of Grenada and the Government of the USSR on deliveries from the USSR to Grenada of Special and Other Equipment," July 27, 1982, article 2, p. 2; CD, Embajada de Granada en Cuba, no title, February 18, 1982, p. 1; CD, Czechoslovak Federal Ministry of Foreign Trade, "Invoice," no date.

69. CD, "Meeting at the Ministry of Communications," November 9, 1982, p. 3.

70. CD, "Report on the General Congress of the World Center for the Resistance of Imperialism, Zionism, Racism, and Reaction," June 26, 1982, pp. 1–5.

71. CD, "Report on Meeting of Secret Regional Caucus held in Managua from 6th.–7th. January 1983," no date, p. 1.

72. CD, "Draft Workplan of the International Relations Committee, NJM, for 1983," no date, pp. 1–2.

73. CD, "Minutes of the Political Bureau," December 9, 1981, p. 1; CD, Chris De Riggs, "Report on Meeting of Secret Regional Caucus held in Managua from 6th.–7th. January 1983," no date, pp. 1–6.

74. CD, "Minutes of the Political Bureau," December 29, 1982, p. 3.

75. CD, Head Special Branch, "To Minister of National Security: Situation Report—Grenada International Airport," July 14, 1981; CD, "Minutes of the Political Bureau," April 7, 1982, pp. 1–2; CD, "Minutes of the Political/Economic Bureau," August 10, 1983, p. 8; CD, Trevor Noel, "Report on the Anti-Cuban Statement and Sentiments on the Airport Site," no date (probably August 1983); interviews in Havana, June 1986.

76. CD, Rita B. Joseph, "Report of Party Collective of Six-Month Course in Moscow Nov.–May 1983," no date, p. 6; CD, "Minutes of the Central Committee of the New Jewel Movement," April 21, 1982, p. 2; CD, "Minutes of the Political Bureau," September 15, 1982, p. 1; Luna, *Granada,* p. 133; CD, "Minutes of the Political/Economic Bureau," August 10, 1983, p. 5.

77. CD, "Minutes of the Political Bureau," April 27, 1983, pp. 2–3.

78. CD, "Extraordinary General Meeting of Full Members," September 25, 1983, p. 22.

79. CD, "Minutes of the Political Bureau," June 22, 1983, p. 2; and two interviews in Havana, March 1985.

80. *Granma Weekly Review,* November 20, 1983, p. 3; CD, "Letter from Fidel Castro Ruz to the Central Committee, New Jewel Movement," October 15, 1983, p. 2; interviews in Havana, March 1985.

81. CD, "Minutes of Emergency Meeting of NJM Central Committee," August 26, 1983, pp. 1–2.

82. Interview with José Antonio Arbesú, March 28, 1985.

83. Interviews in Havana, March 1985 and June 1986.

84. CD, "Letter from Fidel Castro Ruz to the Central Committee, New Jewel Movement," October 15, 1983, p. 2.

85. CD, "On Cuba's Response to the Issue," October 21, 1983, pp. 1–2.

86. *Granma Weekly Review,* October 30, 1983, p. 1.

87. Ibid., November 6, 1983, p. 1; November 20, 1983, p. 4.

88. Ibid., November 13, 1983, pp. 4–5.

89. "Indicaciones metodológicas," *Verde olivo* 24, no. 47 (November 24, 1983): 52–53; interviews in Havana, March 1985.

90. *Granma Weekly Review,* November 6, 1983, p. 2.

91. Jiri Valenta and Virginia Valenta, "Leninism in Grenada," *Problems of Communism,* July-August 1984, pp. 1–23.

92. CD, Embassy of Grenada in the USSR, "Relations with the CPSU," no date (probably late 1982), p. 2.

93. CD, "Protocol to the Agreement between the Government of the USSR of October 27, 1980 on deliveries from the USSR to Grenada of Special and Other Equipment," February 9, 1981, and its annex; CD, "Agreements Concluded between the Governments of the USSR and Grenada," May 29, 1982.

94. CD, "Extraordinary General Meeting of Full Members," September 25, 1983, pp. 21–22.

95. CD, "Minutes of the Political Bureau," June 22, 1983, p. 2; CD, "Letter

from General Hudson Austin to Division General Arnaldo Ochoa," May 16, 1982.

96. CD, undated, untitled handwritten notes of the plenary meetings of the NJM Central Committee, September 1983, p. 116.

97. CD, letter from Gail, the Cuban ambassador's wife, to Maurice Bishop, no date; CD, Richard Jacobs, "Grenada's Relations with the USSR," July 11, 1983, p. 4.

98. CD, "Foreign Relations Report," no date (probably mid-1981), p. 3; CD, "Summary of the Prime Minister's Meeting with Soviet Ambassador," May 24, 1983, p. 3.

99. *Current Digest of the Soviet Press* 30, no. 42 (1983): 16; ibid., 30, no. 43 (1983): 1–8.

100. Compare Nikolai Mostovets, "Introducción: No se podrá doblegar al pueblo de Granada," pp. 9–13, with Eduard Nitoburg, "Washington contra Granada: El Pentágono amenaza, la CIA actúa," p. 87, both in *Granada: Historia, revolución, intervención de Estados Unidos* (Moscow: Soviet Academy of Sciences, 1984).

101. Interviews in Havana, March 1985.

102. *Granma Weekly Review,* September 19, 1982, p. 8; November 11, 1984, p. 5; September 14, 1986, p. 9; September 21, 1986, p. 10; August 9, 1987, p. 10; November 16, 1980, special supplement, p. 4; *Granma,* February 7, 1987, p. 3; Frank Agüero, "La educación: Obra de todos," *Verde olivo* 24, no. 52 (December 29, 1983): 57; Felipe, "Cuba y la colaboración económica," p. 95.

103. *Granma Weekly Review,* December 11, 1983, special supplement, p. 15; *Granma* January 5, 1980, p. 6; February 7, 1987, p. 6; Martínez de Salsamendi, "El papel de Cuba en el Tercer Mundo," p. 145.

104. *Granma,* August 28, 1982, p. 1; July 4, 1983, p. 3; July 13, 1983, p. 3; October 9, 1984, p. 3; November 14, 1984, p. 2; *Granma Weekly Review,* September 19, 1982, p. 8; November 18, 1984, p. 3; September 6, 1987, p. 3.

105. Paul Grundy and Peter Budetti, "The Distribution and Supply of Cuban Medical Personnel in Third World Countries," *American Journal of Public Health* 70, no. 7 (July 1980): 717–719; Martínez de Salsamendi, "El papel de Cuba en el Tercer Mundo," p. 184; interviews in Havana, June 1986.

106. *Granma,* July 8, 1983, p. 1; *Granma Weekly Review,* February 11, 1979, p. 7; April 8, 1984, special supplement, p. 12.

107. *Granma,* August 9, 1982; *Granma Weekly Review,* August 9, 1981, p. 2; January 26, 1986, p. 12.

108. Regla Zulueta, "Libia: Con nuestros constructores internacionalistas," *Verde olivo* 24, no. 23 (June 9, 1983): 26; *Granma Weekly Review,* April 19, 1981, p. 7; July 4, 1982; February 27, 1983, p. 9; Díaz Vázquez, "Cuba: Colaboración," p. 34; Cazañas and López, "El aeropuerto de Granada," p. 59; Felipe, "Cuba y la colaboración económica," p. 97.

109. The most complete though still insufficient source is Díaz Vázquez, "Cuba: Colaboración," pp. 30–43.

110. *Granma Weekly Review,* January 22, 1984, p. 1; April 15, 1987, p. 3;

Granma, July 30, 1976, pp. 1, 3; February 7, 1987, p. 6; Ramón Martínez, "Colaboración azucarera cubana," *Verde olivo* 24, no. 51 (December 22, 1983): 18.

111. *Granma Weekly Review,* April 29, 1984, p. 8; *Granma,* February 7, 1987, p. 6.

112. *Granma,* October 1, 1984, p. 5; *Granma Weekly Review,* November 23, 1986, p. 9.

113. *Granma Weekly Review,* October 2, 1983.

114. Ibid., April 18, 1982, p. 12; July 18, 1982, p. 2; September 19, 1982, p. 8; November 30, 1980, special supplement, p. 4; *Bohemia,* 76, no. 21 (May 25, 1984): 72–73; Felipe, "Cuba y la colaboración económica," p. 97.

115. Grundy and Budetti, "The Distribution and Supply of Cuban Medical Personnel," p. 718; *Granma Weekly Review,* November 4, 1973, p. 7; Martínez de Salsamendi, "El papel de Cuba en el Tercer Mundo," pp. 150–151.

116. *Granma Weekly Review,* October 28, 1978, p. 9.

117. Ibid., August 5, 1984, p. 3; *Granma,* February 7, 1987, p. 6; Isaac Owusu, "Ghana: The Cubans Move In," *Afriscope* 12, no. 8 (August 1982): 8.

118. *Granma,* February 7, 1987, p. 6.

119. *Granma Weekly Review,* September 19, 1982, p. 8; *Granma,* February 7, 1987, p. 6.

120. Grundy and Budetti, "The Distribution and Supply of Cuban Medical Personnel," p. 718; Felipe, "Cuba y la colaboración económica," p. 94. For an analysis of Cuban-Libyan relations, see Damián Fernández, *Cuba's Foreign Policy in the Middle East* (Boulder, Colo.: Westview Press, 1988), chap. 4.

121. *Granma,* February 7, 1987, p. 6.

122. Ibid., January 10, 1983, p. 8; February 7, 1987, p. 6.

123. *Granma Weekly Review,* March 22, 1981, p. 9: *Granma,* February 7, 1987, p. 6.

124. *Granma,* February 7, 1987, p. 6.

125. *Granma Weekly Review,* November 4, 1984, p. 6; December 13, 1987, p. 4.

126. Ibid., January 17, 1982, p. 5.

127. Ibid., September 19, 1982, p. 8; *Granma,* February 7, 1987, p. 6.

128. *Granma Weekly Review,* September 19, 1982, p. 8; June 27, 1987, p. 4; Martínez de Salsamendi, "El papel de Cuba en el Tercer Mundo," p. 150, denies that Cuba ever aided Idi Amin, though Amin had so requested.

129. August 30, 1987, p. 11.

130. *Granma,* June 26, 1986, p. 6.

131. *Granma Weekly Review,* March 23, 1986, p. 4; April 13, 1986, p. 3; July 20, 1986, p. 9.

132. Serafín Marrero, "La colaboración cubano-afgana," *Bohemia* 76, no. 48 (November 30, 1984): 33.

133. *Granma Weekly Review,* September 19, 1982, p. 8; August 17, 1986, p. 10; Felipe, "Cuba y la colaboración económica," p. 94.

134. *Granma,* January 12, 1983, p. 6; January 3, 1986, p. 6.

135. Ibid., February 7, 1987, p. 6.

136. Ibid., December 27, 1982, p. 5; January 3, 1986, p. 6; November 21, 1986.

137. *Granma Weekly Review,* February 28, 1988, p. 3.

138. *Granma,* January 19, 1983, p. 3; October 13, 1986, p. 3; *Granma Weekly Review,* December 21, 1980, p. 12.

139. *Granma Weekly Review,* February 24, 1974, p. 5.

140. *Granma,* February 7, 1987, p. 6.

141. *Granma Weekly Review,* June 21, 1987, p. 1.

142. Ibid., March 15, 1987, p. 1.

143. Ibid., November 30, 1980, special supplement, p. 4; *Granma,* February 7, 1987, p. 6.

144. Felipe, "Cuba y la colaboración económica," p. 98; *Granma,* February 7, 1987, p. 6; *Granma Weekly Review,* April 24, 1988, special supplement, p. 10.

145. *Granma,* February 7, 1987, p. 6.

146. Interviews in Havana, March 1985; *Fidel Castro Speeches 1984–85,* pp. 134–135.

147. *Granma Weekly Review,* August 3, 1980, p. 3; November 30, 1980, special supplement, p. 3; March 22, 1981, p. 3; Díaz Vázquez, "Cuba: Colaboración," pp. 28–30; Martínez de Salsamendi, "El papel de Cuba en el Tercer Mundo," p. 144; Felipe, "Cuba y la colaboración económica," p. 89.

148. Interviews in Havana, June 1986; William J. Durch, "The Cuban Military in Africa and the Middle East: From Algeria to Angola," professional paper no. 201 (Arlington, Va.: Center for Naval Analysis, 1977), pp. 14–16. My earlier suggestion that they had not fought was wrong; see "The Armed Forces and Foreign Relations," in *Cuba in the World,* ed. Cole Blasier and Carmelo Mesa-Lago (Pittsburgh: University of Pittsburgh Press, 1979), p. 70.

149. *Granma,* July 2, 1966, p. 12; García Márquez, "Operation Carlota," pp. 9–11; Limbania Jiménez Rodríguez, "Heroines of Angola," *Tricontinental,* no. 3 (1986): 29; interviews in Havana, March 1985.

150. Juana Carrasco, "Encuentro entre hermanos de lucha," *Verde olivo* 22, no. 37 (September 13, 1981): 55; *Granma,* October 21, 1976, p. 2; August 3, 1983, p. 1.

151. Keith Somerville, "The U.S.S.R. and Southern Africa since 1976," *Journal of Modern African Studies* 22, no. 1 (1984): 86; François Soudan, "Benin: Les potions magiques de Kerekou," *Jeune afrique,* no. 1242 (October 24, 1984): 47; *Granma Weekly Review,* November 16, 1986, p. 10.

152. *Granma Weekly Review,* August 3, 1980, p. 3; November 30, 1980, special supplement, p. 3.

153. *Granma Weekly Review,* April 18, 1982, p. 12.

154. Fidel Castro, "Main Report: Third Congress of the Communist Party of Cuba" (mimeo, Havana, 1986), p. 50.

155. *Granma Weekly Review,* April 8, 1979, p. 2.

156. *Fidel Castro Speeches 1984–85,* p. 135; *Granma Weekly Review,* May 15, 1988, p. 8.

157. *Granma,* July 30, 1984, p. 6.

158. *Granma Weekly Review,* November 18, 1979, p. 1.

159. Ibid., March 25, 1984, p. 3; August 5, 1984, p. 10.

160. *Granma,* August 3, 1983, p. 1; *General del Pino Speaks,* p. 28.

161. *Granma Weekly Review,* September 19, 1982, p. 8.

162. *Granma,* November 28, 1984, p. 5.

163. Theodore Schwab and Harold Sims, "Relations with Communist States," in *Nicaragua: The First Five Years,* ed. Thomas W. Walker (New York: Praeger, 1985), pp. 447–452.

164. U.S. Department of State and Department of Defense, *The Soviet-Cuban Connection in Central America and the Caribbean* (Washington, D.C., 1985), p. 27; U.S. Department of State, Bureau of Public Affairs, "An End to Tyranny in Latin America," *Current Policy,* no. 777 (1985): 3; *New York Times,* July 10, 1986, p. A10.

165. *Verde olivo* 20, no. 31 (August 5, 1979): 9–12; *Granma Weekly Review,* August 3, 1980, p. 2.

166. *Fidel Castro Speeches 1984–85,* p. 129; Castro's speech before the closing of the Third Party Congress, February 1986; and *Granma Weekly Review,* November 6, 1983, p. 2.

167. Ricardo Acciaris, "Les relations economiques de Cuba avec l'Amerique Latine et les Caraibes," *Courier de pays de l'est,* no. 278 (November 1983): 47.

168. *Granma,* January 12, 1985, p. 1; January 14, 1985, p. 6; *Fidel Castro Speeches 1984–85,* pp. 89–91.

169. *Granma Weekly Review,* October 7, 1984, p. 10.

170. Tomás Borge, interview, 1984, "Central America Project," WGBH-TV Educational Foundation.

171. Theodore Schwab and Harold Sims, "Revolutionary Nicaragua's Relations with the European Communist States, 1979–1983," *Conflict Quarterly* 5, no. 1 (Winter 1985): 5–14; *Nicaragua: Glorioso camino a la victoria* (Moscow: Soviet Academy of Sciences, 1981).

172. Jorge I. Domínguez, "It Won't Go Away: Cuba on the U.S. Foreign Policy Agenca," *International Security* 8, no. 1 (Summer 1983): 116–121.

173. Interviews in Havana, June 1986.

174. Mohamedi Musa Mawani, "Nkomati's False Dawn," *New African,* no. 205 (October 1984): 14–15; *Granma,* August 14, 1984, p. 6; September 12, 1984, p. 5; November 29, 1984, p. 3; November 30, 1984, p. 3.

175. *Revolución,* June 28, 1965, p. 4; *Granma,* June 25, 1967, p. 2.

176. *Verde olivo* 18 (October 1977): 4–5; ibid., 18 (October 1978): 10; Hugo Rius, "Cuba y Yemen Democrático," *Bohemia,* October 12, 1979, p. 69; *Granma Weekly Review,* June 16, 1978, p. 1; July 9, 1978, p. 9; July 16, 1978, p. 10; August 13, 1978, p. 9; September 24, 1978, p. 4; October 1, 1978, p. 3; October

8, 1978, p. 12. Steven David and others have argued that the Cubans helped to depose Ali and that there were no differences in the Cuban and Soviet response to these events. See his *Third World Coups d'Etat and International Security* (Baltimore: Johns Hopkins University Press, 1987), pp. 89–91. Though the facts of what happened in South Yemen are murky, Cuba did not condemn Ali at the time of the coup and, though the Cuban press referred to the existence of a rift between Ali and the USSR, it did not associate Cuba with that dispute. A month after Ali's overthrow, the Cuban foreign minister failed to express public solidarity with the new government of South Yemen, even though the subject of his speech lent itself well to such expression. Cuban relations with South Yemen did not become close again until September 1978.

177. *New York Times*, January 19, 1986, p. 9; February 9, 1986, pp. 1, 16. See also Fernández, *Cuba's Foreign Policy in the Middle East*, pp. 69–70.

178. *Bohemia* 71 (August 24, 1979): 73; ibid., 71 (September 7, 1979): 75; ibid., 71 (September 28, 1979): 70–71; Martínez de Salsamendi, "El papel de Cuba en el Tercer Mundo," pp. 150–151.

179. *Granma*, April 6, 1984, p. 5; interviews in Havana, March 1985; *Granma Weekly Review*, October 25, 1987, p. 5.

180. *Granma Weekly Review*, July 6, 1980, p. 11; May 24, 1981, p. 9; April 8, 1984, special supplement, pp. 6–12; *Granma*, July 1, 1980, p. 7; December 17, 1981, pp. 3, 5.

181. *Granma*, July 2, 1966, p. 12; July 5, 1966, p. 1; interviews in Havana, March 1985; Hector de Arturo, "Una amistad sin fronteras," *Verde olivo* 17 (September 21, 1975); García Márquez, "Operation Carlota"; Samuel Decalo, *Coups and Army Rule in Africa* (New Haven: Yale University Press, 1976), pp. 142, 151, 154–155; Okechukwu Onyejekwe, "Congo: The Rule of Armed Saviors," in *The Performance of Soldiers as Governors*, ed. Isaac J. Muwoe (Washington, D.C.: University Press of America, 1980), pp. 179–181.

182. Interview with Cuba's last ambassador in Suriname, Osvaldo Cárdenas, Havana, June 19, 1986; see also Elsa Blaquier and José Cazañas, "Cuba: Donde la salud es para todos," *Verde olivo* 24, no. 28 (July 14, 1983): 59.

7. Cuba's Relations with Capitalist Countries

1. Stanley Hoffmann, *State of War: Essays in the Theory and Practice of International Politics* (New York: Praeger, 1965); Robert O. Keohane and Joseph S. Nye, Jr., *Power and Interdependence: World Politics in Transition* (Boston: Little, Brown, 1977).

2. Susan Eckstein, "Capitalist Constraints on Cuban Socialist Development," *Comparative Politics*, April 1980, pp. 253–274.

3. Edward A. Hewett, "Cuba's Membership in the CMEA," in *Revolutionary Cuba in the World Arena*, ed. Martin Weinstein (Philadelphia: Institute for the Study of Human Issues Press, 1979); Edward A. Hewett, *Foreign Trade Prices in*

the Council for Mutual Economic Assistance (Cambridge: Cambridge University Press, 1974).

4. *Comercio exterior* 2, no. 3 (1964).

5. Computed from Dirección Central de Estadística, *Compendio estadístico de Cuba, 1968* (Havana: Junta Central de Planificación) p. 26.

6. "Conversación del Comandante Fidel Castro con un grupo de periodistas franceses," *Verde olivo* 24, no. 33 (August 18, 1983): 12.

7. *Compendio, 1968*, p. 26; Economist Intelligence Unit, *Quarterly Economic Review: Cuba, Dominican Republic, Haiti, Puerto Rico*, no. 45 (March 1964): 2.

8. *Revolución*, January 21, 1960, p. 2; January 22, 1960, p. 1; Philip W. Bonsal, *Cuba, Castro, and the United States* (Pittsburgh: University of Pittsburgh Press, 1971), p. 119. I saw the television broadcast. Lojendio left Cuba.

9. Manuel Fernández, *Religión y revolución en Cuba* (Miami: Saeta Ediciones, 1984), pp. 111–115.

10. *Compendio, 1968*, p. 26.

11. Alberto Recarte, *Cuba: Economía y poder (1959–1980)* (Madrid: Alianza Editorial, 1980), pp. 164–165.

12. Interviews in Havana with staff of the Centro de Estudios de Europa Occidental, March 21, 1985.

13. Computed from Junta Central de Planificación, *Censo de población y vivienda, 1970* (Havana: Editorial Orbe, 1975), table 8.

14. *Granma Weekly Review*, December 19, 1971, p. 13.

15. Recarte, *Cuba*, pp. 166–167.

16. *Compendio, 1968*, p. 26.

17. Recarte, *Cuba*, pp. 167–170.

18. *El país*, January 21, 1985, p. 7.

19. Royal Institute of International Affairs, *Documents on International Affairs* (London, 1963), pt. 4, statements of January 21 and May 15, 1959.

20. Fidel Castro, *Discursos para la historia* (Havana: Impresa Emilio Gall, 1959), pp. 51–52; *New York Times*, October 22, 1958, p. 54.

21. Castro, *Discursos*, pp. 50–81.

22. Royal Institute, *Documents*, pt. 4, statements of May 15, November 4, November 18, and December 14, 1959; *New York Times*, October 17, 1959, p. 1; *Revolución*, October 19, 1959, p. 1; November 14, 1959, p. 18.

23. *Compendio, 1968*, p. 26.

24. Economist Intelligence Unit, *Quarterly Economic Review: Cuba, Dominican Republic, Haiti, Puerto Rico*, no. 45 (March 1964): 1.

25. Ibid., no. 46 (June 1964): 5.

26. I am very grateful to E. Andres, counselor of the Swiss embassy in Washington, for making the following published Swiss government reports available: *Annual Report of the Swiss Federal Council to the Federal Assembly, 1960*, pp. 142, 161; *1961*, pp. 84, 109–110; *1962*, pp. 91–92, 110–111; *1963*, pp. 105–106, 131; *1964*, pp. 36, 59–60; *1965*, pp. 33, 54; *1966*, pp. 29, 53; *1967*, pp. 24, 33;

1968, pp. 28–29, 31; *1969*, pp. 16–17; *1970*, pp. 17, 19; *1971*, p. 17; *Feuille federale*, 119th year, vol. 1 (June 1, 1967): 932–940.

27. "La convention entre la France et Cuba," *Journal officiel de France*, October 4, 1967, doc. no. 9762.

28. Canadian Department of External Affairs, *Communiqué*, January 14, 1971, p. 30; *Granma Weekly Review*, December 12, 1971, p. 11; *Canada Weekly* 1, no. 36 (September 12, 1973): 2; and written communication from Andrew Palmer, British ambassador to Cuba, March 10, 1987.

29. Raúl León Torras, "XXV aniversario del Banco Nacional de Cuba," *Economía y desarrollo*, no. 33 (January–February 1976): 45; Morris H. Morley, *Imperial State and Revolution: The United States and Cuba, 1952–1986* (Cambridge: Cambridge University Press, 1987), pp. 309, 491.

30. Recarte, *Cuba*, pp. 170–171; Jorge Pérez-López, *The 1982 Cuban Joint Venture Law: Context, Assessment and Prospects* (Coral Gables: Institute of Inter-American Studies, University of Miami, 1985), p. 52.

31. Computed from Comité Estatal de Estadísticas, *Anuario estadístico de Cuba, 1978* (Havana), pp. 165–168.

32. Ibid., pp. 68, 181.

33. Computed from Comité Estatal de Estadísticas, *Anuario estadístico de Cuba, 1982* (Havana), p. 364.

34. *Anuario, 1978*, p. 163.

35. Banco Nacional de Cuba, *Economic Report*, February 1985, pp. 6, 13.

36. Fumio Nakagawa, "Japanese-Latin American Relations since the 1960s: An Overview," *Latin American Studies* (Tokyo) no. 6 (1983): 68.

37. Akio Hosano, "Economic Relationship between Japan and Latin America," ibid., pp. 76, 78.

38. Recarte, *Cuba*, p. 181.

39. *Granma Weekly Review*, January 22, 1984, p. 11; October 28, 1984, p. 5; and interview in Havana, April 1988.

40. Computed from Comité Estatal de Estadísticas, *Anuario estadístico de Cuba, 1986* (Havana).

41. Recarte, *Cuba*, pp. 177–184.

42. Statement by Deputy Prime Minister Carlos Rafael Rodríguez to *Le monde*, January 16, 1975, pp. 1, 4.

43. *Anuario, 1978*, pp. 165, 167.

44. *Le monde*, July 4, 1975, pp. 1, 24; July 11, 1975, pp. 1, 8; *The Times* (London), July 11, 1975, pp. 1–2.

45. *New York Times*, May 19, 1978, pp. A1, A10; Pablo Piacentini, "Habla Carlos Rafael Rodríguez," *Cuadernos del Tercer Mundo* 2, no. 14 (July 1977): 22.

46. *Granma Weekly Review*, November 27, 1983, p. 4; January 22, 1984, p. 11; Marcelo Fernández, "Las relaciones económicas entre la Comunidad Económica Europea y América Latina: Opiniones de Cuba," *Economía y desarrollo*, no. 24 (July–August 1974): 173.

47. Interviews in Havana, March 1985; *New York Times,* August 31, 1986, p. 9; *Le monde,* September 27, 1986, p. 5; *Granma,* September 26, 1986, p. 3.

48. *Granma Weekly Review,* March 24, 1974; March 31, 1974, p. 11; *International Canada* 5, no. 2 (February 1974): 21.

49. *Granma,* March 19, 1975, p. 3; March 20, 1975, p. 4.

50. Banco Nacional de Cuba, *Economic Report,* August 1982, p. 46.

51. *Granma,* January 26, 1976, p. 7; January 30, 1976, pp. 1–2; *New York Times,* January 25, 1976, p. 20; Theodore H. Moran, "The Political Economy of Cuban Nickel Development," in *Cuba in the World,* ed. Cole Blasier and Carmelo Mesa-Lago (Pittsburgh: University of Pittsburgh Press), 1979.

52. *New York Times,* January 13, 1977, p. 6.

53. *Granma Weekly Review,* May 22, 1977, p. 1; *Granma,* January 7, 1984, p. 3; April 26, 1984, p. 2; September 10, 1984, p. 3; February 24, 1987, p. 3; Pérez-López, *The 1982 Cuban Joint Venture Law,* p. 52; data on Shell of Cuba, from written communication from Andrew Palmer, British ambassador to Cuba, March 10, 1987.

54. *New York Times,* December 22, 1985, sec. 4, p. 3; *Granma,* December 14, 1985, p. 1.

55. *Granma Weekly Review,* November 23, 1986, p. 9; *Granma,* November 17, 1986, p. 3; Congreso de los Diputados, *Boletín oficial de las Cortes Generales: III Legislatura,* no. 116-1 (May 22, 1987): 1–3; *ABC,* May 5, 1987, pp. 24–25. I am grateful to Francisco Parra, of the Spanish embassy in Washington, for mailing me the text of the agreement.

56. *Granma Weekly Review,* December 12, 1986, p. 9; December 28, 1986, p. 1.

57. Ibid., November 16, 1986, p. 1; April 5, 1987, p. 3; *Granma,* November 15, 1986, p. 8.

58. *Granma,* June 28, 1975, p. 8; *Granma Weekly Review,* July 6, 1975, p. 3.

59. *New York Times,* May 23, 1976, p. 111.

60. Interviews in Havana, March 1985.

61. Fulvio Fuentes, "Países nórdicos," *Bohemia* 76, no. 19 (May 11, 1984): 66–67; *Granma Weekly Review,* January 8, 1984, p. 4.

62. Banco Nacional de Cuba, *Economic Report,* August 1982, p. 46.

63. *Granma Weekly Review,* August 19, 1984, p. 2.

64. Ibid., April 16, 1978, p. 1.

65. See Exchange of Notes in United Kingdom, *Treaty Series,* no. 20 (London: Her Majesty's Stationary Office, 1979); and written communication from Andrew Palmer, British ambassador to Cuba, March 10, 1987.

66. *Granma Weekly Review,* October 24, 1984, p. 5.

67. Serafín Marrero, "Cuba-RDA: Dos decenios de colaboración," *Bohemia* 76, no. 20 (May 18, 1984): 35; Rafael Borges, "Cuba-RDA: Consideraciones de un amigo," *Verde olivo* 24, no. 5 (February 3, 1983): 18–19; and interviews in Havana, March 1975.

68. *Anuario, 1978,* p. 165.

69. Interviews in Havana, March 1985.

70. *Granma Weekly Review,* December 9, 1984, p. 9; February 3, 1985, p. 3.

71. Banco Nacional de Cuba, *Economic Report,* March 1986, p. 9; Banco Nacional de Cuba, *Economic Report,* May 1987, p. 14.

72. Abdessatar Grissa, *Structure of the International Sugar Market* (Paris: Organization for Economic Cooperation and Development, 1976), pp. 1, 12.

73. Computed from Cuban Economic Research Project, *A Study on Cuba* (Coral Gables: University of Miami Press, 1965), pp. 508, 511; *New York Times,* February 21, 1960, sec. 4, p. 4.

74. Grissa, *Structure of the International Sugar Market,* pp. 2–4.

75. Vincent A. Mahler, "The Political Economy in North-South Commodity Bargaining: The Case of the International Sugar Agreement," *International Organization* 38, no. 4 (Autumn 1984): 712–719; Reinaldo Silva León, *Cuba y el mercado internacional azucarero* (Havana: Editorial de Ciencias Sociales, 1975).

76. U.S. Department of State, *Treaties and Other International Acts Series,* no. 4389 (Washington, D.C.: U.S. Government Printing Office, 1958), articles 14, 33, and 34.

77. Raúl Cepero Bonilla, "La conferencia azucarera de Ginebra," *Cuba socialista* 7 (1962): 47–61; Cuban Economic Research Project, *A Study on Cuba,* pp. 700–710.

78. Cuban Economic Research Project, *Cuba: Agriculture and Planning* (Coral Gables: University of Miami Press, 1965), p. 142.

79. Grissa, *Structure of the International Sugar Market,* pp. 31–37.

80. Silva León, *Cuba y el mercado internacional azucarero,* pp. 172–173.

81. *Granma Weekly Review,* November 3, 1968, p. 12; Grissa, *Structure of the International Sugar Market,* pp. 62–68.

82. Marcelo Fernández Font, *Cuba y la economía azucarera mundial,* Estudios e Investigaciones, no. 5 (Havana: Instituto Superior de Relaciones Internacionales "Raúl Roa García," 1986), pp. 173–175.

83. Ibid., pp. 176–177; José Vázquez, "Cuba y el convenio azucarero," *Cuba internacional* 6, no. 54 (February 1974); *Granma Weekly Review,* May 20, 1973, p. 11; June 24, 1973, p. 11; October 21, 1973, p. 11; December 2, 1973, p. 8; "Conferencia da UNCTAD para renegociação de acordo internacional do açúcar em Genebra," *Brasil açucareiro* 41, no. 5 (May 1973): 7–8; "Reuniu-se em Genebra a primera sessão da conferencia internacional do açúcar," ibid., 41, no. 6 (June 1973): 17–18.

84. *Granma,* April 9, 1975, p. 3; April 25, 1975, p. 7; April 26, 1975, p. 7.

85. Mahler, "The Political Economy of North-South Commodity Bargaining," pp. 719–722; Fernández, *Cuba y la economía azucarera mundial,* pp. 124–125, 177–182; *Granma Weekly Review,* July 8, 1984, p. 6.

86. *Granma Weekly Review,* March 13, 1977, p. 3; February 27, 1977, p. 12; June 26, 1977, p. 6.

87. Mahler, "The Political Economy of North-South Commodity Bargaining,"

pp. 722–728; Raúl Lazo, "Cuba y el mercado mundial azucarero," *Bohemia* 74, no. 29 (July 16, 1982): 28–31; Banco Nacional de Cuba, *Economic Report,* February 1985, p. 26.

88. Jasper Womach, *Agriculture: The U.S. Sugar Program,* Congressional Research Service Mini Brief no. MB82239 (Washington, D.C.: Library of Congress, 1983).

89. Computed from Banco Nacional de Cuba, *Economic Report,* February 1985, p. 31.

90. *Granma Weekly Review,* July 12, 1987, p. 3; August 30, 1987, p. 11.

91. *Granma Weekly Review,* July 8, 1984, p. 6; July 22, 1984, p. 4; August 26, 1984, p. 8; *Granma,* December 14, 1984, p. 3; Fernández, *Cuba y la economía azucarera mundial,* pp. 186–187.

92. Computed from *Anuario, 1986,* pp. 427–431; Banco Nacional de Cuba, *Economic Report,* March 1986, p. 23; and Banco Nacional de Cuba, *Economic Report,* May 1987, pp. 23–24. In a computation for 1982 based on preliminary statistics, José Luis Rodríguez underestimated the high weight of sugar and derivatives and overestimated the nontraditional share, in which he counted also crude oil "exports." See his "Un enfoque burgués del sector externo de la economía cubana," *Cuba socialista,* no. 14 (2d ser.) (March–April 1985): 86.

93. A point well argued by Claes Brundenius, *Revolutionary Cuba: The Challenge of Economic Growth with Equity* (Boulder, Colo.: Westview Press, 1984), pp. 63–64.

94. *Anuario, 1986,* pp. 426–435; Carmelo Mesa-Lago, *The Economy of Socialist Cuba* (Albuquerque: University of New Mexico Press, 1981), pp. 68, 70.

95. *Anuario, 1986,* pp. 426–435.

96. Fidel Castro, "Main Report: Third Congress of the Communist Party of Cuba" (mimeo, Havana, 1986), p. 28. List in Cámara de Comercio de la República de Cuba, *Empresas cubanas relacionadas con el comercio exterior* (Havana, 1984).

97. *Granma Weekly Review,* July 8, 1984, p. 5; May 18, 1986, p. 12; July 6, 1986, p. 7.

98. Rafael García, "Langosteras de Cárdenas," *Bohemia* 76, no. 44 (November 2, 1984): 7.

99. *Granma,* December 11, 1984, p. 2.

100. Ibid., January 18, 1984, p. 4.

101. Interview with Antonio Villaverde, secretary-general, Chamber of Commerce of Cuba, March 27, 1985; and *Granma Weekly Review,* April 12, 1987, p. 4.

102. Interview with Antonio Villaverde, March 27, 1985. List of Cuban requests of tariff and nontariff trade concessions from industrialized countries in Banco Nacional de Cuba, *Economic Report,* February 1985, pp. 47–54.

103. For a general argument by a Polish economist that centrally planned economies find it "virtually impossible . . . to attain an export orientation," see Jan Winiecki, "Central Planning and Export Orientation," *Eastern European Economics* 24, no. 4 (Summer 1986): 67–89.

104. *Granma Weekly Review,* December 2, 1984, p. 4.

105. Ibid., December 4, 1983, p. 3; *Granma,* April 20, 1984, p. 3.

106. Stephanie Rugoff, "Cuba's Fashion Debut," *Cubatimes* 4, no. 6 (September–October 1984): 9–10; and interviews in Havana, March 1985.

107. *Granma Weekly Review,* October 28, 1984, p. 4; interviews in Havana, March 1985; *Granma,* October 20, 1984, p. 1.

108. Banco Nacional de Cuba, *Economic Report,* February 1985, p. 35; Castro, "Main Report: Third Congress," p. 39; and interviews in Havana, March 1985.

109. Pérez-López, *The 1982 Cuban Joint Venture Law;* Patrick L. Schmidt, "Foreign Investment in Cuba: A Preliminary Analysis of Cuba's New Joint Venture Law," *Law and Policy in International Business* 15 (1983): 689–710.

110. Interviews with the professional staff of the Centro de Investigaciones de la Economía Internacional, Havana, March 22, 1985, and with Antonio Villaverde, secretary-general, Chamber of Commerce of Cuba, March 27, 1985.

111. *Anuario, 1982,* pp. 511–512; Banco Nacional de Cuba, *Economic Report,* May 1987, p. 20; *Granma Weekly Review,* June 15, 1986, p. 1; Alberto Pozo, "Industria turística: Gallina de huevos de oro," *Bohemia* 79, no. 6 (February 6, 1987): 47–54; interviews in Havana and in the United States, March 1985.

112. Banco Nacional de Cuba, *Economic Report,* August 1982, pp. 12, 15, 33, 47. This is also the main source for the next two paragraphs.

113. Computed from *Anuario, 1985,* pp. 396–397.

114. Banco Nacional de Cuba, *Economic Report,* August 1982, p. 45.

115. Banco Nacional de Cuba, *Economic Report,* March 1986, p. 48; Inter-American Development Bank, *Economic and Social Progress in Latin America, 1986* (Washington, D.C.), p. 430. See also Richard Turits "Trade, Debt, and the Cuban Economy," *World Development* 15, no. 1 (January 1987): 163–180.

116. Banco Nacional de Cuba, *Economic Report,* August 1982, p. 44; ibid., 1986, p. 48.

117. *Granma Weekly Review,* April 15, 1984, p. 4; December 23, 1984, p. 4; *Granma,* March 2, 1983, p. 1; July 21, 1984, p. 8; *New York Times,* January 9, 1984, pp. D1, D2; January 10, 1984, p. D6; Banco Nacional de Cuba, *Economic Report,* August 1982, p. 55; interviews in Havana, March 1985.

118. Naciones Unidas, Consejo Económico y Social, Comisión Económica para América Latina (CEPAL), *Balance preliminar de la economía latinoamericana durante 1984,* LC/G.1336 (December 24, 1984), tables 15 and 16; ibid., *Balance preliminar de la economía latinoamericana durante 1985,* LC/G.1383 (December 27, 1985), tables 17 and 18; and ibid., *Balance preliminar de la economía latinoamericana, 1986,* LC/G.1454 (December 18, 1986), table 19.

119. Computed from Banco Nacional de Cuba, *Economic Report,* February 1985, pp. 30, 42, and annexes 4, 5, 8; ibid., March 1986, pp. 32, 46, 48; Banco Nacional de Cuba, *Balance of Payments Highlights for 1986–1987,* April 1986, pp. 3, 8; *Granma Weekly Review,* August 3, 1986, p. 4; José L. Rodríguez, "El desarrollo de Cuba en el contexto de la crisis económica latinoamericana de los años 80," *Revista del CIEM: Temas de economía mundial,* no. 19 (1987): 18.

120. *Granma Weekly Review,* May 11, 1986, p. 1; August 3, 1986, p. 1; February 15, 1987, p. 1; *Wall Street Journal,* May 13, 1986, p. 35; *New York Times,* July 29, 1986, p. D9; interviews in Havana, June 1986.

121. Banco Nacional de Cuba, *Economic Report,* May 1987, pp. 22, 27; Banco Nacional de Cuba, *Report on the Economic and Financial Situation of Cuba during 1987–1988,* January 1988, pp. 3, 7; *Latin America Weekly Report,* WR-87-33 (August 6, 1987): 7; *Latin America Regional Reports: Caribbean Report,* RC-87-09 (November 5, 1987): 4–5; Rodríguez, "El desarrollo de Cuba," p. 18; U.N. Economic Commission for Latin America, *Preliminary Overview of the Latin American Economy, 1987,* LC/G.1485 (December 31, 1987), tables 19 and 20; *Granma,* December 27, 1986, p. 5; December 31, 1987, p. 3; *Granma Weekly Review,* February 21, 1988, p. 2; July 17, 1988, p. 5.

122. *Granma Weekly Review,* January 11, 1987, p. 2.

123. Julio A. Díaz Vázquez, *Cuba y el CAME* (Havana: Editorial de Ciencias Sociales, 1985), pp. 29–31.

8. Cuba's Diplomacy in the Americas and the Third World

1. *Revolución,* September 25, 1959, p. 1; October 23, 1959, p. 9; October 29, 1959, p. 9; December 4, 1959, p. 6; *New York Times,* December 18, 1959, p. 1.

2. *Revolución,* October 26, 1960, p. 8; November 2, 1960, p. 1.

3. "Conferencia de Belgrado (1961)," *Revista cubana de derecho* 8, no. 15 (1979): 12–14; "Presencia de Cuba en el Movimiento de No Alineados (Belgrado 1961 a La Habana 1979)," ibid., pp. 111–112; "La conferencia de países no alineados: Un nuevo golpe al imperialismo," *Cuba socialista* 1, no. 2 (October 1961).

4. "Conferencia de El Cairo (1964)," *Revista cubana de derecho* 8, no. 15 (1979): 24, 31–32, 36.

5. "Conversación del compañero Dorticós con los estudiantes cubanos sobre la conferencia de El Cairo," *Cuba socialista* 4, no. 39 (November 1964): 23.

6. "Conferencia de Lusaka (1970)," *Revista cubana de derecho* 8, no. 15 (1979): 43–49.

7. *Granma Weekly Review,* June 15, 1969.

8. María Amalia Negrín, "Cuba en la UNCTAD," *Economía y desarrollo,* no. 10 (April-May 1972): 63–65.

9. *Granma Weekly Review,* September 16, 1973.

10. "Conferencia de Argel (1973)," *Revista cubana de derecho* 8, no. 15 (1979): 58–59.

11. *Granma Weekly Review,* December 23, 1973, p. 7.

12. *Granma,* December 20, 1974, p. 8; May 7, 1975, p. 8; *Granma Weekly Review,* February 9, 1975, p. 10.

13. Computed from Jorge Pérez-López and René Pérez-López, *Cuban International Relations: A Bilateral Agreements Perspective,* Latin American Monograph Series, no. 8 (Pittsburgh: Northwestern Pennsylvania Institute for Latin American

Studies, 1979), p. 8; see also Carlos Martínez de Salsamendi, "El papel de Cuba en el Tercer Mundo: América Central, el Caribe, y Africa," in *Cuba y los Estados Unidos,* ed. Juan Gabriel Tokatlian (Buenos Aires: Grupo Editor Latinoamericano, 1984), pp. 183–184.

14. "Quinta conferencia de los jefes de estado o de gobierno de los países no alineados," *Revista cubana de derecho* 8, no. 15 (1979): 80, 93–97.

15. *Granma Weekly Review,* July 20, 1969, p. 5; June 20, 1971, p. 5.

16. *Granma Weekly Review,* August 15, 1971, p. 3; November 21, 1971, p. 3; December 12, 1971, p. 1.

17. Ibid., December 19, 1971, p. 15.

18. *Granma Weekly Review,* June 18, 1972, p. 12; July 2, 1972, p. 1; July 30, 1972, p. 4; August 6, 1972, p. 5; December 24, 1972, p. 1.

19. Carlos Moore, *El Caribe y la política exterior de la revolución cubana, 1959–1973,* publication no. 19 (San Germán: Centro de Investigaciones del Caribe y América Latina, Universidad Interamericana de Puerto Rico, 1986).

20. *Granma Weekly Review,* June 3, 1973, p. 1; June 17, 1973, p. 10; December 2, 1973, p. 10; January 13, 1974, p. 16; September 1, 1974, p. 1; September 29, 1974, p. 4; March 16, 1975, p. 1; Lía Ane Aguiloche and Norka Clerch Arza, "El comercio exterior de Cuba con América Latina y el Caribe en la etapa revolucionaria," *Revista del CIEM: Temas de economía mundial,* no. 9 (1984): 118.

21. See U.S. Ambassador Nathaniel Davis's Analysis, *The Last Two Years of Salvador Allende* (Ithaca: Cornell University Press, 1975), pp. 90–91, 190–191, 260, 275, 341–342.

22. *Granma Weekly Review,* June 20, 1971, p. 1; July 18, 1971, p. 2; November 7, 1971, p. 10; December 19, 1971, p. 12; March 19, 1972, p. 10.

23. "Los secuestros: Un boomerang," *Cuba internacional* 2 (November 1970): 53–56; *Granma Weekly Review,* July 15, 1973, p. 2.

24. *Granma Weekly Review,* December 19, 1971, p. 11; Senate Committee on Foreign Relations, Subcommittee on Western Hemisphere Affairs, "U.S. Policy toward Cuba," *Hearings,* 93d Cong., 1st sess. (Washington, D.C.: U.S. Government Printing Office, 1974), pp. 4–7; House Committee on International Relations, *Cuba Study Mission,* 94th Cong., 1st sess. (Washington, D.C.: U.S. Government Printing Office, 1975); Henry Kissinger, *Years of Upheaval* (Boston: Little, Brown, 1982), p. 419.

25. Edward Gonzalez, "Institutionalization, Political Elites, and Foreign Policies," in *Cuba in the World,* ed. Cole Blasier and Carmelo Mesa-Lago (Pittsburgh: University of Pittsburgh Press, 1979), pp. 22–23.

26. U.S. Department of Commerce, Bureau of East-West Trade, Office of Export Administration, "Modification of Restrictions on Export Controls to Cuba," *Export Administration Bulletin,* no. 150 (November 24, 1975).

27. House Committee on International Relations, Subcommittees on International Trade and Commerce and on International Organizations, "U.S. Trade Embargo on Cuba," *Hearings,* 94th Cong., 1st sess. (Washington, D.C.: U.S.

Government Printing Office, 1976), pp. 360–361, 562–564, 607; Gonzalez, "Institutionalization," p. 22; and discussions with William D. Rogers.

28. Cyrus Vance, *Hard Choices* (New York: Simon and Schuster, 1983), pp. 70–71, 133; U.S. Department of State, "U.S.-Cuban Relations," *Gist,* July 1978, 1–2.

29. Wayne Smith, *The Closest of Enemies* (New York: Norton, 1987), pp. 137–142.

30. *New York Times,* November 17, 1977, p. 1; conversation with Robert Pastor, member, National Security Council staff for Latin America.

31. U.S. Department of State, "U.S.-Cuban Relations," *Gist,* November 1979, 1–2: *Granma Weekly Review,* January 29, 1978, p. 9; John S. Martin, "Cuba and Drugs: The Real Dope," *Cubatimes* 4, no. 3 (March-April 1984): 4.

32. Interviews in Havana, March 1985, with Ricardo Alarcón, deputy minister for foreign relations, and alternate member, Communist party Central Committee; José Antonio Arbesú, deputy chief, Americas Department, member, Central Committee staff; Carlos Martínez de Salsamendi, adviser to Council of State Vice President Carlos Rafael Rodríguez.

33. Wayne Smith, "Dateline Havana: Myopic Diplomacy," *Foreign Policy,* no. 48 (Fall 1982): 169–173; A. Dane Bowen, Jr., "Rebuttal to Wayne Smith's 'Dateline Havana: Myopic Diplomacy'" (unpublished); conversations with Robert Pastor, Wayne Smith, and Dane Bowen. See also Smith. *The Closest of Enemies.*

34. Comité Estatal de Estadísticas, *Anuario estadístico de Cuba, 1983* (Havana), p. 171; Ane Aguiloche and Clerch Arza, "El comercio exterior de Cuba con América Latina y el Caribe," p. 118.

35. *Granma,* October 16, 1976; Nicanor León Cotayo, *Crime in Barbados* (Budapest: Interpress, 1978). See also Seymour M. Finger, "Security of International Civil Aviation: The Role of ICAO," *Terrorism* 6, no. 4 (1983): 523.

36. *Granma Weekly Review,* May 11, 1980, p. 2; June 22, 1980, p. 6; October 5, 1980, p. 1; Carlos A. Romero, "La diplomacia de proyección y el caso cubano en el contexto nacional y regional: Las relaciones entre Cuba y Venezuela, 1979–1981," *Fragmentos* (Caracas), no. 11. (1982).

37. *Granma Weekly Review,* May 11, 1980, p. 2.

38. Ibid., February 24, 1985, special supplement, p. 2.

39. Interviews and personal observation in Havana, August 1980; Lourdes Casal, "Cuba, abril-mayo 1980: La historia y la histeria," *Areíto* 6, no. 23 (1980): 15–25; U.S. Department of State, Bureau of Public Affairs, *Current Policy,* no. 193 (June 20, 1980); Alejandro Portes, Juan Clark, and Robert Manning, "After Mariel: A Survey of the Resettlement Experiences of 1980 Cuban Refugees in Miami," *Cuban Studies* 15, no. 2 (Summer 1985): 38–39, 42; and Rafael Hernández and Redi Gomis, "Retrato del Mariel: El ángulo socioeconómico," *Cuadernos de nuestra América* 3, no. 5 (January–June 1986): 138–140.

40. *Granma Weekly Review,* December 21, 1980, p. 1; March 1, 1981, p. 12.

41. *Anuario, 1983,* p. 171; interviews in Havana, June 1986; Alexander Haig,

Caveat: Realism, Reagan, and Foreign Policy (New York: Macmillan, 1984), p. 278.

42. Interview with Osvaldo Cárdenas, formerly on the Cuban Communist Party's Central Committee staff for Caribbean relations, Havana, June 1986.

43. Robert Paarlberg, "The Costs and Benefits of Paying More Attention to Latin America," in *Economic Issues and Political Conflict: U.S.-Latin American Relations,* ed. Jorge I. Domínguez (London: Butterworth, 1982), p. 222; *Granma,* July 14, 1975, pp. 3–4; *Granma Weekly Review,* August 17, 1975, p. 11; November 8, 1981, p. 12.

44. *Granma Weekly Review,* May 18, 1980, pp. 1–2; interview with Carlos Martínez de Salsamendi, March 1985; text of the agreement from the Bahamian Ministry of External Affairs.

45. Marcelo Fernández, *Cuba y la economía azucarera mundial,* Estudios e Investigaciones, no. 5 (Havana: Instituto Superior de Relaciones Internacionales "Raúl Roa García," 1986), pp. 84–85; Comité Estatal de Estadísticas, *Anuario estadístico de Cuba, 1986* (Havana), pp. 414–417.

46. Wayne Smith, *Castro's Cuba: Soviet Partner or Nonaligned?* (Washington, D.C.: Latin American Program, Wilson Center, 1984).

47. Texts in *Revista cubana de derecho* 8, no. 15 (1979).

48. Ibid., and Juan Sánchez, Mario del Cueto, and Raúl Lazo, "La Habana: Capital del mundo no alineado," *Bohemia* 71, no. 36 (September 7, 1979): 36–45; Juan Sánchez, Mario del Cueto, and Raúl Lazo, "Victoria de la Unidad," *Bohemia* 71, no. 37 (September 14, 1979): 36–49, 53.

49. Four years later, Cuba had a modest aid program in Afghanistan. See Serafín Marrero, "La colaboración cubano-afgana," *Bohemia* 76, no. 48 (November 30, 1984): 33.

50. Jorge I. Domínguez, "Political and Military Limitations and Consequences of Cuban Policies in Africa," in *Cuba in Africa,* ed. Carmelo Mesa-Lago and June Belkin, Latin American Monograph and Document Series, no. 3 (Pittsburgh: Center for Latin American Studies, University of Pittsburgh, 1982), pp. 115–120.

51. *New York Times,* January 13, 1980, sec. 4, p. 2; *Granma,* January 5, 1980, p. 7.

52. For Cuba's version, see Jesús Montané Oropesa, "VII cumbre: Significación y resultados," *Cuba socialista,* no. 7 (June–August 1983): 23–47; Martínez de Salsamendi, "El papel de Cuba en el Tercer Mundo," pp. 153–165.

53. *Granma Weekly Review,* December 17, 1981, pp. 3, 5; April 8, 1984, special supplement.

54. Ibid., July 19, 1981, p. 4; December 20, 1981, p. 8; July 11, 1982, p. 11; June 24, 1984, p. 1; *Granma,* September 14, 1984, p. 6.

55. *Granma Weekly Review,* May 9, 1982, p. 1; May 2, 1982, p. 1; June 13, 1982, p. 1; September 26, 1982, p. 3; Haig, *Caveat,* pp. 278, 294; interviews in Havana, June 1986.

56. *Granma Weekly Review,* August 19, 1984, p. 3; April 6, 1986, p. 1; October 26, 1986, p. 1; November 16, 1986, p. 10; *Granma,* June 8, 1984, p. 1.

57. *Granma Weekly Review,* August 22, 1982, p. 15; October 23, 1983, p. 10; November 6, 1983, p. 1; May 27, 1984, p. 3; October 14, 1984, p. 8.

58. Ibid., February 13, 1983, p. 10; January 12, 1986, p. 1; December 28, 1986, p. 1.

59. Ibid., December 19, 1982, p. 4; August 26, 1984, p. 7. See also Olga Nazario, "Brazil's Rapprochement with Cuba: The Process and the Prospect," *Journal of Inter-American Studies and World Affairs* 28, no. 3 (Fall 1986): 67–86.

60. *Granma Weekly Review,* January 23, 1983, p. 7; March 16, 1986; May 17, 1987, p. 3; *Granma,* December 7, 1985, p. 8; December 13, 1985, p. 8.

61. Fidel Castro, "Main Report: Third Congress of the Communist Party of Cuba" (mimeo, Havana, 1986), p. 93.

62. *Granma Weekly Review,* September 23, 1984, p. 3; see also ibid., August 10, 1980, pp. 2, 6; July 5, 1981, p. 1; June 3, 1984, p. 3; *Granma,* December 6, 1980, p. 1; November 2, 1983, p. 4; *Anuario, 1986,* pp. 416–417.

63. "Conversación del Cdte. en Jefe Fidel Castro con un grupo de periodistas franceses," *Verde olivo* 24, no. 33 (August 18, 1983): 15.

64. *Granma Weekly Review,* December 4, 1983, p. 3. On the invasion's popularity in this region, see Robert Pastor, "Grenada, The Caribbean, and the World: The Large Impact of a Small Island," in *Caribbean Perspectives,* ed. Anthony Bryan (Boulder, Colo.: Westview Press, forthcoming).

65. Interview with Osvaldo Cárdenas, Cuba's last ambassador to Suriname, in Havana, June 19, 1986.

66. *Granma,* January 13, 1984, p. 5.

67. See also Heraldo Muñoz and Boris Yopo, "Cuba y las democracias latino-americanas en los ochenta," *Documento de Trabajo PROSPEL* (Santiago), no. 9 (1987).

68. For overviews of Cuban policies by Cuban authors, see Luis Suárez Salazar, "La política de la Revolución Cubana hacia América Latina y el Caribe: Notas para una periodización," *Cuadernos de Nuestra América* 3, no. 6 (July–December 1986): 137–180; Viñas Alfonso, "Las relaciones con el Caribe," *Bohemia* 79, no. 50 (December 11, 1987): 74–75.

69. *Granma,* September 28, 1983, p. 6; October 15, 1983, p. 6; *Granma Weekly Review,* October 14, 1984, p. 5.

70. On the PLO, see *Granma Weekly Review,* December 4, 1983, p. 3; on the FPL, ibid., December 25, 1983, p. 10; on Grenada, Chapter 6.

71. U.S. Department of State, Bureau of Public Affairs, "Secretary Shultz: Southern Africa, Toward an American Consensus," *Current Policy,* no. 685 (April 16, 1985): 1–5.

72. "Editorial Notes: What the Nkomati Accord Means for Africa," *African Communist,* no. 98 (Third Quarter 1984): 5–16; Colin Legum, "Challenge for the ANC," *New African,* no. 201 (June 1984): 12–13; Mohamedi Musa Mawani, "New African, no. 201 (June 1984): 12–13; Mohamedi Musa Mawani, "Nkomati's False Dawn," *New African,* no. 205 (October 1984): 14–15; *Granma,* June 16, 1984, p. 2; August 14, 1984, p. 6; September 12, 1984, p. 5; November 28, 1984, p. 3;

November 29, 1984, p. 3; December 3, 1984, p. 3; interviews in Havana, June 1986.

73. U.S. Department of State, Bureau of Public Affairs, *Realism, Strength, Negotiation: Key Foreign Policy Statements of the Reagan Administration* (Washington, D.C., 1984), pp. 134–137.

74. *Granma Weekly Review,* December 28, 1980, p. 13.

75. "Twenty-five Years of Aggression," *Tricontinental,* no. 88 (April 1983): 30–37; *Granma Weekly Review,* December 19, 1971, pp. 12, 15.

76. Sidney Freidberg, "The Measure of Damages in Claims against Cuba," *Inter-American Economic Affairs* 23, no. 1 (Summer 1969); Lynn Darrell Bender, "U.S. Claims against the Cuban Government: An Obstacle to Rapprochement," *Inter-American Economic Affairs* 27, no. 1 (Summer 1983).

77. U.S. Department of State, Bureau of Public Affairs, *Current Policy,* no. 881 (1986): 1–4.

78. Texts in House Committee on Foreign Affairs, *Inter-American Relations,* 93d Cong., 1st sess. (Washington, D.C.: U.S. Government Printing Office, 1973), pp. 665–671.

79. For a Cuban author's overview, see Rafael Hernández, "La lógica de la frontera en las relaciones E.U.-Cuba," *Cuadernos de Nuestra América* 4, no. 7 (January–June 1987): 6–53.

80. U.S. Department of State, Bureau of Public Affairs, "Dealing with the Reality of Cuba," *Current Policy,* no. 443 (December 14, 1982): 2.

81. *Cuban Economic News* 2, no. 14 (August 1966): 7; ibid., 8, no. 56 (1972): 1; *Granma Weekly Review,* December 22, 1974, p. 5; March 4, 1984, p. 5; March 18, 1984, p. 8; December 21, 1986, p. 9; November 8, 1987, p. 9; *Granma,* September 26, 1984; Hilda Puerta Rodríguez, "Análisis crítico de la organización de Naciones Unidas para la agricultura y la alimentación (FAO)," *Economía y desarrollo,* no. 71 (November–December 1982): 86, 89–90; Raúl Lazo, "El centro de investigaciones pesqueras," *Bohemia* 67, no. 4 (October 3, 1975): 37; Edith Felipe, "Cuba y la colaboración económica con el mundo subdesarrollado," *Revista del CIEM: Temas de economía mundial,* no. 15 (1985): 99–101.

82. Elaine Fuller, "Ban on Cuban Nickel," *Cubatimes* 4, no. 3 (March-April 1984): 9.

83. Kirby Jones, "Economic Notes," *Cubatimes* 1, no. 1 (Spring 1980): 34–35; Philip Brenner, "U.S.-Cuba: Ambiguous Signals," *Cubatimes* 3, no. 2 (Summer 1982): 6–10; John Griffiths, "Cuba-Europe Trade Breaks Blockade," *Cubatimes* 2, no. 4 (Winter 1982): 4–7; interviews in Havana, March 1985 and June 1986.

84. Summary in República de Cuba, "Acciones tomadas por el Gobierno de Estados Unidos en sus relaciones con la República de Cuba," *Economía y desarrollo,* no. 68 (May–June 1982): 167–171.

85. For a discussion of earlier cooperation when bilateral relations were very hostile, see Gordon Dunn, "The Hurricane Season of 1963," *Monthly Weather Review* 92, no. 3 (March 1964): 135–136.

86. Interviews with U.S. government officials; *Granma,* February 11, 1985, special supplement, p. 3.

87. Interview with José Fernández de Cossio, National Bank of Cuba, March 26, 1985.

88. Haig, *Caveat,* pp. 130–137; Smith, "Dateline Havana"; U.S. Department of State, Bureau of Public Affairs, "Dealing with the Reality of Cuba," p. 2.

89. *Granma Weekly Review,* September 30, 1984.

90. U.S. Department of State, Bureau of Public Affairs, "The United States and Cuba," *Current Policy,* no. 646 (December 17, 1984); *Granma,* December 15, 1984; U.S. District Court for the Northern District of Georgia, Atlanta Division, Government's Motion for a Stay of the Court's October 15, 1984, Order Pending Appeal, in *Rafael Fernández Roque et al. versus William French Smith et al.,* Civil Action no. C 81-1084 A (1984), declaration by Michael Kozak, deputy legal adviser of the U.S. Department of State.

91. Cited in Samuel Flagg Bemis, *The Latin American Policy of the United States* (New York: Harcourt, Brace and World, 1943), p. 27.

9. How Cuban Foreign Policy Is Made

1. Cited in Alexander Alexeev, "Cuba después del triunfo de la revolución: Primera parte," *América Latina,* no. 10 (October 1984): 63.

2. *Granma Weekly Review,* December 28, 1980, p. 13.

3. Fidel Castro, *Obras escogidas, 1953–1962,* vol. 1 (Madrid: Editorial Fundamentos, 1976), p. 131.

4. Quoted in Jorge I. Domínguez, *Cuba: Order and Revolution* (Cambridge, Mass.: Harvard University Press, 1978), pp. 197–198.

5. "Playboy Interview: Fidel Castro," *Playboy* 32, no. 8 (August 1985): 183.

6. Ibid.

7. On the latter, see Domínguez, *Cuba: Order and Revolution,* pp. 405–407.

8. Self-portraits in "Playboy Interview: Fidel Castro," pp. 57–68; Frank Mankiewicz and Kirby Jones, *With Fidel* (Chicago: Playboy Press, 1975), pp. 75, 79–80. See also Edward Gonzalez and David Ronfeldt, *Castro, Cuba, and the World,* report R-3420 (Santa Monica, Calif.: Rand Corporation, 1986).

9. Hugh Thomas, *Cuba: The Pursuit of Freedom* (New York: Harper and Row, 1971), pp. 1355–71.

10. On this dating, see "The National Liberation Movement in Latin America and the Caribbean," *Tricontinental Bimonthly,* no. 75 (February 1981): 94; interviews in Havana, March 1985.

11. Interviews in Havana, March 1985.

12. I am grateful to Michael Mandelbaum, Miguel Alfonso, and Rafael Hernández for making this point forcefully (even if they disagree with other points in this book).

13. Gabriel García Márquez, "Operation Carlota," *Tricontinental Bimonthly*, no. 53 (1977): 20.

14. *Granma Weekly Review*, May 11, 1980, p. 2.

15. See also Wayne Smith, *The Closest of Enemies* (New York: Norton, 1987), pp. 206–208.

16. *Granma Weekly Review*, October 30, 1983, p. 3; November 6, 1983, p. 1. I am grateful to the Cuban Interests Section in Washington for copies of all the communiqués; the seventh, eighth, and eleventh communiqués are quoted.

17. Interviews in Havana, March 1985.

18. *Verde olivo* 25, no. 2 (January 12, 1984): 37.

19. Documents captured by the U.S. armed forces in Grenada (and now available in the U.S. National Archives): Embassy of Grenada in the USSR, "Relations with the CPSU," no date (probably late 1982), p. 2.

20. *Granma Weekly Review*, January 15, 1984, p. 4.

21. Walters, Interview, 1984, "Central America Project," WGBH-TV Educational Foundation.

22. Raúl Valdés Vivó, *Etiopía: La revolución desconocida* (Havana: Editorial de Ciencias Sociales, 1977).

23. Interviews in Havana, March 1985, at the various centers.

24. *Granma*, August 30, 1982, p. 2; September 1, 1982, pp. 2–3; September 2, 1982, p. 2; October 12, 1982, p. 2; February 19, 1983, p. 2; Katia Valdés and Francisco Pérez Guzmán, "En la emboscada de Vado del Yeso," *Verde olivo* 23, no. 34 (August 26, 1982): 28, 30.

25. *Granma*, February 1, 1985, p. 1.

26. This section rests in part on Domínguez, *Cuba: Order and Revolution;* and Jorge I. Domínguez, "Revolutionary Politics: The New Demands for Orderliness," in *Cuba: Internal and International Affairs,* ed. Jorge I. Domínguez (Beverly Hills: Sage Publications, 1982).

27. *Granma Weekly Review*, March 26, 1978, p. 4.

28. *Granma*, February 1, 1985, p. 1.

29. Interview with Eloy Valdés, deputy chief, General Department for International Relations, and member, Communist party Central Committee staff, March 26, 1985.

30. Interview with Ricardo Alarcón, in Havana, March 25, 1985.

31. *Revolución*, September 16, 1959, p. 1.

32. Ibid., October 9, 1961, p. 1.

33. Ibid., July 18, 1963, p. 2.

34. Ibid., July 13, 1963, p. 5; July 18, 1963, p. 2.

35. *Obra Revolucionaria*, no. 19 (1963): 8.

36. *Revolución*, April 26, 1960, p. 1; July 16, 1960, p. 1; Ernesto Guevara, "La industrialización en Cuba," *Economía y planificación*, 1961, p. 64; Julio Fumero Marta and Ramón Juliá Milanés, *Comercio exterior: Organización y técnica* (Havana: Editorial de Ciencias Sociales, 1985), pp. 181–191.

37. *Granma*, March 14, 1966, pp. 4–5.

38. Ibid., March 16, 1966, p. 6; *New York Times,* March 15, 1966, p. 3; March 17, 1966, p. 53; March 18, 1966, p. 1; March 19, 1966, p. 6; June 21, 1966, p. 6.

39. Ministerio de Relaciones Exteriores, *Relación de las oficinas del servicio exterior cubano en el extranjero* (Havana: MINREX, 1960); *Revolución,* October 9, 1961, p. 1.

40. *Bohemia* 67, no. 23 (June 6, 1975): 83; Fidel Castro, "Main Report: Third Congress of the Communist Party of Cuba" (mimeo, Havana, 1986), p. 102.

41. *Granma,* January 3, 1975, p. 4; February 8, 1984, p. 2.

42. *Granma,* April 1, 1986, p. 3.

43. *Granma Weekly Review,* April 30, 1967, p. 4.

44. Interview with Eloy Valdés, March 26, 1985.

45. Interview with Ricardo Alarcón, deputy minister for foreign relations, Havana, March 25, 1985.

46. *Granma,* May 3, 1984, p. 3.

47. Fumero and Juliá, *Comercio exterior,* pp. 191–195; *Granma,* April 12, 1984, p. 3; *Granma Weekly Review,* November 18, 1981, p. 5.

48. Chamber of Commerce of the Republic of Cuba, *Directory of Cuban Exporters,* 2d ed. (Havana, n.d.); Chamber of Commerce of the Republic of Cuba, *Cuban Enterprises Related to Foreign Trade* (Havana, 1984).

49. "XV aniversario de la creación de la Junta Central de Planificación," *Economía y desarrollo,* no. 30 (July–August 1975): 238; *Granma Weekly Review,* September 12, 1971, p. 7.

50. *Granma,* November 29, 1976, pp. 4–5; see also Fumero and Juliá, *Comercio exterior,* pp. 195–206.

51. José Pedraza Chapeau, *El CAME y la integración económica socialista* (Havana: Editorial de Ciencias Sociales, 1984), p. 67.

52. Ibid., pp. 64–67; Roberto Villar, "A propósito de los diez años de Cuba en el CAME," *Economía y desarrollo,* no. 68 (May–June 1982): 146–150; *Granma Weekly Review,* October 28, 1984, p. 3.

53. Carlos Martínez Trujillo, José Mellado Sánchez, and Isabel María González, "Las organizaciones internacionales multilaterales de los países miembros del CAME y la participación de Cuba," *Economía y desarrollo,* no. 81 (July–August 1984): 92–103.

54. Julio A. Díaz Vázquez, "Cuba: Integración económica socialista y especialización de la producción," *Economía y desarrollo,* no. 63 (July–August 1981): 148; and Julio A. Díaz Vázquez, *Cuba y el CAME* (Havana: Editorial de Ciencias Sociales, 1985), p. 71.

55. Edith Felipe Duyos, "Los cambios más recientes en los sistemas de dirección económica en Europa socialista," *Revista del CIEM: Temas de economía mundial,* no. 12 (1984): 80–116.

56. Jorge Valdés Miranda, "Acerca de la compraventa de plantas completas u objetivos industriales," *Economía y desarrollo,* no. 71 (November–December 1982): 168–169.

57. Fidel Castro, "Acerca de Haydée Santamaría y la Casa de las Américas,"

Casa de las Américas 24, no. 142 (January–February 1984): 3; *Granma Weekly Review,* April 29, 1984, p. 6.

58. See Haydée Santamaría's frank discussion in *Granma,* October 7, 1967, p. 5.

59. *Granma Weekly Review,* May 9, 1972, p. 9; Lourdes Casal, ed., *El Caso Padilla: Literatura y revolución en Cuba* (Miami: Ediciones Universal, 1971); Dominguez, *Cuba: Order and Revolution,* pp. 391–394; Jorge Edwards, *Persona non grata* (Barcelona: Barral Editores, 1973): Seymour Menton, *Prose Fiction of the Cuban Revolution* (Austin: University of Texas Press, 1975), pp. 123–156.

60. "Prensa Latina cumple 25," *Bohemia* 76, no. 23 (June 8, 1984): 56.

61. *Granma Weekly Review,* October 19, 1975, p. 11; February 6, 1977, p. 3; *Bohemia* 67, no. 41 (October 10, 1975): 54.

62. *Tricontinental Bulletin,* no. 2 (May 1966); ibid., no. 27 (July 1968): 46–47; *Granma Weekly Review,* March 29, 1981, p. 3.

63. *Tricontinental Bulletin,* no. 2 (May 1966); ibid., no. 27 (July 1968): 46–47.

64. "Creation of the OLAS," *Tricontinental Bulletin,* no. 1 (April 1966): 8–9; *Granma Weekly Review,* August 20, 1967, p. 7.

65. *Tricontinental Bimonthly,* no. 10 (January–February 1969): 127.

66. "Interview with Paulo Jorge from the MPLA," *Tricontinental Bimonthly,* no. 7 (July–August 1968): 154–156.

67. *Granma Weekly Review,* November 20, 1966, p. 1; *Tricontinental Bulletin,* no. 27 (July 1968): 6, 34.

68. Manuel González Bello, "Luchas de hoy: XV aniversario de la OCLAE," *Bohemia* 73, no. 42 (August 7, 1981): 75–76; "XV aniversario de la OCLAE," *OCLAE* 15, no. 8 (1981): 9, 11.

69. Jesús Montané and Manuel Piñeiro, "Dramatic Stage in the History of a Continent," *World Marxist Review* 25, no. 5 (May 1982): 15–17; Manuel Piñeiro, "La crisis actual del imperialismo y los procesos revolucionarios en América Latina y el Caribe," *Cuba socialista,* no. 4 (2d ser.) (November 1982): 15–53; *Granma,* April 29, 1982, p. 2.

70. *Granma,* June 8, 1976, p. 1.

71. José M. Ortiz, "Angola: From the Trenches," *Tricontinental,* no. 96 (June 1984): 50.

72. *Granma,* March 27, 1984, p. 2.

73. Ibid., January 30, 1968, p. 2.

74. José Cazañas, "En cada palmo de nuestras costas," *Verde olivo* 24, no. 9 (March 3, 1983): 24–27; José Cazañas, "Guardafronteras," *Verde olivo* 22, no. 23 (June 7, 1981): 4–8; Joel Vilariño, "Veinte años de heroísmo," *Verde olivo* 22, no. 45 (November 5, 1981): 30–33.

75. Carlos Rivero Collado, *Los sobrinos del Tío Sam* (Havana: Editorial de Ciencias Sociales, 1976).

76. *Granma,* March 27, 1984, p. 1.

77. Domínguez, *Cuba: Order and Revolution,* p. 319.

78. Interviews in Havana, June 1986; *Granma,* December 3, 1985, p. 1.

79. *Granma Weekly Review,* June 27, 1982, p. 2; *Granma,* December 13, 1982, p. 2.

80. U.S. Departments of State and Defense, *The Soviet-Cuban Connection in Central America and the Caribbean* (Washington, D.C., 1985), p. 9.

81. *Granma,* January 4, 1985, special supplement, p. 6; Castro, "Main Report: Third Congress," p. 51.

82. *Granma Weekly Review,* February 1, 1981, p. 2; *Verde olivo* 25, no. 10 (March 8, 1984): 37.

83. *Granma Weekly Review,* June 22, 1980, p. 3; March 28, 1981, p. 3; December 19, 1982, p. 3; Pablo Noa, "En el IPUEC 'Capt. Jesús Suárez Gayol,'" *Verde olivo* 24, no. 4 (January 27, 1983): 40–43.

84. Claes Brundenius, *Revolutionary Cuba: The Challenge of Economic Growth with Equity* (Boulder, Colo.: Westview Press, 1984), pp. 125–138; Carmelo Mesa-Lago, *The Economy of Socialist Cuba* (Albuquerque: University of New Mexico Press, 1981), pp. 110–112; Domínguez, *Cuba: Order and Revolution,* pp. 345–350.

85. *Granma,* July 11, 1975, p. 2; December 8, 1975, p. 5; February 4, 1983, p. 2; *Granma Weekly Review,* July 3, 1977, p. 3; December 28, 1980, p. 10; "Algunos aspectos relacionados con la ley del servicio militar general y su reglamento," *Verde olivo* 17, no. 4 (January 26, 1975): 54.

86. Computed from *Granma Weekly Review,* November 6, 1983, p. 1.

87. Fidel Castro, *Nada podrá detener la marcha de la historia* (Havana: Editora Política, 1985), p. 99.

88. Rubén Placeres, "Raúl y los tanquistas," *Verde olivo* 22, no. 20 (May 17, 1981): 8.

89. Eugenio Suárez Pérez, "Para el estudio de una tradición," *Verde olivo* 24, no. 48 (December 1, 1983): 24–27.

90. "Convocatoria del MINFAR," *Verde olivo* 17, no. 11 (March 16, 1975): 43; "Convocatoria," ibid., 18, no. 7 (February 15, 1976): 36–39.

91. *Granma,* February 27, 1982, p. 5; December 22, 1982, p. 2; Jesús González, "Veinte años formando cuadros para las FAR," *Verde olivo* 23, no. 33 (August 19, 1982): 11–13.

92. *Granma,* January 29, 1983, p. 4.

93. Juan Almeida, "El suboficial en las FAR," *Verde olivo* 24, no. 1 (January 6, 1983): 40–41.

94. Computed from *Granma Weekly Review,* November 20, 1983, p. 4.

95. Joaquín Benavides Rodríguez, "La ley de la distribución con arreglo al trabajo y la reforma de salarios en Cuba," *Cuba socialista* 1, no. 2 (2d ser.) (March 1982): 70–73; *Granma Weekly Review,* December 28, 1980, p. 12.

96. Cuban workers in Grenada came disproportionately from the western provinces, which have fewer blacks as a percentage of the population than Cuba's eastern provinces. Therefore, for the sake of comparison, the racial distribution of

Cuba's population was recalculated to match exactly the distribution by province of Cubans killed in Grenada. Computed from Comité Estatal de Estadísticas, Oficina Nacional del Censo, *Censo de población y viviendas, 1981: República de Cuba,* vol. 16 (Havana), p. cxi, hereafter cited as *Censo, 1981; Granma Weekly Review,* November 20, 1983, p. 4.

97. Interviews in Havana, March 1985. Nonwhites are also probably overrepresented in the construction sector but there are no census data on this point.

98. *Granma Weekly Review,* November 20, 1983, pp. 9–11.

99. Computed from ibid., pp. 9–11, and from *Censo, 1981,* p. 242.

100. Maurice Zeitlin, *Revolutionary Politics and the Cuban Working Class* (New York: Harper Torchbooks, 1970); Domínguez, *Cuba: Order and Revolution,* pp. 485–494.

101. Computed from *Granma,* August 29, 1983, p. 6.

102. *Granma Weekly Review,* March 28, 1981, p. 3.

103. Ibid., November 25, 1979, p. 1; *Censo, 1981,* pp. 251, 253.

104. Computed from *Granma Weekly Review,* April 1, 1979, p. 4.

105. Computed from ibid., April 29, 1984, p. 1; *Censo, 1981,* p. cxi.

106. Castro, "Main Report: Third Congress," p. 34.

107. Oscar Rego, "¿Estudias algún idioma?" *Bohemia* 73, no. 40 (October 2, 1981): 80–81.

108. *Bohemia* 73, no. 39 (September 25, 1981): 66.

109. *Granma Weekly Review,* November 4, 1984, p. 6.

110. *Censo, 1981,* p. cxi.

111. Comité Estatal de Estadísticas, Dirección de Demografía, *Estadísticas de migraciones externas y turismo* (Havana: Editorial Orbe, 1982), pp. 49–60.

112. Reinaldo Peñalver, "Mensajeros del internacionalismo," *Bohemia* 76, no. 30 (July 27, 1984): 52–55.

113. Interviews in Havana, March 1985.

114. *Granma Weekly Review,* October 30, 1983, p. 9.

115. *Granma,* September 17, 1983, p. 2; October 8, 1983, p. 2; on poor phone service, see *Granma Weekly Review,* January 1, 1984, p. 2.

116. *Granma,* September 21, 1984, p. 3.

117. Marifeli Pérez-Stable, "Politics and Conciencia in Revolutionary Cuba, 1959–1984," (Ph.D. diss., State University of New York at Stony Brook, 1985), chap. 6 and apps. 1 and 2.

118. *Granma,* November 30, 1983, p. 3; Comité Estatal de Estadísticas, *Anuario estadístico de Cuba, 1986* (Havana), p. 546.

119. Raúl Castro, "El diversionismo ideológico: Arma sutil que esgrimen los enemigos contra la revolución," *Verde olivo* 14, no. 30 (July 23, 1972): 4–15; *Granma Weekly Review,* May 9, 1971, p. 3; May 9, 1972, p. 5.

120. *Granma Weekly Review,* April 17, 1977, p. 5.

121. Interviews in Havana, August 1980.

122. Comité Estatal de Estadísticas, Dirección de Demografía, *Estadísticas,* pp.

61, 71; Comité Estatal de Estadísticas, *Anuario estadístico de Cuba, 1982* (Havana), p. 87.

123. *Granma,* May 17, 1984, p. 5.

124. *Granma Weekly Review,* January 11, 1976.

125. Ibid., February 9, 1986, p. 1; *Granma,* December 21, 1975, p. 1; December 20, 1980, pp. 1, 5.

126. *Granma,* April 16, 1977, p. 2; June 3, 1977, p. 3; March 26, 1982, p. 3; December 22, 1982, p. 3.

127. Interviews with the staff of the Center for Research on International Economics, March 22, 1985.

128. Fidel Castro, "Marxism-Leninism and the Cuban Revolution," *World Marxist Review* 22, no. 1 (January 1979): 17–18.

Appendix B

1. Jorge Pérez-López, private communication, September 19, 1985, noted that additional Cuban sugar sales to market-economy countries might depress the world price, thereby affecting anew the opportunity cost calculations of the Soviet sugar price subsidy.

2. Marcelo Fernández Font, *Cuba y la economía azucarera mundial,* Estudios e Investigaciones, no. 5 (Havana: Instituto Superior de Relaciones Internacionales "Raúl Roa García," 1986), pp. 126–127.

3. Comité Estatal de Estadísticas, *Anuario estadístico de Cuba, 1986* (Havana).

4. Computed from Carmelo Mesa-Lago and Jorge Pérez-López, "A Study of Cuba's Material Product System, Its Conversion to the System of National Accounts, and Estimation of Gross Domestic Product per Capita and Growth Rates," in *World Bank Staff Working Papers,* no. 770 (Washington, D.C.: World Bank, 1985), pp. 59–66; Banco Nacional de Cuba, *Economic Report,* February 1985, annex 10, p. 3; Banco Nacional de Cuba, *Economic Report,* March 1986, p. 50; Banco Nacional de Cuba, *Economic Report,* May 1987, p. 47.

5. U.S. Central Intelligence Agency, National Foreign Assessment Center, *The Cuban Economy: A Statistical Review,* ER 81-10052 PA 81-10074 (March 1981), pp. 39–40.

Index

Abrantes, José, 272
Acuña, Juan, 136, 259–260
Afghanistan, 105, 111, 220; Cuban aid to, 174, 340n49
Africa, 1, 114, 116, 128, 132, 142, 149, 154, 169, 183, 197, 219–224, 229–230, 255, 270; Cuban troops in, 78, 133, 135; Cuban relations with countries in, 119, 129, 139, 152, 159–160, 162, 171, 234, 257, 264; revolutionaries in, 125, 144; governments in 135; subversion in, 139
African National Congress (ANC), 133, 180, 242
Agramonte, Roberto, 16, 19
Aid: from Cuba, 1, 127–146, 147, 171–180, 201, 206, 234, 236–237, 340n49; from USSR to Cuba, 4, 27, 31, 58, 63–67, 71–73, 75, 77, 79–94, 96–104, 107, 112, 133, 144–145; to Batista, 11, 189; from U.S. to Cuba, 16–19; from socialist countries to Latin America, 69, 71; from Eastern Europe to Cuba, 84, 92–104, 107, 133; to Cuba, 116; to Angola, 152–159; to Ethiopia, 157–162; to Grenada, 163–171, 173; donations from Cuba, 163, 166, 173–175, 177, 238, 244; to Nicaragua, 171–173, 175–178; to Algeria, 172–173, 175, 180, 187, 273, 328n148; from Canada to Cuba, 197; from the Netherlands to Cuba, 199; from Sweden to Cuba, 199. *See also* Angola; Ethiopia; Nicaragua
Aircraft: bombers (IL-28), 37–38, 43, 46, 48, 51, 53; MiGs, 37, 43, 46, 49, 51–53, 57–58, 78, 228, 301n18; civilian, 131, 157, 188, 211, 230, 280
Airport: in Grenada, 163, 165, 169–170; in Guinea, 173; in Havana, 211
Alarcón, Ricardo, 132, 257, 263, 287–288
Alexeev, Alexandr, 20–21, 36
Algeria, 7, 15, 128, 180–181, 222, 234–235; revolution in, 130, 221. *See also* Aid, to Algeria
Ali, Salem Robaya, 181, 329–330n176
Alignment and alliances, 6, 7, 8, 14–16, 20–21, 28–29, 32–33, 63, 70, 75, 78, 84, 99, 104–106, 111–112, 113–114, 120, 127, 133–134, 143–146, 147–149, 151, 156, 158–160, 162–163, 169, 175, 182, 184, 221–223, 227, 229, 235, 251, 271. *See also* Nonaligned Movement
Allende, Salvador, 182, 199, 223, 225–226
Alliance for Progress, 25, 120
Alves, Nito, 158–159, 170–171, 323n44
Ambassadors, 16, 127, 159, 161–162, 164, 166, 169–170, 187, 189, 253, 262–266, 323n44
Amoedo, Julio, 23
Angola, 2, 5, 138, 144–146, 148, 151, 158, 160, 162, 169–171, 177–178, 182, 197–198, 206, 208, 210, 213, 229, 232, 234–235, 244, 261, 279; Cuban troops in, 1, 4, 51, 56, 84, 108, 111, 129, 131–134, 141–142, 152–154, 156–157, 159, 161, 176, 199, 217, 220, 224, 227, 241, 245–246, 251, 259,

Angola (*continued*)
271, 273, 278; Soviets in, 108; Cuban advisers in, 131, 152–156, 161, 172–173, 175–176, 278, 317n59; conflicts with Cuba, 156–157, 180, 241–242, 259, 323n44. *See also* MPLA
Antigua-Barbuda, 168, 240
Arab governments, 221, 223–225, 236
Arafat, Yasser, 130
Argentina, 15, 23, 28, 97, 122, 143, 211, 222, 224, 226–227, 230, 232, 237–238, 315n19
Armed forces: troops, 1, 6, 7, 47, 56, 72, 84, 148, 151–154, 156, 159, 162, 175–177, 181, 197, 229, 243, 272–276, 282; advice to, 12, 44, 53; Air Force, 12, 19, 25, 40, 51, 232–233, 257, 275; Army, 12–13; preparedness of, 34–35, 45, 73, 226, 251–252, 273; policy views of, 39, 71, 73; Anti-Aircraft Defense (DAAFAR), 40, 42; capacity of, 47, 53–57, 79–80, 148, 167, 176–177, 246, 273, 275; Navy, 50, 53, 118, 139, 276; civic soldier, 154, 168, 177; of Grenada, 167; Ministry of, 168; officers, 168–169, 261, 275; reservists, 168–169, 176–177, 253, 273–275; politics in, 272, 275–276. *See also* Angola; Ethiopia; Military
Armed struggle, 70–71, 76, 124–126, 129–130, 132, 135, 137, 221, 223
Asia, 116, 221; Cuban relations with countries in, 119, 135, 219, 224, 257, 264
Assassination, 25–26, 35, 48–49, 115, 181, 260
Asylum: in embassies, 10, 16, 197, 230–232, 237, 252–253; in the U.S., 19; in Cuba, 119, 227
Atwood, William, 48
Austin, Hudson, 166–167, 170
Australia, 205, 207, 212
Autonomy, 4, 6, 41, 62–63, 70, 78, 81–82, 84, 105–106, 111–112, 132, 134, 144–145, 148, 158, 162, 165, 171, 180, 207, 220

Bahamas, Cuba's conflict with, 232–233, 257
Ball, George, 45

Banks: private, 5, 10, 25, 28, 88, 184, 190, 210–211, 213–218, 244; National Bank of Cuba, 18, 20, 67, 89, 210–214, 216; Inter-American Development Bank, 27, 237; World Bank, 27
Barbados, 167–168, 226, 230, 233, 240
Barco, Virgilio, 124
Bargaining, 5, 7, 45–46, 67, 114, 143–146, 164, 180, 190–191, 204, 206, 214–216, 225, 242; rule of, 115, 120–124, 127, 134–135, 138
Batista, Fulgencio, 8–13, 16, 21, 29–30, 48, 68, 189, 250, 260, 272
Bay of Pigs, invasion of, 1, 25–26, 34–35, 37. *See also* Invasion(s)
Belgium, 24, 129, 154
Ben-Bella, Ahmed, 180–181
Benefits: general, 45, 60, 184; to U.S. 46–47, 50, 55–56; to Cuba, 50, 55, 64–67, 82, 84–88, 90–104, 107–112, 113–114, 120, 122, 165, 207, 218, 222, 267–268; to USSR, 50, 55; to Grenada, 165; shared, 188, 191, 218
Benin, 173, 175
Berlin (West), 200–201
Betancur, Belisario, 124, 238
Bishop, Maurice, 163, 166–167, 169–171
Blockade, 37, 42, 104
Bofill, Ricardo, 197
Bolivia, 28, 97, 121, 126, 278; Communist party in, 76, 124; subversion of, 135–136, 141, 143, 259–260, 262, 272; Cuban aid to, 174
Bonsal, Philip, 16–17
Borge, Tomás, 136, 178
Bourgeoisie, 21, 30, 74
Braddock, Daniel, 23
Bravo, Douglas, 125
Bravo, Flavio, 30
Brazil, 73, 97, 122, 205, 207, 227, 238, 240
Brazzaville, 135
Brezhnev, Leonid, 84, 255–256
Broker role, 4, 22–23, 158, 163–164, 169, 182
Brundenius, Claes, 100
Budget, 71, 77, 110, 218, 273–274
Bulgaria, 22, 92, 94–95, 99, 102, 107, 203
Bundy, McGeorge, 44–46

Bureaucracies, 62, 261–276, 281–282; co-ordination between, 67, 80–82, 84, 93–96, 102, 111, 263, 267–268
Burkina Faso, 173, 181
Burundi, 173

Cabinda, 131, 153, 259
Cabinet, 16, 24–25, 166
Cabrera, Francisco, 257–258
Caldera, Rafael, 121, 225
Camagüey, 19
Canada, 5, 12, 62, 184, 185–186, 190–194, 197–199, 201, 211, 218, 224, 227, 235, 255, 272, 290–291
Cape Verde, 172–173, 209
Capitalism, 10, 67–68, 102, 109, 249, 259; and capitalist countries, 6, 25, 29, 33, 103–104, 106, 184–202, 207, 218, 219
Careers, 149
Caribbean, 1, 39, 43–44, 46, 57, 76, 90, 134, 142, 144, 183, 205, 211, 220, 226; Cuban relations in, 219, 230, 232–233, 237, 240, 264, 268. See also Organization of Eastern Caribbean States
Caribbean Common Market (CARICOM), 167
Carter, Jimmy, administration of, 51–52, 55, 59, 145, 227–230, 233, 257
Casa de las Américas, 268–269
Castro, Fidel, 4, 5, 26, 48, 51–52, 58, 63, 244, 259–260, 278, 281–282; ideas of, 3, 8, 16, 18, 20, 29–34, 185, 243, 248–251, 259; as rebel leader, 10–14; and relations with U.S., 16–20, 23, 35, 37, 230, 243, 245; power of, 19, 22, 34, 42, 254–255, 261, 263, 279; as public speaker, 19–20, 250; and relations with USSR, 20–22, 64–65, 72, 75–77, 78, 81, 88–90, 101, 103–105, 107–110, 307n42; skill of, 22–23, 32–33, 229, 251–253, 258–259; during missile crisis, 38–43; and relations with China, 69; and relations with CMEA, 92–93, 96; and revolutionary movements, 116–126, 128–133, 136–138, 144; and relations with African countries, 153, 158–160; and relations with Grenada, 166–168; and relations

with Nicaragua, 177; and relations with capitalist countries, 187–189; and relations with Nonaligned Movement, 222–223, 236; and relations with Latin America, 223, 238–240
Castro, Raúl, 12, 19, 22, 25, 30, 36, 38, 50–52, 68, 71, 73–74, 108, 128, 160, 254–256, 260, 275, 280
Casualties in combat, 19–20, 40, 57, 106, 136, 152, 168, 171, 175–176, 182, 252–253, 262, 276, 281, 348n96
Cement, 151, 161, 208, 210
Center for American Studies (CEA), 258, 285–288
Central America, 1, 2, 4, 122–126, 134, 136, 142–145, 177, 201, 230, 238–240, 242–243, 251, 261, 271
Central Intelligence Agency, 12, 24–26, 35, 48–49, 59, 230, 293
Cepero Bonilla, Raúl, 23, 203–204
Chernenko, Konstantin, 108
Chile, 2, 28, 69, 73, 120, 126, 143, 164, 182, 199, 223, 225–228, 269–270
China, 7, 14, 21–22, 27, 66–69, 71, 109, 113, 191, 207, 217, 221
Choices, 7, 32–33, 65, 75–76, 91, 105, 108, 113, 129, 132, 175, 184, 218, 229–230, 250
Chomón, Faure, 254, 260
Christian Democrats, 69, 165, 200–201, 225
Cienfuegos, 50, 58–59, 90, 97, 209, 246

Citrus fruits, 85, 95–97, 103, 208–210
Civilians overseas, 149–151, 154–156, 159, 163, 168, 171–180, 210, 217, 232, 240, 267, 277–282. See also Angola; Ethiopia; Grenada; Labor; Nicaragua
Client role, 9, 61–63, 147, 158, 165
CMEA. See Council for Mutual Economic Assistance
Coalitions, 8, 29, 259–261
Coard, Bernard, 166–167, 170–171
Coercion, 4, 39, 61, 72–77, 78, 84, 105, 107, 111, 121, 145, 158, 186
Cold War, 11, 220
Colombia, 10, 15, 27, 71, 73, 110, 139–141, 226, 230, 233, 237–240, 249; subversion of, 123–134, 135, 165, 232,

Colombia (*continued*)
270; Communist party in, 124–125. *See also* M-19

Colomé, Abelardo, 152, 257, 260

Colonialism, 24, 188, 270; and anticolonialist movements, 114, 127, 130–135; and decolonization, 130, 220–224, 237; and neocolonialism, 197

Communications and transportation, 173–175, 188, 196–197, 211, 228, 230, 245, 254, 269, 279–280, 282

Communist party of Cuba, 9, 13, 19, 22, 32, 36, 51, 68, 70–71, 76–77, 118, 129, 163, 243, 265, 267, 278, 281; Political Bureau of, 30, 75, 84, 128, 254, 256–257, 260, 262, 272, 276; Central Committee of, 58–59, 72–75, 108, 119, 133, 136, 166, 257–261, 262, 266, 272–273, 275–276, 279, 285; Americas Department of, 166–167, 262–263, 271–272; Secretariat, 254, 261, 276; General Department for International Relations, 262–263, 271–272

Communists, 8, 19, 25, 27, 30, 132, 242–243; and Communist countries, 14, 21, 29, 46, 63, 68–69, 105, 113, 133, 137, 191, 202, 219, 225, 261, 267; and Communist parties, 68, 71, 74–75, 116, 121, 134–135, 137, 144, 165, 255; and Communist parties in Latin America, 70–71, 76, 124–126, 143–144, 260–261

Communist Youth Union (UJC), 267, 272, 276–278

Compensation: for Swiss, 190–191, 205, 217; for Canadians, 190, 198; for French, 190–191, 205, 217; for Spaniards, 191, 198; for U.S. firms, 191; for British, 200; for Bahamians, 233. *See also* Expropriation

Concessions, 5, 8, 9, 49–50, 52, 54–55, 82, 123

Congo, 131, 135, 139, 142, 181; Cuban relations with, 171–173, 175

Conservatives, 8, 54, 56, 189, 238, 240

Constitution: of 1901, 8; of 1940, 19, 72; of 1976, 77, 261–272

Construction, 1, 5, 149, 161, 210, 232,

274, 279, 282, 348n97; Cuban workers overseas in, 3, 151, 154–156, 172–178, 253, 277–278; by Soviets, 50, 90; by Cubans in Grenada, 163, 168–169; and profit-making, 172

Contadora Group, 238–240

Contras, 177

Cornwall, Leon, 166, 170

Costa Rica, 13, 27, 136, 230–233, 240, 253

Costs: to U.S., 45, 114, 251–253; to Eastern Europe, 78; to USSR, 78, 81, 84, 91–92, 107, 109, 349n1; to Cuba, 81, 96, 107, 111, 172, 182, 191, 200, 229, 282; to CMEA, 84, 92, 96, 107

Council for Mutual Economic Assistance (CMEA): trade with Cuba, 64, 67, 78, 81–84, 90, 92–109, 111–112, 133, 185, 193–195, 197, 201–202, 204–205, 207, 217–218, 255, 267–268, 291; advisers in Cuba, 98–99

Cuban Americans, 211, 228, 231, 245, 272, 281

Cuban Institute for Friendship with Peoples (ICAP), 139, 269

Cultural relations, 73, 80, 173, 237–239, 266, 268–270, 280–281

Currencies: hard, 5, 189, 202; convertible, 22, 64–65, 82–85, 90–91, 93, 95, 104, 108, 155, 172–173, 185, 189, 194, 208, 210–218, 264, 291; rubles, 82, 90; pesos, 88, 292–293; nonconvertible, 97; transferable rubles, 185, 210, 291; dollars, 292–293. *See also* Exchange rates

Czechoslovakia, 22, 76, 92–99, 102, 107, 164, 203; Communist party in, 74. *See also* Invasion(s)

Daniel, Jean, 48

Debt(s): to banks, 5, 90, 184, 211–218; to USSR, 79, 81–82, 90, 255; rescheduling of, 88, 91, 211–218, 244; service, 90, 202, 212–214; to socialist countries, 90, 110; cancellation of, 178; to market-economy governments, 211–218. *See also* Interest rates; Loans

Deception, 16–17, 21, 29, 31–33, 46, 115

Decision making, 4, 14, 18, 24, 32–33,

39–41, 53, 65, 103–105, 115, 117, 132–133, 143, 151–152, 156–158, 187, 191, 206, 210, 229, 248–53; individuals engaged in, 254–261, 282; organizations engaged in, 261–276. *See also* Castro, Fidel

Defectors, 19, 39, 152, 176, 198, 272

de Gaulle, Charles, 187, 196, 221

del Pino, Rafael, 152, 176

Demand, 148, 154, 202, 204–205

Democracy, 16, 25, 30, 72, 119, 242–243

Demography, 149–150, 276–278, 347n96

Dependency, 1, 10, 23, 63, 81, 84, 99, 112, 143, 207, 210–211; and associated development, 9, 101–103; and vulnerability, 69, 72–73, 75, 100–102, 112, 218; deepening of, 85, 92, 100–104, 185, 194, 201

Deterrence, 44–45, 54–55, 114, 121, 168–169, 251–253

Díaz Lanz, Pedro Luis, 19–21

Dictators, 10, 15, 117–120, 126, 188

Diplomatic isolation, 118–119, 184, 186, 188, 201, 233. *See also* Asylum

Diplomatic relations, 13, 16, 20–21, 25, 28–29, 105, 117, 119–124, 127–130, 135, 163, 167, 181, 188, 191, 200, 219, 223–226, 230–233, 238, 240, 257, 264–265, 269. *See also* Asylum

Dobrynin, Anatoly, 50–52

Dominica, 168, 233, 240

Dominican Republic, 10, 26–27, 70, 116, 118, 141, 238, 249, 270; Cuban aid to, 174

Dorticós, Osvaldo, 19, 24, 133–134, 221–222, 254–256, 262, 264

Drug trafficking, 139–141, 228, 245

Dulles, John Foster, 11

Eastern Europe, 6, 14, 21–22, 27, 63–64, 69, 72–77, 81, 92–99, 102, 105–109, 112, 124, 159, 162, 169–170, 179–180, 200, 202, 205, 213, 255, 268, 290

Economy: stagnation of, 2, 91, 101–103, 142, 187, 195, 199, 212–213, 216; international, 5, 6, 89, 101–104, 185, 187, 191, 195, 212, 267; growth of, 9, 82, 90–92, 101–104, 107, 142, 185, 213; development of, 22, 64–67, 71,

82, 89–90, 93, 96–97, 103, 105–106, 109–110, 268; planning for, 30, 65, 71, 77, 86, 195, 218; hegemony over, 62; crisis in, 65, 250; recession in, 88, 91, 102, 109, 216–218

Ecuador, 225, 230, 232–233, 238, 240

Education, 1, 99, 149–151, 154–155, 161–163, 168–169, 171, 173–175, 237, 265, 271, 275, 278–280, 282

Efficiency, 81–82, 91, 94, 103–104, 112, 195, 209–210, 218, 309n30

Egypt, 7, 14, 15, 234–236; and United Arab Republic, 270

Eisenhower, Dwight, 17, 23–25, 33

Elites, 2; and nonelites, 115, 122. *See also* Leadership

El Salvador, 7, 27, 53, 114, 197, 201, 237, 239–242, 271; subversion of, 122–123, 136–137, 141, 143–145, 164–165, 177; Communist party in, 124–126, 135, 137

Embargo, 11–13, 27–28, 35, 42, 75, 104, 186, 188–189, 191, 195, 197, 199, 201, 212, 227–228, 244–245

Equatorial Guinea, 171–173, 181

Eritrea, 134, 160–162, 323n52

Escalante, Aníbal, 36, 73–74, 260

Escalation, 33, 132

ETA, 119

Ethics, 33, 67, 110, 115, 122, 136, 138, 141, 167–168

Ethiopia, 1, 164, 169–170, 171, 234, 258, 261, 265; Cuban troops in, 56, 157–162, 176, 199, 228–229, 244, 251, 262, 273, 323n52; and war with Somalia, 57, 157–160, 180, 182, 217, 275; government of, 134, 148, 158; Cuban civilians in, 161, 172–173; subversion of, 160–161, 180

European Economic Community (EEC), sugar policies of, 202, 205–207, 212, 218, 290; protectionism of, 209; exports to, 234

Exchange rates, 292–293. *See also* Currencies

Exiles, 1, 24–26, 35, 49, 129, 138, 156, 188, 197, 211, 228, 231

Exports, 5, 10, 13, 22–23, 25, 64–67, 69, 82–91, 94–97, 100–104, 107–111,

Exports (*continued*)
186–196, 200–206, 212–213, 217–218,
227, 230, 235, 237, 239, 261, 290–
292; Soviet, 73; nontraditional, 96,
154, 161, 207–211, 335n92; of services, 149–151, 155–156, 162, 172–
175, 177–178, 207, 210, 234, 267;
problems with, 208–210
Expropriations of property: British, 13,
189, 200; U.S., 16–17, 19, 25, 29–31,
243; Cuban, 72, 209; Spanish, 187,
198; Canadian, 190, 198; French, 190,
217; Swiss, 190, 217. *See also* Compensation

Factions, 13, 68, 72–75, 170, 259–261,
262
Fernández, José Ramón, 99
Fernández, Marcelo, 194, 205, 256, 264,
266
Films, 226, 280
Finance, 71, 82, 89–93, 96–97, 100–101,
129, 134, 177, 187, 194, 198, 207,
210, 212–213, 215–218, 245, 271,
291, 293
Fishing, 149–150, 163, 166, 173–175,
188, 198, 208–210, 226, 228, 230,
233, 238–239, 244
Florida, 56–58, 139, 281
Foreign exchange, 75, 82, 93, 98, 172–
173, 175, 196, 210, 292. *See also* Currencies; Exchange rates
Foreign Relations Ministry, 263–267
Foreign Trade Ministry, 194, 256, 263–
267
France, 15, 17, 129–130, 134, 154, 187,
189–194, 199, 201, 209, 218, 221,
223; and military conflict with Cuba,
196–197; Interior Ministry of, 196, 272
Franco, Francisco, 5, 119–120, 188–189
Franqui, Carlos, 39–40, 42
Frei, Eduardo, 69, 120, 225

García, Guillermo, 254, 260, 275
Gender, 277–279
Generations, 276–278, 280
Germany, East (Democratic Republic),
92–95, 97–99, 133, 161, 200, 203,
268, 279; technicians from in Cuba, 74

Germany, West (Federal Republic), 15,
17, 93, 186, 192–194, 200–201, 209,
211, 214, 218
Ghana, 173, 182
Global social product (GSP), 86–87, 89,
91, 93–94, 101–102, 107, 195, 216,
291
Goals: Cuba's, 3, 5, 7, 55, 103, 106,
113–115, 119, 138, 187, 218, 220,
225, 229, 236, 240; Castro's, 11, 41,
250–251; U.S., 47–48, 55; Soviet, 55
González, Felipe, 198
Gorbachev, Mikhail, 108–111, 255
Governments: of Cuba, 4, 5, 6, 8, 23,
25–27, 33, 38, 49, 58, 62, 64, 71–72,
74, 77–78, 81, 91, 111–112, 113–120,
129, 132, 135, 139, 149–150, 155,
184–185, 188, 203, 216, 229, 243,
282, 291; Cuban relations with, 6–7,
26, 33, 113–115, 117–124, 130, 135,
182, 213, 225
Granma, 73, 75
Grants, 66, 89, 91, 107, 155–156, 175,
210; from capitalist countries, 197, 199
Grenada, 107, 232–233, 238, 240, 243,
249; Cubans in, 3, 163, 167–168, 253,
257, 275–277, 347n96; U.S. and English Caribbean forces in, 3, 106, 162;
government of, 4, 148, 164, 167–168;
Cuban relations with, 162–171, 173,
175–176, 180, 182; lessons of, 177
Guantánamo naval base, 8, 12–13, 36, 42,
57, 68, 106, 221–224, 243, 272. *See
also* New Jewel Movement
Guatemala, 15, 24, 26–27, 114, 117,
126, 221; Communist party in, 76,
124–125, 135, 144; Thirteenth of November Revolutionary Movement of,
125; subversion of, 136–137, 143, 270
Guerrillas, 28, 76, 114, 120–126, 131,
133–137, 139–141, 143, 156, 165,
233, 240–242, 270–271
Guevara, Ernesto (Che), 20, 22, 24, 27,
30, 38, 66–68, 92, 109, 116–117, 121,
124–126, 131, 135–136, 141, 143,
259–260, 262, 270, 272
Guillot Lara, Jaime, 139–140
Guinea, 131, 172–173, 175, 181, 259,
270, 282

Guinea-Bissau, 131, 281; and PAIGC (African Party for the Independence of Guinea-Bissau and Cape Verde), 133, 135, 141; Cuban aid to, 171–172, 174–175

Gutiérrez Menoyo, Eloy, 198

Guyana, 172, 175, 180–181, 226, 233, 237, 240, 259

Haig, Alexander, 53, 245

Haiti, 26–27, 118

Handal, Schafik Jorge, 126, 137

Hart, Armando, 131, 281

Havana, 16, 19, 24, 36, 43, 106–107, 249, 270–271, 277; Declarations of, 27–28, 116

Health, 1, 149–151, 197; Cuban aid in, 127–128, 131, 133, 142, 154–155, 161–163, 168–169, 172–177, 232, 238, 278, 282; and convertible currency earnings, 172

Hegemony, 3–4, 6, 8–11, 15–16, 18, 32, 34, 61–63, 76–112, 144–145, 147, 158, 162, 165, 180, 184, 237, 288

Herter, Christian, 18

Hijacking, 122, 146, 226–227, 230, 237–238, 245

History, meaning of, 3, 20, 30, 106, 117, 146, 248–249, 251

Homosexuals, 231

Honduras, 27

Hostility, 5, 6, 14, 20, 25, 29–30, 32, 36, 67–69, 73, 79, 112, 113–114, 116–118, 120, 123, 145, 147, 191, 195, 212, 217, 225–227, 230, 237–238, 248–249, 261, 269

Human rights, 2, 26, 54, 73, 197, 240–241, 273; and political prisoners, 72, 74, 189, 198, 228, 243, 246, 269, 281; and censorship, 269, 280–281

Hungary, 14, 74, 92–95, 98–99, 203, 268

Ideology, 3, 4, 5, 24, 27, 29–34, 61–63, 70–73, 76–77, 84, 102–103, 105–106, 109, 111–112, 113–117, 121, 123–127, 132, 135, 137, 139, 146, 147, 158, 162, 170, 182, 187, 210, 212, 216–217, 243, 248–250, 261, 264, 269, 280–281. See also Marxism-Leninism; Rectification

Imperialism, 3, 8–9, 30, 67, 70, 76, 104–105, 116, 119, 126, 134, 160, 167, 223–224, 243, 248–249, 269, 280

Imports, 10, 22, 64, 67, 69, 72–73, 82–83, 85–89, 94, 100–104, 107, 151, 186–190, 192–200, 202–203, 205–207, 212–213, 217, 226, 230, 232, 244–245, 264, 267, 291–292, 315n19; substitution of, 9, 100, 104

Incentives, 78, 90–91, 103, 149, 207, 216, 273–274, 276, 281–282

Independence, 4, 8, 23, 69, 71, 75, 77, 114, 121, 128–129, 131–135, 137, 145, 147, 153, 157, 184, 186–187, 217, 220, 223–225, 236, 243, 247, 272, 307n42. See also Autonomy

India, 14, 162, 234, 258

Indochina, 114, 142, 144, 224

Indonesia, 14

Influence, 6, 7, 13, 15, 53, 65, 114, 146–147, 151, 152, 160, 169, 171, 175, 178, 180–181, 183, 219–221, 223–224, 229–230, 235–236, 240, 266, 269, 272

Innovation, 5, 148–151, 162, 175, 183, 210, 225

Inspection and intelligence, 37–38, 43, 45–46, 52, 58–59, 221; by U-2, 40–42, 50; by satellites, 49, 59; by Soviets, 51, 58, 78, 80; by SR71, 59; by human means, 169, 198; by Cuba, 271–273

Institutionalization, 62, 261–276, 282

Insurgencies, 121, 165, 270–271; in Cuba, 10–14, 30, 275; in Latin America, 70, 135, 141, 143; in Colombia, 110; in Eritrea, 134; in Nicaragua, 136, 178; in Angola, 148, 152–153; in Ethiopia, 160

Intellectuals, 73–74, 268–269, 280–281

Inter-American system, 26–27

Inter-American Treaty for Reciprocal Assistance (Rio Treaty), 26–28

Interest rates, 22, 66, 81–82, 88–92, 96–97, 107, 177, 199, 212, 215–216, 218, 238, 309n20

Interests: Cuban, 7, 42, 58, 78, 103, 106,

Interests: Cuban (*continued*)
111, 113, 146–147, 158, 182, 202,
217, 243, 247–248, 267; Soviet, 13,
58, 62–63, 71, 78, 84, 105, 111, 133,
144, 152, 158; U.S., 13, 58, 145, 228,
243, 247–248; Castro's, 14; self-, 54,
55; of revolutionaries, 70; of CMEA,
84; Portugal's, 134; shared, 180, 184,
199, 206; of capitalist countries, 185–
186; Sections, 228, 244, 246, 256, 288;
of Cubans, 280–282
Interior Ministry, 73–74, 168, 176, 254,
260, 271–273, 275–276, 282; troops of,
131, 228, 271–272
International Monetary Fund, 17–18, 218
International Sugar Agreement, 5; quotas
under, 203–204; and Communist countries, 203–205, 207; and international
sugar conferences, 203–207, 217
International system: structure of, 3, 8,
14–16, 21, 24, 32–33, 61–63, 152,
176, 182–186, 218, 220, 223, 242,
247, 249; Cuba's place in, 132; U.S.
role in, 147
Interpersonal relations, 98–99, 165, 167,
211, 228, 231, 245, 254, 256, 259–
261, 279–282
Intervention, 25, 27–29, 56, 74, 76, 119–
120, 132, 140, 145, 157–159, 161–162,
181–182, 198, 213, 217, 219–221,
224, 227–228, 232, 240, 251–252, 273;
and nonintervention, 23, 117–119, 139,
167, 188
Invasion(s): of Cuba, 35–37, 41–43, 45–
46, 48–49, 51, 55–56, 58–59, 71, 108,
110, 145, 272; of Czechoslovakia, 76,
105, 121; of Afghanistan, 105, 111,
219, 236, 241; of Grenada, 106, 167–
168, 171, 182, 240–241, 253; of Panama, 117–118; of Nicaragua, 119, 177;
of Angola, 127, 132; of Ethiopia, 134,
148; of Shaba, 138, 153–154, 156,
197, 228. *See also* Bay of Pigs
Investment: from U.S., 9, 17, 30, 61–62,
209; from USSR, 62, 102; from
CMEA, 95–97, 102; from Canada,
197; efficacy of, 210; from other foreigners, 211
Iran, 15, 52

Iraq, 172–174, 234–235
Isle of Youth, 128, 155, 161, 171, 173–
174, 279
Israel, 7, 15, 105, 127, 209, 223, 236;
and 1967 Arab-Israeli war, 130

Jamaica, 2, 164, 168, 180, 182, 226,
232–233, 240, 245, 282
Japan, 5, 62, 93, 104, 184–186, 191–196,
201, 212, 216, 218, 224, 235, 244–
245, 290–291
Johnson, Lyndon, 71; administration of,
48–49
Joint commissions, Cuban-Soviet, 67, 81,
267

Kampuchea, 2, 174, 182, 235–236
Katanga (Shaba), gendarmes of, 127,
138–139, 153–154
Kennedy, John, 25, 35–38, 41–46, 48
Khrushchev, Nikita, 25, 37–39, 41–43,
46, 255–256
Kidnapping, 12, 115, 198, 272
Kissinger, Henry, 45–46, 49–51, 227
Korea, 76, 235, 270
Kosygin, Aleksei, 71
Kuwait, 174, 210

Labor, 19, 72–74, 110, 148, 165, 263–
264, 266–267, 273–274, 276–278,
280–282; in Eastern Europe, 98–99;
and labor-intensive strategies, 151; in
earning foreign exchange, 155–156,
173, 177, 209
La Coubre, 24
Language, knowledge of, 17–18, 30, 36,
98, 155, 161, 165, 176, 178, 268–269,
278–279, 281
Laos, 173–174
Latin America, 1, 10, 15–16, 18–19, 71,
96–97, 114, 116, 130, 134, 141, 143–
144, 186–187, 190, 205–208, 211,
213–226, 230–233, 235, 237–241,
255–256, 259, 261, 263–264, 268–271;
governments in, 2, 5, 6, 7, 26–29, 69,
91, 120, 128, 135, 184, 191, 201; revolutionaries in, 120, 125; Economic
System of (SELA), 230, 238

Law: Cuban, 19, 24, 29, 245; U.S., 54, 197, 215, 227, 231; international, 118

Leadership: Cuba's 3–4, 19–20, 22–24, 29, 34, 36, 68, 70, 74, 77, 107, 109–110, 112, 117, 121, 125, 127, 136–137, 146–147, 157, 164, 166, 184–185, 195, 217, 219, 235–237, 248–261, 282; small countries', 15, 251; Soviet, 64, 158; of Communist world, 68, 70–71, 75, 143; Latin America's, 74; by Cuba of USSR, 114, 132–133, 144–145, 158, 162, 164, 169, 178, 182; revolutionary, 115, 124, 144, 161, 229; of Sandinistas, 126; of Third World, 236. *See also* Castro, Fidel; Castro, Raúl; Decision making

Learning, 77, 98–99, 110, 116, 182, 240, 242, 258–259, 265–266, 268, 281

Lebanon, 15

Lechuga, Carlos, 43, 46, 68

Legitimacy, 61–62, 77–78, 112, 127, 129, 137

Le Monde, 75

LeoGrande, William, 100–101, 157

Liberation, 66, 70, 77, 134, 220, 222–224, 270

Libya, 5, 128; Cuban relations with, 164, 172–174, 180, 210, 234, 259

Linkage, 152–153, 156–157, 245

Loans, 17, 19, 22, 66, 68–69, 72–73, 81–82, 86, 89–92, 97, 107, 177, 187, 189, 197–200, 213–214, 238, 244, 309n30

Lojendio, Juan Pablo de, 187–188, 331n8

López Portillo, José, 122

M-19, 110, 123–124, 139–141, 143, 165, 232

Machado, José Ramón, 71, 260

Macías, Nguema, 173, 181

Malagasy Republic, 174

Mali, 172, 174

Malmierca, Isidoro, 256

Malvinas (Falkland) Islands, 224, 237

Management, 194–195, 211, 213–214, 216, 229, 250–253, 256–257, 261, 263–268

Manley, Michael, 232

Manufacturing, 9, 17, 20, 25, 28, 66, 80, 94, 102, 163, 273, 291; and industriali-

zation, 65, 90, 93, 100, 197; exports of, 154, 161, 209–210, 234

Mariel, emigration through, 88, 211, 230–231, 239

Markets, 5, 18, 71–72, 76–77, 102, 110, 202–207; Cuba's responsiveness to international, 82–86, 88, 90, 104, 149–151, 155–156, 172–173, 175, 177–178, 185, 187, 191–192, 194, 209–210, 217; and market economy countries, 88, 93, 95–96, 101, 109, 119, 184–202, 210, 216–218, 239, 261, 268–269, 290, 292, 349n1; and oligopolies, 148, 151; politics and, 187–191, 193, 196–197, 200, 209, 213, 216, 218. *See also* Capitalism

Martí, José, 75

Marxism-Leninism, 3, 6, 18, 20–21, 27, 29–32, 34, 71, 73, 124, 132, 135, 137, 151, 170, 197–198, 248–249, 282. *See also* Ideology

Massemba-Debat, Alphonse, 181

Matos, Huber, 19, 21

Matthews, Herbert, 11, 38

McNamara, Robert, 45

Meetings of Consultation, 26–27

Mengistu Haile Mariam, 157, 160–162

Mesa-Lago, Carmelo, 100–101

Mexico, 11, 27–29, 68, 106, 119–120, 122, 135, 140, 211, 222, 225–226, 230, 237–239, 269

Microfaction, 72–75, 260, 262, 272

Migration, 2, 53, 59, 72, 88, 98, 140, 150, 211, 226, 230–231, 243, 245–246, 253, 257, 281; and foreign migrants in Cuba, 188, 195, 228, 269, 279. *See also* Cuban Americans; Exiles

Mikoyan, Anastas, 20–23, 43

Militancy, 4, 28, 71, 135, 148, 191, 205, 218, 224–225, 276

Military: coups, 8, 122, 158–159, 161, 166, 169–171, 180–182, 259, 329n176; advisers, 10–11, 17, 22, 163; officers, 69, 253, 256–257, 259, 273; rule, 97, 120–121

Mining, 12, 128–129; exports, 207

Miret, Pedro, 260

Miró Cardona, José, 16, 35

Missiles: ballistic, 3, 25, 28–29, 34, 36–

Missiles: ballistic (*continued*)
39, 41–43, 45, 49–51, 256; surface-to-
air (SAMs), 36–38, 40–41, 46. *See
also* Weapons
Missile crisis, 1, 3, 5, 28, 34–48, 53, 63–
64, 67, 72, 74, 187, 251, 253, 255–
256, 258
Mitterrand, François, 197
Mobutu, Joseph, 125
Modernization, 56–57, 66, 94
Mongolia, 93, 96, 109
Monroe Doctrine, 45, 55
Montané, Jesús, 122, 263
Mora, Alberto, 194, 256, 264
Morocco, 7, 127–129, 154, 175, 181,
196, 209, 234–236, 273, 328n148
Moscow, 36
Mozambique, 5, 133; FRELIMO (Front
for Mozambique's Liberation) in, 133;
Cuban relations with, 171, 174–175,
180, 241–242, 259
MPLA (Popular Movement for the Libera-
tion of Angola), 127, 130–132, 135,
138, 141, 144, 148, 152, 157, 252,
270, 317n59. *See also* Angola
Mulele, Pierre, 125
Multinational firms, 1, 28, 148–149, 155,
172–173, 197, 227, 244–245, 267;
owned by Cuba, 210–211, 239

Namibia, 127, 129, 139, 153, 156–157,
171, 245, 316n52
National Assembly, 72, 77, 198, 265; and
Council of State, 262
Nationalism, 2–3, 9–10, 16, 20, 29, 32,
223, 248–249
Negotiations, 23–24, 33, 43, 54, 57–59,
64–67, 81, 93, 122–123, 153, 156,
177, 188–190, 204, 207, 214–217,
229, 238–246, 255, 257, 267, 291
Netherlands, 198–199
Neto, Agostinho, 132, 156, 158–159,
161, 170
New Jewel Movement (NJM), 162–164,
170–171, 241, 273; Political Bureau of,
165–167; Central Committee of, 166–
167. *See also* Grenada
New York Times, 11

Ngouabi, Marien, 181
Nicaragua, 26–27, 114, 137, 148, 169–
170, 182, 199, 201, 206, 208, 227,
232, 237–238, 242–244, 277, 280; subversion of, 118, 136, 143–144; Sandinista government of, 122, 145, 176,
239–240; Communist party in, 125,
135, 143; Cuban aid to, 171–173, 175–
178, 210, 279; Cuban military in, 176–
178, 180, 271; and France, 197
Nickel, 82, 85, 88–90, 93, 96–97, 103–
104, 197, 208, 244–245
Nigeria, 174, 206
Nixon, Richard, 15, 17; administration of,
49
Nkomati accord, 180, 242, 259
Nonaligned Movement, 1, 15, 104–105,
127, 129, 133, 137, 184, 201, 220–
224, 233–234, 241, 256, 259, 264; Havana summit of, 123, 128, 234–236;
Cuba's leadership of, 130, 219, 224,
235–237, 255, 257
North Atlantic Treaty Organization
(NATO), 56–57, 75, 197
Novosti, 74
Nuclear power plants, 58–59, 90, 238,
246

OAS. *See* Organization of American
States
Ochoa, Arnaldo, 257
OCLAE (Continental Organization of
Latin American Students), 271
Ogaden, 148, 159–160, 176
Operation Mongoose, 48
Opposition: domestic, 2–3, 13, 48, 182,
220, 252, 261; to USSR, 4, 67, 70–71,
75, 77–78, 105–112, 129, 144–145;
from U.S., 5, 228; to U.S., 6, 160,
184, 197, 239; to hegemony, 62; to
China, 75; to colonial rule, 130; within
Communist parties, 137; in Grenada,
167, 169; in Guyana, 181; in Spain,
188; to terrorism, 196; to racism, 221;
to Cuba, 227; in U.S., 230; to negotiations, 259
Organization for Latin American Solidarity (OLAS), 270
Organization for Solidarity of the Peoples

of Africa, Asia, and Latin America
(OSPAAL), 130–131, 134, 270–271
Organization of African Unity (OAU),
159
Organization of American States (OAS),
16, 18, 26, 28, 116, 118, 221, 225–
226, 255
Organization of Eastern Caribbean States,
167
Orthodoxy, 71, 77, 102, 135, 137, 218

Padilla, Heberto, 269
Palestine Liberation Organization (PLO),
127, 129–130, 241, 271
Panama, 26–27, 123, 175, 210–211, 226,
238–239, 245; Canal Zone, 68, 106,
223; subversion of, 117
Paraguay, 27, 227
Paris Club, 214
Partnership: of Cuba and USSR, 63, 100,
158, 182; of Cuba and Communist
countries, 84, 101; of Cuba and Spain,
119, 199; of Cuba and non-Communist
countries, 187–188, 191
Pawley, William, 13
Pazos, Felipe, 18, 20
Peace, 76, 123, 262
Pérez, Faustino, 20
Pérez, Humberto, 91, 102, 108, 195, 254
Pérez Herrero, Antonio, 254, 258, 261–
262, 265, 280
Pérez-López, Jorge, 101
Pérez Novoa, José, 161–162, 258
Pérez-Stable, Marifeli, 280
Perón, Juan, 10
Peru, 15, 27, 120–121, 126, 143, 172,
175, 222–223, 225, 230–233, 238–
239, 252–253, 270; Communist party
in, 124; armed conflict with, 231
Petroleum, 5, 22–23, 72–75, 85, 87–89,
102, 107, 185, 237, 239, 291–292,
307n42; refineries for, 10, 12, 24–25,
90, 189; reexports of, 90–91, 100,
207–208, 216; countries rich in, 151; in
Angola, 153, 155, 259
Piñeiro, Manuel, 74, 166, 260, 262, 272
Pinochet, Augusto, 2
Platt Amendment, 8–9
Poland, 22, 92, 95, 203, 221

Polisario, 7, 127–129, 235–236, 271. See
also Sahara
Pol Pot, 2, 182, 235
Popular Movement for the Liberation of
Angola. See MPLA
Population, 1, 2, 149–150, 152, 161, 176,
276–277, 279
Portugal, 2, 130, 134, 142, 205, 223
Portuguese Africa, 1, 2, 6, 114, 133, 141,
147, 175, 220–222, 224, 270, 279. See
also Angola; Guinea-Bissau; Mozam-
bique
Pragmatism, 4, 5, 190–191, 200, 205,
217, 240. See also Markets
Prensa Latina, 269
Prices, 5, 9, 22, 64–67, 76, 81–89, 91–
97, 100–104, 107–111, 185–186, 188–
192, 194–196, 200–210, 212–213,
216–218, 234–235, 290–292, 309n30,
349n1
Prío, Carlos, 11
Priorities, 7, 67, 76–77, 80, 108, 113,
120, 122–123, 129, 135, 169, 184, 229
Product differentiation, 150, 162; and
brand names, 148, 151
Profits abroad, 1, 2, 119, 148, 151–152,
155–156, 159, 172–175, 177–178, 210.
See also Markets
Public utilities, 10, 16, 29, 31, 166
Puerto Rico, 42, 68, 106, 133–134, 145,
223, 237, 243, 270
Puppet and proxy, 4, 62, 70–71, 112,
145, 165

Quasi-states, 127–130, 133–135, 171, 271

Race, 132, 149, 276–279, 347n96,
348n97
Radicalism, 31–32, 71–72, 74–75, 109,
125, 145–146, 190, 264
Radio: Havana, 133, 142; Martí, 211,
246, 280
Rationality, 58, 104, 168–169, 251–253
Ray, Manuel, 20
Reagan, Ronald, 46–47, 50, 53–54, 230,
242; administration of, 5, 59, 79, 145,
206, 212, 237, 244–246, 257
Rebellion in Cuba, 10–14, 48

Rectification, 109, 216, 250. *See also* Ideology
Regimes: authoritarian, 2, 184, 243; domestic, 5, 6, 8, 13, 16, 18, 22, 72, 188, 251, 254, 261, 263, 280–282; Marxist-Leninist, 6, 7; international, 8, 61–63; structure of, 118–119; rightwing, 119; Sandinista, 177. *See also* Rules; Security regime
Religion, 134, 166; and Roman Catholic church, 187–188, 261
Remittances, 98–99
Resources, 4, 29, 34, 58, 66, 107–108, 110, 114, 121, 135, 142, 151, 220, 273
Revolución, 16–17, 19, 22, 24, 36, 39, 43, 118
Revolution: Cuba's, 2–3, 6, 18, 32–34, 74, 92, 112, 217, 243, 282; in the world, 3, 6, 7, 27–28, 33, 70, 115–117, 119, 126, 146, 147, 218, 249, 282; vanguard in a, 10; in Nicaragua, 136, 141; in Ethiopia, 160, 162; in Eritrea, 160; in Grenada, 167
Revolutionary Directorate, 48, 260
Revolutionary movements, 2–3, 5, 6, 7, 164, 219–220; Cuban support for, 26, 28–29, 33, 35, 45–47, 56, 70–71, 76, 113–146, 147, 177, 184, 191, 217, 225, 232, 234–236, 239, 243, 250–251, 259–260, 262, 270–272, 316n52; Soviet support for, 71; unity of, 126, 134, 137, 162, 241; untrustworthy, 127, 137–141, 143, 165, 196; worthwhile, 127, 135–137, 143. *See also* Colonialism; Quasi-states
Revolutionary states, 6, 219; Cuban support for, 33, 35, 147–183, 184
Rice, 69, 306n26
Risquet, Jorge, 131, 153, 156, 254
Rivero Collado, Carlos, 272
Roa, Raúl, 221, 254–256, 263–264
Roca, Blas, 254, 260
Rodríguez, Carlos Rafael, 22, 30, 74, 81, 84, 93–95, 106–107, 110, 121, 195, 197, 206, 224, 240, 245, 256–258, 260, 267–268, 288
Rodríguez, José Luis, 103, 288
Rodríguez, Marcos, 68
Rogers, William D., 227

Rubottom, R. Richard, 17–18
Rules, 9, 34, 45, 54–57, 60, 121–126; of internationalism, 115–116, 120, 146; of precedence, 115, 117–120, 127, 130, 134, 137–139, 188, 239; "Panama," 118–119. *See also* Bargaining; Regimes; Security regime; Vanguard
Rum exports, 209
Rumania, 92, 95, 97, 105, 203
Rusk, Dean, 45

Sabotage, 24, 42, 48–49, 108, 115, 160, 217
Sahara (former Spanish), 127–129, 171, 236; and Democratic Saharawi Arab Republic (RASD), 127–129. *See also* Polisario
Saint Lucia, 167–168, 230, 233, 240
Saint Vincent and the Grenadines, 168, 233, 240
SALT II, 52, 228, 230
Sánchez, Celia, 30, 248, 252
Sánchez, Díaz, Antonio, 136, 259
Sanctions against Cuba: Soviet, 4, 72–76, 145; Latin American, 5, 27–28, 195, 206, 225, 227, 230, 268; U.S., 5, 28, 64, 76, 243–245; Chinese, 69
Sandinista Front for National Liberation (FSLN), 124–126, 141, 143, 177, 197. *See also* Nicaragua
São Tomé and Principe, 171–172, 174
Satellites, 164, 269, 280. *See also* Inspection and intelligence
Scholarships: for Cubans in USSR, 66, 75, 82, 99, 110; for Cubans in Eastern Europe, 99; for foreigners in Cuba, 128–131, 133, 136, 155, 161, 163, 171–176, 242
Seaga, Edward, 2, 182, 232
Security: Cuba's, 6, 34–36, 39, 56–67, 59, 60, 62, 104–105, 112, 113, 117–118, 122, 147; U.S., 9, 37, 51, 53, 56, 60, 229; internal, 175, 177, 211, 271; mutual, 243
Security regime, 34–60
Setbacks, Cuba's, 2, 5, 136, 161, 180–183, 199, 219–220, 226, 229–233, 240, 242, 250–251
Seychelles, 174

Shaba: province, 129, 138, 154, 176, 196; exiles, 129, 138–139, 197, 228

Shell, Royal Dutch, 24, 189, 198, 200

Shevchenko, Arkady, 39, 132

Siad Barre, 2, 158, 180

Smith, Earl, 11, 13, 16

Socialism, 20, 34, 77, 106, 114, 182, 237, 264, 280; and socialist countries, 25, 64, 66–67, 69–71, 74, 76, 89, 94, 96, 102–105, 108–110, 130, 133, 137, 190, 263, 268; and Social Democratic parties, 164–165, 198; and Socialist International, 164; and socialist realism, 269. See also Ideology

Solidarity, 69, 105, 119, 121–122, 134, 147, 189, 223, 270–271, 330n176

Somalia, 2, 134, 148, 157–160, 162, 180, 182, 228–229, 258

Somoza, 118, 125, 136, 176, 178

South AFrica, 5, 128–129, 133, 139, 165, 180, 223, 229, 241–242, 259; troops in Angola, 85, 127, 131–132, 148, 152–154, 156, 160–161, 176, 246

Southern Africa, 5, 183, 198, 241–243, 246

South West Africa People's Organization. See SWAPO

Soviet-Cuban relations, 4, 6, 18, 20–23, 27, 29, 31–33, 34, 36–47, 49–59, 61–77, 78–94, 96–112, 113–114, 116–117, 121, 124, 129–133, 136, 142–145, 147–149, 151–153, 162, 178–183, 184, 187–196, 211, 217–218, 219–223, 225, 228–230, 242–247, 260–261, 268–269, 279, 288; economic, 3, 22, 25, 75, 107, 202–204, 207, 213, 216, 256–257, 290–293, 307n42; military, 3, 22, 25–26, 28, 38, 49–51, 54, 57, 75, 79–80, 107–108, 233, 256, 273, 302n52; political 3, 229, 235–237, 251–252, 255–259, 329n176; crises in, 72–77, 78–79, 81, 89, 106–112, 252, 256, 258, 262, 271–272; over Angola and Ethiopia, 157–160; over Grenada, 163–166, 169–171; over Nicaragua, 177–178. See also Hegemony; Missile crisis; Security regime

Soviet Union, 1, 5, 13–16; Communist party of, 22; military advisers in Cuba,

36, 38, 44, 51, 53, 74, 78–80; troops in Cuba, 36, 38–42, 44, 46, 49, 52–53, 55, 58, 63, 76, 78–80, 228; technicians in Cuba, 66, 75, 82, 99; embassy in Havana, 74

Spain, 5, 8, 93, 104, 119–120, 187–194, 196, 198–201, 211–212, 217–218, 235, 238, 272, 290–291

Sports, 1, 149, 171, 173–175, 208, 237–238, 282; in Olympics, 105, 150

Sri Lanka, 174

Stability, 9–10, 55, 61–63, 126, 203–204, 270, 273

State Committee for Economic Collaboration (CECE), 266–267

State enterprises, 1, 73, 110, 151, 155, 166, 172, 264, 267, 273, 280

Steel products, 90, 208, 239, 244

Strategy, 5, 20–21, 113, 116, 132, 139, 145–146, 147, 168–169, 182, 201, 204, 207, 229–230, 248–249; and crisis management, 251–253

Subsidies: Eastern European, 1, 81, 229; Soviet, 1, 3, 5, 22, 64–67, 77, 81–97, 100–103, 107–111, 147, 151, 202, 208, 210, 213, 229, 235, 288, 290–291, 293, 309n30, 349n1; U.S., 9, 23, 25, 202; CMEA, 93–97, 104, 107, 202, 208, 210; Canadian, 197; Dutch, 199; from Cuba, 291

Sugar: exports, 1, 9, 21–22, 24–25, 64–67, 69, 77, 82–89, 91–97, 100–103, 107–111, 185, 188–196, 200–208, 210–213, 217–218, 234–235, 239, 290–293, 349n1; world market for, 5, 22, 64–65, 81–82, 93, 101, 107–109, 184–186, 196, 202–208, 210, 217, 234–235, 290–291, 349n1; quotas, 9, 23–25, 203; refined, 9, 234; mills, 9–10, 25, 66, 72, 94, 177–178, 206, 250; donation of, 127; industrial exports, 149, 173–175, 177–178, 239. See also International Sugar Agreement

Supply, 148, 150–152, 154, 157, 160, 175, 188, 195, 202–203, 205

Suriname, 182, 230, 240

Surprise, 21, 41–42, 166, 171, 241, 251–253; and predictability, 58, 81

Surrender, 168–169, 251–253

SWAPO, 127, 129, 156, 165, 241, 271
Sweden, 192–194, 199
Switzerland, 187, 190–191, 220
Syria, 174, 234, 270

Tanzania, 172, 174, 282
Tass, 20, 50, 74
Technology, 76, 110, 134, 185, 208, 217, 239, 291
Television, 11, 30, 42, 76, 187, 238, 261, 280
Terrorists, 138, 196, 199, 201, 228, 230, 245, 272
Thant, U, 41, 43
Third World, 6, 29, 63, 97, 105–106, 129, 147, 148–149, 151–152, 172, 180, 182, 211, 219–223, 236, 241–242
Tobacco, 187, 207–209
Tortoló, Pedro, 168–169, 253, 257
Touré, Sekou, 175, 181, 259
Tourism, 163, 201, 211–212, 228, 238–239, 245, 292
Trade, 5, 6, 7, 15, 21–22, 25, 27–28, 35, 64–65, 69, 72–73, 90–97, 100–104, 107–112, 119–120, 124, 129, 134, 140–141, 143, 148, 175, 183, 184–211, 217–218, 225–227, 229–232, 234–235, 237–239, 245, 264, 267–268, 290–293; and tariffs, 9; barter, 64, 85–86, 104, 185, 291–292; deficit, 66, 68–69, 82, 85, 88–95, 101, 107–108, 192–195, 211–213, 215–216; surplus, 66, 85, 88, 92, 154, 291; terms of, 66–67, 85–89, 92, 101–102, 107, 213, 291–292; competitiveness, 104, 111–112, 151, 156
Treaties: U.S.-Cuban, 11–12, 36, 122, 140, 226–227, 243, 257; Soviet-Cuban, 22, 39, 64–66, 81–82, 84–85, 87, 90, 93; multilateral, 26–27, 106; Nuclear Test Ban, 67; on Latin American nuclear weapons, 68, 106; CMEA-Cuban, 81, 93–94, 96, 108; Nonproliferation, 106; Angolan-Cuban, 154, 160; Grenadan-Cuban, 163, 167; Spanish-Cuban, 188–189; French-Cuban, 190; Swiss-Cuban, 190; with others, 223–224; antihijacking, 227, 237; Mexican-Cuban, 239; ratifying, 262. See also International Sugar Agreement

Tricontinental Conference, 69–70, 116, 131, 270
Trinidad and Tobago, 167, 226, 233, 240
Trotskyites, 125
Trudeau, Pierre, 197
Trujillo, Rafael, 10, 26, 118
Tshombe, Moise, 135
Turcios Lima, Luis, 125
Twenty-sixth of July Movement, 10, 18–19, 257, 260

Uganda, 174, 327n128
Underdevelopment: Cuba's, 1, 93, 103, 151, 166, 220; Grenada's, 166
Understandings, U.S.-Soviet, 5–6, 34, 37–38, 44–60, 258. See also Missile crisis; Security regime
UNECA (Caribe Union of Construction Enterprises), 155, 172–173
UNITA (National Movement for the Total Independence of Angola), 131–132, 152–153, 242; and Jonas Savimbi, 131
United Kingdom, 13, 15, 17, 24, 75, 104, 130, 167, 186–187, 189–190, 192–194, 199–200, 205, 210, 223–224, 237
United Nations, 16, 25, 37, 41, 48, 118, 127, 133, 137, 214, 221, 224, 237, 240–241, 244, 257; Economic Commission for Latin America, 121; Security Council, 123, 233, 236–237; Conference for Trade and Development, 222; Development Program, 222, 244; Group of 77, 222; Latin American caucus in, 222–223, 241
United States, 5, 6, 7, 14–16, 29–30, 32, 290; government, 1, 3, 10, 12, 17, 25–26, 32, 158, 176–178, 293; policies, 2, 12–13, 15, 70, 195, 197–199, 201, 213–214, 224–225, 233, 239, 242–243, 246–247; firms, 9–10, 19, 25, 28, 31, 61–62, 134; Neutrality Act, 11–12; Navy, 12, 245; State Department, 17, 36, 49; Treasury Department, 18, 24, 28; Senate, 19, 52; Congress, 24–25, 37, 228, 255; House of Representatives, 24; troops, 70, 168–169; as subversive power, 114, 120, 122, 177; Coast Guard, 140, 228, 245, 272
U.S.-Cuban relations, 3–4, 6, 7, 8–14, 16–21, 23–29, 32–33, 34–60, 61–62,

67–68, 76, 79, 104–106, 110, 112, 114–117, 119–123, 129, 132–142, 145–146, 147, 151, 153, 156, 160, 181–182, 184, 186–191, 195–207, 209, 211–215, 217–218, 219–233, 235, 237–247, 248–253, 255–258, 261, 263, 272–273, 280, 285–286, 288–289; over Grenada, 165, 167–170, 240; over Nicaragua, 177–178; improvements in, 227–230, 251, 273
University students, 10, 19, 48, 75, 172, 260, 265, 271, 274–275, 278, 282
Urrutia, Manuel, 16, 19
Uruguay, 28, 227, 238, 269

Valdés, Ramiro, 116, 133, 254, 272
Valdés Vivó, Raúl, 258, 263
Values: U.S., 3, 148, 242–243, 249, 280; Cuban, 7, 113, 117, 243; Castro's, 249; of currencies, 292–293
Vanguard: role, 63, 70–72, 126–127, 133, 135, 137, 139, 249; rule, 115, 124–126
Venezuela, 15–16, 27–28, 71, 120, 181, 230, 232–233, 237, 239, 252; Communist party in, 70, 76, 124–125, 135; subversion of, 119, 141, 143, 262, 270; Armed Forces of National Liberation (FALN) of, 125; Cuban cooperation with, 225–227, 230
Vesco, Robert, 140
Viet Cong, 70, 270; and Provisional Revolutionary Government of South Vietnam, 127, 172
Vietnam, 2, 7, 70–71, 76, 96, 109, 127, 132, 145, 147, 152, 164, 176, 220, 225, 229, 243; Cuban aid to, 172–174, 206, 282; Cuban trade with, 234–235
Violence, 10, 70, 115, 134, 196, 243

Walters, Vernon, 132, 245, 258

War: in Angola, 1, 79, 81, 138, 145, 148–149, 152–154, 156–159, 169, 201, 224, 246, 252, 273, 275, 280; in Ethiopia, 1, 79, 149, 157–162, 201, 252, 273; in the Caribbean, 5; in Cuba, 11–

14, 25–26, 30–31, 39, 57, 248; colonial, 15; nuclear, 15, 34–35, 37, 39–41, 45, 47, 251; conventional, 39–41, 52, 56–57; in the Horn of Africa, 52, 145, 156, 160, 180, 224, 228–229, 255; threats of, 54–57, 110, 115, 145, 251–252; in Europe, 56–58; unconventional, 118; civil, 141, 181, 236; Algerian-Moroccan, 175, 181, 273, 328n148; in Central America, 177, 238; in Africa, 219, 273; British-Argentine, 237; declaring, 262
Warsaw Pact, 57–58, 63, 76, 79, 201
Weapons: strategic, 6, 29, 36–37, 39, 41, 44–49, 51–52, 63, 251, 255; to Cuba, 10–13, 22, 24, 26, 29, 36, 43, 47, 53, 56–57, 75, 79–80, 136, 189, 273, 291; nuclear, 14–15, 37, 39–40, 43, 45, 52, 56; from Cuba, 28, 137, 142; antiaircraft, 40–42; submarine, 46, 50–51, 53, 57–58, 78; to M-19, 123, 139–141; to Angola, 131, 138, 157; to Guinea-Bissau, 133; to Nicaragua, 136, 141, 177–178; to Grenada, 163, 170; to Chile, 226. See also Aircraft; Missiles
Western European countries, 5, 6, 15, 44, 56–58, 62–63, 98, 104, 184–186, 188–191, 199–201, 207, 209, 224, 231, 234, 244–245, 255–256, 261, 263–264, 269
Western Hemisphere, 11, 27–29, 45, 68, 224–233, 237–242, 263
West Indies, 119, 135

Yemen (South), 161, 181, 329n176; Cuban aid to, 171–172, 174–175, 279
Yon Sosa, 125
Yugoslavia, 70, 207, 221

Zaire, 125, 127, 131, 135, 138, 153–154, 156, 176, 221, 228, 270; Moroccan troops in, 129, 154, 196; Cuban aid to, 174, 206
Zambia, 174
Zeitlin, Maurice, 277
Zimbabwe, 114, 139; Cuban aid to, 174

Publications of the Center for International Affairs, Published by Harvard University Press

Created in 1958, the Center for International Affairs fosters advanced study of basic world problems by scholars from various disciplines and senior officials from many countries. The research at the Center focuses on economic, social, and political development, the management of force in the modern world, the evolving roles of Western Europe and the Communist nations, and the conditions of international order.

The Soviet Bloc, by Zbigniew K. Brzezinski (Sponsored jointly with the Russian Research Center), 1960. Revised edition, 1967.

United States Manufacturing Investment in Brazil, by Lincoln Gordon and Engelbert L. Grommers, 1962. Harvard Business School.

The Economy of Cyprus, by A. J. Meyer, with Simos Vassiliou (sponsored jointly with the Center for Middle Eastern Studies), 1962.

Communist China 1955–1959: Policy Documents with Analysis, with a foreword by Robert R. Bowie and John K. Fairbank (sponsored jointly with the East Asian Research Center), 1962.

Somali Nationalism, by Saadia Touval, 1963.

The Dilemma of Mexico's Development, by Raymond Vernon, 1963.

The Arms Debate, by Robert A. Levine, 1963.

Africans on the Land, by Montague Yudelman, 1964.

Democracy in Germany, by Fritz Erler (Jodidi Lectures), 1965.

The Rise of Nationalism in Central Africa, by Robert I. Rotberg, 1965.

Pan-Africanism and East African Integration, by Joseph S. Nye, Jr., 1965.

Germany and the Atlantic Alliance: The Interaction of Strategy and Politics, by James L. Richardson, 1966.

Political Change in a West African State, by Martin Kilson, 1966.

Planning without Facts: Lessons in Resource Allocation from Nigeria's Development, by Wolfgang F. Stolper, 1966.

Export Instability and Economic Development, by Alasdair I. MacBean, 1966.

Europe's Postwar Growth, by Charles P. Kindleberger, 1967.

Pakistan's Development: Social Goals and Private Incentives, by Gustav F. Papanek, 1967.

Strike a Blow and Die: A Narrative of Race Relations in Colonial Africa, by George Simeon Mwase, ed. Robert I. Rotberg, 1967.

Korea: The Politics of the Vortex, by Gregory Henderson, 1968.

The Brazilian Capital Goods Industry, 1929–1964 (sponsored jointly with the Center for Studies in Education and Development), by Nathaniel H. Leff, 1968.

The Process of Modernization: An Annotated Bibliography on the Sociocultural Aspects of Development, by John Brode, 1969.

Agricultural Development in India's Districts: The Intensive Agricultural Districts Programme, by Dorris D. Brown, 1970.

Taxation and Development: Lessons from Colombian Experience, by Richard M. Bird, 1970.

Lord and Peasant in Peru: A Paradigm of Political and Social Change, by F. LaMond Tullis, 1970.

The Kennedy Round in American Trade Policy: The Twilight of the GATT? by John W. Evans, 1971.

Korean Development: The Interplay of Politics and Economics, by David C. Cole and Princeton N. Lyman, 1971.

Development Policy II—The Pakistan Experience, edited by Walter P. Falcon and Gustav F. Papanek, 1971.

Studies in Development Planning, edited by Hollis B. Chenery, 1971.

Political Mobilization of the Venezuelan Peasant, by John D. Powell, 1971.

Peasants Against Politics: Rural Organization in Brittany, 1911–1967, by Suzanne Berger, 1972.

Transnational Relations and World Politics, edited by Robert O. Keohane and Joseph S. Nye, Jr., 1972.

Latin American University Students: A Six Nation Study, by Arthur Liebman, Kenneth N. Walker, and Myron Glazer, 1972.

The Politics of Land Reform in Chile, 1950–1970: Public Policy, Political Institutions, and Social Change, by Robert R. Kaufman, 1972.

The Boundary Politics of Independent Africa, by Saadia Touval, 1972.

Becoming Modern: Individual Change in Six Developing Countries, by Alex Inkeles and David H. Smith, 1974.

Big Business and the State: Changing Relations in Western Europe, edited by Raymond Vernon, 1974.

Economic Policymaking in a Conflict Society: The Argentine Case, by Richard D. Mallon and Juan V. Sourrouille, 1975.

New States in the Modern World, edited by Martin Kilson, 1975.

No Easy Choice: Political Participation in Developing Countries, by Samuel P. Huntington and Joan M. Nelson, 1976.

Storm over the Multinationals: The Real Issues, by Raymond Vernon, 1977.

Insurrection or Loyalty: The Breakdown of the Spanish American Empire, by Jorge I. Domínguez, 1980.

On the Autonomy of the Democratic State, by Eric A. Nordlinger, 1981.

Two Hungry Giants: The United States and Japan in the Quest for Oil and Ores,
by Raymond Vernon, 1983.

To Make a World Safe for Revolution: Cuba's Foreign Policy, by Jorge I.
Domínguez, 1989.